Palgrave Studies in African Leadership

Series Editors

Faith Ngunjiri, Global Leadership Development LLC, Windham, NH, USA

Nceku Nyathi, Royal Holloway University of London, Egham, UK

Almost every continent has solid representation in the field of leadership studies except for Africa, despite its rapid growth. A groundbreaking series, Palgrave Studies in African Leadership fills a gap in the production of knowledge and scholarly publishing on Africa and provides a much needed outlet for the works of scholars interested in African leadership studies around the world. Where many studies of leadership in Africa focus solely on one country or region, this series looks to address leadership in each of the different regions and countries of the continent. This comes at a time when business and academic discourse have begun to focus on the emerging markets across Africa. The wide-ranging scholarly perspectives offered in this series allow for greater understanding of the foundation of African leadership and its implications for the future. Topics and contributors will come from various backgrounds to fully explore African leadership and the implications for business, including scholars from business and management, history, political science, gender studies, sociology, religious studies, and African studies. The series will analyze a variety of topics including African political leadership, women's leadership, religious leadership, servant leadership, specific regions, specific countries, specific gender categories, specific business entities in Africa, and more.

Samuel Adomako · Albert Danso ·
Agyenim Boateng
Editors

Corporate Sustainability in Africa

Responsible Leadership, Opportunities,
and Challenges

Editors
Samuel Adomako
University of Birmingham
Birmingham, UK

Albert Danso
De Montfort University
Leicester, UK

Agyenim Boateng
De Montfort University
Leicester, UK

ISSN 2945-6673 ISSN 2945-6681 (electronic)
Palgrave Studies in African Leadership
ISBN 978-3-031-29272-9 ISBN 978-3-031-29273-6 (eBook)
https://doi.org/10.1007/978-3-031-29273-6

© The Editor(s) (if applicable) and The Author(s), under exclusive license to Springer Nature Switzerland AG 2023

This work is subject to copyright. All rights are solely and exclusively licensed by the Publisher, whether the whole or part of the material is concerned, specifically the rights of translation, reprinting, reuse of illustrations, recitation, broadcasting, reproduction on microfilms or in any other physical way, and transmission or information storage and retrieval, electronic adaptation, computer software, or by similar or dissimilar methodology now known or hereafter developed.
The use of general descriptive names, registered names, trademarks, service marks, etc. in this publication does not imply, even in the absence of a specific statement, that such names are exempt from the relevant protective laws and regulations and therefore free for general use.
The publisher, the authors, and the editors are safe to assume that the advice and information in this book are believed to be true and accurate at the date of publication. Neither the publisher nor the authors or the editors give a warranty, expressed or implied, with respect to the material contained herein or for any errors or omissions that may have been made. The publisher remains neutral with regard to jurisdictional claims in published maps and institutional affiliations.

Cover illustration: Alex Linch/shutterstock.com

This Palgrave Macmillan imprint is published by the registered company Springer Nature Switzerland AG
The registered company address is: Gewerbestrasse 11, 6330 Cham, Switzerland

Acknowledgements

At Palgrave, we want to thank Supraja Yegnaraman and Marcus Ballenger for their encouragement and consistent support, and understanding.

Dr. Samuel Adomako
Associate Professor in Strategy and Innovation
Birmingham Business School
University of Birmingham, UK

Dr. Albert Danso
Associate Professor in Accounting and Finance
Leicester Castle Business School
De Montfort University, UK

Professor Agyenim Boateng
Professor in Finance & Director, Finance & Banking Research Centre
Leicester Castle Business School
De Montfort University, UK

CONTENTS

Overview and Structure of the Book   1
Samuel Adomako, Albert Danso, and Agyenim Boateng

SDGs and Africa

**Enhancing Circular Economy and Sustainable
Environmental Practices—Opportunities and Challenges
for Tyre Pyrolysis in Africa**   9
Rexford Attah-Boakye, Elvis Hernandez-Perdomo,
Mike Tooke, Honglan Yu, and Kweku Adams

Africa's Response to SDGs: Barriers and Challenges   47
Antoinette Yaa Benewaa Gabrah, George Kofi Amoako,
and George Oppong Appiagyei Ampong

**Multinational Enterprises, Sustainability Activities,
and Implementation of Sustainable Development Goals
in Africa**   65
Edmund Osei Afriyie and Nadia Zahoor

**Financing Sustainable Development Goals in Africa: The
Role of Remittances—Evidence from Nigeria**   81
Chioma N. Nwafor

viii CONTENTS

Natural Resources, Sustainable Entrepreneurship, and Poverty Reduction in Resource-Rich African Countries: The Missing Link 101
Deji O. Olagboye, Oluwasoye P. Mafimisebi, Demola Obembe, and Kassa Woldesenbet Beta

Institutions and Sustainability

Institutional Pressures, Firm Resource Context and SMEs' Sustainability in Africa 127
Kassa Woldesenbet Beta and Olapeju Ogunmokun

Bribery, Corruption and Sustainability Activities in African Countries 151
Alessio Faccia and Zeenat Beebeejaun

Organizational Culture and Corporate Sustainability in Africa 187
Dhawal Sharad Jadhav

Entrepreneurship and Sustainability

Sustainability Activities and Business Model Innovation 209
Alessio Faccia, Zeenat Beebeejaun, and Narcisa Roxana Mosteanu

Understanding the Impact of the Entrepreneurial Ecosystem on Sustainability in Africa 229
Joseph Kwadwo Danquah, Mavis Serwah Benneh Mensah, William Yamoah, and Qazi Moinuddin Mahmud

Strategic Entrepreneurship Approach for a Sustainable African Ecosystem 255
Narcisa Roxana Moşteanu and Albert Dans Michael Ngame Mesue

Promoting Sustainability in Africa Through Entrepreneurial Branding 281
Samuel Yaw Kusi, Arinze Christian Nwoba, Adedapo Adebajo, and Osei Yaw Adjei

CONTENTS ix

Gender and Sustainability

Beyond Mere Rhetoric: Gender Diversity and Corporate Sustainability Policies   297
Priscilla Akua Vitoh

Gender and Sustainability in Africa   319
Esther Aseidu, Afia Nyarko Boakye, George Kofi Amoako, and Ebenezer Malcalm

Corporate Governance and Sustainability

The Role of Accountability in Corporate Environmental Sustainability Framework   349
Mfon S. Jeremiah and Kassa Woldesenbet Beta

Sustainability: Concept Clarification and Theory   375
Sara Omair, Hafiz Muhammad Usman Khizar, Omair Majeed, and Muhammad Jawad Iqbal

Corporate Governance and Sustainability Reporting in Africa   405
Waseem Ahmad Khan, Muhammad Farooq Shabbir, Hafiz Muhammad Usman Khizar, and Dacosta Omari

Green Human Resource Practices and Sustainability Performance: Evidence from Ghana   427
Gladys Esinu Abiew, George Kofi Amoako, and Emem Anwana

Index   445

Notes on Contributors

Gladys Esinu Abiew is a lecturer in Human Resource Management at the Koforidua Technical University in Ghana. Gladys's research have been published in International Journal of Innovation Science and Open Journal of Leadership. Her research focuses on diversity, innovation, leadership, sustainability, imposter syndrome, employee well-being and organizational behaviour. Gladys have attended and participated in a number of conferences in Ghana, an act that is sharpening her research skills. Her teaching interest includes human resource management, strategic management and organizational behaviour. She is currently pursuing her Ph.D. in Business and Management (Human Resource Management) at the Kwame Nkrumah University of Science and Technology, Ghana.

Kweku Adams Ph.D., LLM, M.B.A., SFHEA, is Associate Professor in International Business & Management at the Bradford School of Management. A Senior Fellow of the Higher Education Academy, he holds an M.B.A. (University of Bedfordshire), Master of Laws (University of York), and Ph.D. (Swansea University), among others. His research has been published in journals including *Tourism Management, Journal of International Management, Technological Forecasting & Social Change, IEEE-Transactions on Engineering Management, Journal of Environmental Management, Journal of Business Research*, etc. He is on the Editorial Review Boards of the *Thunderbird International Business Review* and the *Africa Journal of Management*.

Adedapo Adebajo is a lecturer in Marketing at the School of Management and Marketing, Greenwich Business School, Marketing Research Group, University of Greenwich, London—UK. His research expertise encompasses the academic realms of marketing, innovation, and public management. He received his Ph.D. degree in Management from the University of Edinburgh, United Kingdom, with a thesis on open innovation in public services. He was awarded a doctoral scholarship in co-production by the Centre for 'Service Excellence and has presented his research works at reputable academic international conferences. Adedapo's research is underpinned by his passion for social change, individual and collective well-being, and sustainable development.

Osei Yaw Adjei is a practising Marketing professional and Entrepreneur. He has served as a Senior Investment Analyst and Marketing Manager with Databank, the premier investment Bank in Ghana. Currently, he is an Executive Director in charge of Marketing and Channels at Pesewa ONE PLC; a business incubator with the core mandate of grooming young entrepreneurs in Africa. He is a holder of an M.B.A. in Marketing, a Finalist of the Professional Postgraduate Diploma level in Marketing of the Chartered Institute of Marketing-UK, and a Postgraduate Certificate holder in Management Studies with The Int. Professional Managers Association-UK. Osei has research works in Service Quality Delivery in the Investment Banking Sector in Ghana, The Role and Impact of Service Providers in The Introduction of the 3 Tier pension Scheme in Ghana. The Effective Use of Sales Promotion Tools in Increasing the Patronage of Fast Moving Consumer Goods.

Samuel Adomako is an Associate Professor of Strategy at the Birmingham Business School at the University of Birmingham, UK.

Edmund Osei Afriyie is a Ph.D. student in Strategy and International Business (Management) at the University of Birmingham, UK. He completed his MSc. International Business at Brunel University London, UK and pursued his undergraduate program in Business Administration at Ashesi University, Ghana. At Brunel University London, he gained an understanding of sustainability in Africa during his dissertation period. He is also particularly interested in exploring the triple-bottom-line sustainability development of multinational enterprises throughout Africa during his higher education.

NOTES ON CONTRIBUTORS xiii

George Kofi Amoako is the Director at the Office of Research Innovation and Consultancy and Associate Professor at Ghana Communication Technology University Accra. He is an academic practising Chartered Marketer (CIM-UK) with specialization in, Marketing Sustainability, Branding, CSR, and E-Business. He was educated at Kwame Nkrumah University of Science and Technology in Kumasi Ghana and the University of Ghana and the London School of Marketing (UK). He has completed Ph.D. at London Metropolitan University UK. He also has a postgraduate certificate in academic practice from Lancaster University. He has considerable research, teaching, consulting, and practice experience in Marketing Theory application.

George Oppong Appiagyei Ampong is Associate Professor in Management and Dean of the Business School at Ghana Communication Technology University in Ghana. He holds Ph.D. in Business Administration and PGCert in International Higher Education Academic Practice. His research interest includes Business and Sustainability strategies, entrepreneurship and SME development, and organizational leadership, His research has been published in reputable journals such as VINE Journal of Information and Knowledge Management Systems, Journal of Hospitality and Tourism Insights, Journal of Technological Forecasting & Social Change, Journal of Business Research among others.

Emem Anwana is a lawyer by profession. She is a senior lecturer in the Applied Law Department of the Durban University of Technology. She is currently the Faculty Research Co-coordinator, in charge of postgraduate studies in the Faculty of Management Sciences of the university. Her area of expertise is in business law, commercial law, corporate governance, social justice, supply chain management, entrepreneurship, and women/gender issues. Her interest also lies in research and higher education development in emerging economies. She has published several articles, conference proceedings, and book chapters in the area.

Esther Aseidu is a lecturer of management at Ghana Communication Technology University (GCTU). She holds a Ph.D. in Business Administration. She has seven years of undergraduate and postgraduate teaching in diverse management courses. Her research focuses on management and organizational behaviour, leadership, supply chain, graduate employability studies, procurement, corporate sustainability, small and medium-sized enterprises, the maritime industry, higher education, green human

xiv   NOTES ON CONTRIBUTORS

resource, procurement, and gender-related issues. In addition to her academic expertise, she has been providing the University and the community with invaluable services in the areas of youth mentoring, business planning, and gender advocacy.

Rexford Attah-Boakye is Assistant Professor of Accounting at the University of Nottingham Business School. He is a qualified chartered accountant (ACCA), an associate member of the institute of credit management (AICM), and a certified quantitative risk management expert (CQRM). His specialty is in financial accounting and reporting, auditing, and assurance, environmental accounting, accounting for cyber-security and artificial intelligence, corporate governance, taxation, and risk management. His research has appeared in the *British Journal of Management, International Journal of Finance & Economics, European Journal of Finance, Technological Forecasting and Social Change, IEEE Transactions on Engineering Management, Journal of environmental management*, etc.

Zeenat Beebeejaun is Assistant Professor in Law at the Dubai Campus and a doctoral researcher at the University of Birmingham. She has a range of publications in world-leading peer-reviewed journals in commercial law, dispute resolution in oil and gas disputes, and equity and trusts. Zeenat also has extensive experience teaching Law at the undergrad and post-grad levels, having taught at various British universities in Dubai. She has also designed several Law modules and led many modules in these universities. Before joining academia, she practised as a legal consultant in Dubai, mainly advising clients on real estate matters and commercial transactions.

Dr. Kassa Woldesenbet Beta Ph.D., is Associate Professor in Research and Deputy Director of the Centre for Enterprise and Innovation at the Leicester Castle Business School, De Montfort University, UK. He is a leading authority on inclusive entrepreneurship. His research and scholarship span across various themes including entrepreneurship in context, gender, SMEs, resources and capabilities, supplier diversity, institutions, and sustainability. He has strong track records in conducting impactful research that contributes to business practice and policy.

Afia Nyarko Boakye is a lecturer of human resource management at Ghana Communication Technology University (GCTU). She holds Ph.D. in Human Resource Management and has eight years of undergraduate and postgraduate teaching. Her research focuses on human resource planning, organizational behavior, leadership, graduate employability studies, and gender-related issues. Apart from her academic background, she has been rendering valuable services to the University and the community on women empowerment, youth mentorship, and gender advocacy. She has been researching with colleagues on issues related to organizational behavior, higher education, artificial intelligence, green human resource, and gender.

Agyenim Boateng is Professor of Finance and Director of Finance and Banking Research Centre at the Leicester Castle Business School at De Montfort University, UK.

Dr. Joseph Kwadwo Danquah is Assistant Professor of Human Capital Development, Innovation and Entrepreneurship. He holds a Ph.D. in Human Resource Development, and a master's in Human and Organisational Capacity for Development, both from the University of Bradford—UK. **Joseph** is a fellow of the Higher Education Academy (HEA) and an academic member of the Chartered Institute of Personnel and Development (CIPD). **Joseph** is a researcher and currently a lecturer in human resource management and human resource development at the School of Management, Law, and Social Sciences. His research interest focuses on Human Resource Management/Development, SMEs development, managerial effectiveness, innovation, entrepreneurship, and Strategic human resource.

Albert Danso is an Associate Professor of Accounting and Finance at the Leicester Castle Business School at De Montfort University, UK.

Alessio Faccia Assistant Professor in Finance, qualified as an auditor and chartered Accountant since 2009. He ran his independent audit firm for 10+ years and started his career previously at Accenture. He gained International Experience in Italy (Università LUISS Guido Carli, Università Roma TRE, Università di Roma La Sapienza), UAE (The University of Birmingham Dubai Campus, American University of the Emirates, De Montfort University Dubai), UK (Coventry University), and Malta (American University of Malta). Dr. Alessio served as an expert and trainer for the Italian Tax Police (Guardia di Finanza) and as a court-appointed technical consultant in White-Collar Crime and Bankruptcy. His research interests range from accounting and finance to technology and innovation, enjoying multidisciplinary research as he believes it ensures novelty and innovation.

Antoinette Yaa Benewaa Gabrah is a Ph.D. candidate at the University of Professional Studies Accra. She holds an MPhil in Marketing from the University of Ghana. She is currently an adjunct faculty at Akenten Appiah-Minka University of Skills Training and Entrepreneurial Development in Kumasi Ghana. Antoinette has published in Scopus Indexed journals. Her research interest includes e-business, services marketing, and digital marketing strategies.

Elvis Hernandez-Perdomo Ph.D. (Fin.), Ph.D. (EngSc.), MIF, M.Sc., B.S., CQRM, AFHEA, is the Executive Director of OSL Risk Management (UK), Vice-Chairman of the International Institute of Professional Education and Research (US). Dr. Hernandez has over 20 years of experience in risk management, corporate governance, project management, and real options valuations. Formerly Central Banker's Economist and Senior VP of Consulting, specialized in Monte Carlo Risk Simulation, optimization, data analytics, ESG Risk, and business intelligence. He has done Ph.D. in Finance (University of Hull) and Ph.D. in Engineering Science. Fellow of the Energy Institute. Visiting Professor and Associate Fellow at the Academy of Higher Education with several academic articles published in international peer-review journals.

Dr. Muhammad Jawad Iqbal is Professor, Dean Faculty of Management, and Director Institute of Business Management and Administrative Sciences (IBMAS), at The Islamia University of Bahawalpur. He received his Ph.D. from the University of Technology, Malaysia. His current research interests include sustainable entrepreneurship, business strategy, and leadership. His research has appeared in leading journals, including the Journal of Business Research, Computers & Education, Sustainable Development, and Sustainability.

Dhawal Sharad Jadhav is an FPM (Fellow Program in Management) scholar at MICA, Ahmedabad (India). He is Company Secretary (CS) and has a Master of Law (LLM) in the area of Business law. His research portfolio focuses on Strategic Management, Corporate Sustainability, Corporate Governance, Business Ethics, and Digitalization. His research interests broadly include corporate sustainability, digitalization, and strategy. He has ten years of experience, including five years in the industry and more than five years of academic experience teaching Legal aspects of business, Corporate laws, Business ethics, Corporate governance, and Strategic management.

Mfon S. Jeremiah Ph.D., is Senior Lecturer at the Department of Accounting, University of Uyo, Nigeria where he teaches both at the undergraduate and postgraduate levels. His research interest revolves around context-specific corporate social responsibility, environmental accountability, and sustainability in transition economy. Before joining the University of Uyo in 2008 he worked in industry for over five years and also worked in private auditing and consulting firm for four years.

Dr. Waseem Ahmad Khan has a Ph.D. in Accounting from Xiamen University, China, and is currently working as a Lecturer at The Islamia University of Bahawalpur, Pakistan. Dr. Waseem has more than ten years of teaching and research experience, and his research interests include FDI in One Belt Road, Financial Development, Corporate Governance, Sustainable Development, and reporting.

Dr. Hafiz Muhammad Usman Khizar is working as a full-time faculty member at the Institute of Business, Management, and Administrative Sciences (IBMAS), the Islamia University of Bahawalpur. He has more than 12 years of teaching and research experience. His research interests are in strategy, sustainable entrepreneurship, and organizational behaviours. He is an expert in conducting Systematic Literature Reviews (SLR). His research has appeared in cross-disciplinary journals, including Journal of Business Research, Sustainable Development, Sage Open, Kybernetes, and Journal of Public Affairs.

Samuel Yaw Kusi is a lecturer in Marketing at the School of Management and Marketing, Greenwich Business School, Marketing Research Group, University of Greenwich, London—UK. He teaches postgraduate subjects: Strategic Marketing Management, Global Marketing & Emerging Issues. His research interest is in international marketing and the interface of entrepreneurship and branding. His research has appeared in journal outlets such as *Journal of World Business* and *International Business Review*.

Dr. Oluwasoye P. Mafimisebi Ph.D., is Associate Professor & Reader in Strategic Management; Faculty Head of Research Students at Leicester Castle Business School and has active ambitious research agenda around

Risk and Resilience, Fintech, Global Challenges and Tackling Crises in the Global South. He's currently the Research Degrees Leader for Business and Law and Chair of the Faculty Research Degrees Sub-Committee. Dr. Oluwasoye is a Senior Consulting Editor—Review of Management Literature and has published widely in top journals and acted as external examiner for UK business schools as well as a reviewer for several top-tier journals.

Dr. Qazi Moinuddin Mahmud associate fellow of the Higher Education Academy (AFHEA) has been working in academia for fourteen years and currently serves as an Assistant Professor of Management at the University of Dhaka in Bangladesh. As a commonwealth doctoral scholar, he completed Ph.D. in Human Resource Management from the University of Bradford School of Management. He received Dean's prize for innovation and impact in doctoral research for his highest-scoring Ph.D. research. Earlier he completed his bachelor's in management, postgraduate diploma in marketing, and master's in Humane Resource Management. He became a Bradford Graduate Fellow in 2020 and an Associate Fellow of the Advance HE, UK in 2023.

Omair Majeed is an adjunct lecturer at Bahauddin- Zakariya University Multan, Pakistan. His research interests include firm sustainability, organizational communications, and Islamic Banking & Finance.

Ebenezer Malcalm is the Dean of the School of Graduate Studies and Research at Ghana Communication Technology University (GCTU). He is a trained Instructional Designer and Technologist and Communication and Development Specialist. About his educational background, Dr. Malcalm obtained a Bachelor's degree in Publishing Studies at Kwame Nkrumah University of Science and Technology Kumasi, Ghana, and a Master's degree in Population Studies, from the University of Ghana. He also graduated and earned a Master's degree in International Affairs with a major in Communication and Development at Ohio University. He earned his Ph.D. in Curriculum/ Instruction and Instructional Technology at Ohio University, USA.

Dr. Mavis Serwah Benneh Mensah is Senior Lecturer of Entrepreneurship and the founding Director of the Centre for Entrepreneurship and Small Enterprise Development (CESED) at the School of Business, University of Cape Coast, Ghana. She holds a Ph.D. in Development Studies from the University of Cape Coast, Ghana, an M.B.A.

in Small and Medium-sized Enterprise Development from the University of Leipzig, Germany, and a Diploma in SMEs Management and Development from the Galilee College in Israel. She is a Certified CEFE entrepreneurship trainer. She had her secondary education at Holy Child School, in Cape Coast, Ghana, between 1994 and 1996.

Albert Dans Michael Ngame Mesue is a social scientist with a keen interest in the sustainability of businesses and entrepreneurial ventures, particularly in Africa. With a background in Economics and an M.B.A. from the American University of Malta, he has research experience in certain fields like Corporate Social Responsibility, environmental reporting, sustainability, and compliance. Driven by the desire to sustainably grow businesses from start-up, Michael has occupied several positions in growing and already established organizations and has worked with cross-functional teams across different corporations and continents. He currently works as the compliance officer for a Pharmaceutical based in Malta while pursuing research in business philosophy.

Dr. Narcisa Roxana Mosteanu is a Full Professor at the American University of Malta, on Finance and Business Management Specialization, and during the last two years, she was the chief academic officer and the Provost of the same university. Her area of expertise and education comes from prestigious universities in Romania, the UK, the USA, and the UAE. Over 25 years of professional finance, banking, taxation, management, and higher education globally, make Professor Narcisa an excellent ambassador for the higher education and international financial management industry. She has an extensive academic background, spending considerable time as a professor and academic researcher, with more than scientific 100 articles, and 24 books

Chioma N. Nwafor received her M.Sc. and Ph.D. degrees in Financial Services and Monetary Economics, respectively, from the Adam Smith Business School University of Glasgow, Scotland. She leads the Quantitative Research team at CEDAF Ltd and is a lecturer in Quantitative Risk Modelling at Glasgow Caledonian University. Chioma has published her work in leading academic journals, including the International Review of Economics and Finance, the International Journal of Finance and Economics, and Finance Research Letters. She has also presented her research at local and international conferences. Her research interests include applying machine learning-induced artificial intelligence systems in financial risk, among others.

Arinze Christian Nwoba is a lecturer (Assistant Professor) in Marketing at the School of Business and Economics at Loughborough University, United Kingdom. Arinze's research centres around International Marketing Strategy, Social Marketing and Social Entrepreneurship, Corporate Sustainability, Emerging Markets, and International Marketing. Specifically, Arinze's research is focused on how emerging market firms survive in the face of institutional adversity and emerging markets phenomena. Arinze has published his research findings in the European Journal of Marketing; International Marketing Review; Business Strategy and the Environment; Production, Planning & Control; Asia Pacific Journal of Management; Telematics and Informatics, among others.

Dr. Demola Obembe Ph.D., is Associate Professor of Strategic Management and Head of the School for Leadership, Management and Marketing at De Montfort University, UK. Over a 20-year period, he has been involved in academic teaching, research, and leadership. His research interests are in the areas of; strategy processes and practice, entrepreneurship and SMEs, knowledge and innovation management, and social capital.

Dr. Olapeju Ogunmokun is a lecturer in the Department of Leadership, Management and Marketing at De Montfort University. She has a breadth and depth of experience in coordinating business management modules, supervising business management research, and teaching at both undergraduate and postgraduate levels. Her research interests and expertise centre around finance, risk, entrepreneurship, and sustainability.

Dr. Deji O. Olagboye Ph.D., is Lecturer in Business Management at the School for Leadership, Management and Marketing at Leicester Castle Business School, De Montfort University, UK. Dr. Deji is an early career researcher with over 15 years of industry experience. He is involved in academic teaching and research. His research interests are in the areas of; entrepreneurship and SMEs, business development and sustainability, change management and innovation, and institutions.

Dacosta Omari is a Ph.D., candidate at Durham University Business School, UK. Dacosta's research interests are in the areas of R&D, Quality

Management, Innovation Management, SMEs, and Human resource management.

Sara Omair is a lecturer of Management at the National University of Modern Languages Islamabad, Multan campus, Pakistan, and a doctoral student at the Islamia University of Bahawalpur. Her primary research interests include leadership communication, organizational behavior, and sustainability.

Dr. Muhammad Farooq Shabbir is Assistant Professor at the Institute of Business, Management, and Administrative Sciences (IBMAS), at The Islamia University of Bahawalpur. He has more than 15 years of teaching and research experience. His research interests are in Corporate Governance and Sustainable Finance.

Mike Tooke CEng, MEI, is the Director of 2G BioPOWER, Chartered Engineer, and Member of the Energy Institute. He is an international expert in circular economy with over 30 years of professional experience, mainly in pyrolysis technologies to turn waste into valuable products. He has participated in many international engineering projects on technology commercialization, evaluation, and selection. Mike conducts Techno-Economic Assessments, risk-based operational and financial modelling for project development. He has created a 100k tpa tyre pyrolysis project working with Scandinavian Enviro Systems, covering technical, commercial, and regulatory issues. He has represented a German gasification company in the UK.

Priscilla Akua Vitoh is a Doctoral Candidate at the University of Warwick School of Law and is Associate Fellow of the Higher Education Academy, United Kingdom. She integrates conceptual and theoretical understanding with empirical research techniques to research the intersection of Financial regulation, landed property rights, labour law and Bank financing of women-owned and women-led Small and medium-scale enterprises (SMEs). She also has a keen interest in the effect of legal and regulatory frameworks on the socio-economic development of Anglophone West African women.

Mr. William Yamoah is a result-oriented person with professional qualifications in Project Management and Education. **Mr. William** is currently a second-year Ph.D. student in Public Administration and Policy Management at the University of Ghana Business School. He holds a master's in project management from Northeastern University, Boston USA and a Bachelor of Education from the University of Winneba, Ghana. He has over twenty (20) years of working experience, holding managerial positions such as Director of Finance and Administration at the Ruling New Patriotic Party Headquarters, Deputy Director, Program Manager, and instructor. **Mr. William** is keen to leverage his managerial skills and professional experiences to bring a desired outcome to his role.

Honglan Yu Ph.D., M.Sc., is a lecturer in Management (Strategy) at Huddersfield Business School, with research interests in corporate turnaround and organizational learning. Prior to joining the University of Huddersfield, Honglan worked as a Graduate Teaching Assistant at Adam Smith Business, University of Glasgow. Honglan obtained his Ph.D. in Management from the University of Glasgow and MSc in International Business and Emerging Markets from the University of Edinburgh. Honglan's research interests lie in antecedents, changing processes and outcomes of corporate turnaround actions, and changes of organizational learning in internationalization. His Ph.D. research investigated how and why firms achieve a successful corporate turnaround by collaborating with eleven international SMEs in the high-tech manufacturing industry.

Nadia Zahoor is a senior lecturer in Strategy at the Queen Mary University of London, UK. She completed her Ph.D. in Management at the University of Huddersfield, UK. Her research interests are strategic alliances, global strategy, innovation, and organizational resilience. She is particularly interested in the context of small and medium-sized enterprises in emerging markets. Her research has been published in mainstream journals, including *British Journal of Management, Technovation, International Journal of Management Reviews, International Business Review, International Marketing Review, International Small Business Journal, Business Strategy and the Environment*, among others.

LIST OF FIGURES

Enhancing Circular Economy and Sustainable Environmental Practices—Opportunities and Challenges for Tyre Pyrolysis in Africa

Fig. 1   Waste pyrolysis approach (*Source* Chew et al. [2021] and Zabaniotou et al. [2014])   13

Africa's Response to SDGs: Barriers and Challenges

Fig. 1   Conceptual framework of the study   56

Multinational Enterprises, Sustainability Activities, and Implementation of Sustainable Development Goals in Africa

Fig. 1   Summary of roles by MNEs   70
Fig. 2   Summary of a framework for local development sustainability   72

Financing Sustainable Development Goals in Africa: The Role of Remittances—Evidence from Nigeria

Fig. 1   Africa progress snapshot (*Source* Africa UN Data Development. Available at https://ecastats.uneca.org/uns dgsafrica/SDGs/SDG-progress)   85
Fig. 2   Progress at indicator level (poverty) (Available at https://ecastats.uneca.org/unsdgsafrica/SDGs/SDG-progress)   87

xxiv LIST OF FIGURES

Fig. 3 Multidimensional poverty measure and deprivation
by indicators (*Source* Poverty and Inequality Platform.
Available at https://pip.worldbank.org/country-profiles/
NGA) 91

Fig. 4 Top remittance recipients in Sub-Saharan Africa, 2020 95

Fig. 5 Variable trend graphs 97

Institutional Pressures, Firm Resource Context and SMEs' Sustainability in Africa

Fig. 1 Conceptual framework on the role of internal and external
factors on SMEs sustainability practice and performance 141

Organizational Culture and Corporate Sustainability in Africa

Fig. 1 Triple I approach of corporate sustainability 193

Fig. 2 Three levels of culture 194

Understanding the Impact of the Entrepreneurial Ecosystem on Sustainability in Africa

Fig. 1 Entrepreneurial Ecosystem (EE) factors for sustainability
in developing countries (*Source* Compiled by Authors 2022) 242

Strategic Entrepreneurship Approach for a Sustainable African Ecosystem

Fig. 1 PESTEL external evaluation chart 262

Fig. 2 SWOT analysis 263

Fig. 3 Threats, weakness, and environmental challenges
of entrepreneurs in Africa—biggest obstacles 265

Fig. 4 Diagrammatic illustration of the decision stage 268

Fig. 5 Generic strategic plan digital entrepreneurship in Africa 273

The Role of Accountability in Corporate Environmental Sustainability Framework

Fig.1 Four-step model of corporate environmental sustainability
(*Source* Developed by the researchers from literature reviewed) 355

Fig. 2 The model of stakeholder's engagement in environmental
accountability system (*Source* Developed by the researchers) 358

Green Human Resource Practices and Sustainability Performance: Evidence from Ghana

Fig. 1 Conceptual model   437

LIST OF TABLES

Enhancing Circular Economy and Sustainable Environmental Practices—Opportunities and Challenges for Tyre Pyrolysis in Africa

Table 1	Summary of articles published tyres pyrolysis and circular economy in Africa (2008–2022)	16
Table 2	Project drivers in tire pyrolysis and circular economy literature in Africa (2008–2022)	28

Multinational Enterprises, Sustainability Activities, and Implementation of Sustainable Development Goals in Africa

Table 1	Categories of roles played by MNEs	71

Financing Sustainable Development Goals in Africa: The Role of Remittances—Evidence from Nigeria

Table 1	Mapping of clusters/pillars to SDGs	84
Table 2	Poverty headcount ratio at $1.90/day 2021 and 2022	88
Table 3	2021 SDG overall score for African countries	89
Table 4	SDGs 1, 2, and 8 dashboards for Nigeria	92
Table 5	Expected gap: Nigeria	93
Table 6	Correlation matrix 2000–2019	97

xxvii

xxviii LIST OF TABLES

Natural Resources, Sustainable Entrepreneurship, and Poverty Reduction in Resource-Rich African Countries: The Missing Link

Table 1	EDBI in RRDCs and poverty levels	108
Table 2	Other resource-rich countries	110

Bribery, Corruption and Sustainability Activities in African Countries

Table 1	Theoretical and empirical mapping and implications	161

Organizational Culture and Corporate Sustainability in Africa

Table 1	Top 5 companies in 2021	198

Sustainability Activities and Business Model Innovation

Table 1	Innovative African solutions and sharing economy	221

Understanding the Impact of the Entrepreneurial Ecosystem on Sustainability in Africa

Table 1	The six schools of thought on entrepreneurship	237

Overview and Structure of the Book

Samuel Adomako, Albert Danso, and Agyenim Boateng

1 Introduction

The concept of sustainability first became the focus of international policymaking after the publication of the influential report of Brundtland in 1987, which opened the international policy debate on environment and development. However, a significant change in thinking emerged with the adoption of the United Nations Sustainable Development Goals (SDGs), leading to intense international advocacy around the globe on the need to pay urgent attention to issues associated with environmental sustainability and development.

S. Adomako
Birmingham Business School, University of Birmingham, Birmingham, UK
e-mail: S.Adomako@bham.ac.uk

A. Danso (✉)
Leicester Castle Business School, De Montfort University, Leicester, UK
e-mail: Albert.danso@dmu.ac.uk

A. Boateng
Finance and Banking Research Centre, Leicester Castle Business School, De Montfort University, Leicester, UK
e-mail: Agyenim.boateng@dmu.ac.uk

© The Author(s), under exclusive license to Springer Nature
Switzerland AG 2023
S. Adomako et al. (eds.), *Corporate Sustainability in Africa,*
Palgrave Studies in African Leadership,
https://doi.org/10.1007/978-3-031-29273-6_1

Despite the renewed interest among policymakers in the corridors of power in both developed and developing countries, unsustainability practices continue to persist and, at best, governments of major polluting countries have pursued selective programmes and policies to maintain their economic competitiveness and dominance on the global stage. Increasingly, academics, practitioners, and environmental activists have realized that many of the sustainability challenges such as air pollution, biodiversity loss, climate change, energy and food security, disease spread, species invasion, water shortages, and pollution are intertwined and require cooperation and concerted efforts among governments, consumers/individuals, and companies. Although it is important to point out that companies are only one of the vehicles of environmental problems facing the globe, the sheer volume of company activities, financial resources, and technological knowledge makes it imperative for them to be at the forefront of the fight for net zero. Indeed, companies are primary engines of economic development and growth, yet their activities have unintended negative consequences for the planet we live on.

2 Sustainability and Africa

In the context of Africa, weak institutions, poor corporate governance systems, lack of resources and technical capabilities to tackle sustainability, and environmental management issues have driven environmental and sustainability issues to the bottom of the agenda of African governments and corporate entities. Several cases of environmental degradation, hazards, and public health problems have been reported on the continent including poor gold mining practices (galamsey) leading to water pollution in Ghana, oil spillage in the Niger Delta in Nigeria and Angola, and malnutrition in Somalia. In addition, with the promotion of industrialization to achieve economic development in Africa, carbon emissions have quadrupled in the last decade (Adekunle, 2020). All these have put pressure on governments and firms across Africa to improve their sustainability practices. Specifically, the environmental challenges have amplified the expectations of firms operating in developing countries of being visible in integrating sustainable business practices for their employees and business partners along their global supply chains (Gardiner, 2020). However, these challenges remain consistently under-researched in the African context in comparison to developed countries. Given the critical role that both indigenous African firms and foreign subsidiaries in Africa play in contributing to economic growth across the continent, there is a great societal expectation of these firms towards enhancing environmental stewardship and social responsibility. In fact, ignoring sustainability could be detrimental (Adomako et al., 2019, 2020) to the enterprising efforts of these firms because of environmental, social, and economic expectations to continue to grow. In the main, sustainability, social responsibility, society, and ethics motivate scholarship from diverse disciplines—e.g., management, finance, accounting, marketing, operations, supply chain, political science, sociology, psychology, and economics (Danso et al., 2019, 2020). Each discipline makes significant contributions to this topical area, and most researchers agree that interdisciplinary research can be highly revelatory. Surprisingly, and perhaps regrettably, the limited number of truly interdisciplinary studies, including in special issues, suggests that more can and should be done to intensify cross-boundary sustainability research, especially in Africa (Amankwah-Amoah et al., 2019).

Against the above backdrop, this book sheds light on corporate sustainability in Africa where about one-quarter of the world's natural resources are located, and good sustainable practices are key for companies to maintain long-term viability and contribute to the continent's economic development. Thus, the need and expectation for companies to pursue more sustainable strategies appear more pronounced and urgent, given that companies are major producers that convert natural resources into usable products and are therefore better situated to implement policies and sustainable strategies to reduce pollution (Shrivastava, 1995). Moreover, African governments lack resources to tackle environmental problems largely caused by multinational companies from the developed North exploiting the continent's vast natural resources. Thus, the vast resources (both financial and non-financial) available to these companies place them in a unique position to make major contributions that impact the society and environment in which they operate (Haugh & Talwar, 2010).

3 Themes of the Book

In our edited book we have compiled a diversity of chapters that explore issues such as SDGs, institutions, corporate governance, gender, entrepreneurship, and their impact on sustainability in Africa, grouped under five main themes as follows. Under Part I, the authors consider

4 S. ADOMAKO ET AL.

opportunities, challenges, and implementation of sustainable environmental practices that may influence the achievement of sustainable development goals (SDGs) in Africa. The next section, Part II, explores the effects of institutions on sustainability. Here, the authors deal with the effects of institutional pressures, culture and corruption on corporate sustainability practices. Following that is Part III, which examines the relationship between entrepreneurship and sustainability practices. The chapters in this section tackle entrepreneurship design, promotion, business model innovation, and how they affect sustainability. In Part IV, the roles of gender and gender-inclusive policies in achieving sustainable practices are considered. The final part (Part V) deals with the effects of corporate governance on sustainability in Africa. In this part, the authors present conceptual clarification of sustainability, the impact of sustainability reporting, and green human resource practices on sustainability strategies.

REFERENCES

Adekunle, I. A. (2020). On the search for environmental sustainability in Africa: The role of governance. *Environmental Science and Pollution Research*, 1–14.

Adomako, S. (2020). Environmental collaboration, sustainable innovation, and small and medium-sized enterprise growth in sub-Saharan Africa: Evidence from Ghana. *Sustainable Development, 28*(6), 1609–1619.

Adomako, S., Amankwah-Amoah, J., Danso, A., Konadu, R., & Owusu-Agyei, S. (2019). Environmental sustainability orientation and performance of family and nonfamily firms. *Business Strategy and the Environment, 28*(6), 1250–1259.

Adomako, S., Ning, E., & Adu-Ameyaw, E. (2020). Proactive environmental strategy and firm performance at the bottom of the pyramid. *Business Strategy and the Environment*.

Amankwah-Amoah, J., Danso, A., & Adomako, S. (2019). Entrepreneurial orientation, environmental sustainability and new venture performance: Does stakeholder integration matter? *Business Strategy and the Environment, 28*(1), 79–87.

Danso, A., Adomako, S., Amankwah-Amoah, J., Owusu-Agyei, S., & Konadu, R. (2019). Environmental sustainability orientation, competitive strategy and financial performance. *Business Strategy and the Environment, 28*(5), 885–895.

Danso, A., Adomako, S., Lartey, T., Amankwah-Amoah, J., & Owusu-Yirenkyi, D. (2020). Stakeholder integration, environmental sustainability orientation and financial performance. *Journal of Business Research, 119*, 652–662.

Gardiner, B. 2020. Why COVID-19 will end up harming the environment. https://www.nationalgeographic.com/science/article/why-covid-19-will-end-up-harming-the-environment. Accessed 30 March 2021.

Haugh, H. M., Talwar, A. (2010). How do corporations embed sustainability across the organisation? *Academy of Management Learning & Education, 9*(3), 384–396.

Shrivastava, P. (1995). The role of corporations in achieving ecological sustainability. *The Academy of Management Review, 20*(4), 936–960.

World Commission on Environment and Development. (1987). *Our common future*. Oxford University Press.

SDGs and Africa

Enhancing Circular Economy and Sustainable Environmental Practices—Opportunities and Challenges for Tyre Pyrolysis in Africa

Rexford Attah-Boakye, Elvis Hernandez-Perdomo, Mike Tooke, Honglan Yu, and Kweku Adams

1 INTRODUCTION

With the increasing growth, studies forecast that the global population will increase significantly to around 12.3 billion by 2100 (Seto, 2011). The overuse of natural energy resources, particularly non-renewable ones,

---

R. Attah-Boakye (✉)
Nottingham University Business School, Nottingham, UK
e-mail: Rexford.Attah-Boakye@nottingham.ac.uk

E. Hernandez-Perdomo · M. Tooke
International Institute of Professional Education and Research (IIPER), Hull, UK
e-mail: elvis.hernandez@oslriskmanagement.com

M. Tooke
e-mail: miketooke@2gbc.co.uk

© The Author(s), under exclusive license to Springer Nature Switzerland AG 2023
S. Adomako et al. (eds.), *Corporate Sustainability in Africa*,
Palgrave Studies in African Leadership,
https://doi.org/10.1007/978-3-031-29273-6_2

is one of several unsustainable practices linked to global overpopulation. Also, the global-north economic growth surge vis-a-vis the social-economic inequalities and environmental degradations in the global-south (north–south dichotomy) continue to exacerbate the global warming and climate change challenges (Creutzig et al., 2015). Overpopulation also accelerates the pace of urbanisation, consumption, transportation, and waste (Steffen et al., 2015). If economic development continues to base on a linear trend, it has been estimated that the world will need at least 30% more fresh water, 50% more food, and 50% more energy (Albrecht et al., 2018; World Economic Forum, 2011), and society will demand unprecedented levels of natural resources and produce an extremely high volume of waste (Di Maio & Rem, 2015).

Africa is already facing more severe climate change than the rest of the world, despite bearing the least responsibility for the problem of climate change. With nearly one-fifth of the world's population today, Africa accounts for less than 3% of the world's energy-related carbon dioxide (CO_2) emissions and has the lowest emissions per capita of any region (Senyagwa, 2022). Nevertheless, Africans are already disproportionately experiencing the adverse effects of climate change, including water stress, reduced food production, increased frequency of extreme weather events, and lower economic growth—all fuelling mass migration and regional instability.

Besides, while the world population is projected to grow to approximately 12.3 billion by 2100, the highest percentage of this growth will come from the Global South, particularly in Africa, Asia, and Latin America (Abuzukhar, 2021; Ullah et al., 2021). Rapid population growth is usually associated with increasing urbanisation, demand, productivity, and consumption, and the like (Abuzukhar, 2021; Mokoele & Sebola, 2018). These phenomena exacerbate the challenges faced by Africa in

---

H. Yu
Huddersfield Business School, University of Huddersfield, Huddersfield, UK
e-mail: H.Yu2@hud.ac.uk

K. Adams
Faculty of Management, Law & Social Sciences, University of Bradford, Bradford, UK
e-mail: K.Adams3@bradford.ac.uk

areas such as waste disposal, environmental degradation, and global warming. Since most of Africa's inhabitants continue to migrate to the cities in search of work and a better standard of living, transportation has become a necessity, not a privilege. Most Average and middle-income workers are now buying cars as their primary means of transport. Those who cannot afford to buy cars are now using public transport such as buses, motorbikes, and others. Therefore, Tyre waste disposal is a critical challenge facing most African cities, towns, councils, and individuals.

Despite these issues, accepted circular economy practices have proven to reduce wastes from food production, transportation, industrial, manufacturing, electronics, automobiles, construction, and design (Benachio et al., 2020; EMF, 2017; Jia et al., 2020) is lacking. In addition to these challenges, Africa has been used as a dumping ground for electronic and industrial wastes. These antecedents have meant that several African governments continue to grapple with the challenges arising out of unsustainable practices of local and foreign businesses (Adams et al., 2018).

The main aim of this chapter is to discuss a circular economy practice that has been recognised in developing countries as plausible solutions to waste management in the transport sector. While the widely used waste management programmes in China to recycle batteries and the use of e-buses is popular (EMF, 2019), the Western Cape Industrial Symbiosis Programme in South Africa (EMF, 2020) and water recycling practices in Indian companies (Sohal et al., 2022) are among few of the best practices Africa can learn from. To address tyre waste in Africa, this chapter answers the question of how pyrolysis can be integrated into production plants and associated businesses to minimise waste in Africa. Though there are multiple challenges, risks, and impacts for investors and stakeholders, pyrolysis presents the best pathway for dealing with tyre and transport waste in Africa.

The rest of the chapter is organised and proceeds as follows: the next section presents a systematic literature review to delineate what a pyrolysis production plant business entails. The subsequent sections would demonstrate how to implement pyrolysis by converting waste into alternative by-products and the associated challenges. A discussion of implications and areas for future research concludes the chapter.

Circular Economy

Circular economy is opposite to the linear economy with the fundamental logic of "make-use-throw" (Lacko et al., 2021). The critical premise of the circular economy is *"the products of today are the materials of tomorrow at yesterday's price"* (Stahel, 2016, p. 437). Circular economy aims to reduce waste, maximise the use of natural resources, and regenerate economic systems (EMF, 2017). Recent development in circular economy specified the concept into 4R principles: reduce the consumption of primary energy and raw materials (Reduce), use by-products and waste as production inputs (Reuse), recycle water (Recycle), and redesign business models (Renew) (Vasiljevic-Shikaleska et al., 2017). In other words, it is an overall strategy of changing business models, management approaches, and managerial mindsets to realise economic benefits with less reliance on drawing resources from natural resources (Murray et al., 2017). Adopting a circular economy can help firms and countries to meet better responsible production and consumption goals (i.e. Sustainable Development Goal 12).

Waste Tyre Pyrolysis

The pyrolysis-circular economy recycling methodology (albeit a relatively new tyre recycling procedure in Africa) is gaining popularity as an effective measure of dealing with the challenges associated with the tyre waste disposal problems in Africa. Pyrolysis is a thermal decomposition process that converts used tyres into a solid residue (char), liquid oil (pyro-oil), and gas at temperatures between 300 and 900 °C (Dick et al., 2020). More importantly, it causes the feed materials to thermally decompose without using reactive gases, such as oxygen. As a result, its thermal efficiency can be improved from 70 to 90% if pyrolysis oil is further used in the thermochemical process (Nkosi & Muzenda, 2014). We use the conceptual model Zabaniotou et al. (2014) developed to illustrate how pyrolysis is implemented in practice in five key steps: pre-treat raw materials, slow pyrolysis, solid product activation, marketable end-product collection, and energy recycling, as shown in Fig. 1.

According to Zabaniotou et al. (2014), the pre-treatment of raw materials of end-of-life tyres (ELTs) pertains to steel chord removal and shredding. The primary equipment for preparing feedstocks is divided into two categories: ambient processing and cryogenic processing. Ambient

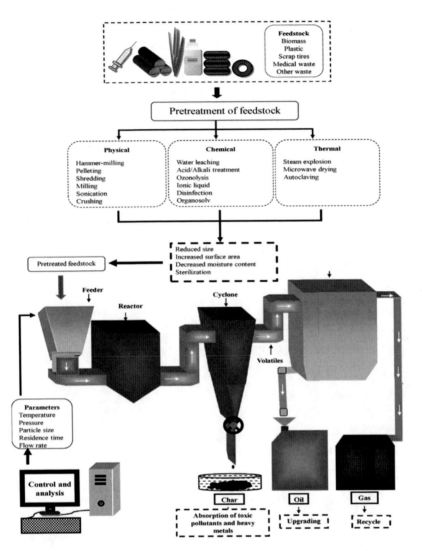

Fig. 1 Waste pyrolysis approach (*Source* Chew et al. [2021] and Zabaniotou et al. [2014])

processing of tyres is a common practice for raw material size reduction. Therefore, cryogenic grinding creates fragile, low-elastic particles by utilising liquid nitrogen and a low temperature (190 °C). On the other hand, slow pyrolysis can be made to run in batch or continuous mode. For smaller capacity, a batch pyrolysis system is typically implemented. The process cycle follows the loading of raw materials, pre-heating of the system, pyrolysis, temperature reset (cooling), and collection of end-products. Slow pyrolysis often requires significant manual labour. Finally, the raw material is processed by solid production activation, distinguished into different categories of marketable products and energy efficiency and optimisation.

Figure 1 provides a generic view of the application of pyrolysis to waste. As such, the pre-treatment and post-treatment options cover a wide range of wastes. According to the authors, for tyres pyrolysis based on emergent commercial solutions, the following treatment methods are applicable:
Pre-treatment:

- De-wiring
- Washing
- Shredding—typically including wire typically to 20–150 mm
- Crumbing (de-wired tyres) typically to 1–5 mm
- Metals removal (magnets)

Post-treatment:

- Volatiles:
  - Condensation (into 1 or more fractions)
  - Water separation
  - Centrifuge
  - Compression (gases)
  - De-sulphurisation (gases)
- Char:
  - Metals removal (magnets)
  - Milling, beading, and pelletising (if producing recovered Carbon Black)

The volatiles include non-condensing gases. These are typically used to deliver process heat for the pyrolysis reactor and post-treatment of the carbon char. The balance of the products (steel, oil, and carbon char) can be re-used.

As a result, pyrolysis is a circular economy practice that provides a reliable mechanism for dealing with the urgent tyre disposal challenges in the world, including Africa (Sohal et al., 2022), while adding value to potential investors and producing economic growth (employment, GDP, consumption, etc.). Thus, our systematic literature review of twenty-one studies on pyrolysis in 16 African countries from 2008 to 2022 offers critical references for adopting strategies for dealing with tyre waste disposal and providing decision-making support in Africa.

2   SYSTEMATIC LITERATURE REVIEW

Data Sources

At the beginning of December 2022, a search using the Thomson Reuters' Web of Knowledge-based Web of Science, Google Scholar, and EBSCO was undertaken for a multi-year period (2008–2022) across 16 countries in Africa. The initial search criterion used was based on the words "tyre pyrolysis" (OR "tyre waste") AND "circular economy" AND "Africa" in the title of the journal article relating to this multi-year period. Initial searches yielded 125 documents, including published articles, book reviews, editorial materials, and letters to the editor. This initial search was refined to include only published articles and book reviews, excluding editorial material and editor letters. This search revealed 55 published interdisciplinary journal articles, of which 21 articles were selected after verifying their coverage across African countries (see Table 1).

Tyre Pyrolysis and Sustainable Practices in Africa

The compendium of studies presented in Table 1 illustrates that many disposal routes either have detrimental environmental impacts (e.g. combustion) or questionable viability (e.g. use in concrete). Six of the papers focus on pyrolysis and support this route as a reasonable and sustainable means of solving Africa's increasing tyre waste disposal problem. It is a circular economy route that uses thermal methods of recycling tires. At the same time, the associated project can give the project

Table 1 Summary of articles published tyres pyrolysis and circular economy in Africa (2008–2022)

Authors	Focus/title	Country	Methods	Findings/conclusion	Limitations
Senthil Kumar et al. (2017)	This study reviews the feasibility of using waste tires as chips and fibres of different sizes in concrete to improve, strengthen, and protect the environment	Rwanda	Literature review	The study shows that reducing compressive and tensile strength can be increased by adding some super plasticisers and industrial wastes as partial cement replacement will increase the strength of waste tyre rubber-modified concrete	The study did not test for the effects of fire on the product
Vanessa Linganzi (2008)	This study explores how firms make gains from recycling solid industrial waste, including tyres	Burkina Faso	Survey response	Tyres can be recycled into making footwear tyre sandals which provide income to many low-income families	Some of the tyre-footwears eventually end up in a scrap causing further waste
Sanneh et al. (2011)	This study examines the recycling system in the Gambia to enhance sustainable municipal solid waste management	Gambia	Literature review	Open burning of solid waste, including vehicle tyres, is common in the cities of Gambia. These represent significant harm to humans	The prevailing open dumping and open burning constitute a significant challenge for the government

Authors	Focus/title	Country	Methods	Findings/conclusion	Limitations
Eldred et al. (2012)	The study examines the effects of toxic air pollutants of solid waste, such as the burning of car tyres and its impact on human health	Sierra Leone	Simulation of sample data	The concentration levels, health risks, and seasonal variation of polycyclic aromatic hydrocarbons pose a significant threat to humans in Freetown	Another solid waste was included in the analysis
Garrido et al. (2012)	This study explores the application of activated recycled rubber from used tyres in oil spill clean-up	Nigeria	Experimental Research	The carbonisation and activation of recycled carbon from scrap tyres resulted in particles of different and higher surface areas. In addition, activated carbon particles exhibit higher oil removal efficiency when compared with non-activated particles	Limited sample in the experiment. The research appears to be about the "carbonisation" of rubber, i.e. its pyrolysis. This means the material then being activated is carbon, not rubber
Pilusa et al. (2014)	This study is a PFD to potentially evaluate the viability of pyrolysis technology as a treatment process for waste tyres intending to produce alternative fuel and other high-value products	South Africa	Processed flow diagram	It was discovered that pyrolysis technology becomes more viable when there is a guarantee on the product offtake at a given price. Further processing of the crude tyre oil and carbon black is essential to produce consistent quality products	The study concentrated on the financial feasibility of pyrolysis technology with minimal focus on environmental sustainability

(continued)

Table 1 (continued)

Authors	Focus/title	Country	Methods	Findings/conclusion	Limitations
Dodoo-Arhin et al. (2015)	The study explores discarded Rubber Car Tyres as Synthetic Coarse Aggregates in Light Weight Pavement Concretes	Ghana	Experimental Research	This study shows that it is possible to use recycled rubber tyres in concrete construction as a partial replacement for coarse aggregates	Limited sample sizes were used in this analysis
Negm et al. (2015)	The study assesses the Life Cycle of Vehicles Tyres on the Egyptian Road Network	Egypt	Life cycle impact assessment	Egyptian road tyres contribute mainly to global warming problems and human health	Limited data used in the study
Garlapalli et al. (2016)	The study examines the Economic benefits of extended producer responsibility initiatives in tyre waste in South Africa	South Africa	General equilibrium model	Findings from the study show that extended producer responsibility initiatives for waste tyres will lead to positive economic benefits and new jobs that favour lower-skilled people	The environmental benefits associated with recycling were not quantified and hence accounted for
Jimoda et al. (2018)	The study assesses the environmental impact of open burning of scrap tyres on ambient air quality	Nigeria	Experimental research and simulation	The study significantly established gaseous pollutants (CO, NO_2, and SO_2) are present at varying concentrations in all categories of tyres which causes a significant threat to human health	No beneficial recycling method is provided

Authors	Focus/title	Country	Methods	Findings/conclusion	Limitations
Rambau et al. (2018)	The study explores the Mechanochemical approach in the synthesis of activated carbons from waste tyres, including hydrogen storage applications	South Africa	Mechanochemical structural analysis	The synthesis of carbon materials from waste tyre solid char following the mechanochemical strategy was successful. Compared to the conventional activation method, the application of the compactivation method was observed to lead to an increase in surface area between 3 and 24%	Limited sample sizes were used in this analysis
Sulaymon et al. (2017)	Examines Toxicity potential of the emitted aerosols from open burning of scrap tyres	Zimbabwe	Experimental Research	This study has shown that open-burning scrap tyres (OBST) could increase aerosols' concentration in an environment with significant toxic effects on humans	Limited dataset used in the experiment

(continued)

Table 1   (continued)

Authors	Focus/title	Country	Methods	Findings/conclusion	Limitations
Rekhaye and Jeetah (2018)	Assessing Energy Potential from Waste Tyres in Mauritius by Direct Combustion, Pyrolysis and Gasification	Mauritius	Experimental research	Findings from the study show that direct combustion will increase CO_2 emission by 26% if shredded waste tyres as a replacement for coal. Pyrolysis gave 35% char, 33% heavy pyrolytic oil, 17% light pyrolytic oil, and 15% gas by mass per cent. Thus, gasification is not best to waste-to-energy conversion technology	Limited sample used for the experiment. Some analyses and conclusions cannot be extrapolated to gasification as it is a different thermal process
Dorr et al., (2019	The study examines the effects of recycled tyre steel fibres and palm kernel shells on the compressive, splitting tensile and flexural strengths of lightweight structural concrete, using recycled tyre steel fibres for reinforcement and palm kernel shells as partial replacement of coarse aggregates	Uganda	Experimental research	The results of this study show that an increase in recycled steel fibres from 20 to 80 aspect ratios increases the compressive strength and splitting tensile strengths of normal-weight concrete	Other solids waste materials were included in the analysis

Authors	Focus/title	Country	Methods	Findings/conclusion	Limitations
Quaicoe et al. (2020)	This study sought to examine how to transform waste vehicle tyres into fuel which invariably minimises or eliminates its environmental impact	Ghana	Experimental research	Treated pyrolysis oil could be used as blended with other diesel fuels in cars	Limited sample sizes were used in this analysis
Okafor et al. (2020)	This paper review discussed challenges and opportunities offered by post-consumer management of end-of-life tyres in Nigeria. End-of-life tyres (ELTs) cause a multi-faceted problem in Nigeria	Nigeria	Literature review	Circular management of post-consumer product such as tyres are essential to the economic sustainability	Substantial scarcity of data and methodological challenges in differentiating the economic impacts
Kumar and Siagi (2021)	The study examines the Optimisation of Liquid Fuel Production from Microwave Pyrolysis of Used Tyres	Kenya	Experimental research using microwave pyrolysis	The liquid fuel properties obtained from the experiment meet the required international standards and can be used as an alternative to diesel fuel	Research is still needed to refine the liquid fuel used directly in internal combustion engines

(continued)

Table 1 (continued)

Authors	Focus/title	Country	Methods	Findings/conclusion	Limitations
Hu et al. (2021)	The paper examines waste tyre problems and sustainable waste management in the Tunisian context	Tunisia	Mixed methods analysis	Strict legislation coupled with sustainable finance for waste disposal is imperative in dealing with the problems of tyre waste disposal in Tunisia	Limited data on tyre disposal
Sakri et al. (2021)	The study examines the potential production and utilisation of refuse-derived fuel (RDF) from MSW to be used as a substitute fuel in cement kilns in Algeria	Algeria	Experimental research	The results show that refused-derived fuel (RDF) and cement can be produced from municipal solid waste such as car tyres	The study did not examine in detail if the use of RDF in cement manufacturing is cost-beneficial and environmentally friendly
Bwalya et al. (2022)	The study examines used tyres as a resource for concrete production	Zambia	Experimental Research	There is potential for rubber-modified concrete products in Zambia, which in turn mitigates adverse impacts resulting from over-exploitation of natural aggregates and disposal of used rubber tires	However, in this research, a replacement of coarse aggregates was used to determine the suitability of using rubber aggregates in concrete production

owners and stakeholders monetary value on the products obtained (pyrolysis oil, char, and metals). Many of these studies have investigated if using activated recycled rubber from old tyres in fuel and carbon charcoal is possible. For example, Aisien and Aisien (2012) conducted an experiment that involved recycling waste car tyres into oil in Nigeria. They discovered that recycling rubber from discarded tyres and carbonising and activating it produced particles with various and more significant surface areas. They further emphasised that, compared to carbon particles that have not been activated, activated rubber-derived carbon particles demonstrate better effectiveness in oil removal.

Dodoo-Arhin et al. (2015) conducted an experiment in Ghana that discovered that disposable car tyres could be recycled to produce synthetic coarse aggregates in lightweight pavement concretes. They demonstrated that it is feasible to substitute coarse aggregate in concrete buildings with recycled rubber tyres. Moreover, Abuzukhar (2021) conducted a study in Tunisia to investigate if the waste tyre can be used for oil, cement for construction, and the like. The findings from the survey show that pyrolysis can yield a sustainable result of producing oil, cement, and carbon charcoal from waste car tyres. However, the study underscores the need for tight laws and long-term waste financing in addressing the tyre disposal challenges and their associated environmental problems in Tunisia. Other studies, including Asma et al. (2021), argue that cement and refused-derived fuel (RDF) may be made from municipal can be extracted from recycled automobile tyres. Their study shows that pyrolysis represents a sustainable means of recycling the many waste automobile tyres that pollute the environment in most Algerian cities. They demonstrated how fuel could be extracted from recycled car tyres or used in the manufacture of cement.

Circular economy approaches have been emphasised as sustainable solutions to the tyre waste challenges in African countries. Senthil Kumar et al. (2017) acknowledged the problem associated with tyre waste in Africa. They examined the possibility of incorporating scrap tyres in concrete as chips and fibres to reinforce concrete for construction work in Rwanda. Their research demonstrates that adding certain super plasticisers and industrial waste as a partial cement replacement can boost the strength of waste tyre rubber-modified concrete while reducing compressive and tensile strength degradation. The study did not, however, examine how the fire might affect the product. By utilising a study in Burkina Faso, Linganzi (2008) investigated how businesses profit from recycling solid industrial waste, including tyres. He discovered that tyres could be recycled to create footwear called tyre sandals and give many disadvantaged people an income. To improve sustainable municipal solid waste management, Sanneh et al. (2011) assessed the recycling system in the Gambia. They suggested that the open burning of solid garbage, including car tyres, be practised often in the country's towns. However, these pose severe risks to people and complex problems for the administration.

Also, using simulation data from Sierra Leone, Taylor and Nakai (2012) investigated the effects of toxic air pollutants from solid waste, such as burning car tyres, and their impact on human health. They discovered that the concentration levels, health risks, and seasonal variation of polycyclic aromatic hydrocarbons in Freetown pose a significant threat to people's health. Moreover, Elkafoury et al. (2015) evaluated the life cycle of automobile tyres on the Egyptian road network and discovered that they are primarily responsible for the mid-point effect of global warming problems, as well as for the harm caused by terrestrial acidification and nitrification, including adverse effects on human health. Finally, to assess the economic advantages of the expanded producer responsibility initiative in tyre trash in South Africa, Hartley et al. (2016) used a computational general equilibrium model. According to their results, expanded producer responsibility programmes for discarded tyres will have a positive economic impact and create up to 1448 net new full-time equivalent (FTE) employment that is more favourable to those with lower skill levels.

Therefore, Jimoda et al. (2018) evaluated the environmental effects of open burning of waste tyres using process modelling and found that gaseous pollutants (CO, NO_2, and SO_2) are present in all kinds of tyres at variable amounts, posing a serious hazard to human health. In an experiment conducted in Zimbabwe, Sulaymon et al. (2017) demonstrated how open-burning scrap tyres (OBST) might increase the environment's aerosol concentration, which has harmful consequences for people. Khavharendwe et al. (2017) employed mechanochemical structural analysis to investigate if the mechanochemical approach to producing carbon compounds from waste tyre solid char was effective. Thus, the compactivation process improved the surface area by between 3 and 24% compared to the standard activation method. The problems and possibilities presented by post-consumer management of end-of-life tyres (ELTs) in Nigeria are reviewed by Elem et al. (2020). They stated that

ELTs and other post-consumer products require circular management to be sustainable.

Tyre Pyrolysis into Oil and Charcoal for Sustainable Energy

While energy efficiency is recognised as one cost-effective way to meet sustainable development demands, most African countries are still saddled with acute energy problems. With the need for energy services in Africa snowballing, exploring new avenues for securing more affordable and sustainable energy sources is imperative. Besides, increased energy efficiency is essential for economic growth since it reduces fuel imports, eases strains on existing infrastructure, and reduces production costs. Furthermore, studies show that the pyrolysis-circular economy approach can provide a more sustainable and partially renewable source of cheaper energy and alleviate energy problems.

The circular economy ideas should also be applied better with the support from thermal technologies. For example, Pilusa et al. (2014) formulated a process flow diagram using South African data. They evaluated the viability of pyrolysis technology as a treatment process for waste tyres to produce alternative fuel and other high-value oil products for energy. They discovered that pyrolysis technology could produce oil and carbon black and be a reliable energy source but also, critically, identified that the resultant products needed further treatment to achieve a quality that would sustain a project. Similarly, Quaicoe et al. (2020) argue that treated pyrolysis oil could be blended with diesel fuel for cars and other vehicles. Kumar and Siagi (2021) developed microwave pyrolysis and argued that the liquid fuel properties obtained from their experiment meet the required international standards and can be used as an alternative to diesel fuel.

Pyrolysis is a promising chemical solution to manage waste effectively, energy deficits and material recovery (Nkosi et al., 2020) and turn waste into renewable energy sources (Adeniyi et al., 2018, 2019; Ighalo & Adeniyi, 2019). It is one circular economy practice to create a sustainable society and encompasses all operations, from garbage recycling to recovering components from worn goods (Ighalo et al., 2021). Examples include the recycling of textile wastes (Shirvanimoghaddam et al., 2020), the production of bioenergy from food wastes (Ingrao et al., 2018), the use of olive pomace for renewable energy (Nunes et al., 2020), and the conversion of waste into biogas (Kapoor et al., 2020). In addition, pyrolysis offers many key benefits, including the ability to reduce water pollution through alternative pollutant conversion, the potential to reduce reliance on imported energy resources, cost savings over landfills, and the provision of public health benefits through cleaned-up wastes (Ighalo et al., 2021).

Besides, Zabaniotou et al. (2015) demonstrated the possibility of bridging the divide between agriculture and the circular economy while focusing on converting agricultural leftovers to liquid fuel, gas fuel, and biochar. Vaskalis et al. (2019) adopted an experiment employing fluidised bed gasification systems that combined the production of heat and power and were fuelled using wastes obtained from the processing of rice. The results demonstrated that the suggested model might be used to properly exploit waste flows from various rice value chains by using wastes as fuels. Somoza-Tornos et al. (2020) studied the recovery of ethylene monomers through the pyrolysis of polyethene. They found that polyethene pyrolysis might close the ethylene manufacturing operations' loop. The findings also demonstrated the necessity for additional research on pre-treatment polyethene waste to obtain more accurate environmental assessments, and the opportunity to lower hazardous emissions into the environment is provided by waste pyrolysis.

Finally, Pilusa et al. (2014) studied the financial feasibility of pyrolysis technology with minimal focus on environmental sustainability. Although pyrolysis has been proposed as promising in existing literature, we still lack a comprehensive understanding of how waste tyre pyrolysis is implemented and, more importantly, what the challenges are associated with pyrolysis implementation in African countries.

Although circular economy is impactful in developing sustainability, emerging economies still need more successful examples in waste collection, recycling, repair, and refurbishment (Murray, et al., 2017). For instance, evidence suggests that circular economy has primarily remained a vague concept in African countries where the most emphasis has been placed on economic development and natural resource maximisation (Desmond & Asamba, 2019). However, research-based feasibility projects still need to produce more consistent findings for decision-making support (investors, stakeholders, and government representatives). As a result, developing a circular economy is even more difficult in a developing country.

Similarly, establishing a waste tyre pyrolysis plant in practice has many challenges that discourage adoption and implementation. So, analysts, researchers, and decision-makers need to identify critical project drivers and link them to actionable strategies, plans, and decision support. For example, (a) technology readiness (technical maturity of pyrolysis technologies at the implementation phase), (b) risk identification (detection of potential risks that adversely affect projects and business performance), (c) carbon footprint analysis (generation or reduction of greenhouse gases, including carbon dioxide and methane), (d) supply chain and procurement factors (processes of getting and transforming tyres feedstock into products and distributing them to customers), and (e) financial risk quantification (practice for creating, quantifying, protecting economic value under risk and uncertainty).

3 FINDINGS AND DISCUSSIONS

Current Limitations and Contributions of Tyre Pyrolysis Research

Table 2 shows that most of the literature reviewed underscores the environmental sustainability arguments in pyrolysis in Africa. However, significant and rapid progress has been made in other parts of the world. Critically the progress encompasses: uses for both recovered Carbon Black (tyre manufacturers) and tyre pyrolysis oil (refiners producing fuel and plastics manufacturers); regulations (e.g. waste status and legislation); and incentives (mainly biofuels). These factors have massively increased the focus on tyre pyrolysis as a solution.

In doing these have also highlighted the many issues that need to be addressed to realise tyre pyrolysis projects. The decision-makers must advance such projects to support tyre pyrolysis as one solution for a more circular and long-lasting solution for tyres disposal needs to cover product quality and end-use, investment, project management, technological challenges, risk management, supply chain management, and the like. Besides, pyrolysis is only beginning to gain popularity in Africa. Nonetheless, the existing research streams on tyre pyrolysis still need to identify other critical project drivers, including carbon footprint analysis, risk management, and techno-economic requirements, in an integrated way to satisfy project owners and stakeholders. These drivers can help scholars fill research gaps in future studies. Furthermore, it could be supported by working and

Table 2 Project drivers in tire pyrolysis and circular economy literature in Africa (2008–2022)

Authors	Focus of study	Country	Environmental benefits	Technology readiness	Risk identi-fication	Carbon footprint	Supply chain & procurement	Risk quan-tification
Senthil Kumar et al. (2017)	Waste tyre for cement chips for concrete	Rwanda	Y	Y	Y	Y	Y	N
Vanessa Linganzi (2008)	Recycling industrial waste tyres in footwear sandals	Burkina Faso	Y	Y	Y	Y	Y	N
Sanneh, et al. (2011)	Examine waste disposal problems, including car tyres	Gambia	Y	Y	Y	Y	Y	N
Eldred et al. (2012)	Examines the effects of burning car tyres and its toxic effects on humans	Sierra Leone	Y	Y	Y	Y	Y	N
Garrido et al. (2012)	This study explores the application of activated recycled rubber from used tyres in oil spill clean-up	Nigeria	Y	Y	N	Y	N	N
Pilusa et al. (2014)	This study evaluates the viability of pyrolysis technology as a treatment process for waste tyres	South Africa	Y	Y	N	Y	Y	N
Dodoo-Arhin et al. (2015)	The study explores discarded Rubber Car Tyres as Synthetic Coarse Aggregates in Light Weight Pavement Concretes	Ghana	Y	Y	N	Y	N	N
Negm et al. (2015)	The study assesses the Life Cycle of Vehicles Tyres on the Egyptian Road Network	Egypt	Y	Y	N	Y	Y	N

Authors	Focus of study	Country	Environmental benefits	Technology readiness	Risk identi-fication	Carbon footprint	Supply chain & procurement	Risk quan-tification
Garlapalli et al. (2016)	The study examines the Economic benefits of extended producer responsibility initiatives in tyre waste in South Africa	South Africa	Y	Y	N	Y	N	N
Jimoda et al. (2018)	The study assesses the environmental impact of open burning of scrap tyres on ambient air quality	Nigeria	Y	Y	N	Y	N	N
Rambau et al. (2018)	The study explores the mechanochemical approach in the synthesis of activated carbons from waste tyres and their hydrogen storage applications	South Africa	Y	Y	N	Y	N	N
Sulaymon et al. (2017)	Examines Toxicity potential of the emitted aerosols from open burning of scrap tyres	Zimbabwe	Y	Y	Y	Y	N	N
Rekhaye and Jeetah (2018)	Assessing Energy Potential from Waste Tyres in Mauritius by Direct Combustion, Pyrolysis, and Gasification	Mauritius	Y	Y	Y	Y	Y	N

(continued)

Table 2 (continued)

Authors	Focus of study	Country	Environmental benefits	Technology readiness	Risk identi-fication	Carbon footprint	Supply chain & procurement	Risk quan-tification
Dorr et al., (2019	The study examines the effects of recycled tyre steel fibres and palm kernel shells on concrete	Uganda	Y	Y	N	Y	N	N
Quaicoe et al. (2020)	It examines how to transform waste vehicle tyres into fuel	Ghana	Y	Y	Y	Y	N	N
Okafor et al. (2020)	It discusses the challenges and opportunities offered by a waste tyre in Nigeria	Nigeria	Y	Y	Y	Y	Y	N
Kumar and Siagi (2021)	The study examines the optimisation of Liquid Fuel Production from Microwave Pyrolysis of Used Tyres	Kenya	Y	Y	N	Y	N	N
Hu et al. (2021)	It examines waste tyre problems and sustainable waste management in the Tunisian context	Tunisia	Y	Y	Y	Y	Y	N
Sakri et al. (2021)	It examines the potential production of refuse-derived fuel (RDF) from used car tyres	Algeria	Y	Y	N	Y	N	N
Bwalya et al. (2022)	The study examines used tyres as a resource for concrete production	Zambia	Y	Y	N	Y	Y	N

interviewing engineering specialists about the challenges in tyre pyrolysis projects and potential managerial implications.

Other Challenges in Tyre Pyrolysis, from Industry to Academia

In this report, along with the systematic literature review, we have identified other critical criteria for installing a waste tire pyrolysis plant through consultation and collaboration with engineering experts in the UK, the US, Europe, and Africa. The underlying recommended topics, complemented with literature, should be considered in any research-based feasibility study, financial decision, front-end engineering design, construction, or project risk management analysis. Otherwise, they may hinder the acceptance and implementation of pyrolysis projects and, consequently, have potential implications for business performance; for example, operational costs, technological assurance, end-product quality, shareholder integration, project management and execution, risk management, hazardous and environmental assessment, plant optimisation, process modelling, and regulatory framework.

a) Operational costs: developing and operating pyrolysis plants, firms often have a heavy burden of operational costs of establishing proper infrastructure and ensuring a safe working environment (Kozub et al., 2021). Many expenses derive from the reactor systems, condensers and heat exchangers, burner and furnace systems, oil loading stations and pumps, oil storage, water system, thermal oil system, and carbon-black silos. Apart from tangible equipment, contractor's fees, commissioning, testing, and training costs also constitute high costs and are expected to grow. For African firms, overcoming the higher costs of adopting such a circular economy business is a big concern to be considered as part of the risk quantification process.

b) Technological assurance: it is evident that waste tyre pyrolysis requires advanced technologies, and these must be ready to deploy at a commercial scale—i.e. have achieved Technology Readiness Level 7 (process proven at commercial scale). Such a level of development presumes the technology employs stringent control mechanisms, suitable automation systems, and reliable safety circuits. Managers and engineers must also consider alternative designs to cope with unplanned disruption, such as a gas evacuation system. Therefore, high-quality materials and standards must be ensured in reactor systems, storage tanks, assembly and mechanical equipment for blowers and pumps (Martines, 2021). All these require evaluating superior manufacturing techniques and technical expertise to judge, support, and enable obtaining crucial data for system design and maintenance. To strengthen the confidence in the technology, the pyrolyser suppliers should provide adequate and verifiable technical descriptions of all plant components, including functional descriptions, flow diagrams, operational instructions, mass and volumetric flow rates, pressure and temperature profiles and emissions.

It has also been advised to test and identify reliable pyrolysis technologies before purchasing and verifying the supplier's information. Note that pyrolysis plants consider experimental data to support the process' nominal operating characteristics and aid in more accurately developing the business model. Another crucial factor to consider is the demonstration of facilities, which helps reduce technical ambiguity and build up the confidence of prospective customers in the technology and the qualities of end-products. Establishing and demonstrating an appropriate technology also need to include well-designed plans for corrective, preventive, and predictive maintenance and be dependable throughout the medium and long term in a regular manner. These characteristics contribute to increased trust in providers of pyrolysers and enhance better project outcomes.

Furthermore, industrial-scale pyrolysis facilities must be fitted with desulphurisation abatement systems, primarily because of the sulphur (H_2S) entering the gas portion. The ability to prove that a supplier's technology complies with specific regulatory air emissions criteria, especially those related to occupational health, is mandatory. Technological consideration and standard regulations need to be established to make sure that no plant employees should come into touch with potentially harmful chemicals like fumes and vapours. Pyrolysis plants need to identify all elements involved, including intermediates, by-products, and effluents, for their hazardous characteristics (physical, chemical, and health). Each material should be categorised using a banding system that connects the substance's dangers to the required engineering controls. The process's dangers (exothermic reaction, gas evolution, etc.) should be recognised, quantified, and recorded to recommend the degree of control corresponding to each hazard. The pyrolysis facility must be risk-free for workers and guests and should not violate environmental, health, and safety regulations. All these technological insurance considerations are complex and resource-demanding for African firms but help to address the gap between expenditures and sales in reality (ETRMA, 2018a, 2018b).

c) End-product quality: it is worth noting that pyrolysis technologies and products in African countries are still in the early stages of development. The technological maturity of the pyrolyser significantly impacts the quality of end-products, including chemical properties, which may be caused by various reasons, such as lacking the technical tools to guarantee safe operating circumstances. A slight difference in inputs and materials used in pyrolysis can significantly change end-product quality, aspects associated with supply chain management. For example, different types of tyres contain different grades and reliability of materials. Note that all pyrolysis techniques and types of machinery can produce end-products with other chemical characteristics and qualities. For example, one end-product of all recovered carbon black (rCB) comprises numerous CB grades (Martínez et al., 2019) and both inorganic and carbonaceous components. Therefore, ensuring the same qualities in a virgin CB (Mastral et al., 2019) is difficult. As one of the end-products, tyres pyrolysis oil (TPO) is a viable replacement for petroleum-derived goods, such as heating oil, valuable chemical compounds, and motor fuels. This discrepancy in the properties of TPO and rCB has undermined a reputation and given urgency for pyrolysis manufacturers to improve.

To make TPO meet the fuel criteria, applications in the plants need to establish further upgrading steps (Geerken et al., 2019). Moreover, more rigorous refinement techniques, such as milling and acid treatment, are required to enhance the characteristics of other end-product rCBs and improve the intended use (Ighalo et al., 2022). All the technological and chemical demonstration indicates how crucial it is to have appropriate safety data sheets and regulations for both TPO and rCB. Safety data sheets also need to be enacted during shipping and handling. The development of established certifications and standards, as is happening with bio-oil, biochar, and bio-oil from biomass pyrolysis, are recommended to support the market acceptability of these products (ETRMA, 2018a, 2018b). Therefore, standardisation prevents traditional methods' performance limitations and attracts investors and entrepreneurs (Zabaniotou et al., 2014).

To accurately forecast how the pyrolysis process functions in detail by using new characterisation techniques based on structure, surface area, sieve residue, pellet characteristics, and concentrations of ash and sulphur (ASTM, 2018). However, it has also been observed that TPO and rCB made with their pyrolysers may be sold as virgin CB and diesel-like fuel, establishing a negative reputation with prospective interested parties.

Proofs-of-concept enables tackling this difficulty by small-scale testing in goods and processes and is often conducted in cooperation with possible end markets to confirm the practicality of the pyrolysis product. As a result, the TPO and/or rCB must be set based on the clients' requirements of quality and options provided by the pyrolyser. As a solution, some ELT pyrolysis providers have customised their solution to meet the qualities required by the clients to substitute rCB for virgin CB in tyres and automobile components (Prnewswire, 2018).

d) Stakeholder integration: pyrolysis project execution and business management require convergence among project owners and stakeholders. Collaborating with multiple stakeholders, such as product clients, investors, technicians, researchers in the subject, type and rubber enterprises, tyre collectors, national and local environmental entities and government, is difficult. These stakeholders can support the effective implementation of ELT pyrolysis facilities but also have their interests. As we discussed above, pyrolysis is a resource-intensive business. It often requires substantial financial support to handle the high plant construction and commissioning expenses and to ensure development and environmental compliance.

Also, persuading investors and guaranteeing a quick break-even is a challenge for shareholders, which are aspects to be considered during the scenario analysis for risk quantification. Therefore, joint venture agreements between seasoned businesses involved in designing and installing industrial-scale plants, waste-to-energy (WtE) processes, and petroleum and chemical products can improve the project deployment and the marketability of the products produced through pyrolysis. How to carry out collaborative activities related to research institutes and universities is also challenging. How to manage suppliers and clients to ensure a resilient and sustainable supply chain is a general concern in African countries. The promotion or subsidies of recycling goods by governments and other authorities can have a favourable impact on pyrolysis but requires social network support (Yang, et al., 2021). The marketability barriers for end-products tend to be diminished if external stakeholders involved in recycling, clean production, and environmental protection do not recognise these products as alternative energy sources and sustainable value-added outputs in line with sustainable production.

e) Project management and execution: in addition to the technical system, various project management procedures should be considered during the project implementation stage, such as FEED, detailed design, procurement, installation/construction and plant commissioning. They have relevant cost, schedule, and financial risk implications that need to be analysed during the risk quantification process.

For instance, it has been suggested that the Front End Engineering Design (FEED) be assigned to a single engineering design firm that would continue to develop the facility's design. The FEED contractor will be in charge of developing the engineering design to a degree of specificity enough to eliminate any sizable uncertainty about the facility's technical needs. Get vendor quotes, improve the cost estimates, and help manage long lead equipment items to be prepared in conjunction with the design. Due to the nature of the reactor systems, it could be necessary to initiate a distinct contract to develop their design further, give the details required for the facility's overall design, and establish the costs of the reactor systems. The major FEED contract should be reimbursed against a target cost, although fixed price arrangements are possible based on a scope correctly specified (Yussef et al., 2018).

In a pyrolysis project, the project owner can choose an EPCm (Engineering, Procurement, Construction, and Management) business with the expertise and experience necessary to complete the project effectively. The EPCm contractor will ensure that the project's engineering and design adhere to its technical and functional requirements. Its primary duty is to oversee, manage, and coordinate the construction interface following a de-risked timetable. The EPCm contractor can negotiate contracts with other contractors, suppliers, subcontractors, and sub-vendors through a tendering procedure. They will also oversee the management of the equipment delivery orders from order placement to equipment delivery to guarantee that suppliers' technical and commercial responsibilities are met.

Finally, construction must also be supervised by the EPCm contractor under an EPCm contract. They are responsible for creating the construction scope, choosing the most qualified installation contractor(s), and managing these firms throughout the building process. Due to the diverse extent of the installation, there may be more than one installation contractor, including civil/structure; mechanical/piping; and electrical/instrumentation.

f) Risk management: This topic is highly related to risk identification and quantification. Note that decision-makers can only manage risk events if they quantify their impacts. So, a quantitative cost-risk analysis helps identify, simulate, quantify, and analyse the primary cost-risk variables and

risk drivers should be organised and conducted (WBCSD, 2019). At the same time, risk management requires a consistent and well-defined phase of Design Verification and Engineering (including FEED) to facilitate risk quantification on costs, asset integrity, safety, operability, maintainability, availability and procurement, construction, and commissioning (Del Cano & De la Cruz, 2002).

To reduce uncertainty on cost and capital expenditure and potential impact across the supply chain and procurement during plan execution, more project risk analysis and quantification is needed in FEED; for example, integrating capital expenditures with the project timeline and variable costs must align with budgeting, capital allocation, and procurement strategies. In pyrolysis projects, it is essential to understand the economic effects of the reactor system and increase expense confidence by considering multiple possibilities early and doing further risk analysis on the incoming energy supply (supplier capacity, building needs, project consequences, etc.) following plant and products specifications.

g) Hazardous and environmental assessment: Consistent with our discussion above, pyrolysis is not always risk-free. Although pyrolysis provides flexibility to convert wastes into economically usable products, feedstock availability tends to emerge as an essential concern. Transporting, storing, and processing feedstock before thermochemical conversion provides additional difficulties (Effendi et al., 2008; Zhang et al., 2019) and negative environmental impacts do exist as well. So, Important parameters during the production process must be carefully measured and calibrated to cope with adverse environmental impacts, including particle size, vapour residence time, carrier gas flow rate, moisture content, and pressure. However, the process is complex, requiring careful comprehension and in-depth investigation (Chemerys & Baltrėnaitė, 2018). To cope with potentially hazardous and environmental issues, managers and plants need to accurately plan and structure the process in the refineries. A cleaner production environment and more understanding of the reaction parameters need to be explored in detail to maximise the product, lessen the environmental effect, and achieve economic efficiency.

h) Plant optimisation: Managers also need to consider several issues and options related to future optimisation, including process heat options, onsite power generation, standard equipment sizing, pumped export oil pipeline, and heat recovery and utilisation. For example, power or natural gas may provide a more economic source of process heat. Using power may reduce CAPEX, however, power rates may still not make this an economic option. Equally product fractionation can be an option as selling light and heavy oil products may deliver a higher economic worth. In addition to pyro-gas and ultralight oil, the heat might also be produced using electricity, but further research is needed in these areas because some options might require changing the entire production process, which is infeasible for a plant manager.

Depending on process location, transferring the oil produced by tyre pyrolysis to a neighbouring oil refinery may be more economic using pipelines than tankers. The drawback is that it limits the plant's commercial flexibility by tying it to supplies to that refinery. However, whenever additional data is easily accessible, a cost–benefit and risk analysis will need to be carried out at the FEED stage.

Regarding heat recovery and utilisation, some tyre pyrolysis process flow diagrams demonstrate that there are options for waste heat recovery and use. For instance, the heat from the flue gas may be recovered and utilised to operate an organic Rankine system or an absorption chiller refrigeration system, which might be used to create energy or replace the electric chillers, lowering the process's electrical power usage. Additionally, there is the potential to use production waste heat to heat office rooms, reducing the need for HVAC power. Using heat recovery in more depth remains a future challenge as well.

i) Process Modelling: Any feasibility study has to provide an accurate heat and material balance report for any particular process (modelling and simulation). In addition, these reports give valuable data to size essential process equipment. Then, high-level heat and material balance information should be collected and provided to size pieces of process equipment. The entire process's material and energy balance will be completed during the FEED phase. This will be done by carefully modelling and simulating the tyre pyrolysis process in the simulation programme.

As a result, a lot of data and feedback are required for process modelling, such as ultimate and approximate analysis of the tyre feedstock, reactor size, temperature and pressure, product stream flow rate and composition, among other details of the operating parameters, including composition and properties of the pyrolysis gas, ultralight, light, and heavy oils.

j) Regulatory framework: The equipment in pyrolysis must comply with local laws and regulations to be imported and used safely and lawfully. Although they are not required, design standards and codes provide direction to promote the adoption of best practices. Technology and equipment used in pyrolysis plants need to be reviewed at a high level to ensure conformation with applicable regulations (Zabaniotou et al., 2014); for example, pressure systems safety regulations, supply of machinery regulations, provision and use of work equipment regulations, electrical equipment regulations, control of major accident hazards regulations, planning (hazardous substances) regulations, environmental permitting regulations, and town and country planning (environmental impact assessment) regulations, among others.

Moreover, design codes are a special kind of in-depth design advice that adopts best practices to speed up workflows, produce products of higher quality, and promote some degree of industry standardisation. While design codes alone are not required, specific laws stipulate that particular equipment must be built following a globally recognised design code. In addition, all equipment must comply with local regulations following internationally recognised design codes. The institutional environment is fast shifting. Thus, the most recent directives and rules should be examined to guarantee that the equipment will comply with legislation before ordering.

In summary, research-based feasibility or circular economy pyrolysis projects need to advance in a more long-lasting analysis to address decision-making problems (investment, project management, technological challenges and readiness, risk management, supply chain management, and the like). So, to strengthen the opportunities in Africa, not only project owners and stakeholders do need to be aligned and integrated, but also scholars need to start filling research gaps and answer managerial questions around operational costs, technological assurance, end-product quality, project management and execution, risk management, future optimisation, process modelling, and regulatory framework, and the like.

4   Conclusions

The main message of the findings of this paper has two aspects. The first is that waste tyre pyrolysis research-based applications and feasibility studies have had limited focus within literature in African countries, especially in addressing the multiple challenges, risks, and impacts faced by investors and stakeholders in Africa. Meanwhile, the growing population has resulted in increasing demand for non-degradable products, especially tyre waste. So, the circular economy approach that tyre pyrolysis promises requires underscoring in environmental sustainability and driving discussions that support decision-makers on more long-lasting solutions (technology readiness, risk identification, carbon footprint, supply chain and procurement, and risk quantification).

Second, research-based literature on pyrolysis projects and associated businesses must consider industry requirements and specifications to support project finance and investments decision around front-end engineering design, operational costs, technological assurance, end-product quality, shareholder integration, project management and execution, risk management, hazardous and environmental assessment, plant optimisation, process modelling, and regulatory framework.

Although pyrolysis projects, investments and businesses are only beginning to gain popularity in Africa, further insight into circular economy and waste tyres management can also address some of the concerns within the sustainable energy literature, including corporate sustainability, policy-making, risk-based business decisions (i.e. project financing, commercial scale of the technologies selected, product offtake contracts, site planning and conditions, government incentives, engineering and construction services providers, and the like), and environmental management issues.

References

Abuzukhar, M. U. N. I. R. (2021). *Exploring waste tyre problems and sustainable waste management in the Tunisian context* (Doctoral dissertation). University of Salford. Retrieved from https://www.proquest.com/docview/268928 9638?pqorigsite=gscholarfromopenview=true

Adams, K., Nayak, B. S., & Koukpaki, S. (2018). Critical perspectives on "manufactured" risks arising from Eurocentric business practices in Africa. *Critical Perspectives on International Business, 14*(2–3), 210–229.

Adeniyi, A. G., Adewoye, L. T., & Ighalo, J. O. (2018). Computer aided simulation of the pyrolysis of waste lubricating oil using aspen Hysys. *Environmental Research Engineering and Management, 74*, 52–57.

Adeniyi, A. G., Odetoye, T. E., Titiloye, J., & Ighalo, J. O. (2019). A thermodynamic study of rice husk (oryza sativa) pyrolysis. *Europeam Journal of Sustainable Development Research, 3*, 1–10.

Aisien, F. A., & Aisien, E. T. (2012). Application of activated recycled rubber from used tyres in oil spill clean-up. *Turkish Journal of Engineering and Environmental Sciences, 36*(2), 171–177.

Albrecht, T. R., Crootof, A., & Scott, C. A. (2018). The Water-Energy-Food Nexus: A systematic review of methods for nexus assessment. *Environmental Research Letters, 13*(4), 043002.

American Society for Testing and Materials (ASTM). (2018). *ASTM standardisation news. Recycling rubber into rCB.* https://sn.astm.org/features/recycling-rubber-rcb-ma17.html

Benachio, G. L. F., Freitas, M. D. C. D., & Tavares, S. F. (2020). Circular economy in the construction industry: A systematic literature review. *Journal of Cleaner Production, 260,* 121046.

Bwalya, T., Mulenga, M., & Chizyuka, C. (2022). *Used Tyre as a resource in concrete production in Zambia.*

Chemerys, V., & Baltrėnaitė, E. (2018). A review of lignocellulosic biochar modification towards enhanced biochar selectivity and adsorption capacity of potentially toxic elements. *Ukrainian Journal of Ecology, 8*(1), 21–32.

Chew, K. W., Chia, S. R., Chia, W. Y., Cheah, W. Y., Munawaroh, H. S. H., & Ong, W.-J. (2021). Abatement of hazardous materials and biomass waste via pyrolysis and co-pyrolysis for environmental sustainability and circular economy. *Environmental Pollution, 278,* 116836.

Creutzig, F., Baiocchi, G., Bierkandt, R., Pichler, P. P., & Seto, K. C. (2015). Global typology of urban energy use and potentials for an urbanization mitigation wedge. *Proceedings of the National Academy of Sciences, 112*(20), 6283–6288.

Del Cano, A., & de la Cruz, M. P. (2002). Integrated methodology for project risk management. *Journal of Construction Engineering and Management, 128*(6), 473–485.

Desmond, P., & Asamba, M. (2019). *Accelerating the transition to a circular economy in Africa.*

Di Maio, F., & Rem, P. C. (2015). A robust indicator for promoting circular economy through recycling. *Journal of Environmental Protection, 6*(10), 1095.

Dick, D. T., Agboola, O., & Ayeni, A. O. (2020). Pyrolysis of waste tyre for high-quality fuel products: A review. *AIMS Energy, 8*(5), 869–895.

Dodoo-Arhin, D., Mensah, S. A., Yaya, A., & Agyei-Tuffour, B. (2015). Application of discarded rubber car tyres as synthetic coarse aggregates in light weight pavement concretes. *American Journal of Materials Science, 5*(4), 75–83.

Dorr, B. J., Kanali, C. L., & Onchiri, R. O. (2019). *Effects of recycled tyre steel fibres on the compressive, splitting tensile and flexural strengths of structural lightweight concrete using palm kernel shells as partial replacement of coarse aggregates.*

Effendi, A., Gerhauser, H., & Bridgwater, A. V. (2008). Production of renewable phenolic resins by thermochemical conversion of biomass: A review. *Renewable and Sustainable Energy Reviews, 12,* 2092–2116.

Eldred Tunde, T., & Satoshi, N. (2012). The levels of toxic air pollutants in kitchens with traditional stoves in rural sierra leone. *Journal of Environmental Protection*.

Elem, I. M., Chukwuemeka, C. P., Onyia, A. I., Elem, I. N., Ngozi, E. C., & Iheanyichukwu, C. A. (2020). Estimation of the calorific value and electrical energy potential of waste generated biomass within abakaliki meteropolis Ebonyi State, Nigeria. *American Journal of Nano Research and Applications*, *8*(3), 42–49.

Elkafoury, A., Negm, A. M., Bady, M. F., & Aly, M. H. (2015). Modelling vehicular CO emissions for time headway based environmental traffic management system. *Procedia Technology*, 19, 341–348.

European Tyre and Rubber Manufacturers Association (ETRMA). (2018a). *Tyre recycling*. http://www.etrma.org/tyres/ELTs/material-recovery

European Tyre and Rubber Manufacturers Association (ETRMA). (2018b). *ETRMA position paper on circular economy*. https://www.etrma.org/wp-con tent/uploads/2019/09/2015-09-29_etrma-position-paper-on-circular-eco nomy_vf.pdf

Garlapalli, R. K., Wirth, B., & Reza, M. T. (2016). Pyrolysis of hydrochar from digestate: Effect of hydrothermal carbonization and pyrolysis temperatures on pyrochar formation. *Bioresource Technology*, *220*, 168–174.

Garrido, R., Ruiz-Felix, M. N., & Satrio, J. A. (2012). Effects of hydrolysis and torrefaction on pyrolysis product distribution of spent mushroom compost (SMC). *International Journal of Environmental Pollution and Remediation (IJEPR)*, *1*(1), 98–103.

Geerken, T., Schmidt, J., Boonen, K., Christis, M., & Merciai, S. (2019). Assessment of the potential of a circular economy in open economies–Case of Belgium. *Journal of Cleaner Production*, *227*, 683–699.

Hartley, F. A. A. I. Q. A., Caetano, T. A. R. A., & Daniels, R. C. (2016). *The general equilibrium impacts of monetising all waste streams in South Africa*. Energy Research Centre, University of Cape Town.

Hu, Y., Attia, M., Tsabet, E., Mohaddespour, A., Munir, M. T., & Farag, S. (2021). Valorization of waste tire by pyrolysis and hydrothermal liquefaction: a mini-review. *Journal of Material Cycles and Waste Management*, *23*(5), 1737–1750.

Ighalo, J. O., & Adeniyi, A. G. (2019). Thermodynamic modelling and temperature sensitivity analysis of banana (Musa spp.) waste pyrolysis. *SN Applied Sciences*, *1*, 1086–1095.

Ighalo, J. O., et al. (2021). Regenerative desulphurisation of pyrolysis oil: A paradigm for the circular economy initiative. *Journal of Environmental Chemical Engineering*, *9*, 106864.

Ighalo, J. O., et al. (2022). Flash pyrolysis of biomass: A review of recent advances. *Clean Technologies and Environmental Policy*, *24*, 2349–2363.

Ingrao, C., Faccilongo, N., Di Gioia, L., & Messineo, A. (2018). Food waste recovery into energy in a circular economy perspective: A comprehensive review of aspects related to plant operation and environmental assessment. *Journal of Cleaner Production, 184*, 869–892.

Jia, F., Peng, S., Green, J., Koh, L., & Chen, X. (2020). Soybean supply chain management and sustainability: A systematic literature review. *Journal of Cleaner Production, 255*, 120254.

Jimoda, L. A., Sulaymon, I. D., Alade, A. O., & Adebayo, G. A. (2018). Assessment of environmental impact of open burning of scrap tyres on ambient air quality. *International Journal of Environmental Science and Technology, 15*(6), 1323–1330.

Kapoor, R., et al. (2020). Valorisation of agricultural waste for biogas based circular economy in India: A research outlook. *Bioresource Technology, 304*, 123036.

Kozub, B., Bazan, P., Gailitis, R., Korniejenko, K., & Mierzwiński, D. (2021). Foamed geopolymer composites with the addition of glass wool waste. *Materials, 14*(17), 4978.

Kumar, A., & Siagi, Z. O. (2021). Optimisation of liquid fuel production from microwave pyrolysis of used tyres. *Journal of Energy, 2021*.

Lacko, R., Hajduova, Z., & Zawada, M. (2021). The efficiency of circular economies: A comparison of visegrád group countries. *Energies, 14*, 1–13.

Linganzi, V. (2008). *Making gains from industrial scrap: Small-scale production in Ouagadougou, Burkina Faso* (Doctoral dissertation). Northwestern University.

Martínez, J. D., Cardona-Uribe, N., Murillo, R., García, T., & Lopez, J. M. (2019). Carbon black recovery from waste tire pyrolysis by demineralisation: Production and application in rubber compounding. *Waste Management, 85*, 574–584.

Mastral, A. M., Alvarez, R., Callen, M. S., Clemente, C., & Murillo, R. (2019). Characterisation of chars from coal-tire copyrolysis. *Industrial & Engineering Chemistry Research, 38*, 2856–2860.

Mokoele, J., & Sebola, M. (2018). Unplanned urbanisation in South African cities: The emergence of urban environmental problems. *The Business & Management Review, 9*(3), 574–584.

Murray, A., Skene, K., & Haynes, K. (2017). The circular economy: An interdisciplinary exploration of the concept and application in a global context. *Journal of Business Ethics, 140*, 369–380.

Negm, N. A., Ahmed, S. A., Badr, E. A., Ghani, M. A., & El-Raouf, M. A. (2015). Synthesis and evaluation of non-ionic surfactants derived from tannic acid as corrosion inhibitors for carbon steel in acidic medium. *Journal of Surfactants and Detergents, 18*, 989–1001.

Nkosi, N., & Muzenda, E. (2014). A review and discussion of waste tyre pyrolysis and derived products. *Proceeding of the World Congress on Engineering, 2,* 2–14.

Nkosi, N., Muzenda, E., Mamvura, T. A., Belaid, M., & Patel, B. (2020). The development of a waste tyre pyrolysis production plant business model for the Gauteng region, South Africa. *Processes, 8,* 1–17.

Nunes, L. J. R., Loureiro, L. M. E. F., Sa, L. C. R., & Silva, H. F. (2020). Thermochemical conversion of olive oil industry waste: Circular economy through energy recovery. *Recycling, 5,* 1–8.

Okafor, C., Ajaero, C., Madu, C., Agomuo, K., & Abu, E. (2020). Implementation of circular economy principles in management of end-of-life tyres in a developing country (Nigeria). *AIMS Environmental Science, 7,* 406–433.

Pilusa, J., Shukla, M., & Muzenda, E. (2014). Economic assessment of waste tyres pyrolysis technology: A case study for Gauteng Province, South Africa. *International Journal of Research in Chemical, Metallurgical and Civil Engineering, 1*(1), 41–49.

Prnewswire. (2018). *The first tire pyrolysis plant in the world to receive cradle-to-cradle certification.* https://www.prnewswire.com/news-releases/the-first-tire-pyrolysis-plant-in-the-world-to-receive-cradle-to-cradle-certification-300 440959.html

Quaicoe, I., Souleymane, A. A., Kyeremeh, S. K., Appiah-Twum, H., & Ndur, S. A. (2020). Vacuum pyrolysis of waste vehicle tyres into oil fuel using a locally, fabricated reactor. *Ghana Mining Journal, 20*(1), 59–65.

Rambau, K. M., Musyoka, N. M., Manyala, N., Ren, J., & Langmi, H. W. (2018). Mechanochemical approach in the synthesis of activated carbons from waste tyres and its hydrogen storage applications. *Materials Today: Proceedings, 5*(4), 10505–10513.

Rekhaye, A., Jeetah, P. (2018). Assessing energy potential from waste tyres in mauritius by direct combustion, pyrolysis and gasification. In *The nexus: Energy, environment and climate change* (pp. 113–125). Springer.

Sakri, A., Aouabed, A., Nassour, A., & Nelles, M. (2021). Refuse-derived fuel potential production for co-combustion in the cement industry in Algeria. *Waste Management & Research, 39*(9), 1174–1184.

Sanneh, E. S., Hu, A. H., Chang, Y. M., & Sanyang, E. (2011). Introduction of a recycling system for sustainable municipal solid waste management: A case study on the greater Banjul area of the Gambia. *Environment, Development and Sustainability, 13*(6), 1065–1080.

Senthil Kumar, P., Bharathikumar, M., Prabhakaran, C., Vijayan, S., & Ramakrishnan, K. (2017). Conversion of waste plastics into low-emissive hydrocarbon fuels through catalytic depolymerization in a new laboratory scale batch reactor. *International Journal of Energy and Environmental Engineering, 8,* 167–173.

Senyagwa, J. (2022). *Africa energy outlook 2022.* https://www.iea.org/reports/africa-energy-outlook-2022/key-findings. Accessed 1 December 2014.

Seto, K. C., Fragkias, M., Güneralp, B., & Reilly, M. K. (2011). A meta-analysis of global urban land expansion. *PloS One, 6*(8), e23777.

Shirvanimoghaddam, K., Motamed, B., Ramakrishna, S., & Naebe, M. (2020). Death by waste: Fashion and textile circular economy case. *Science of the Total Environment, 718,* 137317.

Sohal, A., Nand, A.-A., Goyal, P., & Bhattacharya, A. (2022). Developing a circular economy: An examination of SME's role in India. *Journal of Business Research, 142,* 435–447.

Somoza-Tornos, A., Gonzalez-Garay, A., Pozo, C., Graells, M., Espuña, A., & Guillén-Gosálbez, G. (2020). Realizing the potential high benefits of circular economy in the chemical industry: Ethylene monomer recovery via polyethylene pyrolysis. *ACS Sustainable Chemistry & Engineering, 8*(9), 3561–3572.

Stahel, W. R. (2016). The circular economy. *Nature, 531*(7595), 435–438.

Steffen, W., Richardson, K., Rockström, J., Cornell, S. E., Fetzer, I., Bennett, E. M. ... & Sörlin, S. (2015). Planetary boundaries: Guiding human development on a changing planet. *Science, 347*(6223), 1259855.

Sulaymon, I. D., Adebayo, G. A., Sulaymon, Z. O., & Oyehan, I. A. (2017). Toxicity potential of the emitted aerosols from open burning of scrap tyres. *Zimbabwe Journal of Science and Technology, 12*(1), 99–109.

Taylor, E. T., & Nakai, S. (2012). Prevalence of acute respiratory infections in women and children in Western Sierra Leone due to smoke from wood and charcoal stoves. *International Journal of Environmental Research and Public Health, 9*(6), 2252–2265.

Ullah, S., Adams, K., Adams, D., & Attah-Boakye, R. (2021). Multinational corporations and human rights violations in emerging economies: Does commitment to social and environmental responsibility matter? *Journal of Environmental Management, 280,* 111689.

Vasiljevic-Shikaleska, A., Gjozinska, B., & Stojanovikj, M. (2017). The circular economy–a pathway to sustainable future. *Journal of Sustainable Development, 7*(17), 13–30.

Vaskalis, I., Skoulou, V., Stavropoulos, G., & Zabaniotou, A. (2019). Towards circular economy solutions for the management of rice processing residues to bioenergy via gasification. *Sustainability, 11*(22), 6433.

World Business Council for Sustainable Development (WBCSD). (2019*). Global ELT management—A global state of knowledge on regulation, management systems, impacts of recovery and technologies.* https://docs.wbcsd.org/2019/12/Global_ELT_Management-A_global_state_of_knowledge_on_regulation_management_systems_impacts_of_recovery_and_technologies.pdf

World Economic Forum. (2011). Unlocking entrepreneurial capabilities to meet the global challenges of the 21st century: Final report on the entrepreneurship education work stream. In *World economic forum global education initiative*. World Economic Forum.

Yang, Q., et al. (2021). Prospective contributions of biomass pyrolysis to China's 2050 carbon reduction and renewable energy goals. *Nature Communications, 12*, 1–12.

Yussef, A., Gibson G. E., Jr., Asmar, M. E., & Ramsey, D. (2018). Front end engineering design (FEED) for large industrial projects: FEED maturity and its impact on project cost and schedule performance. In *Construction Research Congress 2018* (pp. 1–8).

Zabaniotou, A., Antoniou, N., & Bruton, G. (2014). Analysis of good practices, barriers and drivers for ELTs pyrolysis industrial application. *Waste Management, 34*, 2335–2346.

Zabaniotou, A., Rovas, D., Libutti, A., & Monteleone, M. (2015). Boosting circular economy and closing the loop in agriculture: Case study of a small-scale pyrolysis–biochar based system integrated in an olive farm in symbiosis with an olive mill. *Environmental Development, 14*, 22–36.

Zhang, A., Venkatesh, V. G., Liu, Y., Wan, M., Qu, T., & Huisingh, D. (2019). Barriers to smart waste management for a circular economy in China. *Journal of Cleaner Production, 240*, 118198.

Africa's Response to SDGs: Barriers and Challenges

Antoinette Yaa Benewaa Gabrah, George Kofi Amoako[iD]*, and George Oppong Appiagyei Ampong*

1 INTRODUCTION

There are several calls for research across disciplines to further explore issues related to sustainable development in Africa (Hübscher et al., 2022). This is because the challenges faced in implementing sustainable development practices are context-specific and its implementation

---

A. Y. B. Gabrah (✉)
University of Professional Studies, Accra, Ghana

Akenten Appiah-Menka University of Skills Training and Entrepreneurial Development, Kumasi, Ghana

G. K. Amoako · G. O. A. Ampong
Ghana Communication Technology University, Accra, Ghana
e-mail: gamoako@gctu.edu.gh

G. O. A. Ampong
e-mail: gampong@gctu.edu.gh

G. K. Amoako
Durban University of Technology, Durban, South Africa

© The Author(s), under exclusive license to Springer Nature Switzerland AG 2023
S. Adomako et al. (eds.), *Corporate Sustainability in Africa,*
Palgrave Studies in African Leadership,
https://doi.org/10.1007/978-3-031-29273-6_3

48   A. Y. B. GABRAH ET AL.

continues to be one of the biggest barriers to firms operating in developing countries (Boso et al., 2017; Danso et al., 2020; Voola et al., 2022). In Africa, SDGs present a unique opportunity to address the continent's development challenges and achieve sustainable growth. However, despite the significant progress in some areas, many African countries continue to face significant barriers to achieving the SDGs (Danso et al., 2020; Voola et al., 2022). These barriers include increased poverty, inequality, conflict, and poor institutional and technical capabilities. This makes it difficult to tackle sustainability and environmental management issues in African nations and firms operating in this context often find it difficult to cooperate with stakeholders and governments to address environmental sustainability problems (Kolk & Lenfant, 2013).

Despite these challenges, African countries have demonstrated their commitment to the SDGs and are taking steps to integrate them into their national development plans. The African Union, in particular, has been actively promoting the SDGs and has adopted Agenda 2063, which aims to accelerate the implementation of the SDGs in Africa. Nevertheless, such barriers or challenges are under-researched (Voola et al., 2022). Voola et al. (2022), based on their systematic review of the literature, suggested that potential challenges and opportunities for implementing SDG initiatives in emerging economies should be further explored.

This search mainly focused on barriers and challenges of SDGs or sustainable development goals, barriers, challenges of SDGs, and sustainable development goals (SDGs). This research, therefore, explores the barriers and challenges faced in the implementation of SDGs using the dependency theory to achieve this objective and is structured as follows: the next section focuses on barriers to SDGs; the challenges of measuring progress towards SDGs in Africa; how to overcome such challenges; and financing SDGs in Africa. In the subsequent section, the policy contributions, and managerial and theoretical implications are discussed, followed by the conclusion, limitations, and future studies.

The study proposes that African nations face several barriers and challenges in implementing SDGs due to their dependence on developed economies and that such an over-dependence on developed economies breeds situations of increasing poverty, inequality, environmental degradation, corrupt practices, and the lack of partnership among stakeholders, which affect sustained development negatively. Furthermore, African nations face a high rate of demographic pressures and insufficient data and information to aid the achievement of SDGs. The findings of the study encourage managers of firms operating in African nations to recognize such challenges to help them operate effectively and invest wisely to aid the achievement of SDGs in such areas.

2   LITERATURE REVIEW

Dependency Theory

Dependency theory is a school of thought in modern social science that aims to comprehend underdevelopment, analyse its origins, and, to a lesser extent, suggest ways to overcome it. The dependency theory was put forth by Schank in 1972 (Sonntag, 2001). According to dependency theory, capital intervention directly causes underdevelopment that is seen throughout Latin America and worldwide. According to the theory, developing economies operate as providers of raw materials and low-cost labour for developed economies because of the disparity in unequal interaction with advanced nations (Ghosh, 2019). This leads to developing economies experiencing poor economic growth. However, the industrialized economies also provided aid to these nations in the form of significant debts. According to the argument, developing economies rely on assistance from developed nations (Palma, 1981). Per this argument, developing nations may exploit their resources to boost their economies. According to this idea, developing nations—including many African nations—are dependent on wealthy nations for resources and investments, which limits their ability to meet the SDGs due to a shortage of resources (Sonntag, 2001; Kay, 1998). The dependency theory aims to explain the unfair link between developed and developing nations. Dependency theorists contend that rich countries control and manipulate the economy of developing nations, preventing these nations from escaping poverty and achieving sustainable development.

Critics claim that the theory lacks logical coherence and empirical validity (Ahiakpor, 1985). This is due to the fact that it presents an overly simplistic and deterministic perspective of economic growth, contending that dependency on industrialized economies is the principal impediment to the economic progress of developing nations. The theory, however, did not take into consideration the complicated realities of economic development and international commerce, as well as the initiative and agency of developing countries (Manyara & Jones, 2008). Again, critics argue that the dependency theory makes broad claims about the relationship between developed and developing countries and the impact of this relationship on economic development. However, it is challenging to design empirical studies that can test claims conclusively. Also, the theory fails to account for how domestic elements like political institutions, social structures, and cultural norms influence the economic development. (Saad-Filho, 2005). It is important therefore to state dependency theory relates to sustainability in several ways. First, the theory suggests that developing countries are often exploited by developed countries, leading to environmental degradation and a lack of sustainability. Second, the theory highlights the importance of economic and political power imbalances in shaping development and sustainability. This situation forces developing economies to rely on unsustainable practices like overexploiting natural resources to ensure their economic needs are met. This reveals that it is important to establish and strengthen the relationship between developed and developing economies to promote equitable and sustainable development practices (Manyara & Jones, 2008).

Sustainable Development Goals

The UN created the Sustainable Development Goals (SDGs) in September 2015. By the year 2030, all countries, both developed and developing, are expected to have accomplished the 17 sustainable development goals. The SDGs' universality, indivisibility, and transformative nature are its three defining characteristics (Bebbington & Unerman, 2018; D'Alessandro & Zulu, 2017). Along with these 17 goals, it is hoped that by 2030, 169 targets and 263 indicators would also be accomplished. The SDGs offer a multidimensional and holistic perspective on development, in contrast to conventional development agendas, which concentrate on a limited number of factors (Fukuda-Parr, 2016). The government, agencies, businesses, and the entire community must work together to achieve these goals because no single entity can do it alone (Bebbington & Unerman, 2018; sdgcafrica.org, 2023).

The worldwide initiative to implement a plan of action for people, the environment, and prosperity was made possible by the SDGs (Bebbington & Unerman, 2018). SDGs promote sustainability by balancing the three sustainable development components, namely the economic, social, and environmental (Leal Filho et al., 2019). The sustainable development goals serve as a road map for improving and sustaining society (Perrigot & Gbetchi, 2022). Creating goods that satisfy consumer demands and desires without endangering the environment or future generations is what is meant by sustainability (Amoako et al., 2022; World Commission on Environment and Development, 1987).

The Africa Context: Unique Barriers to Achieving the SDGs

According to the literature, the SDGs face some obstacles, including a lack of funding, poor governance, corruption, infrastructure, a lack of capacity and skills, poverty, inequality, conflict, climate change, demographic pressures, and a lack of data and knowledge (Nunes et al., 2022; Togo & Gandidzanwa, 2021). In light of dependence theory, this section analyses the main obstacles to fulfilling the sustainable development goals in Africa.

Limited Control Over Resources and Over-Dependence on Foreign Aid

Resources are readily available in the environment, are economically viable, are culturally sustainable, and help to satiate human needs and desires (Togo & Gandidzanwa, 2021). There is evidence that many African countries experience severe resource shortages as a result of their poor ability to manage their resources (Hansen et al., 2021; Hinson et al., 2019). These limitations include a lack of skilled workers, poor infrastructure, and restricted financial access. Lack of funding is a significant obstacle to implementing the SDGs (Masuda et al., 2021; Mawonde & Togo, 2021; Togo & Gandidzanwa, 2021). Both locally owned African businesses and foreign affiliates in Africa are impacted by these difficulties. This is because African nations frequently rely on industrialized nations for resources like finance, technology, and knowledge, which hinders their independence in achieving the SDGs. Once more, their lack of basic infrastructure, like roads and electricity, limits their capacity to meet the SDGs. Again, one major barrier to achieving SDGs is dependence on foreign aid. It is crucial to acknowledge that many African nations significantly rely on foreign aid to fund their development objectives, including the SDGs. This reliance may lead to a lack of ownership and sustainability as well as a restricted influence from development initiatives (Aust et al., 2020).

52   A. Y. B. GABRAH ET AL.

Governance and Corruption

A significant and particular challenge to the accomplishment of SDGs in Africa is governance and corruption (Kim, 2016). According to the dependence theory, aid-dependent nations have the worst records of ineffective leadership and corruption (Ahiakpor & James, 1985). The rule of law is threatened by corruption and poor governance, which also reduces the efficiency of public institutions. This serves to further deter investment in many African nations. As a result, it is argued that implementing the SDGs presents significant implementation issues connected to policy (Del Rio Castro et al., 2021). Creating inclusive decision spaces for stakeholder interaction across many sectors is one of the primary governance problems affecting SDG implementation. The reason for this is competing interests. Making challenging trade-offs while concentrating on equity, justice, justice, and fairness is also included. When both cannot be fully attained at once, this entails giving up one component of a goal in exchange for advancements in another (Barbier & Burgess, 2019; Zhao et al., 2021). The challenge of ensuring accountability for commitments made by countries, communities, organizations, and other parties to agreements related to the SDGs is another major challenge in governance; as a result, mechanisms to hold societal actors accountable for investment, and outcomes must exist (Bowen et al., 2017).

Partnership

A partnership is a type of collaboration that uses the resources, abilities, and qualities of both parties to work towards common objectives (Eweje et al., 2021). Partnership issues have an impact on SDG implementation. In Africa, partnerships between NGOs, CSOs, private actors, and the local community are typically weak, despite the importance of multistakeholder participation in the localization of the SDGs. This makes it challenging for multiple stakeholders to work together in Africa (Lauwo et al., 2022). According to Katuwawala and Bandara (2022), the SDGs' implementation is hampered by poor teamwork and ineffective collaborative policies. As a result, to execute and achieve the SDGs, relevant shareholders must pool their expertise, skills, and resources and share risks and associated costs and rewards (Eweje et al., 2021).

Poverty

Poverty is the lack of the necessities of life—food, shelter, and clothing. It is the situation or state where individuals, groups, or communities are unable to maintain a minimal level of living due to a lack of enough resources. As a result, it is a condition of the human being that is characterized by a persistent or chronic lack of resources, talents, choices, security, and authority. This is a problem that affects both the individual and the larger society. Although some African nations have made tremendous progress in eliminating poverty, poverty is still pervasive in many of these nations. This makes it challenging for many people to get essential services like food, healthcare, and education. This makes it much more challenging to engage in the economy. As a result, one of the primary hurdles to the SDGs' implementation is poverty. To the extent that poverty transforms synergies into trade-offs for some SDGs, poverty limits synergies and intensifies trade-offs among SDGs (Wei et al., 2023). According to the dependency theory, developing economies are becoming poorer and more dependent on foreign capital as a result of the enormous rise in capital mobility and availability (Kay, 1998).

Income Inequality
Income inequality, according to the OECD (2023), is the degree to which income is divided inequitably among a population. The distribution of income among people, organizations, populations, social classes, or nations, thus, exhibits a huge discrepancy. Notably, there are still significant income disparities in many African nations. This worsens poverty even more and retards economic development. Consequently, initiatives to reduce poverty are undermined. Due to this, certain people have less equal access to services including healthcare, education, and other necessities. Additionally, this is because international financial institutions have forced structural adjustment programmes on Africans due to their heavy debt loads. Their chances of achieving the SDGs are so substantially diminished.

Environmental Degradation
Deforestation, soil erosion, and pollution make it difficult for residents to acquire clean water and grow food, which poses a serious problem for many African nations. These environmental problems also contribute to climate change, which endangers global and African sustainable development. Africa is significantly impacted by climate change. Increasing temperatures, decreasing precipitation, and more frequent and severe weather occurrences are examples of this. Thus, the local, regional, and global climates of the earth are the result of long-term changes in

the average weather patterns. These have detrimental effects on human health, water resources, and agriculture. For example, environmental elements like abrupt changes in the weather and severe weather events may contribute to hunger (Jacob-John et al., 2022). Even though this is a worldwide phenomenon, Africa is the continent most susceptible to climate change. This makes it harder for African countries to accomplish the SDGs and has an additional negative impact on entrepreneurial businesses (Toukabri & Youssef, 2022).

Demographic Pressures

The indicator of demographic pressure considers pressure on the state either from the population itself or its surroundings. The population of Africa is expanding quickly, placing more demands on infrastructure and resources. The SDGs become more challenging for African nations to implement as a result. All residents should have access to quality healthcare, education, and work opportunities. Bhargava (2019), for example, claims that the high population expansion in many developing nations is impeding the achievement of sub-goals including eradicating hunger and food insecurity, enhancing the quality of education, and providing appropriate sanitation. To increase global sustainability, it is crucial to guarantee that resources are preserved and that regulations are upheld (Bhargava, 2019).

Data and Information

The lack of data and information is a distinct hurdle preventing the SDGs from being realized in Africa. According to the literature, there is a dearth of trustworthy and current statistics and information about how the SDGs are doing in Africa. This makes it more challenging for African nations to track their progress and determine where more work needs to be done. This hinders the ability of governments, civic society, and the corporate sector to create policies and initiatives that are supported by data to accomplish the SDGs. As a result, there are proposals for using big data and artificial intelligence to correct these inequities (Abaku et al., 2021; Del Rio Castro et al., 2021).

Challenges of Measuring Progress Towards SDGs in Africa

Data-Related Issues

Many African countries lack comprehensive and reliable data on key indicators of the SDGs. This makes it difficult to measure progress and identify areas for improvement. This is particularly true in areas such as poverty, inequality, health, and education, where data collection and analysis can be challenging. Hence, the quality of data and information is poor. This makes it difficult to use the data to monitor progress and inform policy decisions. Again, this is due to factors like weak data collection systems, inadequate funding for data collection and analysis, and the lack of trained personnel. This is also attributed to the lack of standardization—different African countries use different methodologies and data sources to measure progress towards the SDGs (Abaku et al., 2021). This leads to difficulty in comparing progress across countries and regions. Furthermore, it limits the ability of African countries to learn from each other and share the best practices. Subsequently, this leads to poor data dissemination. Furthermore, many African countries lack the technical capacity to collect, analyse, and use data to monitor the progress of SDGs. This problem includes a shortage of trained personnel and a lack of investment in data collection and analysis systems (Del Rio Castro et al., 2021; Hansen et al., 2021; Hinson et al., 2019) (Fig. 1).

Implications of the Study

Theoretical Implications

There are numerous and significant theoretical implications of the dependence theory for Sustainable Development Goals (SDGs). This research fills the knowledge gap on the challenges and obstacles encountered in Africa. Per the dependency theory, the balance of power between rich and developing nations has a significant impact on how well those nations can accomplish the SDGs. As a consequence, it emphasizes the necessity of a more equitable allocation of authority and wealth so that emerging nations can take part in the international system on an equitable basis. The necessity for structural transformation rather than just addressing the related side effects of poverty and inequality is also highlighted by the dependence theory. Because of this, it will be vital to address the underlying causes of inequality and encourage increased economic and political independence for African nations.

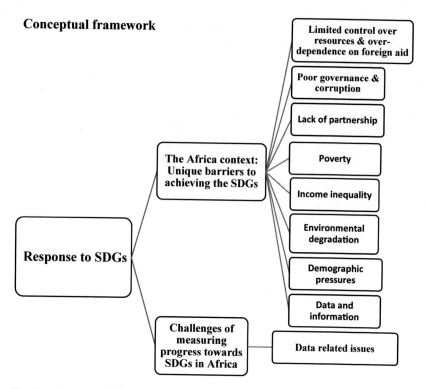

Fig. 1 Conceptual framework of the study

According to the dependency theory, relying solely on market-based solutions would not be sufficient to achieve the SDGs because they frequently serve the interests of developed countries and fail to address the structural inequalities that prevent developing countries from achieving sustainable development. The concept that all nations will inevitably pass through the same stages of development and those industrialized nations are inherently superior to developing nations is contested by the dependency theory. Instead, it emphasizes how crucial it is to consider the unique historical and economic circumstances that influence each country's growth trajectory. It also implies that the current system of international relations is fundamentally unfair and encourages wealthy nations' dominance over poorer nations. This viewpoint emphasizes the need for a more equitable and sustainable type of globalization that considers the requirements and objectives of each African nation.

The theory highlights the significance of considering the historical background of each country and region as well as the effects of colonialism, imperialism, and other forms of exploitation on their development paths. This viewpoint contributes to the explanation of why some nations have succeeded more readily in fulfilling the SDGs than others. Finally, even though the dependence theory is sometimes connected to a worldview that divides nations into developed and developing ones, it does emphasize the significance of interdependence and the necessity for developed and developing nations to collaborate to accomplish the SDGs. This viewpoint acknowledges that global challenges like sustainable development call for cooperation and coordinated action from all nations.

Policy Implications
According to reports, corruption and bribery have an impact on how the SDGs are implemented, hinder development outcomes, and seriously jeopardize efforts to fulfil the SDGs in Africa. Because of this, authorities in Africa must prioritize fighting corruption, including the prevention of money laundering, bribery, and other illegal activities, to achieve sustainable development. This will enhance good governance, and the creation of institutions that are inclusive and effective, as required by the SDGs. This will further offer financial support for achieving the SDGs (Hope, 2022). The African leadership should offer political backing for a multi-stakeholder collaboration (Lauwo et al., 2022). Again, stakeholders and investors should push businesses to take social responsibility seriously and manage climate change risks, specifically through Greenhouse Gas (GHG) disclosure.

Policymakers should encourage GHG disclosure as it is an important tactic for addressing climate change and global warming challenges. GHG disclosure in the form of industry-specific disclosure criteria should be developed and put into practice (Toukabri & Youssef, 2022). Biermann et al. (2017) assert that it is crucial to guarantee consistent and predictable resource mobilization. Consequently, the achievement of the SDGs depends on public–private and private–private partnerships as well as other types of action networks. Leadership in Africa should therefore promote effective partnerships, especially regional cooperation. Given that foreign direct investment is essential for accomplishing nearly all of the

SDGs and their underlying targets, policymakers must promote this type of external finance. Furthermore, as it is not usually apparent how this financing is disbursed among the many SDG goals in Africa, its allocation needs to be tracked and reported on (Lopes et al., 2020; Aust et al., 2020). Policymakers must support efficient and cutting-edge funding methods, such as impact investment and blended finance, to fund the SDGs in Africa (Aust et al., 2020).

Managerial Implications

Managers must take a comprehensive approach to tackle the core causes of inequality and poverty to accomplish the SDGs, as opposed to only focusing on the symptoms. The ability to create and execute complete and integrated solutions is necessary for this, as is a thorough awareness of the intricate connections that exist among the economic, political, and social systems. Second, managers must be dedicated to fostering greater equality and eliminating poverty, both within and across nations. This calls for a focus on underrepresented populations and organizations, as well as an understanding that tackling inequality is necessary for sustainable development. Third, managers need to be open to embracing innovation and cutting-edge technologies that can enhance people's lives and save the environment. This calls for a commitment to research and development as well as a readiness to try out and evaluate novel concepts. Fourth, managers must be motivated to interact with stakeholders at all stages, from neighbourhood associations to global corporations. This calls for a thorough comprehension of the wants and needs of all parties involved as well as a willingness to collaborate to discover solutions that advance sustainable development for all.

Managers need to understand that global challenges like sustainable development call for cooperation and coordinated action from all nations. Focusing on interdependence and being willing to collaborate with partners from other countries to design and execute solutions that support sustainable development for everybody are necessary for this. They must also be willing to collaborate with a variety of stakeholders, including governments, civil society organizations, the commercial sector, and international organizations. They must likewise understand the value of partnerships in attaining the SDGs. This calls for a dedication to developing trust and cooperation between partners as well as good leadership and communication abilities. This necessitates an emphasis on community-based strategies and a readiness to collaborate with regional partners to create and implement solutions that are adaptable to regional conditions and needs. Finally, managers must be dedicated to transparency and accountability as well as be willing to provide frank and straightforward reports on their progress and impact if they are to succeed in achieving the SDGs. This calls for a concentration on monitoring and assessment as well as a dedication to ongoing improvement so that initiatives promote sustainable development.

Conclusion, Limitations, and Future Studies

The Sustainable Development Goals (SDGs) offer African nations a road map for achieving a more sustainable future; however, achieving these objectives would necessitate overcoming considerable obstacles and challenges. The SDGs' financing presents a significant issue for African nations, which are constrained by factors like inadequate government budget allocation, an unfriendly business climate, and restricted access to capital markets. The rise of digital finance, the growth of impact investing, and increased donor assistance all present substantial prospects for financing the SDGs in Africa. Innovative approaches and best practices are needed to address these issues, including bolstering domestic resources, encouraging private sector investment, enhancing access to capital markets, fostering regional cooperation, utilizing novel financing mechanisms, and putting best practices in program design and implementation into practice. A sustained commitment to the SDGs and the courage to overcome obstacles and challenges are necessary for Africa to advance towards a sustainable future. This entails tackling the underlying reasons for these difficulties and coming up with fresh, creative ways to fund the SDGs. Africa can help realize the SDGs' vision for a more sustainable future for all people if given the necessary tools and resources. The propositions made could be tested in further studies using empirical data. Further propositions could be made based on a different theory apart from the dependency theory.

REFERENCES

Abaku, T., Calzati, S., & Masso, A. (2021). Exploring digital sustainability of/ through Estonia's e-residency: Africa's case and the importance of culture for sustainability. *Digital Policy, Regulation and Governance, 23*(3), 300–313.

Ahiakpor, J. C. (1985). The success and failure of dependency theory: The experience of Ghana. *International Organization, 39*(3), 535–552.

Amoako, G. K., Dzogbenuku, R. K., Doe, J., & Adjaison, G. K. (2022). Green marketing and the SDGs: Emerging market perspective. *Marketing Intelligence & Planning, 40*(3), 310–327.

Aust, V., Morais, A. I., & Pinto, I. (2020). How does foreign direct investment contribute to sustainable development goals? Evidence from African countries. *Journal of Cleaner Production, 245*, 118823.

Barbier, E. B., & Burgess, J. C. (2019). Sustainable development goal indicators: Analyzing trade-offs and complementarities. *World Development, 122*, 295–305.

Bebbington, J., & Unerman, J. (2018). Achieving the United Nations sustainable development goals: An enabling role for accounting research. *Accounting, Auditing & Accountability Journal.*

Bhargava, A. (2019). Climate change, demographic pressures and global sustainability. *Economics & Human Biology, 33*, 149–154.

Biermann, F., Kanie, N., & Kim, R. E. (2017). Global governance by goal-setting: The novel approach of the UN sustainable development goals. *Current Opinion in Environmental Sustainability, 26*, 26–31.

Boso, N., Danso, A., Leonidou, C., Uddin, M., Adeola, O., & Hultman, M. (2017). Does financial resource slack drive sustainability expenditure in developing economy small and medium-sized enterprises? *Journal of Business Research, 80*, 247–256.

Bowen, K. J., Cradock-Henry, N. A., Koch, F., Patterson, J., Häyhä, T., Vogt, J., & Barbi, F. (2017). Implementing the "sustainable development goals": Towards addressing three key governance challenges—Collective action, trade-offs, and accountability. *Current Opinion in Environmental Sustainability, 26*, 90–96.

Castro, G. D. R., Fernandez, M. C. G., & Colsa, A. U. (2021). Unleashing the convergence amid digitalization and sustainability towards pursuing the Sustainable Development Goals (SDGs): A holistic review. *Journal of Cleaner Production, 280*, 122204.

D'Alessandro, C., & Zulu, L. C. (2017). From the millennium development goals (MDGs) to the sustainable development goals (SDGs): Africa in the post-2015 development agenda. A geographical perspective. *African Geographical Review, 36*(1), 1–18.

Danso, A., Adomako, S., Lartey, T., Amankwah-Amoah, J., & Owusu-Yirenkyi, D. (2020). Stakeholder integration, environmental sustainability orientation, and financial performance. *Journal of Business Research, 119*, 652–662.

Eweje, G., Sajjad, A., Nath, S. D., & Kobayashi, K. (2021). Multi-stakeholder partnerships: A catalyst to achieve sustainable development goals. *Marketing Intelligence & Planning, 39*(2), 186–212.

Ghosh, B. N. (2019). *Dependency theory revisited*. Routledge.

Hansen, B., Stiling, P., & Uy, W. F. (2021). Innovations and challenges in SDG integration and reporting in higher education: A case study from the University of South Florida. *International Journal of Sustainability in Higher Education, 22*(5), 1002–1021.

Hinson, R., Lensink, R., & Mueller, A. (2019). Transforming agribusiness in developing countries: SDGs and the role of FinTech. *Current Opinion in Environmental Sustainability, 41*, 1–9.

Hope, K. R., Sr. (2022). Reducing corruption and bribery in Africa as a target of the sustainable development goals: Applying indicators for assessing performance. *Journal of Money Laundering Control, 25*(2), 313–329.

https://sdgcafrica.org/wp-content/uploads/2019/06/AFRICA-2030-SDGs-THREE-YEAR-REALITY-CHECK-REPORT.pdf

https://www.oecd.org/dac/sustainable-development-goals.htm

Hübscher, C., Hensel-Börner, S., & Henseler, J. (2022). Social marketing and higher education: Partnering to achieve sustainable development goals. *Journal of Social Marketing, 12*(1), 76–104.

Jacob-John, J., D'Souza, C., Marjoribanks, T., & Singaraju, S. (2022). Sustainable development practices for SDGs: A systematic review of food supply chains in developing economies. *Environmental Sustainability in Emerging Markets: Consumer, Organisation and Policy Perspectives*, 213–241.

Katuwawala, H. C., & Bandara, Y. M. (2022). System-based barriers for seaports in contributing to sustainable development goals. *Maritime Business Review* (ahead-of-print).

Kay, C. (1998). Relevance of structuralist and dependency theories in the neoliberal period: A Latin American perspective. *ISS Working Paper Series/General Series, 281*, 1–30.

Kim, S. B. (2016). Dangling the carrot, sharpening the stick: How an Amnesty program and Qui Tam actions could strengthen Korea's anti-corruption efforts. *Northwestern Journal of International Law and Business, 36*, 235.

Kolk, A., & Lenfant, F. (2013). Multinationals, CSR and partnerships in Central African conflict countries. *Corporate Social Responsibility and Environmental Management, 20*(1), 43–54.

Lauwo, S. G., Azure, J. D. C., & Hopper, T. (2022). Accountability and governance in implementing the Sustainable Development Goals in a developing country context: Evidence from Tanzania. *Accounting, Auditing & Accountability Journal*.

Leal Filho, W., Tripathi, S. K., Andrade Guerra, J. B. S. O. D., Giné-Garriga, R., Orlovic Lovren, V., & Willats, J. (2019). Using the sustainable development goals towards a better understanding of sustainability challenges. *International Journal of Sustainable Development & World Ecology, 26*(2), 179–190.

Lopes, J., Somanje, A. N., Velez, E., Lam, R. D., & Saito, O. (2020). Determinants of foreign investment and international aid for meeting the sustainable development goals in Africa: A visual cognitive review of the literature. *Sustainability Challenges in Sub-Saharan Africa I: Continental Perspectives and Insights from Western and Central Africa*, 161–187.

Manyara, G., & Jones, E. (2008). Reflecting on tourism development in Kenya through the mirror of dependency theory. *Tourism Review International*, *12*(3–4), 231–242.

Masuda, H., Okitasari, M., Morita, K., Katramiz, T., Shimizu, H., Kawakubo, S., & Kataoka, Y. (2021). SDGs mainstreaming at the local level: Case studies from Japan. *Sustainability Science*, *16*, 1539–1562.

Mawonde, A., & Togo, M. (2021). Challenges of involving students in campus SDGs-related practices in an ODeL context: The case of the University of South Africa (UNISA). *International Journal of Sustainability in Higher Education*, *22*(7), 1487–1502.

Nunes, A. K. D. S., Morioka, S. N., & Bolis, I. (2022). Challenges of business models for sustainability in startups. *RAUSP Management Journal*, *57*, 382–400.

Palma, G. (1981). Dependency and development: A critical overview. In *Dependency theory: A critical reassessment* (pp. 20–78).

Saad-Filho, A. (2005). Structuralism and dependency theory. In *The origins of development economics: How schools of economic thought have addressed development* (p. 128).

Sonntag, R., Lewis, G. J., & Raszkowski, A. (2022). The Importance of implementing SDGs by small and medium size enterprises: Evidence from Germany and Poland. *Sustainability*, *14*(24), 16950.

Togo, M., & Gandidzanwa, C. P. (2021). The role of education 5.0 in accelerating the implementation of SDGs and challenges encountered at the University of Zimbabwe. *International Journal of Sustainability in Higher Education*.

Toukabri, M., & Mohamed Youssef, M. A. (2022). Climate change disclosure and sustainable development goals (SDGs) of the 2030 agenda: The moderating role of corporate governance. *Journal of Information, Communication and Ethics in Society*.

Voola, R., Bandyopadhyay, C., Voola, A., Ray, S., & Carlson, J. (2022). B2B marketing scholarship and the UN sustainable development goals (SDGs): A systematic literature review. *Industrial Marketing Management*, *101*, 12–32.

Wei, Y., Zhong, F., Song, X., & Huang, C. (2023). Exploring the impact of poverty on the sustainable development goals: Inhibiting synergies and magnifying trade-offs. *Sustainable Cities and Society*, *89*, 104367.

Zhao, Z., Cai, M., Wang, F., Winkler, J. A., Connor, T., Chung, M. G., Zhang, J., Yang, H., Xu, Z., Tang, Y., Ouyang, Z., Zhang, H., & Liu, J. (2021). Synergies and tradeoffs among Sustainable Development Goals across boundaries in a meta-coupled world. *Science of the Total Environment, 751,* 141749.

Multinational Enterprises, Sustainability Activities, and Implementation of Sustainable Development Goals in Africa

Edmund Osei Afriyie and Nadia Zahoor

1 INTRODUCTION

Multinational enterprises (MNEs) are key agents in shaping economic growth. It is estimated that MNEs account for half of the foreign direct investment (FDI), which provides job creation and boosts economic growth (Castellani et al., 2022; Nguyen, 2022). Brand reputations of MNEs in the global north are well established as compared to those in the global south where natural resources are heavily exploited. In the global

---

E. O. Afriyie (✉)
Department of Strategy and International Business, University of Birmingham, Birmingham, UK
e-mail: exo212@student.bham.ac.uk

N. Zahoor
Department of Business and Society, Queen Mary University of London, London, UK

InnoLab, University of Vaasa, Vaasa, Finland

N. Zahoor
e-mail: n.zahoor@qmul.ac.uk

© The Author(s), under exclusive license to Springer Nature Switzerland AG 2023
S. Adomako et al. (eds.), *Corporate Sustainability in Africa*, Palgrave Studies in African Leadership,
https://doi.org/10.1007/978-3-031-29273-6_4

south, local institutions denounce such activities of western corporations as being a social and environmental burden. In addition, there has been considerable attention in the global north concerning corporate sustainability compared to the global south (Seuring & Müller, 2008). In this regard, research suggests that MNEs due to their global nature can be powerful actors to promote sustainable development that is in line with SDGs (Ghauri et al., 2021). MNEs can promote corporate sustainability through promoting education and initiating social campaigns in partnership with governments and international organizations (Forum for the Future, 2000). However, there is a lack of attention to the role of MNEs to achieve a breadth of SDGs (Wettstein et al., 2019). This is particularly true in the case of Africa where FDI is a key driver of economic growth and the aim of Africa SDG (Aust et al., 2020) and dashboards report is to "*help each African country identify priorities for action, understand key implementation challenges, and identify the gaps that must be closed to achieve the SDGs by 2030*" (SDGs Center for Africa and SDSN, 2018). Thus, it is essential to discuss the role of MNEs in the achievement of SDGs in Africa and this influence may differ among different SDGs.

Sustainability can best be described as the process of aiding humans in the realization of their potential quality of life without compromising the earth's support system (OECD, 2018). 2015 marked the establishment of the UN SDGs. MNEs are not left out as they feed into the progress on a local, national, and global scale of this initiative by the United Nations. In addition, SDGs provide opportunities to strategize business operations (UNGC, 2015). Indeed, the private sector contributes significantly to goals in the areas of employment, job creation, provision of education, and financing which boosts the host nation's income (Robinson, 2004). To this effect, MNEs across the globe have SDGs embedded in their business operations and play a vital role on the global scale. Thus, there is a lack of investigative research on the contribution of foreign firms toward sustainable development in developing countries in collaboration with local stakeholders (Vazquez-Brust et al., 2014). Furthermore, it is essential for international business (IB) research to explore more sustainability as research by van der Waal and Thijssens (2020) indicates that less than 25% of Forbes Global 2000 companies based in the Global North mentioned SDGs in their annual reports. Thus, this calls for concern about MNEs in the global south implementing sustainability strategies.

The review of this chapter covers the past and current state of SDGs in sub-Saharan Africa, the nexus between MNEs' activities, government partnerships, and SDGs through consulting sustainable reports, and the limitations and future direction of this study.

The State of Sustainable Development Goals in Sub-Saharan Africa

The expectation of MNEs to address sustainability is a huge challenge due to the magnitude of MNEs' responsibilities and operations in local and international markets (Filatotchev & Stahl, 2015). Financial resources are required to execute SDGs but they have fallen short of targets over the past years and have a large funding gap in Africa (SDGCA, 2019). Genuine savings, an indicator of national wealth, is negative in 49 out of 54 sub-Saharan African countries. This suggests an unstable path with negative implications for welfare and development in the long run (Bissoon, 2017). For example, only five African countries met the growth rate of 7% predicted under SDG 8 in 2017 (SDGCA, 2019). Despite the inflows of FDI into the sub-Saharan Africa region in the past decade, the percentage of unemployment remains high. Among nations in the global south, sub-Saharan Africa remains the region with the highest percentage of malnutrition in 2019 (UNNY, 2019).

Furthermore, it is predicted that all sub-Saharan African countries are less likely to meet their SDGs (Begashaw, 2021). In sub-Saharan African countries, poor institutional quality, income inequality, political conflicts, and overdependence on the export of natural resources can negatively influence genuine savings (Nyanzu et al., 2019). Despite these situations, SDGs have been a priority of governments and policymakers in sub-Saharan Africa to alleviate poverty and support economic growth (Selsky & Parker, 2005). To this end, the activities of SDGs by MNEs remain unfulfilled on a large scale. Furthermore, the limited implementation and delayed progress of SDGs by MNEs are a result of the close interaction with government policies. This poses a discussion on what roles MNEs have played in the progression of SDGs, what is expected of them in the future, and the role of International Business reviews in directing the course of this discussion (Tulder et al., 2021). Despite the presence of MNEs in rural and urban areas, the economic spillovers from the companies in Africa fail to reach the most vulnerable and less privileged people (Haglund, 2008). Furthermore, the private sector faces challenges in the sub-Saharan Africa region as they fail to innovate new growth models (B&SDC, 2017). Thus, these states of affairs have raised criticism as to whether SDGs are too ambitious or lack substance (Tulder et al., 2021).

Multinational Enterprises and Sustainable Development Goals

SDGs activities of MNEs are made available through self-published reports on an annual basis about their contribution carried out either on a global, regional, or national level to inform stakeholders of their positive quota to these goals (Sachs, 2012). Large corporations in the *global north* have embraced SDGs, which are linked to their business models (PwC, 2015). MNEs are expected to operate in a sustainable manner *per the sector* they belong to, standards required by the local agencies, and some norms and values held highly by the communities (Lee, 2008).

Some firms do not engage fully in SDGs due to the costs incurred for action taken although sustainability can be good for financial gains. On the other hand, firms can be more competitive with their visibility of sustainability actions to draw more customers and be environmentally friendly. Also, there is a weak link between assessing adherence to SDGs, and the absence of precise metrics of sustainability strategies. In addition, firms usually take a benevolent route toward local or communal development against providing accurate unbiased information about their operations to safeguard their reputation (Lashitew, 2021).

Evidence of Sustainable Development Goals' Activities by MNEs

The private sector has a vital role to play in the implementation of SDGs as it represents 75% of the global GDP. As an essential stakeholder, collaboration with other stakeholders such as governments and civil society actors is required (Sachs, 2015). However, a gap stands in how MNEs translate their local sustainability goals on the ground although there is an admitted desire to carry out these activities (Wilkinson & Mangalagiu, 2012). *Self-reports* published indicate there are positive steps made and being processed to affect the communities and host countries while few are called to book on the negative effects of their operations. However, these positive impacts have fewer progressive measurements based on targets and indicators. On the other hand, scholars have revealed that awareness of SDGs is known among top management level or dedicated sustainability departments. Thus, this awareness is not entirely embedded in the firm's operationalization (Mhlanga et al., 2018).

Sustainability Reporting

Sustainability reporting is providing proof, feedback, response, or evidence to sustainability issues within the global, regional, or national context by the government or an MNE in published documents. However, the outlook of these responses varies across nations and companies. In addition to this, environmental awareness within the nations or localities is a major driver for publishing which displays steps taken to address some of these issues often within their business operation (Kolk, 2018). This is important because MNEs translate their understanding and solutions to stakeholders for easy accessibility and assimilation of the impact made (Higgins & Coffey, 2016). The constant backlash from community members and media houses forces MNEs to disclose their reports because of social and environmental degradation. To this effect, there has been external encouragement from renowned internal bodies such as the United Nations Global Compact and the Global Reporting Initiative to partake in this exercise of publishing their impact on society, the environment, and the economy (Witte & Dilyard, 2017).

Themes Adopted in Sustainability Reporting by MNEs

Firms are most likely to be glued to goals connected to their client's expectations and the operation of the sector or industry. A typical example will be a construction company that tends to resolve challenges related to recycling and waste management. On that note, SDGs are embedded in their publications as strategic goals and achievements (Higgins & Coffey, 2016). Similarly, companies in pharmaceutical companies are most likely and well-positioned to contribute to challenges in health while agriculture companies address issues of food security (Hall & Vredenburg, 2003).

Secondly, standardization is a key theme to ensure uniformity in publication. Standardization is followed by MNEs and accepted by Global Reporting Initiative (GRI) for evaluating the impact of SDGs on firms (GRI, 2017). MNEs are encouraged to have these publications implemented despite the inconsistency or little information in sub-Saharan Africa. Two common issues in these reports include standardization and the use of terminologies. For example, some reports often interchange Triple Bottom Line and Corporate Social Responsibility in their reports. Hence, it distorts the distinct meaning of each word (Buhr & Gray, 2012).

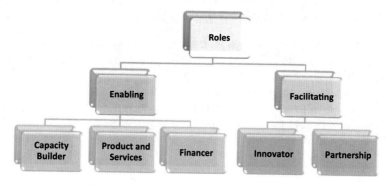

Fig. 1 Summary of roles by MNEs

Role of MNEs in Promoting Sustainable Development

MNEs play a positive or negative role in sustainability development. One is the ability to maximize profit at the expense of environmental preservation (Welford, 1997). However, MNEs contribute to achieving sustainable developments such as the socioeconomic well-being of stakeholders around the globe (Ledgerwood & Broadhurst, 2000). The duties of enabling and facilitating categories will be examined in depth in the following section Fig. 1 and Table 1.

Business-and-Society Relationship

This framework engagement dwells on guidelines or plans for achieving local sustainability development. Plans are implemented based on partnerships, corporate citizenship, and corporate social responsibility at the national or local level (Muthuri et al., 2012). The concept of business society relationship stems from studies by Valente (2012). This deals with mutual agreements or partnerships with governmental agencies, MNEs, and NGOs. Although three partnerships are factored in there, other scholars do not recognize MNEs' engagement. Secondly, a corporate citizen is synonymous with the citizenship duties of an organization or human citizenry. This title is rendered as a result of the active participation of the company in social activities and the provision of goods and services. The positive relationship observed by the community members is welcomed and MNEs are perceived as corporate citizens. This fosters

MULTINATIONAL ENTERPRISES, SUSTAINABILITY ... 71

Table 1 Categories of roles played by MNEs

No	Categories	Roles	Operationalization	Source
1	Enabling	Financer	Capital is raised or injected into the community through microloans, sponsors, donations, grants, etc., to sustain local development	Kolk et al. (2017)
		Capacity builder	Both community members and employees receive the necessary skills, knowledge, training, and education to improve local economic and social development	Newenham-Kahindi (2015)
		Product and service provider	Services or products such as healthcare, education, or infrastructure are handed over to the community either independently or in support of a government agency to fill an institutional void	Newenham-Kahindi (2015)
2	Facilitating	Partner	Partners with individuals, organizations, or communities in multi-stakeholder processes, such as partnerships and joint ventures	Kolk et al. (2008)
		Innovator	Solutions are developed in an innovative way to tackle local sustainable issues through research and development. These solutions benefit the organization, customers, communities, government, and partners	Kraemer and van Tulder (2009)

a voice for the community when political local developments are void. However, they are criticized by some scholars as monopolistic mechanisms to control job creation and economic growth with less government interference (Adelman, 2018). In that regard, MNEs respond to some of these outcries (Crane et al., 2008). Lastly, the focus on CSR activities is seen as corporate gesture to tackle issues of low literacy rate, pollution of water bodies, control of diseases such as malaria which is dominant in developing countries, etc. (Muthuri et al., 2012). However, other scholars perceive that CSR does not take consider the real plights of the communities which will not be conducive to local development (Daouda, 2014). This institutionalized approach also increases market share expansion, social capital, and appropriate networks relevant to sustain the business

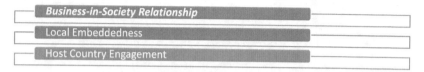

Fig. 2 Summary of a framework for local development sustainability

in the long haul (Newenham-Kahindi, 2015). Brand image or reputation is established through communal partnership (Clarke & MacDonald, 2019). These communal partnerships ensure MNEs operate responsibly. Unfamiliarity with the modus operandi of a locality drains capital from the business in the host country. To address this, the MNEs tread cautiously on social and environmental issues based on country-specific advantages (Pinkse & Kolk, 2008). The engagement of MNEs in local communities has an influence on the industry it operates within. For example, companies in the food and beverage sector have production policies in line with environmental and social safety activities or operations (Codita, 2007). Figure 2 summarises the framework for local development sustainability.

Governments and MNEs

Multinational enterprises are regulated by institutions or governmental bodies at the micro (i.e. company level), meso (i.e. inter-organizational level), and macro (international or national level) (Campbell, 2004). Thus, governments in developing and developed economies have enacted policies to ensure a conducive environment is made accessible to provide social and environmental protection (Wijen et al., 2012). It is essential to have institutional bodies actively engage MNEs as some have grown in influence, power, and finances to distort everything in society in their interest.

However, the activity of these institutions is regarded as less effective in the global south compared to the global north. While some MNEs in Africa are perceived to do less in social and environmental initiatives due to poor institutional framework, other companies are doing quite well. For example, South Africa has in place regulations that require the empowerment of previously disadvantaged people to aid overcome the injustice of the apartheid regime (Arya & Bassi, 2011). To ensure such proactive participation from MNEs, policies from governments must encourage and stimulate such investments (Stephenson et al., 2021).

Furthermore, it is Africa's quest to eliminate extreme poverty and achieve sustainable and inclusive growth. However, Africa faces a variety of complex challenges across all sectors. One critical challenge is the excessive power of the executives, which constrains economic growth. In response to changing the narrative, stronger constraints on government executives could increase the prevalence of growth-enhancing "syndrome-free" regimes (Fosu, 2013). Employment challenges are key issues across African countries hence the implementation of demand-side policies can be rolled out to address job shortages. Rodrik (2013) pointed out that 'two dynamics tend to drive growth: fundamental capabilities and structural transformation. Industrial policy—that is, the prioritization of high-potential sector—is instrumental for structural transformation in sub-Saharan Africa' (Rodrik, 2013). In this regard, new jobs need to be created in productive and employment-intensive sectors in collaboration with well-resourced MNEs.

2 Discussion and Conclusion

The findings of this review show that the activities of MNEs impact the environment and society as a whole. However, there is little or passive interaction of MNEs with government policies which causes a major delay in the implementation of the SDG agenda (Tulder et al., 2021). Therefore, the initiatives of MNEs toward addressing SDGs can be supported through necessary policy reforms and institutional arrangements by governments in sub-Saharan Africa. Further, a commitment by MNEs to the SDGs can be influenced by the home/host country context and industrial sectors they belong to.

The findings are critical for extending sustainability and international literature in two specific ways. First, by identifying and helping to fill theoretical gaps in international business research on MNEs' active participation in driving SDGs in sub-Saharan Africa. The findings of the review suggest that MNEs in sub-Saharan Africa can exploit resources, However, the government and policymakers can introduce institutional reforms that help MNEs to place greater emphasis on addressing SDGs and promoting social and economic growth. Further, a strong linkage between key stakeholders like MNEs, government, non-profit organizations, and community members can help them to undertake social initiatives that are

74   E. O. AFRIYIE AND N. ZAHOOR

conducive to achieving SDGs. Second, extending research questions on which SDGs provide promising platforms for MNEs' visibility in Africa's international business.

Beyond the theoretical implications, this review has practical implications. First, it highlights how MNEs publicly make accessible their SDG activities through their annual reports. Also, it gives vital exercises of their strong leadership in their implementation process given the global influence and managerial capacity (Tulder et al., 2021). Second, policymakers and MNEs managers could benefit from the findings by reviewing and addressing the gaps to establish a stronger relationship and engagement between all stakeholders. This is critical as the role of MNEs remains largely unfulfilled, especially in the global south. While many untapped resources remain to meet SDG targets, billions of dollars may pour in and create millions of jobs to bridge the poverty gap in Africa. To effectively tackle poverty, African countries should adopt appropriate national and regional policies and capitalize on opportunities in the global forum. A partnership both at the global and local level would enable sub-Saharan Africa to meet stringent SDGs targets and deliver value to local communities.

3   LIMITATIONS AND FUTURE RESEARCH DIRECTION

There are some limitations that should be addressed by future studies. First, despite a plethora of studies, there remained a gap in SDGs literature particularly in the context of sub-Saharan Africa and other global south countries. For example, it is worthwhile to study how MNEs influence the achievement of SDGs through sustainable innovation and responsible collaboration. In this regard, researchers can focus on emerging economies such as China, India, and Pakistan and conduct cross-country and cross-industry analysis. Second, the institutional conditions in developing markets make it vital to understand the role of stakeholders in SDGs (Kawai et al., 2018). While there are strong institutions present in western countries, there are weak institutional reforms in developing countries. It would be interesting to understand whether developed countries' MNEs' voluntary participation in sustainable practices is positively perceived by local citizens or actors in host countries located in developing countries, such as sub-Saharan Africa. Third, a recent stream of research is delving into the impact of COVID-19 on developed markets but leaves a caveat in sub-Saharan African countries. This calls for future research on the holistic impact of the triple bottom line and strategies adopted by MNEs and institutional actors to recover from further repercussions. In addition to this limitation, it is important to investigate the ways in which sustainable operational procedures can be established post-pandemic through social innovation. Fourth, scholars can emphasize the role of synergy between local governments, community stakeholders, and MNEs in achieving environmental and social performance in developing economies.

REFERENCES

Adelman, S. (2018). The sustainable development goals, anthropocentrism and neoliberalism. In *Sustainable development goals*. Edward Elgar.

Arya, B., & Bassi, B. (2011). Corporate social responsibility and broad-based black economic empowerment legislation in South Africa: Codes of good practice. *Business and Society, 50*(4), 674–695.

Aust, V., Morais, A. I., & Pinto, I. (2020). How does foreign direct investment contribute to Sustainable Development Goals? Evidence from African countries. *Journal of Cleaner Production, 245*, 118823.

Begashaw, B. (2021). *Africa and the Sustainable Development Goals: A long way to go*. Brookings. https://www.brookings.edu/blog/africa-in-focus/2019/07/29/africa-and-the-sustainable-development-goals-a-long-way-to-go/ (Accessed: 15 September 2021).

Bissoon, O. (2017). Is sub-Saharan Africa on a genuinely sustainable development path? Evidence using panel data. *Margin: The Journal of Applied Economic Research, 11*(4), 449–464.

Buhr, N., & Gray, R. (2012). Environmental management, measurement, and accounting: Information for decision and control? In P. Bansal & J. A. Hoffman (Eds.), *The Oxford handbook of business and the natural environment* (pp. 425–440). Oxford University Press.

Business and Sustainable Development Commission. (2017). *Valuing the SDG prize: Unlocking business opportunities to accelerate sustainable and inclusive growth*. Available at: http://s3.amazonaws.com/aws-bsdc/Valuing-the-SDG-Prize.pdf (Accessed: 10 September 2021).

Campbell, J. L. (2004). *Institutional change and globalization*. Princeton University Press.

Castellani, D., Lavoratori, K., Perri, A., & Scalera, V. G. (2022). International connectivity and the location of multinational enterprises' knowledge-intensive activities: Evidence from US metropolitan areas. *Global Strategy Journal, 12*(1), 82–107.

Clarke, A., & MacDonald, A. (2019). Outcomes to partners in multi-stakeholder cross-sector partnerships: A resource-based view. *Business and Society, 58*(2), 298–332.

Codita, R. (2007). Multinational companies and sustainability practices beyond headquarters—Evidence from foreign subsidiaries in the Romanian food and beverages industry. *Journal of Economic Literature, 2,* 6–26.

Crane, A., Matten, D., & Moon, J. (2008). *Corporations and citizenship.* Cambridge University Press.

Daouda, H. Y. (2014). CSR and sustainable development: Multinationals are they socially responsible in sub-Saharan Africa? The case of Areva in Niger. *Open Edition Journals, 28,* 141–162.

DeSombre, E. R. (2000). The experience of the Montreal protocol: Particularly remarkable, and remarkably particular. *UCLA Journal of Environmental Law and Policy, 19*(49), 49–82. https://doi.org/10.2307/j.ctv18pgn2c.10

Filatotchev, I., & Stahl, G. K. (2015). Towards transnational CSR: Corporate social responsibility approaches and governance solutions for multinational corporations. *Organizational Dynamics, 44*(2), 121–129.

Forum for the Future. (2000). *Annual Report London.* UK: Forum for the Future.

Fosu, A. (2013). Growth of African economies: Productivity, policy syndromes and the importance of institutions. *Journal of African Economies, 22*(4), 523–551.

Ghauri, P., Strange, R., & Cooke, F. L. (2021). Research on international business: The new realities. *International Business Review, 30*(2), 101794.

Ghauri, P., Tasavori, M., & Zaefarian, R. (2014). Internationalisation of service firms through corporate social entrepreneurship and networking. *International Marketing Review, 31*(6), 576–600.

GRI. (2017). *Reporting on the SDGs.* from https://www.globalreporting.org/information/SDGs/Pages/Reporting-on-the-SDGs.aspx

Hadjikhani, A., Elg, U., & Ghauri, P. (Eds.). (2012). *Business, society and politics: Multinationals in emerging markets.* Bingley.

Haglund, D. (2008). Regulating FDI in weak African states: A case study of Chinese copper mining in Zambia. *Journal of African Studies, 46*(4), 547–575.

Hall, J., & Vredenburg, H. (2003). The challenge of innovating for sustainable development. *MIT Sloan Management Review, 45*(1), 61–68.

Higgins, C., & Coffey, B. (2016). Improving how sustainability reports drive change: A critical discourse analysis. *Journal of Cleaner Production, 136,* 18–29.

Kawai, N., Strange, R., & Zucchella, A. (2018). Stakeholder pressures, EMS implementation, and green innovation in MNC overseas subsidiaries. *International Business Review, 27*(5), 933–946.

Kiefner, V., Mohr, A., & Schumacher, C. (2022). Female executives and multinationals' support of the UN's sustainable development goals. *Journal of World Business, 57*(3), 101304.

Kolk, A. (2008). Sustainability, accountability and corporate governance: Exploring multinationals' reporting practices. *Business Strategy and the Environment, 17*(1), 1–15.

Kolk, A., Kourula, A., & Pisani, N. (2017). Multinational enterprises and the sustainable development goals: What do we know and how to proceed? *Transnational Corporations, 24*(3), 9–32.

Kolk, A., Rivera-Santos, M., & Rufin, C. (2018). Multinationals, international business, and poverty: A cross-disciplinary research overview and conceptual framework. *Journal of International Business Policy, 1*, 92–115.

Kraemer, R., & van Tulder, R. (2009). Internationalization of TNCs from the extractive industries: A literature. *Transnational Corporations, 18*(1), 137–157.

Lashitew, A. A. (2021). Corporate uptake of the sustainable development goals: Mere greenwashing or an advent of institutional change? *Journal of International Business Policy.* https://doi.org/10.1057/s42214-020-000 92-4

Ledgerwood, C., & Broadhurst, A. (2000). *Environment, ethics and the corporation.* Macmillan.

Lee, M. D. P. (2008). A review of the theories of corporate social responsibility: Its evolutionary path and the road ahead. *International Journal of Management Reviews, 10*(1), 53–73.

Mhlanga, R., Gneiting, U., & Agarwal, N. (2018). *Walking the talk: Assessing companies' progress from SDG rhetoric to action* (Oxfam Discussion Papers). Oxford, UK.

Muthuri, J. N., Moon, J., & Idemudia, U. (2012). Corporate innovation and sustainable community development in developing countries. *Business and Society, 51*(3), 355–381.

Newenham-Kahindi, A. (2015). Managing sustainable development through people: Implications for multinational enterprises in developing countries. *Personnel Review, 44*(3), 388–407.

Nguyen, Q. (2022). Export intensity of foreign subsidiaries of multinational enterprises. *Management Decision, 60*(12), 3324–3349.

Nyanzu, F., Peprah, J. A., & Ayayi, A. G. (2019). Regulation, outreach, and sustainability of microfinance institutions in sub-Saharan Africa: A multilevel analysis. *Journal of Small Business Management, 57*, 200–217.

OECD. (2018). *Multinational enterprises in the global economy: Heavily debated but hardly measured.* Available at: https://www.oecd.org/industry/ind/MNEs-in-the-global-economy-policy-note.pdf (Accessed: 10 September 2021).

Pinkse, J., & Kolk, A. (2008). A perspective on multinational enterprises and climate change: Learning from "an inconvenient truth"? *Journal of International Business Studies, 39*(8), 1359–1378.

PwC. (2015). *Make it your business: Engaging with the Sustainable Development Goals.* PricewaterhouseCoopers.

Robinson, J. (2004). Squaring the circle? Some thoughts on the idea of sustainable development. *Ecological Economics, 48*(4), 369–384.

Rodrik, D. (2013). The past, present and future of economic growth. In F. Allen et al. (Eds.) (2014), *Towards a better global economy.* Oxford University Press.

Sachs, J. D. (2012). From millennium development goals to sustainable development goals. *The Lancet, 379*(9832), 2206–2211.

Sachs, J. (2015). *The age of sustainable development.* Columbia University Press.

SDGs Center for Africa and SDSN. (2018). *Africa SDG index and dashboards report.* Available at: http://unsdsn.org/resources/publications/africa-sdg-index-and-dashboards-2018/ (Accessed: 19 January 2023).

Selsky, J. W., & Parker, B. (2005). Cross-sector partnerships to address social issues: Challenges to theory and practice. *Journal of Management, 31*(6), 849–873.

Seuring, S., & Müller, M. (2008). From a literature review to a conceptual framework for sustainable supply chain management. *Journal of Cleaner Production, 16*(15), 1699–1710.

Stephenson, M., Hamid, M. F. S., Peter, A., Sauvant, K. P., Seric, A., & Tajoli, L. (2021). More and better investment now! How unlocking sustainable and digital investment flows can help achieve the SDGs. *Journal of International Business Policy.* https://doi.org/10.1057/s42214-020-00094-2

Sustainable Development Goals Center for Africa. (2019). 'Sustainable Development Goals Three-Year Reality Check'. Available at: https://AFRICA-2030-SDGs-THREE-YEAR-REALITY-CHECKREPORT.pdf(sdgcafrica.org)

Tulder, R. V., Rodrigues, S. B., Mirza, H., & Sexsmith, K. (2021). The UN's Sustainable Development Goals: Can multinational enterprises lead the decade of action? *Journal of International Business Policy, 4,* 1–21.

Turcotte, M. F., & Gendron, C. (2011). *Social economy, environment and sustainable development beyond the specialized sector for a social project* (pp. 165–168).

UNGC. (2015). The SDGs explained for business. Available at https://www.unglobalcompact.org/sdgs/about

United Nations New York. (2019). *The Sustainable Development Goals report 2019.* Available at https://unstats.un.org/sdgs/report/2019/The-Sustainable-Development-Goals-Report-2019.pdf (Accessed: 1 September 2021).

Valente, M. (2012). Indigenous resource and institutional capital: The role of local context in embedding 141 sustainable community development. *Business and Society, 51*(3), 409–449. https://doi.org/10.1177/0007650312446680

MULTINATIONAL ENTERPRISES, SUSTAINABILITY ... 79

Van der Waal, J. W., & Thijssens, T. (2020). Corporate involvement in sustainable development goals: Exploring the territory. *Journal of Cleaner Production, 252*, 119625.

van Zanten, J. A., & van Tulder, R. (2020). Beyond COVID-19: Applying "SDG logics" for resilient transformations. *Journal of International Business Policy, 3*(4), 451–464.

Vazquez-Brust, D., Sarkis, J., & Cordeiro, J. (2014). *Collaboration for sustainability and innovation: A role for sustainability driven by the global south? A cross-border, multi-stakeholder perspective* (1st ed.). London: Springer.

Welford, R. (1997). *Hijacking environmentalism: Corporate response to sustainable development*. Earthscan.

Wettstein, F., Giuliani, E., Santangelo, G. D., & Stahl, G. K. (2019). International business and human rights: A research agenda. *Journal of World Business, 54*(1), 54–65.

Wijen, F., Zoeteman, K., Pieters, J., & van Seters, P. (Eds.). (2012). *A handbook of globalisation and environmental policy* (2nd ed.). Edward Elgar.

Wilkinson, A., & Mangalagiu, D. (2012). Learning with futures to realise progress towards sustainability: The WBCSD vision 2050 initiative. *Futures, 44*(4), 372–384.

Witte, C., & Dilyard, J. (2017). Guest editors' introduction to the special issue: The contribution of multinational enterprises to the Sustainable Development Goals. *Transnational Corporations, 24*(3), 1–8.

Yamin, M., & Sinkovics, R. R. (2009). Infrastructure or foreign direct investment? An examination of the implications of MNE strategy for economic development. *Journal of World Business, 44*(2), 144–157.

Financing Sustainable Development Goals in Africa: The Role of Remittances—Evidence from Nigeria

Chioma N. Nwafor

1 INTRODUCTION

The Sustainable Development Goals are a collection of seventeen goals adopted by the United Nations in 2015 to be a "shared blueprint for peace and prosperity for people and the planet, now and into the future" (THE 17 GOALS United Nations). The SDG Goals have an achievement target year of 2030. These Goals, otherwise known as Agenda 2030 (United Nations, 2015), can transform the continent into a global powerhouse of the future. Although the continent has made some progress in achieving some SDG goals over the past two decades (United Nations et al., 2022), the region faces considerable challenges with high poverty levels, high infrastructural deficits, and rising debt crises that could impede the achievement of these goals. In addition, the COVID-19 global pandemic has negatively impacted the progress recorded towards achieving the SDGs. The economic and social disruptions of the pandemic

---

C. N. Nwafor (✉)
Department of Finance, Accountancy and Risk, Glasgow School for Business and Society, Glasgow Caledonian University, Glasgow, Scotland, UK
e-mail: Chioma.Nwafor@gcu.ac.uk

© The Author(s), under exclusive license to Springer Nature Switzerland AG 2023
S. Adomako et al. (eds.), *Corporate Sustainability in Africa*, Palgrave Studies in African Leadership, https://doi.org/10.1007/978-3-031-29273-6_5

81

have pushed between 26 and 40 million people into extreme poverty, and two in every five people living in Africa are still in extreme poverty (United Nations et al., 2022).

For Africa to meet the goals of Agenda 2030, the continent needs to reduce the current poverty levels and infrastructure deficits. While most African governments have enormous fiscal constraints resulting from rising debt-to-GDP ratios, private-sector financing (remittances) could help fund SDG performance gaps. Countries within the continent need innovative financing solutions to fund the current infrastructural deficits to make developmental progress. This chapter explores the effects of remittances on sustainable development goals and forwards thoughts on using them to finance the SDG performance gap. In line with previous remittances and economic growth studies, the chapter uses the Gross Domestic Product (GDP) as a measure of growth in the empirical estimation (Fayissa & Nsiah, 2010; Francois et al., 2022; Sutradhar, 2020; Ziesemer, 2012).

The chapter has three objectives. First, it analyses Africa's progress towards achieving the SDGs less than ten years before the target year 2030. Second, it explores the SDG performance/expected gap in Nigeria. Third, it empirically examines the correlation between SDGs, remittances, GDP, and other variables using data from Nigeria. Using a single-country study allows us to avoid the well-documented challenges of heterogeneities that affects this relationship in panel studies (Francois et al., 2022). The rest of this chapter is structured as follows. Section 2 assesses the progress and challenges faced by the continent in achieving the SDGs. Section 3 explores the SDG performance gaps focusing on Nigeria. In Sect. 4, the paper explores the correlation between the variables. While Sect. 5 is the conclusion and policy recommendations.

2 SDGs Progress and Challenges African Perspective

This section aims to provide a brief overview of the progress and challenges of the SDGs within the continent using data from the SDG Index (Sachs et al., 2022) and Africa UN data for development (Africa UN Data for Development Portal). While the paper considers the overall performance of the countries within the African continent on the 17 SDGs, the primary focus is on SDG 1 (no poverty), SDG 2 (zero hunger), and SDG 8 (decent work and economic growth). Specific SDG metrics explored in this chapter are the SDG overall score which measures the total progress towards achieving all the 17 SDGs (Sachs et al., 2022), and the SDG progress snapshot, which captures the progress made on each of the 17 goals (Africa UN Data for Development Portal). These sources provide important insights into Africa's progress towards Agenda 2030. The Sustainable Development Goals are 17 interlinked goals that guide addressing the world's challenges. Table 1 provides a list of the SDGs mapped according to the African's SDG report 2020 pillars of *People, Prosperity, Planet, Peace and Partnerships* (United Nations et al., 2022). These Pillars correspond to the seventeen sustainable development goals and provide a framework for a holistic analysis of progress made in achieving the continent's SDGs.

As can be seen in Table 1, the **People pillar**, commonly referred to as social goals, comprises goals 1 (*no poverty*), 2 (*zero hunger*), 3 (*good health and well-being*), 4 (*Quality education*), and 5 (*gender equality*). The **Prosperity pillar** comprises goals 7 (*affordable and clean energy*), 8 (*decent work and economic growth*), 9 (*industry, innovation & infrastructure*), 10 (*reduced inequalities*), and 11 (*sustainable cities and communities*). Pillar 1-people is in many ways closely interlinked to pillar 2-prosperity. For example, the prosperity goals reduce poverty and hunger and improve gender equality, health and well-being, and quality education. Also, the prosperity pillar is for development enablers, such as innovative technologies and affordable clean energy. On the other hand, ending poverty requires reducing inequalities which would have a positive spillover effect on food insecurity, thus enhancing the ability of Africans to live healthier lives. The **Planet pillar** comprises SDGs 6 (*clean water and sanitation*), 12 (*responsible consumption and production*), 14 (*life below water*), and 15 (*life on land*). The **Peace pillar** comprises SDG 16 (*peace, justice* and *strong institutions*).

Africa, except for a few states, continues to face significant challenges in peace, governance, and the rule of law. Challenges of Illicit financial flows (IFF) is undermining the continent's progress towards achieving the SDGs. The final pillar, **Partnerships**, focuses on innovative financing models' role in achieving these goals. Specifically, the author considers the effects of inward remittances, using evidence from Nigeria. Finally, the author uses the Pearson correlation to explore the correlation between SDG score, inflow remittances, official development assistance (ODA), external debt, foreign direct investment (FDI), and GDP. The idea is

84   C. N. NWAFOR

Table 1   Mapping of clusters/pillars to SDGs

Five pillars	*SDGs Agenda 2030*
People	• **SDG 1 No Poverty**: End poverty in all its forms everywhere • **SDG 2 Zero Hunger**: End hunger, achieve food security and improved nutrition and promote sustainable agriculture • **SDG 3 Good Health and Well-being**: Ensure healthy lives and promote well-being for all at all ages • **SDG 4 Quality Education**: Ensure inclusive and equitable quality education and promote lifelong learning opportunities for all • **SDG 5 Gender Equality**: Achieve gender equality and empower all women and girls
Prosperity	• **SDG 7 Affordable and Clean Energy**: Ensure access to affordable, reliable, sustainable and modern energy for all • **SDG 8 Decent Work and Economic Growth**: Promote sustained, inclusive and sustainable economic growth, full and productive employment and decent work for all • **SDG 9 Industry, Innovation and Infrastructure**: Build resilient infrastructure, promote inclusive and sustainable industrialization and foster innovation • **SDG 10 Reduced Inequalities**: Reduce inequality within and among States • **SDG 11 Sustainable Cities and Communities**: Make cities and human settlements inclusive, safe, resilient and sustainable
Planet	• **SDG 6 Clean Water and Sanitation**: Ensure availability and sustainable management of water and sanitation for all • **SDG 12 Responsible Consumption and Production**: Ensure sustainable consumption and production patterns • **SDG 13 Climate Action**: Take urgent action to combat climate change and its impacts • **SDG 14 Life Below Water**: Conserve and sustainably use the oceans, seas and marine resources for sustainable development • **SDG 15 Life on Land**: Protect, restore and promote sustainable use of terrestrial ecosystems, sustainably manage forests, combat desertification, and halt and reserve land degradation and halt biodiversity loss
Peace	• **SDG 16 Peace, Justice and Strong Institutions**: Promote peaceful and inclusive societies for sustainable development, provide access to justice for all and build effective, accountable and inclusive institutions at all levels
Partnerships	• **SDG 17 Partnerships for the Goals**: Strengthen the means of implementation and revitalize the global partnership for sustainable development

Source Adapted from 2020 African Sustainable Development Report: Towards Recovery and Sustainable Development in the Decade of Action. Available at https://hdl.handle.net/10855/47554

to determine whether relationships exist among these variables and the strength and direction of such relationships.

Figure 1 is the SDG snapshot of Africa's progress on each of the 17 goals. The length of each bar shows the progress of the region since 2000. The region would have achieved the expected progress to date if a bar reaches or crosses the current year line. As shown in Fig. 1, Africa's SDG progress is mixed. While the content has made some progress in some of the 17 goals, it has regressed in goal 13 (*Climate Action*) and goal 16 (*Peace, Justice and strong institutions*). The goals were significant progress was recorded as of 2020 where goal 1 (*no poverty*), goal 3 (*good health and well-being*), goal 4 (*quality of education*), goal 6 (*clean water and sanitation*), goal 15 (*life on land*), and goal 17 (*partnership for the goals*). The economic and social effects of the COVID-19 pandemic have undermined the progress made in these areas. The SDGs that were affected by the pandemic the most were *good health and well-being* (SDG 3), decent work and economic growth (SDG 8), food security (SDG 2), and poverty (SDG 1).

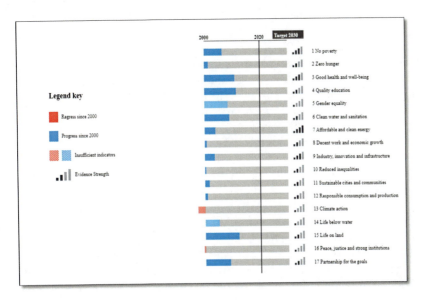

Fig. 1 Africa progress snapshot (*Source* Africa UN Data Development. Available at https://ecastats.uneca.org/unsdgsafrica/SDGs/SDG-progress)

A 2022 study by the African Development Bank estimates that 30 million Africans were pushed into extreme poverty, and about 22 million jobs were lost in the continent due to the economic disruptions of the pandemic (AfDB, 2022). The report posits that these outcomes will likely continue in 2022 and 2023. This development affects other goals due to the interlinkages of the SDGs. For example, a report by the Food Security Information Network and the Global Network Against Food, Crises (2021) estimates that 97.7 million Africans were at risk of hunger and malnutrition in 2020, compared with 70.5 million in 2019.

An analysis of the ten poverty indicators, as shown in Fig. 2, suggests that the regression of the "Economic loss from the disaster" significantly influenced the previous progress achieved in SDG 1 (*no poverty*). Although considerable progress was recorded in adopting and implementing the national *Disaster Risk Reduction* (DRR)[1] score, the proportion of local governments that adopted and implemented local DRR strategies as of 2020 was negligible. According to United Nations Office for Disaster Risk Reduction (UNDRR) (2022), disaster risk indicates poor development. Reducing disaster risk requires integrating DRR policies and disaster risk management (DRM) practices into sustainable development goals. Another indicator of poverty analysed is the poverty headcount ratio at $1.90/day for all 50 States with available data. Analysis of this indicator helps us evaluate the percentage change in poverty between 2021 and 2022. This ratio estimates the percentage of the population living under the poverty threshold of US$1.90 a day, and it represents those living in extreme poverty. The long-term sustainable development goal's objective for this indicator is a value of 0.

Table 2 shows the values for 2021 and 2022. The highlighted red cells are countries that experienced an increase in this indicator. In contrast, the green highlighted cells are countries on track to achieving SDG goal 1 (No poverty) by 2030 based on this indicator. Table 2 suggests minimal progress in poverty reduction across many African states during the review periods. The poverty headcount in 2021 and 2022 was low in most states within Northern Africa. The 2022 values for Algeria (0.33), Egypt (1.92), Morocco (0.20), Tunisia (0.21), and Mauritius (0.27) reveal a significant poverty reduction. Table 2 shows that countries such as Cabo Verde (−35.47), Egypt (−20.25), Ethiopia (−19.47), The Gambia (−12.65),

---

[1] DRR is the policy objective of anticipating and reducing risk. Disaster risk is an indicator of poor development.

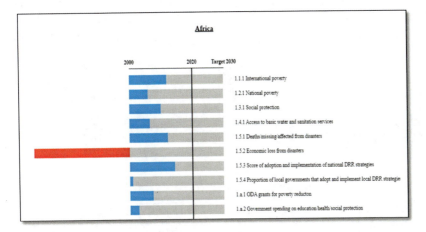

Fig. 2 Progress at indicator level (poverty) (Available at https://ecastats.uneca.org/unsdgsafrica/SDGs/SDG-progress)

and Mauritius (−18.18) experienced a double-digit reduction in poverty levels during the period under review.

The highest incidences of poverty in 2022 were recorded in South Sudan (84.53), Madagascar (76.38), Burundi (74.87), and Congo Dem. Republic (71.74%). Of all the 51 countries reported in Table 3, 17 had poverty headcounts above 40% in 2022. While some positive improvements were observed in poverty reduction across some countries, recent reports suggest that more Africans have fallen into extreme poverty due to the pandemic (AfDB, 2022). Ending extreme poverty in Africa requires massive infrastructural developments, extensive and substantial economic growth, robust peace, and strong institutions. Unfortunately, most countries within the continent have yet to record significant progress in these areas.[2]

Focusing on the SDG overall index, Table 3 shows the Africa SDG Index score, which shows a country's position between the worst (0) and best (100) outcomes. The overall score measures the progress towards

---

[2] Visit African UN Data for Development at https://ecastats.uneca.org/unsdgsafrica/SDGs/SDG-progress. And Sustainable Development Report 2022 at https://dashbords.sdgindex.org for a detailed interactive SDG progress on the 17 goals and more than 100 indicators.

88   C. N. NWAFOR

Table 2   Poverty headcount ratio at $1.90/day 2021 and 2022

S/N	Country	2021 score	2022 score	% change 2021/22	S/N	Country	2021 Score	2022 Score	% change 2021/22
1	Algeria	0.34	0.33	−2.94	26	Mali	37.86	36.34	−4.01
2	Angola	53.67	53.83	0.30	27	Mozambique	61.19	59.85	−2.19
3	Burundi	75.85	74.87	−1.29	28	Mauritania	4.94	4.46	−9.72
4	Benin	47.31	45.46	−3.91	29	Mauritius	0.33	0.27	−18.18
5	Burkina Faso	38.83	36.87	−5.05	30	Malawi	69.73	69.73	0.00
6	Botswana	17.33	16.52	−4.67	31	Morocco	0.23	0.2	−13.04
7	Central African Republic	70.51	69.65	−1.22	32	Namibia	24.32	23.96	−1.48
8	Cote d'Ivoire	21.65	20.08	−7.25	33	Niger	33.07	31.41	−5.02
9	Cameroon	22.7	21.96	−3.26	34	Nigeria	32.87	32.82	−0.15
10	Congo Dem. Republic	73.01	71.74	−1.74	35	Rwanda	50.02	47.52	−5.00
11	Congo Republic	49.82	49.78	−0.08	36	Sudan	17.05	16.34	−4.16
12	Comoros	21.39	20.88	−2.38	37	Senegal	32.06	30.71	−4.21
13	Cabo Verde	3.27	2.11	−35.47	38	Sierra Leone	38.57	36.06	−6.51
14	Djibouti	13.06	12.09	−7.43	39	Somalia	56.09	55.53	−1.00
15	Egypt Arab Rep.	2.42	1.93	−20.25	40	South Sudan	85.57	84.53	−1.22
16	Ethiopia	7.19	5.79	−19.47	41	Sao Tome and Principe	34.46	33.78	−1.97
17	Gabon	3.61	3.34	−7.48	42	Eswatini	32.32	32.24	−0.25
18	Ghana	10.42	9.65	−7.39	43	Chad	44.39	44.56	0.38
19	Guinea	41.23	38.7	−6.14	44	Togo	46.14	44.36	−3.86
20	Gambia, The	7.43	6.49	−12.65	45	Tanzania	47.86	46.53	−2.78
21	Guinea−Bissau	66.28	65.39	−1.34	46	Tunisia	0.23	0.21	−8.70
22	Kenya	18.85	17.43	−7.53	47	Uganda	35.38	34.41	−2.74
23	Liberia	43.15	41.81	−3.11	50	South Africa	26.87	26.73	−0.52
24	Lesotho	30.37	30.13	−0.79	51	Zambia	58.26	58.89	1.08
25	Madagascar	77.36	76.38	−1.27					

Note The highlighted red cells are countries that experienced an increase in this indicator. The green highlighted cells are countries on track to achieving the SDG goal 1 (No poverty) based on this indicator

Data source World data lab, http://worldpoverty.io/

achieving all 17 SDGs. The score can be interpreted as a percentage of SDG achievement. A score of 100 indicates that all SDGs have been achieved. The yellow highlighted cells suggest an improvement in SDG overall score in 2021, while the cells highlighted in red are low-performing states. Low-performing states are countries with an overall score of less than 50. Of all the 51 countries reported in Table 3, 17 had poverty headcounts above 40% in 2022. The main findings from the analysis, if we use 2021 scores as benchmarks on the road to 2030, are as follows: Algeria tops the ranking with a score of 71.47%, indicating that the country is approximately 71% on the way towards achieving the SDGs. The top 10 performing states within the continent are Morocco (68.89),

FINANCING SUSTAINABLE DEVELOPMENT GOALS ... 89

Table 3 2021 SDG overall score for African countries

S/N	Country	2021 score	% change 2020/21	S/N	Country	2021 score	% change 2020/21
1	Algeria	71.47	−0.06	25	Malawi	53.14	−0.11
2	Angola	50.94	−0.12	26	Mali	53.87	−0.11
3	Benin	51.16	−0.70	27	Mauritania	55.72	0.00
4	Botswana	61.22	0.31	28	Mauritius	68.34	−0.18
5	Burkina Faso	54.28	−0.09	29	Morocco	68.89	0.16
6	Burundi	53.94	−0.02	30	Mozambique	53.51	−0.09
7	Cameroon	55.46	0.16	31	Namibia	62.65	0.11
8	Central African Republic	39.12	−0.18	32	Niger	52.03	0.06
9	Chad	41.18	−0.15	33	Nigeria	54.19	0.17
10	Congo Dem. Republic	49.96	0.02	34	Rwanda	59.2	0.07
11	Congo Republic	52.31	−0.11	35	Sudan	49.53	−0.02
12	Cote d'Ivoire	58.23	−0.22	36	Senegal	58.64	0.24
13	Djibouti	50.15	0.26	37	Sierra Leone	52.87	−0.19
14	Egypt, Arab Republic	68.47	0.12	38	Somalia	45.04	−0.11
15	Eswatini	54.49	−0.06	39	South Sudan	38.89	−0.03
16	Ethiopia	57.66	−0.05	40	Sao Tome and Principe	59.38	−0.05
17	Gabon	62.76	0.37	41	Togo	55.49	0.07
18	The Gambia	60.00	0.07	42	Tanzania	57.31	−0.26
19	Ghana	63.04	−0.57	43	Uganda	54.84	0.75
20	Guinea	51.16	0.45	44	Yemen Republic	45.04	−0.13
21	Kenya	60.65	0.48	45	South Africa	63.71	−0.16
22	Lesotho	54.89	−0.02	46	Zambia	54.07	−0.72
23	Liberia	49.83	0.04	47	Zimbabwe	56.47	0.04
24	Madagascar	50.11	−0.06	50	Tunisia		

Notes The overall score measures the progress towards achieving all 17 SDGs. The score can be interpreted as a percentage of SDG achievement. A score of 100 indicates that all SDGs have been achieved. The yellow highlighted cells suggest an improvement in SDG overall score in 2021, while the cells highlighted in red are low-performing states. Low-performing states are countries with an overall score of less than 50

Source Sustainable Development Report 2022, www.sdgindex.org

Egypt (68.47%), Mauritius (68.34), South Africa (63.71), Ghana (63.04), Namibia (62.65), Gabon (62.76), Botswana (61.22), Kenya (60.65), and The Gambia (60.00).

On average, these top-performing states are approximately 32% away from achieving the SDGs by 2030. A comparative analysis of the 2020/2021 SDG overall score reveals a drop in the scores of the following countries—Ghana (−0.57), Mauritius (−0.18), and South Africa (−0.16). Some of the low-performing states of the Central African Republic (39.12), Chad (41.18), Congo Dem. Republic (49.96), Liberia (49.83), Sudan (49.53), Somalia (45.04), South Sudan (38.89), and Yemen

Republic (45.04) are countries with high levels of poverty, as indicated in Table 2. The unfortunate conclusion from the analysis is that most African countries are not on track to achieving the SDG target of 2030. Given the interconnectedness of these 17 goals, regressing in one will have a spillover effect on other goals. The large number of Africans living in poverty will suffer food insecurity, will be less educated and will face challenges of discrimination. The next section explores the expected SDG performance gaps in Nigeria (the chapter's country of study).

3   Expected SDG Gaps: A Single-Country Analysis (Nigeria)

This section focuses on analysing SDG performance gaps in the country of study. Nigeria currently ranks 139/163 in the SDG Index Rank, with an SDG index score of 54.2 (Sachs et al., 2022). The country faces significant challenges in most of the sustainable development goals. The poverty headcount ratios at $1.90/day and $3.20/day (SDG1) in 2022 stood at 32.87% and 32.84%, respectively. In addition, the country's multidimensional poverty headcount ratio as of 2018 was 41.81%. The Multidimensional Poverty Measure (MPM) captures the percentage of households in a country deprived along the three dimensions of monetary poverty, education and infrastructure services). This indicator is a holistic measure of poverty that goes beyond monetary deprivations. Figure 3 shows the 2018 MPM and deprivation indicators in Nigeria.

Each bar chart shows the percentage of the population experiencing deprivation in non-monetary measures of education, access to infrastructure and monetary per capita income at the $1.90 poverty line. For Nigeria to achieve the SDG of eliminating poverty requires these poverty indicators to fall faster to exceed the country's population growth of 2.41%, as estimated by the United Nations (2022). On the current progress status, the dashboard Table 4 shows that since 2000, Nigeria has achieved the most progress in only three indicators relating to SDGs 2 and 8. Out of the eight indicators of SDG 2, Nigeria is on track and maintaining SDG achievement on only 2—"prevalence of obesity, BMI

FINANCING SUSTAINABLE DEVELOPMENT GOALS ... 91

Multidimensional Poverty Measure and Deprivation by Indicator

Indicator	Value
Education Attainment	17.60%
Education Enrollment	20.29%
Electricity	39.44%
Sanitation	44.85%
Water	27.55%
Monetary	30.86%
MPM	41.81%

Fig. 3 Multidimensional poverty measure and deprivation by indicators (*Source* Poverty and Inequality Platform. Available at https://pip.worldbank.org/cou ntry-profiles/NGA)

≥ 30[3] and human trophic level"[4] see Table 4. Another SDG relevant to this study is SDG 8 (*decent work and economic growth*). The country faces significant challenges in five of the six indicators as shown in Table 4. The only indicator in which Nigeria is on track and maintaining SDG achievement is "fatal work-related accidents embodied in imports[5]".

Table 5 shows the expected gap for SDG 1 (*no poverty*), SDG 2 (*zero hunger*), and SDG 8 (*decent work and economic growth*). For Nigeria to achieve the SDG 1 target by 2030, the country needs to accelerate progress in reducing the national and international poverty rates, increase

---

[3] The percentage of the adult population with a body mass index (BMI) of 30 kg/m^2 or higher is based on measured height and weight. https://dashboards.sdgindex.org/pro files/nigeria/indicators.

[4] Trophic levels measure of the energy intensity of diet composition and reflect the relative amounts of plants as opposed to animals eaten in a given country. https://das hboards.sdgindex.org/profiles/nigeria/indicators.

[5] The number of fatal work-related accidents associated with imported goods. The long-term objective for this indicator is a value of 0. Available at https://dashboards.sdgindex. org/profiles/nigeria/indicators.

92 C. N. NWAFOR

Table 4 SDGs 1, 2, and 8 dashboards for Nigeria

SDGs	Indicators		Level of Progress
SDG 1: No Poverty	⬇ Poverty headcount ratio at $1.90/day	🔴	Major challenges remain
	⬇ Poverty headcount ratio at $3.20/day.	🔴	Major challenges remain
SDG 2: Zero hunger	⬇ Prevalence of undernourishment	🟠	Significant challenges remain
	⇨ Prevalence of stunting in children under 5 years of age	🔴	Major challenges remain
	⇨ Prevalence of wasting in children under 5 years of age	🟡	Challenges remain
	⬆ Prevalence of obesity, BMI ≥30	🟢	On track or maintaining SDG achievement.
	⬆ Human trophic level	🟢	On track or maintaining SDG achievement.
	⇨ Cereal yield	🟠	Significant challenges remain
	⬇ Sustainable nitrogen management index	🔴	Major challenges remain.
	Exports of hazardous pesticides (** trend information unavailable)	🟡	Challenges remain.
SDG 8: Decent work and economic growth	Adjusted GDP growth (** trend information unavailable)	🔴	Major challenges remain.
	⬇ Adults with bank accounts, or mobile money service provider.	🔴	Major challenges remain.
	⬇ Unemployment rate	🟠	Significant challenges remain
	⇨ Fundamental labour rights are guaranteed.	🔴	Major challenges remain.
	⬆ Fata work−related accidents embodied in imports.	🟢	On track or maintaining SDG achievement.

Available at Sustainable development report, Sachs et al. (2022)
https://dashboards.sdgindex.org/profiles/nigeria/indicators

the share of the official development assistance grants for poverty reduction, the percentage of its population with access to water and sanitation, and increase its social safety-net to protect more vulnerable citizens. Severe food insecurity, agriculture orientation index[6] and prevalence of undernourishment are vital indicators that Nigeria needs to reverse their trends to achieve the SDG 2 goal of ending hunger. The country needs to double its efforts to reduce the number of stunted children caused by malnutrition. Significant investments in rural infrastructure, agricultural research and extension services, and technology are required in

---

[6] The Agriculture Orientation Index (AOI) for Government Expenditures is defined as the Agriculture Share of Government Expenditures, divided by the Agriculture Share of GDP, where Agriculture refers to the agriculture, forestry, fishing, and hunting sector. https://sdg.tracking-progress.org/indicator/2-a-1-agriculture-orientation-index-for-government-expenditures-2/.

this regard. In terms of SDG 8 (*decent work and economic growth*), the country needs to reverse the trends on the following indicators, unemployment rate, real GDP per capita growth rate, and real GDP per employed person growth. The country also needs to accelerate progress in the number of youths in education, adults with a bank account, the number of bank branches and aid for trade.

At the mid-way to 2030, Nigeria still faces substantial challenges in its bid to achieve the SDGs. The country faces a looming financial crisis caused by rising debt problems, particularly from private external creditors. Achieving SDGs 1, 2, and 8 requires substantial investments in physical infrastructure and human capital. A national plan to finance the SDGs, particularly in reducing poverty, hunger, and human capital development, is needed. The next session forwards some thoughts on using inward remittances to reduce the SDGs' performance gap in Nigeria.

Table 5 Expected gap: Nigeria

Indicators	Trend
SDG 1 Poverty Indicators	
National poverty	
International poverty	
ODA grants for poverty reduction	
Access to water and sanitation services	
Social protection	
SDG 2 Zero hunger Indicators	
Severe food insecurity in the population	
Agriculture orientation index	
Prevalence of undernourishment	
Prevalence of stunting	
Consumer food index	
Plant and animal breeds with sufficient genetic material stored	
Prevalence of malnutrition	
SDG 8 Decent work and economic growth Indicators	
Unemployment rate	
Real GDP per employed person growth rate	
Real GDP per capital growth rate	
Youth not in education	
Adults with a bank account	
Commercial bank branches and automated machines	
Domestic material consumption	
Aid for trade	

Note The bar chart shows the magnitude of the gap between the predicted and target values of indicators that are not likely to achieve the target by 2030. Red bars refer to indicators for which the trend needs to be reversed and yellow bars refer to indicators for which progress needs to be accelerated

4 Financing SDGs 1, 2, and 8: The Role of Remittances

Africa lags behind other continents in their progress towards the 2030 agenda. Closing this performance gap requires a re-evaluation of the SDG financing models. Documented evidence suggests that the diaspora of developing countries contributes to sustainable development in their countries of origin via inward remittances (Benhamou & Cassin, 2021; Chami et al., 2008; Francois et al., 2022). The United Nations identifies remittance as a significant contributor to sustainable development and a vital lifeline to developing economies (United Nations, 2022). The counter-cyclical nature of remittance flow to economic downturns makes them a robust form of social insurance that can enhance a household's ability to withstand economic shocks. The COVID-19 pandemic proved the resilience of global remittance flows. Despite the fact that the earlier forecast of a 7.0% contraction in remittance flows to low-and-middle-income countries (LMICs) in 2020, official remittance flows to LMICs reached $540 billion, only a drop of 1.6% below the $548 billion was seen in 2019 (KNOMAD, 2021). Remittance inflows per region in 2021 rose in Latin America and the Caribbean (25.3%), South Asia (6.9%), the Middle East and North Africa (7.6%), Sub-Saharan Africa (14.1%), and Europe and Central Asia (7.8%) (KONMAD, 2022). The 2022 remittance flows to low- and middle-income countries (LMICs) are expected to increase by 4.2% to reach $630 billion (ibid.). Turning attention to remittances in Sub-Saharan Africa, Nigeria was the highest remittance recipient in the sub-region in 2020. Figure 4 shows that $17.2 billion US dollars were received in the country during the period. Nigeria accounted for over 40% of remittance flows to the region in 2020 (ibid.).

It is worth noting that this amount does not include money sent via informal channels. Remittances exceeded foreign direct investment flows and official development assistance by a wide margin in 2021 (ibid.). Indeed, UNCTAD estimates a decline in foreign direct investment (FDI) of 35–45% in 2020. Remittance flows are the most crucial source of foreign inflows for receiving countries. From a macro-economic perspective, the literature suggests several transmission channels of the effect of remittances on the economy, including investment in human capital, financial inclusion, savings, skills formation, and entrepreneurship (Benhamou & Cassin, 2021; Shapiro & Mandelman, 2016). Remittances can improve the financial resilience of recipient households by

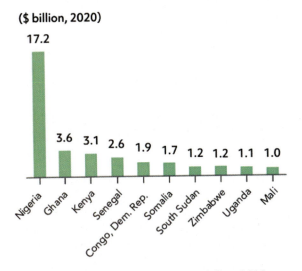

Fig. 4 Top remittance recipients in Sub-Saharan Africa, 2020

allowing credit-constrained households to accumulate assets and business investments (Chatterjee & Turnovsky, 2018).

Based on these remittance transmission channels, it is plausible to conclude that inward remittance contributes to several of the goals set in the 2030 Agenda. Specifically, migrant remittances benefit the following SDGs, SDG 1 (*no poverty*); SDG 2 (*zero hunger*); SDG 3 (*good health and well-being*); SDG 4 (*quality education*); SDG 6 (*clean water and sanitation*); SDG 8, (*decent work and economic growth*); and SDG 10 (*reduced inequality*). Despite the crucial role of remittances in Nigeria, the empirical relationships between remittances and economic growth are unclear, particularly in Nigeria. The current chapter addresses this gap by using correlation to explore the empirical relationship between SDG score, inflow remittances, official development assistance (ODA), external debt, foreign direct investment (FDI), and GDP. Like many developing countries, Nigeria relies on different foreign inflows sources, including ODA, FDI, and external debt stock (multilateral creditors, bilateral and private-sector creditors). We are interested in the signs (direction) and magnitudes of these relationships.

96   C. N. NWAFOR

The data used in this section were sourced from the World Bank's world development indicators and the 2020 African SDG index and dashboards report. The ODA[7] is an aid designed to promote developing countries' economic development and welfare. FDI is a cross-border investment critical to international economic integration because it creates stable and long-lasting links between economies. Total external debt is debt owed to non-residents repayable in currency, goods, or services. It comprises publicly guaranteed and privately nonguaranteed long-term debt, use of IMF credit, and short-term debt. Figure 5 shows the evolution of these variables between 2000 and 2019. The stylised facts reveal three crucial points. First, the overall trend for the SDG score, external debt, and migrant remittances seems to be upward. Second, Nigeria has increased its external debt significantly since 2006. Third, the ODA and FDI are on a downward trajectory, while GDP is improving over time. Finally, FDI has the highest level of volatility among the six variables.

Although the correlation matrix in Table 6 reveals fascinating insights, the author limits the discussion to the variables of interest: remittances, SDG score, and GDP. The result reveals a positive correlation between the SDG index score, GDP, and remittances. Specifically, the result suggests an 84% correlation between remittances and SDG score and a 90% positive correlation between remittances and GDP. Increasing remittances will, on average, positively impact the country's economic development and improve its SDG index score. Diaspora bonds[8] are one of the ways that LMICs can harness the positive effects of the African diaspora in funding development in the continent. The recent redemption of $300 million five-year diaspora bond[9] by the Nigerian government in 2022 has increased investors' confidence in the country's ability to fulfil its debt obligations as they become due.

---

[7] Aid may be provided bilaterally, from donor to recipient, or channelled through a multilateral development agency such as the United Nations or the World Bank, including grants, soft loans, and technical assistance (OECD Library) available at https://www.oecd-ilibrary.org/development/official-development-assistance-oda/indicator-group/english_5136f9ba-en.

[8] Diaspora bonds are bonds funded by Africans living in the diaspora to help drive new investments in the continent (Schneidman et al., 2022).

[9] The diaspora bond was issued on June 27, 2017, for a tenor of five years in the International Capital Market and was redeemed on June 27, 2022. https://dmarketforces.com/nigeria-redeems-300m-diaspora-bond/#:~:text= Nigeria%20has%20redeemed%20its%20300,statement%20posted%20on%20its%20website.

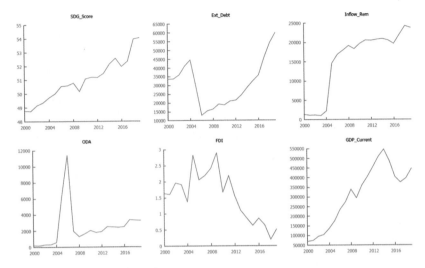

Fig. 5 Variable trend graphs

Table 6 Correlation matrix 2000–2019

	SDG_Score	Ext_debt	GDP_current	Inflow_rem	ODA	FDI
SDG_Score	1.00	0.39	0.83	0.84	0.26	−0.71
Ext_debt	0.39	1.00	−0.05	−0.12	−0.21	−0.67
GDP_current	0.83	−0.05	1.00	0.90	0.16	−0.50
Inflow_rem	0.84	−0.12	0.90	1.00	0.40	−0.32
ODA	0.26	−0.21	0.16	0.40	1.00	−0.06
FDI	−0.71	−0.67	−0.50	−0.31	0.06	1.00

Notes SDG_Score denotes the overall SDG score, Ext_debt denotes the external debt stock, GDP_current denotes GDP in current US$, Inflow_rem denotes migrant remittance inflow, ODA denotes the official development assistance, and FDI denotes the foreign direct investment

5 Conclusion and Implications for Policy

According to the African Development Bank (AfDB), the value of remittances from the African diaspora doubled from $37 billion in 2010 to $87 billion in 2019, reaching $95.6 billion in 2021. While the official development assistance to Africa in 2021 was $35 billion (36%) of the remittances from the diaspora. Nevertheless, remittance transfers remain very expensive. On average, currency conversions and fees account for 7% of the total amounts sent. The so-called "African premium" makes remittance costs in Sub-Saharan Africa the highest in the world. The finding of a positive statistically significant correlation between inflow remittances and SDG index score (84%) and inflow remittances and GDP at (90%) suggests that remittance has become a new form of concessional financing for the livelihood of millions of Africans and could be a significant determinant for economic growth. The long-term objective of SDG 10.C—reducing remittance transfer costs to less than 3% and eliminating remittance corridors with more than 5% costs by 2030 should be a policy priority for Nigeria and other Sub-Saharan African countries. Also, policymakers should explore how to bring informal remittance flows into the formal financial system to capture the value of remittances better. Better-quality remittance data will support the SDG indicators in reducing remittance costs, thus increasing the volume of remittances. Future studies should explore the causal relationship between inflow remittances, GDP, SDG score, and other mediating factors in Nigeria.

References

African Development Bank (AfDB). (2022). *African economic outlook 2022. Supporting climate resilience and a just energy transition in Africa.* Available at https://www.ucl.ac.uk/steapp/sites/steapp/files/african_economic_o utlook_2022-highlights.pdf. Accessed on 04 December 2022.

African Union: Agenda 2023: The Africa we want. Available at https://au.int/en/agenda2063/overview. Accessed on 29 November 2022.

Benhamou, Z. A., & Cassin, L. (2021). The impact of remittances on savings, capital and economic growth in small emerging countries. *Economic Modelling, 94,* 789–803.

Chami, R., Barajas, A., Cosimano, T., Fullenkamp, C., Gapen, M., & Montiel, P. (2008). *Macroeconomic consequences of remittances.* International Monetary Fund.

Chatterjee, S., & Turnovsky, S. J. (2018). Remittances and the informal economy. *Journal of Developing Economics., 133,* 66–83.

Fayissa, B., & Nsiah, C. (2010). The impact of remittances on economic growth and development in African. *American Economist, 55,* 92–103.

Food Security Information Network and Global Network Against Food Crises. (2021). *Global report on food crises.* https://www.wfp.org/publications/global-report-foodcrises-2021

Francois, N. J., Ahmad, N., Keinsley, A., & Nti-Addae, A. (2022). Heterogeneity in the long-run remittance-output relationship: Theory and new evidence. *Economic Modelling, 110,* 1–28.

Global Knowledge Partnership for Migration and Development (KNOMAD). (2021). *COVID-19 crisis through a migration lens* (Migration and development brief 34). World Bank. https://www.knomad.org/sites/default/files/202105/Migration%20and%20Development%20Brief%2034_0.pdf

KONMAD. (2022). *Remittances data.* Available at: https://www.knomad.org/data/remittances

Sachs, J. D., et al. (2022). *From crisis to sustainable development: The SDGs as roadmap to 2030 and beyond. Sustainable development report 2022.* Cambridge University Press. Available at: https://dashboards.sdgindex.org/chapters. Accessed on 09 December 2022.

Schneidman, W., Tadesse, A., & Lissanu, A. (2022). *Diaspora bonds: an innovative source of financing?* Available at https://www.brookings.edu/blog/africa-in-focus/2022/05/27/diaspora-bonds-an-innovative-source-of-financing/. Accessed on 09 December 2022.

Shapiro, A. F., & Mandelman, F. S. (2016). Remittances, entrepreneurship, and employment dynamics over the business cycle. *Journal of International Economics, 103,* 184–199.

Sutradhar, S. R. (2020). The impact of remittances on economic growth in Bangladesh, India, Pakistan and Sri Lanka. *International Journal of Economic Policy Studies, 14,* 275–295.

The 17 Goals | Sustainable Development. Available at https://sdgs.un.org/goals. Accessed on 29 November 2022.

UNCTAD. (2020). *World Investment Report 2020.*

United Nations. (2015). *Resolution adopted by the General Assembly on 25 September 2015, Transforming our world: the 2030 Agenda for Sustainable Development (A/RES/70/1 Archived 28 November 2020 at the Wayback Machine).* https://web.archive.org/web/20201128002202/https:/www.un.org/sustainabledevelopment/sustainable-development-goals/. Accessed on 29 November 2022.

United Nations. (2022). *United Nations department of economic and social affairs population division.* Available at https://population.un.org/wpp/. Accessed on 06 December 2022.

United Nations' Disaster Risk Reduction (UNDRR). (2022). *Understanding disaster risk reduction & disaster risk management.* Available at https://www.preventionweb.net/understanding-disaster-risk/key-concepts/disaster-risk-reduction-disaster-risk-management. Accessed on 04 December 22.

United Nations. Economic Commission for Africa, African Union Commission, United Nations Development Programme, African Development Bank. (2022). *2020 African sustainable development report: Towards recovery and* sustainable development in the decade of action. https://hdl.handle.net/10855/47554

Ziesemer, T. H. (2012). Worker remittances, migration, accumulation and growth in poor developing countries: Survey and analysis of direct and indirect effects. *Economic Modelling, 29*, 103–118.

Natural Resources, Sustainable Entrepreneurship, and Poverty Reduction in Resource-Rich African Countries: The Missing Link

Deji O. Olagboye, Oluwasoye P. Mafimisebi, Demola Obembe, and Kassa Woldesenbet Beta

1 INTRODUCTION

Sustainable development and poverty reduction remain an influential, yet controversial, concept for business and policy alike. Poverty remains a global issue of interest for both multilateral organisations and governments across the globe as evident in the United Nations (UN) Sustainable

D. O. Olagboye (✉) · O. P. Mafimisebi · D. Obembe · K. W. Beta
Leicester Castle Business School, De Montfort University, Leicester, UK
e-mail: deji.olagboye@dmu.ac.uk

O. P. Mafimisebi
e-mail: oluwasoye.mafimisebi@dmu.ac.uk

D. Obembe
e-mail: dobembe@dmu.ac.uk

K. W. Beta
e-mail: kwoldesenbet@dmu.ac.uk

© The Author(s), under exclusive license to Springer Nature
Switzerland AG 2023
S. Adomako et al. (eds.), *Corporate Sustainability in Africa,*
Palgrave Studies in African Leadership,
https://doi.org/10.1007/978-3-031-29273-6_6

Development Goal (SDG) 1—*no poverty*. In parallel, there is renewed awareness and constant reminders about the need for fundamental transformation in the way society consumes natural resources and choice of energy source to address pressing issues such as environmental degradation and global warming. Entrepreneurship is increasingly cited as a significant conduit for bringing about the much-needed transformation in relation to sustainable products and processes. Influential practitioner journals such as Harvard Business Review and the MIT Sloan Management Review advanced the idea that entrepreneurship may be the panacea for many social and environmental concerns (Brugmann & Prahalad, 2007; Wheeler et al., 2005).

Sustainable development was first used at the United Nations Conference on Human Environment in 1972 and gained prominence through the report to the United Nations by the World Commission on Environment and Development (WCED, 1987), referred to as '*The Brundtland Report*' as it was chaired by the then Norwegian Prime Minister Gro Harlem Brundtland. The report defined sustainable development as development that meets the need of the present generation without compromising the ability of future generations to meet their own (WCED, 1987). Such conceptualisation of sustainable development entails balancing present and future societal consumption of resources (including natural resources) and the need to protect the environment whilst addressing poverty. This leads us to the question: *what role entrepreneurship can play in contributing to sustainable development whilst contributing to poverty reduction? How about integrating environmental and social entrepreneurship motives to engage in sustainable-driven entrepreneurship?*

There is a focus on entrepreneurs who integrate both environmental and social purposes into a single venture (Parrish, 2010). Sustainable-driven entrepreneurship is supported by empirical studies that demonstrate a growing movement of such entrepreneurs in practice (Clifford & Dixon, 2006; Parrish, 2010). Drawing on the complementary perspective of the resource curse hypothesis view of nations, we argue that whilst sustainability is a key element for enterprise survival and growth (internal), the wider contribution of entrepreneurship to poverty reduction (external) is determined and influenced by the social and economic environment in which it exists (Hoogendoorn et al., 2019; Silajdžić et al., 2015).

The 'resource curse' hypothesis has emerged to show the negative correlation between the abundance of natural resources and economic growth in countries that export oil, gas, diamond, etc., but remain impoverished and underdeveloped (Auty, 2003; Sachs & Warner, 2001). This chapter reviews research evidence on how resource curse influences entrepreneurs' decision to imbibe sustainability in doing business and how that might affect their contribution to the larger community in the form of employment creation and poverty reduction. First, we lay a theoretical background by examining SE, resource curse, and poverty. We then treatise the influence of sustainability on both entrepreneurship and poverty reduction and reframe SE in the context of poverty reduction. Finally, we develop an agenda for policy and future research. Because the construct of SE, EE, and resource curse are somewhat complementary, yet distinct, first, we examine them separately and outline a few possible impacts and influences on both entrepreneurship and poverty reduction.

2 Theoretical Foundations

Sustainable Entrepreneurship (SE)

Sustainability in the context of entrepreneurship has been viewed in extant literature from three perspectives with the central themes being the need for entrepreneurs to be conscious of the impact of their actions, operations, and processes on business survival, the environment, and the communities in which they operate. The intersection between sustainable development and entrepreneurship has been addressed using various terms and literature such as ecopreneurship, SE, social entrepreneurship and, in an indirect manner such as institutional entrepreneurship. Extant literature reveals that earlier authors addressed sustainability and entrepreneurship exclusively with environmentally focused entrepreneurship, often referred to as 'ecopreneurship' (Hörisch et al., 2017; Lober, 1998; Pastakia, 1998; Schaltegger, 2002) whilst other authors focused on social entrepreneurship which is essentially concerned with achieving the societal goals and securing the funding for it (Bright et al., 2006; Clifford & Dixon, 2006; Prahalad & Hammond, 2002).

The environmental entrepreneurship literature (ecopreneurship), and to some extent social entrepreneurship, both address corporate influence in changing market conditions and regulations as well as initiating societal change. The ambition to change institutional settings created institutional

104   D. O. OLAGBOYE ET AL.

entrepreneurship. As suggested by Schaltegger and Wagner (2011), actors who initiate changes that contribute to transforming existing institutions or to creating new institutions despite pressures towards the status quo are termed institutional entrepreneurs (Battilana et al., 2009; Seo & Creed, 2002; Tina Dacin et al., 2002). Then came SE,which addresses a more comprehensive contribution to sustainable development by entrepreneurship. With SE, organisations are expected to be self-sustaining in addition to contributing increasingly to the sustainable development of the market and society as a whole (Schaltegger & Wagner, 2011).

While the acknowledgement of these antecedents is useful, we note that extant literature on SE has, so far, overlooked a critical issue. Studies are dominantly focused on the contribution of entrepreneurs to preserving the ecosystem, counteracting climate change, reducing environmental degradation, improving farming practices and improving the environment, transporting drinking water, and/or maintaining biodiversity, a construct aligned with environmental entrepreneurship (Cohen & Winn, 2007; Dean & McMullen, 2007; Muñoz & Cohen, 2018a, 2018b). In effect, previous research seems overly concerned with the profitability of businesses without environmental degradation. Whereas, the impact of EE on entrepreneurs is unambiguous (i.e. socio and economic environment), there is limited knowledge about the factors that militate against SE, especially in RRDCs, and how these factors implicitly affect entrepreneurs' choice to adopt sustainable business models for survival and by extension impactful and sustainable contribution to employment creation and the promotion of poverty reduction (Hall et al., 2010; Hoogendoorn et al., 2019; Silajdžić et al., 2015). This chapter attempts to provide such a synthesis and propositions for policy and future research.

Resource Curse and Poverty

The natural resource curse hypothesis represents the ironic dilemma of RRDCs with inimical implications for citizens' well-being and the socio-economic stability of these countries. Scholars empirically argue that RRDCs in most cases develop more slowly, are more corrupt, less diversified, less transparent, more oppressive, run unpredictable economies, and are more susceptible to internal conflict than less endowed countries at similar income levels (Auty, 1990; Gleb, 1988; Robinson et al., 2006; Sachs & Warner, 1999; Siegle, 2005). These empirical studies' support for the natural resource curse is not devoid of criticism, but the argument is compelling. First, logical observation reveals that countries exceptionally rich in natural resources such as oil-rich states like Nigeria, Gabon, Equatorial Guinea or Angola, and Zambia, have not had sustained and/or rapid economic growth. Second, logical observation suggests there is no commonality between the group of countries that have huge natural resources—and the group of countries with high levels of gross domestic product (GDP). Third, the levels of poverty, lack of or deplorable state of basic infrastructure, levels of insecurity, and inefficient institutions in many underdeveloped yet richly endowed countries give credence to the curse of natural resources. The finding in several regressions using data on growth from the post-war era is that high natural resource abundance tends to correlate with slow or stunted economic growth (Sachs & Warner, 2001; Williams, 2011).

Other studies (Alexeev & Conrad, 2011; Kolstad, 2009; Kolstad & Wiig, 2009; Mehlum et al., 2006; Robinson et al., 2006) present findings that point to the fact that RRDCs constitute both growth losers and growth winners. They argue that, natural resource endowment is not directly responsible for the lack of correlation between economic growth and resource endowment, but rather they attribute the diverging experience to the differences in the quality of institutions and political structure. These proponents of institutional quality and political structure agree amongst other things that resource boom results in over-extraction rather than efficient extraction, raises the value of being in power, provides more resources for the political class to influence election outcomes, and essentially results in resource misallocation with the resultant impact of underdevelopment relative to resource endowment.

Findings are consistent in asserting that resource curse hinders typically natural resource-rich countries, especially RRDCs, from developing the enabling entrepreneurship ecosystem (EE) required for sustainable venture creation—infrastructure, institutional structure and support, financial system and incentives, diversified economy, etc.,—and prevent the achievement of the expectation to contribute to poverty reduction through employment creation and economic growth (Bruton et al., 2013; Kimmitt et al., 2019; Maksimov et al., 2017). The richness in natural resources is said to foster the misuse of resources by the political class to sustain political power and weaken the very institutions that should provide checks and balances at the expense of developmental programmes to improve the socio-economic conditions of citizens (Kolstad, 2009;

106   D. O. OLAGBOYE ET AL.

Mehlum et al., 2006; Robinson et al., 2006; Ross, 1999). This chapter seeks to provide insight into the impact of the curse of natural resource on economic growth in RRDCs and make propositions that help addressing this profound problem.

3   Reframing Sustainable Entrepreneurship in the Context of Poverty Reduction

Research in the recent past is concentrated on the role of entrepreneurship in reducing poverty. A 2019 extensive study (Sutter et al., 2019) identified three perspectives that underpin entrepreneurship research in relation to poverty reduction: (i) entrepreneurship as a *remediation* to reduce poverty, highlighting research focused on individuals' entrepreneurial engagements to overcome immediate personal resource concerns (Singh & Dutt, 2019; Sutter et al., 2014); (ii) entrepreneurship as *reform* to reduce poverty, highlighting studies focused on activities leading to important and institutional changes that engender inclusion (Estrin et al., 2013; Mair et al., 2012); and (iii) entrepreneurship as *revolution* to reduce poverty, highlighting studies focused on entrepreneurial activities that provoke actions against a fragmented system (Peredo & Chrisman, 2006; Webb et al., 2013) to institute new measure to promote a more equal and inclusive society (Khavul et al., 2013; Rindova et al., 2009). Sutter et al. (2019) review of entrepreneurship research on poverty reduction does not only point to what we know about the relationship between entrepreneurial activities and poverty reduction, but also the existing gaps between individuals' immediate consequences from entrepreneurship—*remediation*—and the impact of institutional changes on EE—*reforms*—or the entrepreneurial innovations and agitations for system changes—*revolution*.

Ease of Doing Business Index (EDBI) and Poverty reduction in RRDCs

The World Bank and International Monetary Fund data on 30 RRDCs in Table 1 capture the natural resource endowment found in these countries and the comparative gross national income (GNI) per capita in US dollars for the years 2010 and 2019. Based on the 2019 changes to the World Bank classification of countries, 8 of the countries are classified as Low-Income Countries (LIC) with GNI per capita of less than $1,025, while

15 countries are classified as Lower-Middle Income Countries (LMICs) with GNI per capita income of between \$1,026 and \$3,995, and 7 countries are classified as Upper-Middle Income Countries (UMIC) with GNI per capita income between \$3,996 and \$12,375. The table shows that these GNI classifications are not an absolute determinant of the level of poverty in these countries with varying poverty levels as a percentage of the population regardless of classification—LIC, LMIC, and UMIC.

Perhaps, the most important indices from the dataset are the relationship between the ease of doing business index (EDBI) in these RRDCs and the poverty headcount ratio at national poverty lines (% of population) where there seems to be a correlation between the EDBI and the poverty levels in these countries. All the RRDCs with higher EDBI below 80 have significantly lower per centages of the national population below poverty line; Vietnam with EDBI of 70 has 6.7% of its population below the poverty line; Uzbekistan with EDBI of 69 has 14.1% poverty levels, and similarly, Indonesia with EDBI of 73 has 9.8% of its population below the poverty line. In contrast and apart from Lao PDR, Mongolia, Iraq, and Botswana, every other RRDC in Table 1 with EDBI greater than 80 has a poverty headcount ratio of 30% and above. The dataset reveals the fact that most of these RRDCs have significantly high percentages of their national population below the poverty line. Even the RDDCs such as Gabon and Equatorial Guinea who are classified as UMICs in Table 1 have very low EDBI and correspondingly, with over 30% poverty levels like the RRDCs classified as LIC and LMIC. Based on the data from Table 1, we argue that EDBI is a good indicator of poverty levels in these RRDCs.

As argued by some scholars, the existence of natural resource endowment is not the reason why economic development and growth are slow and not commensurate with the revenue that has accrued to countries such as those in Table 1, but rather, they attribute this disparity in development and seemingly impoverishment of citizens of these RRDCs to the quality and efficiency of institutions and political structures—governance (Alexeev & Conrad, 2011; de Medeiros Costa & dos Santos, 2013; Henri, 2019; Kolstad, 2009; Mehlum et al., 2006; Robinson et al., 2006). The institutional quality/efficiency argument points to resource-rich countries (RRC) with presumably negligible or none recorded levels of poverty such as countries in Table 2 classified as High-Income Countries (HIC) with GNI per capita of \$12,375 and above. These growth winners and the economic growth they have been able to achieve with

108   D. O. OLAGBOYE ET AL.

Table 1   EDBI in RRDCs and poverty levels

Country	Country code	Type of natural resources	Gross national income (GNI) per capita (in 2010 US dollars)	Gross national income (GNI) per capita (in 2019 US dollars)	Ease of doing business index (2019)	Poverty headcount ratio at national poverty lines (% of population)[a]
Congo Dem Rep[b]	COD	Minerals and oil	180	520	183	63.9
Liberia[b]	LBR	Gold/ diamond/ iron ore	210	580	175	50.9
Niger[b]	NER	Uranium	360	560	132	44.5
Guinea[b]	GIN	Mining products	390	950	156	55.2
Mali[b]	MLI	Gold	600	880	148	41.1
Chad[b]	TCD	Oil	710	700	182	46.7
Mauritania[c]	MRT	Iron ore	1,000	1,660	152	31.0
Lao PDR[c]	LAO	Copper and gold	1,010	2,535	154	23.4
Zambia[c]	ZMB	Copper	1,070	1,450	85	54.4
Vietnam[c]	VNM	Oil	1,160	2,715	70	6.7
Yemen[b]	YEM	Oil	1,160	940	187	48.6
Nigeria[c]	NGR	Oil	1,170	2,030	131	46.0
Cameroon[c]	CMR	Oil	1,200	1,500	167	37.5
Papua New Guinea[c]	PNG	Oil/ copper/ gold	1,300	2,780	120	39.9
Sudan[b]	SDN	Oil	1,300	590	171	46.5
South Sudan[c]	SSDN	Oil	n.a.	1,090	185	82.3
Uzbekistan[c]	UZB	Gold/gas	1,300	1,725	69	14.1
Cote d'Ivoire[c]	CIV	Oil/gas	1,650	2,290	110	46.3
Bolivia[c]	BOL	Gas	1,810	3,530	150	34.6
Mongolia[d]	MNG	Copper	1,870	4,295	81	28.4
Congo Rep[c]	COG	Oil	2,240	1,750	180	40.9
Iraq[d]	IRG	Oil	2,380	5,740	172	18.9
Indonesia[d]	IDN	Oil	2,500	4,136	73	9.8

(continued)

NATURAL RESOURCES, SUSTAINABLE ENTREPRENEURSHIP ... 109

Table 1 (continued)

Country	Country code	Type of natural resources	Gross national income (GNI) per capita (in 2010 US dollars)	Gross national income (GNI) per capita (in 2019 US dollars)	Ease of doing business index (2019)	Poverty headcount ratio at national poverty lines (% of population)[a]
Timor Leste[c]	TLS	Oil	2,730	1,294	181	41.8
Syrian Arab Rep[c]	SYR	Oil	2,750	1,820	176	35.2
Botswana[d]	BWA	Diamond, gold and copper	5,610	7,660	87	19.3
Guyana[d]	GUY	Gold and bauxite	2,900	5,180	134	n.a.
Angola[c]	AGO	Oil	3,960	3,050	177	47.6
Gabon[d]	GAB	Oil	7,680	7,210	167	33.4
Equatorial Guinea[d]	GNQ	Oil	13,720	6,460	178	76.8

[a]Refers to different years, depending on data availability
[b]Low-Income Country (LIC) based on the July 01, 2019 World Bank changes to the classification
[c]Lower-Middle Income Country (LMIC) based on the July 01, 2019 World Bank changes to the classification
[d]Upper-Middle Income Country (UMIC) based on the July 01, 2019 World Bank changes to the classification
Source World Bank and International Monetary Fund Data

the natural resource revenue endowments contradicts the assertions of the resource curse hypothesis.

Economic Growth and Poverty Reduction

There is convergence in the entrepreneurship literature on the relationship between entrepreneurship and economic growth, employment creation, and poverty reduction. Research points to the transformational contribution entrepreneurial activities make to the developed countries. Multilateral organisations such as the International Monetary Fund (IMF), the World Bank, and their developmental agencies provide support to RRDCs to help them develop an entrepreneurial ecosystem that can lead to improvement in socio-economic conditions through

110   D. O. OLAGBOYE ET AL.

Table 2   Other resource-rich countries

Country	Country code	Type of natural resources	Gross national income (GNI) per capita (in 2010 US dollars)	Gross national income (GNI) per capita (in 2019 US dollars)	Ease of doing business index (2019)[a]	Poverty headcount ratio at national poverty lines (% of population)[a]
Bahrain[b]	BHR	Oil	24,710	22,110	n.a.	n.a.
Brunei Darussalam[b]	BRN	Gas	n.a.	33,230	n.a.	n.a.
Trinidad and Tobago[b]	TTO	Gas	16,700	16,890	n.a.	n.a.
Saudi Arabia[b]	SAU	Oil	17,210	22,850	n.a.	n.a.
Oman[b]	OMN	Oil	17,890	15,330	n.a.	n.a.
United Arab Emirate[b]	UAE	Oil	26,370	43,470	n.a.	n.a.
Qatar[b]	QAT	Gas	69,640	63,410	n.a.	n.a.
Norway[b]	NOR	Oil	84,640	82,500	n.a.	n.a.

[a]Data not available—these resource-rich HICs countries do not have information on this indicator available

[b]High-Income Country (HIC) based on the July 01, 2019 World Bank changes to the classification

Source World Bank and International Monetary Fund Data

employment creation and poverty reduction (Kongolo, 2010; Mamman et al., 2019; Obeng & Blundel, 2015; Rogerson, 2001). Whilst these efforts at stimulating entrepreneurial activities in developing countries are well documented, studies suggest that the transformational impact envisaged have not quite materialised because these RRDCs still have some of the highest poverty levels in the world (Mamman et al., 2019; Poole, 2018; Williams & Shahid, 2016).

Whilst the various efforts aimed at improving entrepreneurial activities and their outcomes in developing countries have undoubtedly achieved some strides by reducing the levels of poverty compared to the figures from 1990, RRDCs are yet to create a conducive entrepreneurial ecosystem that stimulates venture creation, survival, and growth, and impact on poverty reduction. Some scholars argue that some RRDCs have not implemented adequate policies that foster sustainable entrepreneurship (Herrington & Kelley, 2012; Spigel & Harrison, 2018; Williams &

Vorley, 2015) and, consequently, have seen minimal or no reduction in national poverty levels. Based on the foregoing exposition of theoretical perspectives and empirical literature, we develop research propositions in the next subsections.

4 DEVELOPING AGENDA FOR POLICY AND FUTURE RESEARCH

Education and Poverty Reduction

Education, including entrepreneurial education, directly benefits its recipients and by implication improves the society through increased productivity, innovation and invention, and use of new technologies. Research on inequality and education (Bruns et al., 2003) strongly establishes that illiteracy is a major predictor of poverty, which points to the fact that school completion rate is of vital importance to RRDCs. Bruns et al. (2003) argue that completion of five to six years of education, that is, primary education, in most developing countries, is essential for achieving basic level literacy, communication, and numeric skills. Education levels fewer than five to six years are considered inadequate to achieve and sustain economic development.

Research on public spending on education in LICs, LMICs, and UMICs ranges from as low as less than 2% of gross national product (GNP) in Chad, Guinea, and Lao PDR to 10% in Botswana and Guyana (Mingat & Winter, 2002). Whilst greater spending may result in higher quality education, this is not a foregone conclusion (Fuhrer, 2003). Mingat and Winter (2002) note that, whilst Senegal and Burkina Faso spending on education is almost the same (4.8 and 4.2% respectively), achievement is much higher in Burkina Faso. Education at the prescribed level of five to six years contributes to economic growth—human capital, poverty reduction, and individual economic success in RRDCs.

There have been efforts to develop entrepreneurial orientation in developing countries. For example, an initiative implemented by a professional group in South Africa to train secondary-school students on problem recognition and problem-solving skills has resulted in positive outcomes (Meintjes et al., 2015). In contrast, insufficient and inefficient entrepreneurial education programmes in higher education do not lead to new job creation by graduate students (Lebusa, 2014; Popescu et al., 2016). The importance of equitable and quality education—including entrepreneurial education—in developing countries plagued by

112   D. O. OLAGBOYE ET AL.

high unemployment rates is echoed in the United Nations 17 Sustainable Development Goals (SDGs).

Proposition 1: The absence of at least five to six years of education - including some form of entrepreneurial education - is inadequate to achieve and sustain economic development, stable government institutions, and reduce poverty. There needs to be a deliberate and measurable strategy targeting a minimum of five to six years of education for citizens of RRDCs if SDG 1 - No Poverty - is to be achieved and sustained.

Healthcare and Poverty Reduction

Corruption, mismanagement, and a weak public sector hinder improvements in health; and poverty exacerbates the impact as the poor often lack the financial resources necessary to utilise existing interventions (Nallari & Griffith, 2011). Research argues that health and economic growth have a reciprocal relationship in many ways. On the one hand, people with higher incomes can afford better sanitation, nutrition, and healthcare and, on the other hand, a healthier individual is less likely to miss work for health reasons and likely to be more productive. Healthier children also have higher rates of school attendance and better cognitive abilities (Nallari & Griffith, 2011). Notwithstanding, targeted public health care spending increase alone may not be the most prudent use of scarce resources; developments in other high-priority areas such as nutrition, sanitation, water, and other basic infrastructures are also vitally important to promote quality living, improve health, development of productive human capital that result in sustained entrepreneurship and address poverty in RRDCs. Therefore, adopting comprehensive strategy for improving healthcare, its management and institutions should be part of the development of a viable ecosystem. Allocating healthcare spending that aims at improving the well-being of the poor, developing vaccines against preventable diseases, and prenatal care (Gupta et al., 2002) is crucially important.

Proposition 2: The provision of basic healthcare is critical for economic progress and building a viable ecosystem for innovation and entrepreneurship. RRDCs should not only increase public spending on healthcare, but in high-priority areas such as nutrition, sanitation, water, etc., to improve living standards and conditions for sustainable entrepreneurship, poverty reduction, and improved general well-being of citizenry.

Labour Market and Poverty Reduction

Increase in employment and productivity is a prerequisite for economic growth and the labour market is considered one of the major channels through which economic growth can help reduce poverty. On the flip side, studies argue that economies that fail to translate economic growth into jobs and employment creation may experience a slowdown in efforts to reduce poverty as labour is the main asset of the poor, and jobs are a way out of poverty (Nallari & Griffith, 2011). Extant literature identifies labour market conditions and costs as it relates to the availability of the required skills and technological knowhow as factors that affect the dynamic transition from one entrepreneurial stage to the next in developing countries (Guerrero et al., 2020; van Stel et al., 2019). Improvements in human capital development activities and training are required to close the gap between skilled labour supply and demand. Labour market outcomes within countries are increasingly been determined and influenced by external factors such as globalisation and technology (Nallari & Griffith, 2011).

In developing countries with high levels of poverty, social protection for unemployment is inadequate or non-existent in some cases. Therefore, being unemployed is not an option for most people living in poverty. These countries are characterised by working poor people with insufficient and ridiculous compensation which means living below an acceptable poverty line (ILO, 2010). The ILO's (2010) study found that "vulnerable employment'—employment characterised by inadequate earning, low productivity, and difficult working conditions that undermine workers' fundamental rights—are indicative of the informal economy employment in developing regions such as in South Asia and Sub-Saharan Africa (SSA) with over three-quarter of employment classified as vulnerable. The intensity of a country's growth in employment can be determined and explained by labour supply growth, instability, uncertainty, taxes on labour earnings, and the size of the service sector (Kapsos, 2005).

What is important for poverty reduction in RRDCs is the sectoral pattern of growth in employment and productivity. We argue that income accruing from natural resources endowment of RRDCs needs to be

114   D. O. OLAGBOYE ET AL.

channelled into the development of other sectors such as manufacturing, industry, agriculture, and infrastructure to boost employment, productivity, and a conducive ecosystem for venture creation and innovation. Studies (Gutierrez et al., 2007; Kapsos, 2005) have identified that employment-intensive growth in the manufacturing sectors is associated with decreases in poverty, whereas growth in agricultural productivity promotes poverty reduction. They argue that focusing solely on employment intensity of overall growth—which is what tends to happen in RRDCs—subverts the importance of and the emphasis that needs to be placed on employment growth in manufacturing and increase in agricultural productivity.

> *Proposition 3*: The effort and intervention of governments in RRDCs needs to be channelled towards the provision of a conducive ecosystem to engender investment and venture creation that will boost employment in the manufacturing sector and increase productivity in the agricultural sector to decrease levels of poverty and increase productivity. These efforts must be financed from the revenues generated from the extraction of the natural resource endowments.

Science, Technology, and Innovation and Poverty Reduction

If developing countries are to prosper in the global economy, then science, technology, and innovation (STI) capacity-building is a necessity to foster sustainable development and sustained poverty reduction (Watkins & Ehst, 2008). Science, technology, and innovation cannot be seen as a luxury or the exclusive preserve of the more economically dynamic, wealthier countries or regions if developing countries are to improve the quality of life, access to clean water, health care delivery, physical infrastructures, access to affordable and constant energy, and general improvement in the standard of living for the poorest people in the society. STI is decisively important for growth and hence needs to be developed through both foreign direct investment (FDI) and domestic investment to develop innovation and human capital capacity in developing countries.

UNCTAD (2006) identified a few problems in efforts to build STI capacity in local communities that allow for the application of science and technology to local problems and deal with poverty reduction in developing countries. First, local communities should be allowed to actively

NATURAL RESOURCES, SUSTAINABLE ENTREPRENEURSHIP ... 115

participate in the technology development process and not merely be passive observers and recipients of technological development. Second, it is important to identify critical capacities and skills required for the successful diffusion of appropriate technological innovations such as entrepreneurial and marketing skills. And finally, STI should be considered alongside the broader strategy of building the productive capacities of the countries to effectively boost and balance the demand and supply equations for sustained innovation and entrepreneurship that will translate into poverty reduction.

However, in recent years, researchers have examined and argued that economic growth is linked to poverty reduction through entrepreneurship and the development of science, technology, and innovation that has brought new techniques (Ahlstrom, 2010, 2014; Bloom et al., 2016). This technological development and innovation, especially digital technology, has engendered social and economic development that has created new approaches and solutions to poverty alleviation that challenges the existing approaches of handing out financial aid, seeding development, and other traditional poverty reduction measures (Si et al., 2020). Si et al. (2020) argue that the relationship between technology and poverty reduction has been receiving both the academic and policy-makers' interest because of advances and diffusion technology that enable inclusive entrepreneurship to address the growing problem of social exclusion, reduce levels of poverty, and narrow the gap between the haves and have-nots in developing economies. These technological developments notwithstanding, these RRDCs have remained growth losers because of their persistent reliance on the export of unprocessed raw materials that do not add value in product, process, and organisational innovations, and in economic diversification, development of local capacity, and contribution to sustainable development (Watkins & Ehst, 2008).

Proposition 4: The consistent and continuous reliance of RRDCs on exporting unprocessed raw materials has limited the diversification of their economies and productive capabilities to create jobs and alleviate poverty. RRDCs thus need to develop sustainable development strategy that improves the processing, finishing, and exporting of their natural resource endowments using science and technology in order to develop national technical and innovative capabilities for addressing social and economic development issues including reducing poverty and developing successful entrepreneurial eco-system.

5 DISCUSSION AND CONCLUSION

This chapter contributes to the theoretical reframing of sustainable entrepreneurship in the context of poverty reduction in RRDCs in three main respects. First, the chapter theorises the role of education, healthcare, labour market, and science and technology to overcome the challenges RRDCs face in engendering sustainable entrepreneurship with impact on poverty alleviation (Auty, 1990; Brown & Mason, 2017; Gleb, 1988; Isenberg, 2010, 2011; Robinson et al., 2006; Sachs & Warner, 1999; Siegle, 2005). Drawing on the entrepreneurship and economic development literature, we adopt a complementary perspective that shows the subtle interdependence of the above components and hence, the need to develop these areas simultaneously for sustainable development and entrepreneurship in view of achieving equality of opportunities and equity in the process of addressing poverty (Brown & Mason, 2017; Godley et al., 2019; Isenberg, 2010, 2011). The chapter thus provided insight into the link between substantiable entrepreneurship and its enabling factors and reducing poverty levels.

Second, the finding that shows a direct correlation between the ease of doing business index (EDBI) and poverty levels in the RRDCs is of high interest for policymakers and scholars because it implies that RRDCs need to develop conducive and functional environment (business and institutional environments) for venture creation, development and growth as well as putting in place appropriate institutions that support sustainable entrepreneurship and productive capabilities (Ács et al., 2014; Stenholm et al., 2013; Sutter et al., 2019; Szerb et al., 2019; van Stel et al., 2019). In addition, the chapter showed the antecedents of the disparities in economic growth and resource endowment correlation with their EDBI by RRDCs to be the difference in the quality of institutions and political structures governing such institutions. The deficiency in the quality of institutions, lack of check and balance in the political system, and associated misgovernance and corruption significantly impede the development and implementation of policies that enable sustainable entrepreneurship and thereby, alleviating poverty. These findings have pragmatic implications as the relationship between SE and poverty reduction could be significantly shaped by the quality of existing entrepreneurial ecosystem components that facilitate or inhibit the effective utilisation of the natural resource endowments for sustainable development.

The chapter advanced theoretically—and empirically—driven four propositions that guide future research. This is the third contribution of this chapter in that, the propositions guide further research on how the level of education and its apparatus; health and well-being; the labour market conditions; and developments in science and technology act as conduits through which SE fosters and consequently leads to reduction in the level of poverty, developments of quality institutions, national capacity-building, economic diversification, technical and innovative capabilities, stable and sustained employment and finally to sustainable development. These propositions contribute to existing research by integrating various strands of works (Gutierrez et al., 2007; Nallari & Griffith, 2011; Popescu et al., 2016; Si et al., 2020; Watkins & Ehst, 2008).

Limitations and Future Research

The chapter reviewed extant research knowledge on the link between sustainable entrepreneurship and poverty reduction in RRDCs. The chapter has four implications/limitations that can be addressed in future research. First, the chapter's conceptualisation of the resource curse hypothesis along with institutional and political/governance quality on the impact of SE and poverty reduction need empirical examination drawing on real data sources. In doing so, future research opportunities should examine to what extent the entrepreneurial ecosystems in RRDCs and resource curse influence SE and poverty reduction. Second, other factors that may influence the link between SE and poverty reduction in addition to the ease of doing business index (EDBI) and the quality of institutions and political structure need identification to provide a holistic view on these issues. Third, drawing on the recent debates and developments in the area of EE, future studies can explore the components/ actors that play significant roles in the development of robust and functional ecosystems in a particular context; and what factors can act as antecedents for the development of such thriving EEs in RRDCs. Finally, this chapter provides opportunities for future research to examine the propositions presented in the study, offering a complementary and practical approach to sustainable venture creation and poverty reduction in developing countries.

In conclusion, we began by noting that sustainable development and poverty reduction remain an influential, yet controversial, concept for business and policy alike. The ease of doing business and the quality

118 D. O. OLAGBOYE ET AL.

of institutions and political structure are essential in determining which contextual solutions will succeed and result in economic growth and by extension poverty reduction, particularly in RRDCs. Building on the entrepreneurship and economic development literature and the resource curse hypothesis, we propose that SE and poverty reduction are driven by the ease of doing business and the quality of institutions and political structure prevalent in RRDCs. In so doing, we argued for the ease of doing business and the quality of institutions and political structure as core to SE and poverty reduction in RRDCs.

REFERENCES

Ács, Z. J., Autio, E., & Szerb, L. (2014). National systems of entrepreneurship: Measurement issues and policy implications. *Research Policy, 43*(3), 476–494. https://doi.org/10.1016/j.respol.2013.08.016

Ahlstrom, D. (2010). Innovation and growth: How business contributes to society. *Academy of Management Perspectives, 24*(3), 11–24. https://doi.org/10.5465/amp.24.3.11

Ahlstrom, D. (2014). The hidden reason why the first world war matters today: The development and spread of modern management. *Brown Journal of World Affairs, 21*(1), 201–218.

Alexeev, M., & Conrad, R. (2011). The natural resource curse and economic transition. *Economic Systems, 35*(4), 445–461. https://doi.org/10.1016/j.ecosys.2010.10.003

Auty, R. M. (1990). *Resource-based industrialization: Sowing the oil in eight developing countries.* Oxford University Press.

Auty, R. M. (2003). Third time lucky for Algeria? Integrating an industrializing oil-rich country into the global economy. *Resources Policy, 29*(1–2), 37–47. https://doi.org/10.1016/j.resourpol.2004.02.001

Battilana, J., Leca, B., & Boxenbaum, E. (2009). 2 How actors change institutions: Towards a theory of institutional entrepreneurship. *The Academy of Management Annals, 3*(1), 65–107. https://doi.org/10.1080/19416520903053598

Bloom, N., Draca, M., & van Reenen, J. (2016). Trade induced technical change? The impact of Chinese imports on innovation, IT and productivity. *The Review of Economic Studies, 83*(1), 87–117. https://doi.org/10.1093/restud/rdv039

Bright, D. S., Fry, R. E., & Cooperrider, D. L. (2006). *Transformative innovations for the mutual benefit of business, society, and development* (BAWB Interactive Working Paper Series, Vol. 1, Issue 1)

Brown, R., & Mason, C. (2017). Looking inside the spiky bits: A critical review and conceptualisation of entrepreneurial ecosystems. *Small Business Economics, 49*(1), 11–30. https://doi.org/10.1007/s11187-017-9865-7

Brugmann, J., & Prahalad, C. K. (2007, February). Cocreating business's new social compact. *Harvard Business Online*, 1–14. http://harvardbusinessonl ine.hbsp.harvard.edu/hbrsa/en/issue/0702/article/R0702DPrint.jhtml

Bruns, B., Mingat, A., & Rakotomalala, R. (2003). *Achieving universal primary education by 2015.* The World Bank. https://doi.org/10.1596/0-8213-5345-4

Bruton, G. D., Ketchen, D. J., & Ireland, R. D. (2013). Entrepreneurship as a solution to poverty. *Journal of Business Venturing, 28*(6), 683–689. https://doi.org/10.1016/j.jbusvent.2013.05.002

Clifford, A., & Dixon, S. E. A. (2006). Green-works: A model for combining social and ecological entrepreneurship. In J. Mair, J. Robinson, & K. Hockerts (Eds.), *Social entrepreneurship* (pp. 214–234). Palgrave Macmillan.

Cohen, B., & Winn, M. I. (2007). Market imperfections, opportunity and sustainable entrepreneurship. *Journal of Business Venturing, 22*(1), 29–49. https://doi.org/10.1016/j.jbusvent.2004.12.001

Dean, T. J., & McMullen, J. S. (2007). Toward a theory of sustainable entrepreneurship: Reducing environmental degradation through entrepreneurial action. *Journal of Business Venturing, 22*(1), 50–76. https://doi.org/10.1016/j.jbusvent.2005.09.003

de Medeiros Costa, H. K., & dos Santos, E. M. (2013). Institutional analysis and the "resource curse" in developing countries. *Energy Policy, 63*, 788–795. https://doi.org/10.1016/j.enpol.2013.08.060

Estrin, S., Mickiewicz, T., & Stephan, U. (2013). Entrepreneurship, social capital, and institutions: Social and commercial entrepreneurship across nations. *Entrepreneurship Theory and Practice, 37*(3), 479–504. https://doi.org/10.1111/etap.12019

Fuhrer, U. (2003). Cultivating minds. In *Finance and development* (Vol. 42, Issue 2). Routledge. https://doi.org/10.4324/9780203694985

Gleb, A. H. (1988). *Oil windfalls: Blessing or curse?* Oxford University Press.

Godley, A., Morawetz, N., & Soga, L. (2019). The complementarity perspective to the entrepreneurial ecosystem taxonomy. *Small Business Economics.* https://doi.org/10.1007/s11187-019-00197-y

Guerrero, M., Liñán, F., & Cáceres-Carrasco, F. R. (2020). The influence of ecosystems on the entrepreneurship process: A comparison across developed and developing economies. *Small Business Economics.* https://doi.org/10.1007/s11187-020-00392-2

Gupta, S., Clements, B., Guin-Siu, M. T., & Leruth, L. (2002). Debt relief and public health spending in heavily indebted poor countries. *Bulletin of the World Health Organization, 80*(2), 151–157. https://doi.org/10.1590/S0042-96862002000200011

Gutierrez, C., Orecchia, C., Paci, P., & Serneels, P. (2007). Does employment generation really matter for poverty reduction? In *Labor markets and economic development* (No. WPS4432; Policy Research Working Papers, Issue December). The World Bank. https://doi.org/10.1596/1813-9450-4432

Hall, J. K., Daneke, G. A., & Lenox, M. J. (2010). Sustainable development and entrepreneurship: Past contributions and future directions. *Journal of Business Venturing, 25*(5), 439–448. https://doi.org/10.1016/j.jbusvent.2010.01.002

Henri, P. A. O. (2019). Natural resources curse: A reality in Africa. *Resources Policy, 63*, 101406. https://doi.org/10.1016/j.resourpol.2019.101406

Herrington, M., & Kelley, D. (2012). *African entrepreneurship sub-Saharan African regional report.* http://www.babson.edu/Academics/centers/blank-center/global-research/gem/Documents/GEM-2012-Africa-Report.pdf

Hoogendoorn, B., van der Zwan, P., & Thurik, R. (2019). Sustainable entrepreneurship: The role of perceived barriers and risk. *Journal of Business Ethics, 157*(4), 1133–1154. https://doi.org/10.1007/s10551-017-3646-8

Hörisch, J., Kollat, J., & Brieger, S. A. (2017). What influences environmental entrepreneurship? A multilevel analysis of the determinants of entrepreneurs' environmental orientation. *Small Business Economics, 48*(1), 47–69. https://doi.org/10.1007/s11187-016-9765-2

ILO (International Labour Office). (2010). *Global employment trends for youth* (Issue August). International Labour Organisation.

Isenberg, D. J. (2010). How to start an entrepreneurial revolution. *Harvard Business Review, 88*(6), 40–50.

Isenberg, D. J. (2011). The entrepreneurship ecosystem strategy as a new paradigm for economic policy: Principles for cultivating entrepreneurships. *The Babsos Entrepreneurship Ecosystem Project, 1*(781), 1–13.

Kapsos, S. (2005). *The employment intensity of growth: Trends and macroeconomic determinants* (Employment Strategy Paper 2005/12).

Khavul, S., Chavez, H., & Bruton, G. D. (2013). When institutional change outruns the change agent: The contested terrain of entrepreneurial microfinance for those in poverty. *Journal of Business Venturing, 28*(1), 30–50. https://doi.org/10.1016/j.jbusvent.2012.02.005

Kimmitt, J., Muñoz, P., & Newbery, R. (2019, May). Poverty and the varieties of entrepreneurship in the pursuit of prosperity. *Journal of Business Venturing,* 1–18. https://doi.org/10.1016/j.jbusvent.2019.05.003

Kolstad, I. (2009). The resource curse: Which institutions matter? *Applied Economics Letters, 16*(4), 439–442. https://doi.org/10.1080/17446540802167339

Kolstad, I., & Wiig, A. (2009). Is transparency the key to reducing corruption in resource-rich countries? *World Development, 37*(3), 521–532. https://doi.org/10.1016/j.worlddev.2008.07.002

Kongolo, M. (2010). Job creation versus job shedding and the role of SMEs in economic development. *African Journal of Business Management, 4*(11), 2288–2295. http://www.academicjournals.org/AJBM

Lebusa, M. J. (2014). Entrepreneurial intention in advanced undergraduate students. *Mediterranean Journal of Social Sciences, 5*(27), 760–765. https://doi.org/10.5901/mjss.2014.v5n27p760

Lober, D. J. (1998). Pollution prevention as corporate entrepreneurship. *Journal of Organizational Change Management, 11*(1), 26–37. https://doi.org/10.1108/09534819810369554

Mair, J., Martí, I., & Ventresca, M. J. (2012). Building inclusive markets in rural Bangladesh: How intermediaries work institutional voids. *Academy of Management Journal, 55*(4), 819–850. https://doi.org/10.5465/amj.2010.0627

Maksimov, V., Wang, S. L., & Luo, Y. (2017). Reducing poverty in the least developed countries: The role of small and medium enterprises. *Journal of World Business, 52*(2), 244–257. https://doi.org/10.1016/j.jwb.2016.12.007

Mamman, A., Bawole, J., Agbebi, M., & Alhassan, A.-R. (2019). SME policy formulation and implementation in Africa: Unpacking assumptions as opportunity for research direction. *Journal of Business Research, 97*, 304–315. https://doi.org/10.1016/j.jbusres.2018.01.044

Mehlum, H., Moene, K., & Torvik, R. (2006). Institutions and the resource curse. *The Economic Journal, 116*(508), 1–20. https://doi.org/10.1111/j.1468-0297.2006.01045.x

Meintjes, A., Henrico, A., & Kroon, J. (2015). Teaching problem-solving competency in business studies at secondary school level. *South African Journal of Education, 35*(3), 1–11. https://doi.org/10.15700/saje.v35n3a1102

Mingat, A., & Winter, C. (2002, March). Education for all by 2015. *Finance and Development IMF, 39*(1). https://www.imf.org/external/pubs/ft/fandd/2002/03/mingat.htm

Muñoz, P., & Cohen, B. (2018a). Entrepreneurial narratives in sustainable venturing: Beyond people, profit, and planet. *Journal of Small Business Management, 56*, 154–176. https://doi.org/10.1111/jsbm.12395

Muñoz, P., & Cohen, B. (2018b). Sustainable entrepreneurship research: Taking stock and looking ahead. *Business Strategy and the Environment, 27*(3), 300–322. https://doi.org/10.1002/bse.2000

Nallari, R., & Griffith, B. (2011). *Understanding growth and poverty*. The World Bank. https://doi.org/10.1596/978-0-8213-6953-1

Obeng, B. A., & Blundel, R. K. (2015). Evaluating enterprise policy interventions in Africa: A critical review of ghanaian small business support services. *Journal of Small Business Management*, 53(2), 416–435. https://doi.org/10.1111/jsbm.12072

Parrish, B. D. (2010). Sustainability-driven entrepreneurship: Principles of organization design. *Journal of Business Venturing*, 25(5), 510–523. https://doi.org/10.1016/j.jbusvent.2009.05.005

Pastakia, A. (1998). Grassroots ecopreneurs: Change agents for a sustainable society. *Journal of Organizational Change Management*, 11(2), 157–173. https://doi.org/10.1108/09534819810212142

Peredo, A. M., & Chrisman, J. J. (2006). Toward a theory of community-based enterprise. *Academy of Management Review*, 31(2), 309–328. https://doi.org/10.5465/amr.2006.20208683

Poole, D. L. (2018). Entrepreneurs, entrepreneurship and SMEs in developing economies: How subverting terminology sustains flawed policy. *World Development Perspectives*, 9(October 2017), 35–42. https://doi.org/10.1016/j.wdp.2018.04.003

Popescu, C., Bostan, I., Robu, I.-B., Maxim, A., & Diaconu (Maxim), L. (2016). An analysis of the determinants of entrepreneurial intentions among students: A Romanian case study. *Sustainability*, 8(8), 771. https://doi.org/10.3390/su8080771

Prahalad, C. K., & Hammond, A. (Eds.). (2002, September 2). Serving the world's poor, profitably. *Harvard Business Review*, 48–57.

Rindova, V., Barry, D., & Ketchen, D. J. (2009). Entrepreneuring as emancipation. *Academy of Management Review*, 34(3), 477–491. https://doi.org/10.5465/amr.2009.40632647

Robinson, J. A., Torvik, R., & Verdier, T. (2006). Political foundations of the resource curse. *Journal of Development Economics*, 79(2), 447–468. https://doi.org/10.1016/j.jdeveco.2006.01.008

Rogerson, C. M. (2001). In search of the African miracle: Debates on successful small enterprise development in Africa. *Habitat International*, 25(1), 115–142. https://doi.org/10.1016/S0197-3975(00)00033-3

Ross, M. L. (1999). The political economy of the resource curse. *World Politics*, 51(2), 297–322. https://doi.org/10.2307/25054077

Sachs, J. D., & Warner, A. M. (1999). The big push, natural resource booms and growth. *Journal of Development Economics*, 59(1), 43–76. https://doi.org/10.1016/S0304-3878(99)00005-X

Sachs, J. D., & Warner, A. M. (2001). The curse of natural resources. *European Economic Review*, 45(4–6), 827–838. https://doi.org/10.1016/S0014-2921(01)00125-8

NATURAL RESOURCES, SUSTAINABLE ENTREPRENEURSHIP ... 123

Schaltegger, S. (2002). A framework for ecopreneurship. *Greener Management International*, *2002*(38), 45–58. https://doi.org/10.9774/GLEAF. 3062.2002.su.00006

Schaltegger, S., & Wagner, M. (2011). Sustainable entrepreneurship and sustainability innovation: Categories and interactions. *Business Strategy and the Environment*, *20*(4), 222–237. https://doi.org/10.1002/bse.682

Seo, M.-G., & Creed, W. E. D. (2002). Institutional contradictions, praxis, and institutional change: A dialectical perspective. *Academy of Management Review*, *27*(2), 222–247. https://doi.org/10.5465/amr.2002.6588004

Si, S., Ahlstrom, D., Wei, J., & Cullen, J. (2020). Business, entrepreneurship and innovation toward poverty reduction. *Entrepreneurship & Regional Development*, *32*(1–2), 1–20. https://doi.org/10.1080/08985626.2019.164 0485

Siegle, J. (2005). Governance strategies to remedy the natural resource curse. *International Social Science Journal*, *57*, 45–55. https://doi.org/10.1111/j. 1468-2451.2009.00705.x

Silajdžić, I., Kurtagić, S. M., & Vučijak, B. (2015). Green entrepreneurship in transition economies: A case study of Bosnia and Herzegovina. *Journal of Cleaner Production*, *88*, 376–384. https://doi.org/10.1016/j.jclepro.2014. 07.004

Singh, J., & Dutt, P. (2019). Microfinance and entrepreneurship at the base of the pyramid. *Academy of Management Proceedings*, *2019*(1), 1–6. https:// doi.org/10.5465/AMBPP.2019.64

Spigel, B., & Harrison, R. (2018). Toward a process theory of entrepreneurial ecosystems. *Strategic Entrepreneurship Journal*, *12*(1), 151–168. https://doi. org/10.1002/sej.1268

Stenholm, P., Acs, Z. J., & Wuebker, R. (2013). Exploring country-level institutional arrangements on the rate and type of entrepreneurial activity. *Journal of Business Venturing*, *28*(1), 176–193. https://doi.org/10.1016/j.jbusvent. 2011.11.002

Sutter, C. J., Bruton, G. D., & Chen, J. (2019). Entrepreneurship as a solution to extreme poverty: A review and future research directions. *Journal of Business Venturing*, *34*(1), 197–214. https://doi.org/10.1016/j.jbusvent.2018. 06.003

Sutter, C. J., Kistruck, G. M., & Morris, S. (2014). Adaptations to knowledge Templates in base-of-the-pyramid markets: The role of social interaction. *Strategic Entrepreneurship Journal*, *8*(4), 303–320. https://doi.org/10. 1002/sej.1186

Szerb, L., Lafuente, E., Horváth, K., & Páger, B. (2019). The relevance of quantity and quality entrepreneurship for regional performance: The moderating role of the entrepreneurial ecosystem. *Regional Studies*, *53*(9), 1308–1320. https://doi.org/10.1080/00343404.2018.1510481

124   D. O. OLAGBOYE ET AL.

Tina Dacin, M., Goodstein, J., & Richard Scott, W. (2002). Institutional theory and institutional change: Introduction to the special research forum. *Academy of Management Journal, 45*(1), 45–56. https://doi.org/10.5465/amj.2002.6283388

UNCTAD. (2006). *United Nations Conference on Trade and Development Trade and Development Report, 2006.* United Nations Publications. https://unctad.org/en/docs/tdr2006_en.pdf

van Stel, A., Lyalkov, S., Millán, A., & Millán, J. M. (2019). The moderating role of IPR on the relationship between country-level R&D and individual-level entrepreneurial performance. *The Journal of Technology Transfer, 44*(5), 1427–1450. https://doi.org/10.1007/s10961-019-09731-2

Watkins, A., & Ehst, M. (Eds.). (2008). *Science, technology, and innovation.* The World Bank. https://doi.org/10.1596/978-0-8213-7380-4

WCED. (1987). *Our common future.* Oxford University Press. http://www.un-documents.net/wced-ocf.htm

Webb, J. W., Bruton, G. D., Tihanyi, L., & Ireland, R. D. (2013). Research on entrepreneurship in the informal economy: Framing a research agenda. *Journal of Business Venturing, 28*(5), 598–614. https://doi.org/10.1016/j.jbusvent.2012.05.003

Wheeler, D., Mckague, K., Thomson, J., Davies, R., Medalye, J., & Prada, M. (2005). Creating sustainable local enterprise networks. *MIT Sloan Management Review, 47*(1), 32–41.

Williams, A. (2011). Shining a light on the resource curse: An empirical analysis of the relationship between natural resources, transparency, and economic growth. *World Development, 39*(4), 490–505. https://doi.org/10.1016/j.worlddev.2010.08.015

Williams, C. C., & Shahid, M. S. (2016). Informal entrepreneurship and institutional theory: Explaining the varying degrees of (in)formalization of entrepreneurs in Pakistan. *Entrepreneurship & Regional Development, 28*(1–2), 1–25. https://doi.org/10.1080/08985626.2014.963889

Williams, N., & Vorley, T. (2015). Institutional asymmetry: How formal and informal institutions affect entrepreneurship in Bulgaria. *International Small Business Journal: Researching Entrepreneurship, 33*(8), 840–861. https://doi.org/10.1177/0266242614534280

Institutions and Sustainability

Institutional Pressures, Firm Resource Context and SMEs' Sustainability in Africa

Kassa Woldesenbet Beta and *Olapeju Ogunmokun*

1 INTRODUCTION

Sustainability is defined as "development that meets the needs of the present without compromising the ability of future generations to meet their own needs" (World Commission on Environment and Development, 1987). While general awareness on the issue of sustainability has greatly increased, larger businesses have been the focus of research attention when discussing sustainability practices; policies, regulations and incentives thus are directed to them with little consideration given to small and medium enterprises (SMEs) (Masocha & Fatoki, 2018). SMEs, on the other hand, were seen as not proactively practising sustainability (Becherer & Helms, 2014; Eweje, 2020; Higgs & Hill, 2019), thus, making the sustainability practises of SMEs to remain largely unexplored in the literature. It is argued that while the impact of larger enterprises on the environment appears to be more visible, and thus easier

---

K. W. Beta (✉) · O. Ogunmokun
Leicester Castle Business School, De Monfort University, Leicester, UK
e-mail: kwoldesenbet@dmu.ac.uk

O. Ogunmokun
e-mail: olapeju.ogunmokun@dmu.ac.uk

© The Author(s), under exclusive license to Springer Nature
Switzerland AG 2023
S. Adomako et al. (eds.), *Corporate Sustainability in Africa*,
Palgrave Studies in African Leadership,
https://doi.org/10.1007/978-3-031-29273-6_7

to measure, evaluate and held responsible for; SMEs' individual environmental impact is as minuscular as their smallness in size (Schaper, 2002). The United Nations Industrial Development Organization (UNIDO) estimates that SMEs represent more than 90% of enterprises globally, averagely contribute 60% to employment and about 50% to Gross Domestic Product (GDP) of all countries. Despite such remarkable contributions to all economies, SMEs collectively have significant impacts on environmental sustainability. As a sector, SMEs are reported as accounting for up to 70% of all industrial pollution (Hillary, 2004; Revell et al., 2009) and about 60% of all carbon dioxide emissions (Revell et al., 2009). These studies suggest that although SMEs have very little environmental impact individually, collectively their environmental impact is very significant and hence need research, policy, and practice attentions. Hence, this chapter aims to examine, based on the existing research knowledge, factors that enable and/or constrain SMEs behaviours towards sustainability practices and sustainable performance.

Existing studies used a range of perspectives such as institutional theory, resource-based view and stakeholder theory to examine the SMEs' commitment to environmental sustainability (Revell et al., 2009; Simpson et al., 2004). Studies that drew on the resource-based view reported that SMEs for lack of, or limited access to, resources and capabilities are found to often adopt convenient practices that enable them to compete in the market without real focus on sustainability (Famiola & Wulansari, 2020; Songling et al., 2018). Some limited studies have shown SMEs' heightened interest in environmental initiatives (Famiola & Wulansari, 2020) subject to resource and capabilities constraints (McKeiver & Gadenne, 2005; Shields & Shelleman, 2015). From the institutional perspective, it is argued that government can play a major role in being a driver or barrier to corporation's commitment to sustainable practices (Masurel, 2007); but less is known of the influence of government on SMEs adoption of sustainability practices and performance. In addition, plethora of studies examined how coercive, normative, and mimetic institutional forces influence the adoption of innovation, best practices, and systems by organisations. Institutional theory thus offers a valuable lens to understand the pressures that influence SMEs' adoption of sustainability practices (Campbell, 2007; Marquis et al., 2007).

This chapter seeks to advance theoretically and empirically driven propositions drawing on the resource-based view and institutional theory guided by these three questions. (1) How does the resource context of the SMEs influence the types of sustainability practices? (2) How do sustainability-oriented practices affect SMEs' sustainability performance? (3) In what ways do the coercive, normative, and mimetic institutional pressures influence SMEs' sustainability practices. By addressing these questions the chapter makes three contributions. First, it contributes to furthering our understanding of how internal and external factors influence SMEs' adoption of environmental sustainability practices and their effect on sustainability performance (economic, environmental, and social). Second, the chapter develops a theoretical framework that guides further research on the link between institutional forces, firm resource context, mediating factors and SMEs' sustainability performance in Africa.

The rest of the chapter is organised as follows. Section two provides an overview of small- and medium-scale enterprises in Africa drawing on the available sources. Section three develops theoretical and empirically driven propositions that guide future research drawing on the resource-based view, institutional theory, and related literatures. Using the conceptual framework developed from the propositions, the last section discusses the significance of the chapter for future research, practice and policy as well as makes concluding remarks.

2   Small and Medium Enterprises in Africa

In Africa, SMEs provide an estimated 80 percent of jobs across the continent and contribute to economic growth. Sub-Saharan Africa alone has 44 million micro, small, and medium enterprises, of which the majority are classified as micro enterprises (Runde et al., 2021). *In Nigeria for example,* SMEs account for about 98% of all enterprises and employ over 60% of labour force (Iorun, 2014; Kadiri, 2012) and contribute to wealth creation, income generation, poverty reduction, and creation of employment amongst others (Aruwa, 2005; Nnanna, 2001). The new job creation by SMEs in Sub-Saharan African countries have been remarkable. Small enterprises in Kenya, Zambia, Ivory Coast, South Africa, and Cameroon account for 38%, 37%, 33%, 21% and 19% of the new jobs created, respectively (World Bank, 2018). As of December 2017, Nigerian small enterprises created about 3 million jobs (National Bureau of Statistic, 2019).

However, SMEs in Nigeria as well as in other developing economies face serious challenges that limit their potential contributions to economic growth, diversification, and employment as well as to their performance, and sustainability (Ayyagari et al., 2012; Ogunmokun et al., 2022). For instance, SMEs' contribution to Nigeria's GDP has been lower than compared to 40% in Asia, 50% in Europe and US (Eniola, 2014; Okpara, 2011). Existing studies provide evidence that shows worldwide, up to 50% of SMEs fail within the first five years of existence and one-third survive within the first ten years of establishment (Soto-Simeone et al., 2020). The SMEs failure rate experienced in African countries is even more alarming as studies show that five in seven SMEs start-ups fail in their first year (Arinaitwe, 2006), in Uganda—one-third of start-ups fail, in South Africa—50–95% of start-up failure is experienced, in Chad—65% and in Nigeria 80% of business failure is recorded within the first 5 years of establishment (News, 2013; Vanguard Muriithi, 2017). Many reasons may account for such failures including resource scarcity, underdeveloped management and leadership skills, and business environment challenges. It is in such context that we seek to examine the factors that drive or constrain SMEs' adoption of sustainability practices in order to contribute to ongoing debates in this area as existing research findings are inconclusive on the nature of relationship between various aspects of the firm, its adoption of sustainability practices and sustainability performance.

Despite facing challenges of smallness in size and resources constraints, SMEs can be considered as flexible, adaptable and sources of entrepreneurial activities. SMEs can be testbeds for innovation, bringing new products and services that can be scaled up to larger organisations and industry. They engage in innovative activities in unique ways; can tap into technological advances to initiate innovative mechanisms for efficient and effective production and sale of their goods and services (Porter & Kramer, 2019). SMEs could also respond to environmental uncertainties by exploring market opportunities, developing new products, and looking for new market openings for survival and improved performance (Dosi, 1988).

In Africa, however, less attention was given by scholars to study the drivers and practices that enhance SMEs' competitive capabilities and sustainable performance (Aboelmaged, 2018). One of the key questions for the management of SMEs could be how they can optimally use their available scarce resources, compete successfully, and achieve sustainability. Studies such as Günerergin et al. (2012) demonstrate that SMEs that embody sustainability strategies are becoming innovative and more capable of overcoming challenges. Numerous other studies (see for example, Welford & Gouldson, 1993; Welford, 1996) highlight the benefits of sustainability to include increased control of supply chain, increased staff commitment, improved competitiveness, materials efficiency, lower insurance premiums and cheaper finance.

3 Resource Context and Institutional Pressure—Developing Propositions

Resource-Based View and SMEs' Sustainability

Scholars use resource-based view to verify whether small firms can adopt business strategies that enable gaining competitive opportunities from the natural environment using available resources and capabilities. Reyes-Rodríguez et al. (2016) and Leonidou et al. (2017) stated that firms that use such strategies can achieve remarkable positional competitive advantages that, in turn, improve business, market, and financial performance. On the other hand, Halme and Korpela (2014) identified a combination of resources such as equity, research and development cooperation, networks, industry knowledge, and reputation as enabling responsible innovation by SMEs. Bocquet et al. (2017), for example, argued that investment in R&D can help in achieving product and process innovations and CSR activities. Within the scope of this chapter, RBV can provide an explanation for the interplay between the adoption of sustainability practices and internal strength and weaknesses of the organisation (Shibin et al., 2020). RBV states that harnessing external opportunities or fulfilling external requirements is only feasible by deploying existing unique resources within the organisation; this is because internal resources are more easily controlled than external threats or opportunities (Grant, 1991) and the decisions of the organisation is shaped by its economic context (Oliver, 1997). As Glover et al. (2014) argues, RBV could be the best base for conceptualising sustainability adoption by organisations. This subsection identifies the kinds of resources and capabilities SMEs in Africa and in other emerging regions need for achieving economic and noneconomic sustainability. Through the review of existing empirical literatures, the chapter identified socially oriented innovation, lean manufacturing, greening, owner/employee's awareness, knowledge and skills as well as financial resources as strategic resources and capabilities to drive sustainability practices and sustainability performance.

Sustainability-Oriented Innovation

Innovation leads to gaining firms' competitive advantage and performance. Existing literature suggests eco-innovativeness of SMEs plays a significant role in improving efficiency, mitigating risk, increasing firms' bottom lines such as revenue and profit, enhancing reputation and brand value as well as in attracting talents and developing innovative capabilities (Klewitz et al., 2012). Successful innovation activities help SMEs to establish a competitive position in the market, enhance their competitive advantage and, consequently, improve business performance (Marques & Ferreira, 2009). In this chapter, we focus on sustainability-oriented innovation because of its significance for achieving multiple benefits concurrently such as economic, environment and social outcomes. Three types of innovations- product, process and organisational can lead to sustainability-oriented innovation (Klewitz & Hansen, 2014). Sustainability-oriented innovation may take the form of eco-design, green supply chain management and organisational strategy (Dey et al., 2020) and responds to the 'triple-bottom line' by integrating social dimension of innovation with its outcomes (Adams et al., 2016). Eco-design involves producing products efficiently with the use of less resources that can be reused, recycled and recovered; and that can reduce carbon emissions (Dey et al., 2020). Using process innovation such as cleaner production can help firms to implement new or improved production or delivery methods for environmental sustainability (Adams et al., 2016). Hence, we propose:

Proposition 1a: SMEs adoption of sustainability-oriented innovation improves their economic performance.

Proposition 1b: SMEs involvement in sustainability- oriented innovation improves their environmental sustainability performance.

Proposition 1c: SMEs involvement in sustainability- oriented innovation improves their social performance.

Socially Oriented Practices of SMEs

Small and medium enterprises' socially oriented activities tend to be limited and localised given their size and resources constraint. SMEs thus are more likely to engage in CSR initiatives with local impact that help build good image in the local community in a bid to improve their businesses simultaneously. For instance, Burlea-Schiopoiu and Mihai (2019) opined that by developing a sustainable image, firms could achieve a number of benefits including good relationship with various stakeholders, productive alliances and partnership, staff retention, and expansion into new markets, which combined, can increase firms' profitability in the long run. Research also highlighted that SMEs owners' social orientation can influence CSR initiatives and practices (Hemingway, 2005) and that their integrity and ethical practices lead to gaining competitive advantage (Avram & Kühne, 2008). In contrast, other studies documented the fact that SMEs focus on operational tasks, less connected from the general business environment, and reactive to issues that need immediate attention (Spence, 1999); they view CSR as a risky activity with uncertain financial returns (Akben-Selcuk, 2019) and less likely to commit significant money for socially oriented activities (Lee et al., 2016). Hence, we advance the following propositions.

Proposition 2a: SMEs' socially-oriented practices strengthens the relationship between their good image and various performance outcomes.

Proposition 2b: There is a negative relationship between the perceived uncertain financial returns on CSR programmes and SMEs' engagement in CSR activities.

Resources, Environmental Sustainability Practices and SMEs' Sustainability Performance

SMEs' environmental sustainability practices may involve minimising the consumption of resources (raw materials, water, and energy), protecting biodiversity, reducing emissions, residual materials, and minimising the environmental impact of products. Lean manufacturing practice (LMP) is the case in point as it is associated with enabling sustainability performance (economic, environmental, and social sustainability) as well as greening the business. Most often, lean manufacturing practice is considered as a strategic capability for achieving economic performance of the SMEs (Dey et al., 2020) but the recent literature evidence its role also in environmental and social sustainability. These practices aim to achieve cost reduction through 'resource efficiency, waste reduction and productivity enhancement' (Dey et al., 2020; Martínez-Jurado & Moyano-Fuentes,

2014). Environmental sustainability practices of SMEs most often are linked with the utilisation of proficient and cleaner sustainable resources to produce energy in order to reduce carbon dioxide emissions during the operational process (Ghazilla et al., 2015). The existing empirical evidence indicates positive relationship between firms' environmental performance and its market value, market performance and financial performance (Halati & He, 2018). SMEs that implement energy-efficient operating systems, for instance, achieve lean and the desired environmental and social targets that enable achieving overall firm sustainability (Viesi et al., 2017). GreenCare Rwanda, for instance, has been providing sustainable solutions for solid waste management by converting landfills into recycling plants to promote the circular economy, protect the environment, and create green jobs for young men and women.

Some literatures argue that SMEs' adoption of environmental sustainability practices increases their total cost of operation with no commensurate economic benefits and this additional cost is often difficult to transfer to consumers in the form of price increase because of low disposable income of consumers in developing countries like Nigeria (Idoko et al., 2013; Simpson et al., 2004). Some studies show that owners and managers of SMEs believe that adopting environmental practices results in incurring more cost than savings (Purvis et al., 2017; Revell et al., 2009). This reluctance might be due to the potential financial benefits for SMEs adopting resource efficiency strategies maybe quite small and possibly realised easily using means other than environmental practices (Purvis et al., 2017). Thus, SMEs are reported as less likely to adopt high-cost intensive environmental and social sustainability practices such as CSR projects and investment in energy-saving technologies. Such attitudes and behaviours are more likely to be observed in SMEs in Africa because they lack adequate knowledge of environmental management (Musa & Chinniah, 2016). Loucks et al. (2010), for example, reported that most SMEs were unable to assess their negative impact on the environment because of insufficient resources such as finance and skilled labour. Likewise, Journeault et al. (2021) stated that SMEs grapple to incorporate social and environmental concerns into their business practices due to 'a limited awareness of the impacts and benefits associated with sustainability, a lack of time and resources, and a lack of skills and expertise'. SMEs are also less likely to provide formal training and development for their employees because of financial resource constraint and, perceiving training as costly and expensive and the loss of productivity while the employees attend the training (Westhead & Storey, 1996). Consequently, the possibilities of SMEs being involved in activities that are environmentally friendly and socially oriented could be very low. Firm size matters when it comes to going green and adoption of environment-friendly lean management practices. Based on the foregoing analysis, we propose that:

Proposition 3a: Application of lean manufacturing practices contribute to SMEs' sustainability performance.

Proposition 3b: Environmental sustainability practices are positively related with SMEs' sustainability performance.

Proposition 3c: SMEs engagement in environmental and social sustainability practices are subject to them having appropriate resources and capabilities such as financial, skills and expertise.

SMEs Owners' Awareness and Values About Environmental and Social Issues

In recent years, various studies have shown that SMEs are interested in implementing environmental sustainability practices as they become aware of their business impact on the environment. However, their knowledge of specific environmental regulations, formal environmental management systems and the environmental impact of their production activities is generally very limited (Chendo, 2013; Higgs & Hill, 2019; Saka et al., 2020). Unlike in developed countries where existing studies documented increasing adoption of sustainability practices as a result of high levels of awareness, in Nigeria, many SMEs fail to engage with environmental sustainability practices due to lack of awareness, lack of resources and technical know-how (Saka et al., 2020).

In the context of Philippines, Roxas and Chadee (2012) reported that SMEs' environmental sustainability orientation is driven by the owners' awareness of the importance of environmental sustainability. The SMEs owners' consciousness for community and environment (Moyeen & Courvisanos, 2012) and owners' values (Lee et al., 2012) influenced the adoption of CSR activities in Australia and Singapore, respectively. Sancho et al. (2018) established a positive relationship between socially responsible human resource management and competitive performance as well as employees' commitment and relational marketing. Sustainability concerns drove SMEs to implement employee retention initiative in Bangladesh

136   K. W. BETA AND O. OGUNMOKUN

(Huq et al., 2014) and provision of better working conditions in Morocco (El Baz et al., 2016). SMEs in Africa, as it is elsewhere, can demonstrate their social aspects of sustainability through the implementation and standardisation of health and safety policies and practices, building long-term relationships with customers and providing training to employees. They also need to consider donations and charities to the community, social causes, and other philanthropic activities to enhance their image and ethos for social sustainability. Thus, we propose:

> *Proposition 4a*: Social and environmental issues awareness of SMEs' owners influence their environmental and social sustainability performance.
>
> *Proposition 4b*: Positive relationship exist between SMEs' socially responsible employment practices and their economic and social performance.

Institutional Pressures and SMEs' Sustainability

Traditionally, institutional theory is concerned with organisations' conformance to rules, norms, and practices of the environment, as these pressures influence the decision-making and strategies adopted by organisations. We used this theory to explore how institutional pressures influence SMEs' decision and behaviour towards environmentally and socially sustainable practices. The institutional theory perspective helps to explain the motivation behind firm's adoption of policies, practices and procedures (DiMaggio & Powell, 1983) and their responses to external pressures (Grewal & Dharwadkar, 2002) that are beyond economic rationalisation (Oliver, 1997). The institutional theory suggests that firm's actions are defined by predominant social factors within their operating environment which pressurises them to be compliant or to conform in order to gain some form of legitimacy or approval (Famiyeh & Kwarteng, 2018; Oliver, 1997). Thus, the decision to implement sustainability practices is driven by social and institutional contexts of the organisations. The internal and external stakeholders' pressures and expectations define acceptable organisational practices that become homogenised overtime across the organisations within a given environment (DiMaggio & Powell, 1983; Oliver, 1997) and this homogenisation is labelled as institutional isomorphism (DiMaggio & Powell, 1983). According to DiMaggio and

Powell (1983), institutional isomorphism which brings about conformity amongst firms is achieved through coercive, normative and mimetic pressures. Existing studies highlight coercive, normative and mimetic institutional forces to drive firms' to implement sustainability strategies (Christmann, 2000; Delmas, 2003; Famiyeh & Kwarteng, 2018). These pressures come from firm's key stakeholders such as regulatory bodies, competitors, customers, employees, government, policy makers, etc., that impose various pressures on organisations to adopt sustainability practices (Famiyeh & Kwarteng, 2018), and creates expectations that determine appropriate responses and behaviour of organisations (Meyer & Rowan, 1977). We use these three forms of institutional pressures—coercive, normative, and mimetic—to advance propositions on SMEs' sustainability.

Coercive Pressures and SME's Adoption of Sustainability Practices
The regulatory institutions such as laws, sanctions, government rules and regulations coerce organisation for compliance (Famiola & Wulansari, 2020); these pressures are argued to be crucial in driving sustainability practices in organisations (Glover et al., 2014). Scholars such as Zhu and Sarkis (2006), Masocha and Fatoki (2018), and Shibin et al. (2020) all argue that coercive pressures in the form of government rules, sanctions, regulations significantly influence firms' adoption of sustainability practices. The coercive institutional perspective describes pressure on organisation that is exerted by other organisations that they depend on, they are usually cultural or societal expectations. It stems from political influences or government pressures that emphasise firm conformance to the established regulations or laws and which result in punishment for non-conformance and reward for compliance (DiMaggio & Powell, 1983). So, firms are compelled or pressurised to comply with rules and regulations prescribed by the government; the failure to comply or avoidance is subject to punishment (Grewal & Dharwadkar, 2002).

Many studies showed that government rules and regulations drive companies to adopt sustainable practices, as evidenced by European and US firms (Delmas, 2002), Spanish companies (Heras-Saizarbitoria et al., 2011), small and medium enterprises (Williamson et al., 2006) in New Zealand (Dodds et al., 2013) and the manufacturing firms in Malaysia (Zailani et al., 2012). In Malaysia, Hsu et al. (2013) found that government pressure significantly influenced manufacturers to practise environmental sustainability. Williamson et al. (2006), based on the

31 manufacturing small and medium enterprises (SMEs), found that the main driver of environmental sustainability practices amongst SMEs is regulatory requirements.

In Nigeria, many environmental legislations exist. Of these, the National Policy on the Environment (NPE) in 1989, and Environmental Impact Assessment (EIA) introduced by the apex regulatory body Federal Environmental Protection Agency (FEPA) can be considered key environmental policies. Despite regulatory pressures to adopt sustainability practices in some industries have increased, their influence on SMEs adoption of such practices remains controversial. Chendo (2013), for example, showed that NAFAC (National Agency for Food and Drug Administration Control) declaration of a 'gradual' nationwide ban on sachet water as it creates environmental nuisance and hence to change it to bottle packaging was not effectively materialised. In contrast, Saka et al. (2020) reported that firms in construction industry complied to and implemented stipulated government sustainability practices. On the other hand, Idoko et al. (2013) provide evidence that shows the absence of regulatory oversight and laws in Enugu state, Nigeria, as a barrier to SMEs' adoption of environmental sustainability. SMEs were found to adopt unsustainable environmental behaviours as there were no regulatory implications. In the absence of regulatory sustainability requirements, however, organisations tend to be driven by their financial objectives (Glover et al., 2014). Dainty et al. (2017) also suggest that government pressure could have negative impact on SMEs. Hence, we propose:

Proposition 5a: Coercive institutional pressures influence SMEs' adoption of sustainability practices.

Proposition 5b: Relationship exists between the enforcement capacity of regulatory institutions and SMEs' compliance with environmental sustainability practices.

Proposition 5c: Government regulatory pressure has a positive/negative influence on SMEs adoption of environmental sustainability practices.

INSTITUTIONAL PRESSURES, FIRM RESOURCE CONTEXT ... 139

Normative Pressures and SME's Adoption of Sustainability Practices
The normative institutional perspective describes pressure on organisation that stems from adherence to professional codes and conducts. Professionalisation is defined as the collective effort of members of an occupation to establish the processes, conditions of work and to determine the cognitive legitimacy for their occupational autonomy (DiMaggio & Powell, 1983) such as certification, accreditation, etc. Firms are expected to follow the specific guidelines that are aligned with their occupation, professional communities, educational bodies, etc., due to social legitimacy. We argue that SMEs are likely to have health and safety policies, adopt environmental management tools, quality assurance and embrace values and norms that fit cultural, community and professional expectations. Thus, we propose:

Proposition 6: *Normative institutional pressures influence SMEs to implement sustainability practices.*

Mimetic Pressures and SME's Adoption of Sustainability Practices
The mimetic institutional perspective describes pressure on organisation to mimic practices adopted by other organisations especially when in an uncertain situation or faced with problems that are ambiguous (DiMaggio & Powell, 1983). Uncertainties within an organisational procedure or environment pressures an organisation to model their practices after those adopted by other successful firms where those practices have worked competitively towards key stakeholders like customers, suppliers, government, etc. (Famiyeh & Kwarteng, 2018). Organisations in attempt not to cause dissatisfaction to their stakeholders or put their organisation reputation at risk, mimic the actions of other competitive organisations in their social network. Yang (2016) within the Taiwan Maritime power industry found that firms model their environmental practices after the practice of their competitors who are successful to enhance their firm's reputation as well. Chu et al. (2017) also found that mimetic pressure significantly impacts on top managers' performance and effects their adoption of green supply chain management. Hence, we propose:

Proposition 7: Mimetic institutional pressures influence SMEs adoption of sustainability practices.

4 Discussion and Conclusions

We integrated both the resource-based view and institutional theory in a unique way to understand the internal (firm-context) and the external (institutional context) factors that drive SMEs' adoption of sustainability-oriented practices and their sustainability performance. Based on the review of relevant theoretical, empirical, and contextual literature, we advanced several propositions that help further scholarly understanding and guide future research. These propositions can be summarised by the conceptual framework shown below (Fig. 1). The conceptual framework allows: (1) the examination of the relationship between firm resources such as financial, expertise and skills, innovative capabilities, R&D, etc., and the SMEs' engagement in environmental and social sustainability practices, sustainability-oriented innovation, and lean manufacturing practices; (2) exploring how various institutional pressures such as coercive, normative, and mimetic influence the adoption of environmental and social sustainability practices and sustainability-oriented innovation as well as lean manufacturing practices; and, (3) studying a vital role of SMEs owners' awareness of the environmental and social impacts of their business operation and the need to engage in sustainability-oriented innovation, LMP and social sustainability practices. In addition, the conceptual framework establishes connections between the SMEs sustainability-oriented innovation, LMP and sustainability practices and the SMEs' sustainability performance (economic, environmental, and social performance). In essence, the conceptual framework makes the case that, the internal and external factors influence on SMEs sustainability performance in Africa and elsewhere can be much improved/strengthened if they are able to use sustainability-oriented innovations, LMPs, and environmental and social sustainability practices, combined.

The conceptual framework and associated propositions raise many pragmatic challenges to SMEs, policymakers, regulatory institutions, and stakeholders. In the context of Africa, many countries' formal institutional capacity is severely limited; the frameworks that allow access to support services for developing SMEs' awareness of their business impact on environment and society is limited; and high-level trade-offs exist between investing in sustainability practices and financial or short-term performance of SMEs. Conversely, Africa has seen thriving digital transformation, greening the business has seen an increasing attraction and

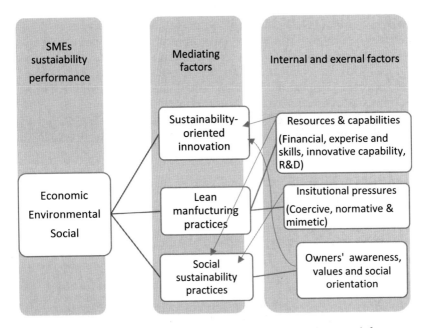

Fig. 1 Conceptual framework on the role of internal and external factors on SMEs sustainability practice and performance

successful case studies exist that show SMEs engaging in greening business, recycling, and caring for the community and the environment. In the presence of supportive institutional environment and availability of internal resources and capabilities, this chapter argues that SMEs in Africa are destined to make a difference in adopting sustainability practices that result in firm economic, environmental, and social performance. The conceptual framework in this chapter contributes to existing research knowledge by showing the fact that SMEs' responses to institutional pressures to conform to sustainability practices and performance are determined by their resource context (Famiola & Wulansari, 2020; Gholami et al., 2013; Shibin et al., 2020). SMEs can be compelled to implement regulatory requirements (Idoko et al., 2013; Saka et al., 2020) in view of sustaining the environment and social context in which they operate but such requirements need to take into account the SMEs' resources and capabilities base (Revell et al., 2009) and their access to relevant information and support services that motivate them to engage in sustainability practices. Regulators and policymakers thus have a role to play in ensuring regulatory oversight over SMEs' environmental sustainability through developing policy initiatives that fit the characteristics and the context of SMEs. Two main conclusions are in order. First, SMEs' contributions to employment, innovation, GDP and sustainable development could be much improved if they engage in sustainable-oriented innovative activities, adopt lean manufacturing practices (as it fits their business context) and implement environmental and social sustainability practices that fit to their operating environment. Second, whilst the institutional environment pressures can drive the SMEs' adoption of sustainability practices, it is the firm's resources and capabilities base that significantly determine their implementation in practice.

REFERENCES

Aboelmaged, M. (2018). The drivers of sustainable manufacturing practices in Egyptian SMEs and their impact on competitive capabilities: A PLS-SEM model. *Journal of Cleaner Production, 175*, 207–221.

Adams, R., et al. (2016). Sustainability-oriented innovation: A systematic review. *International Journal of Management Reviews, 18*(2), 180–205.

Akben-Selcuk, E. (2019). Corporate social responsibility and financial performance: The moderating role of ownership concentration in Turkey. *Sustainability, 11*(13), 3643.

Arinaitwe, S. K. (2006). Factors constraining the growth and survival of small scale businesses. A developing countries analysis. *Journal of American Academy of Business, 8*(2), 167–178.

Aruwa, S. (2005). Empirical evaluation of performance of small and medium industries equity investment scheme. *Nigerian Journal of Accounting Research, 3*(1), 110.

Avram, D. O., & Kühne, S. (2008). Implementing responsible business behavior from a strategic management perspective: Developing a framework for Austrian SMEs. *Journal of Business Ethics, 82*(2), 463–475.

Ayyagari, M., Demirguc-Kunt, A., & Maksimovic, V. (2012) *Financing of firms in developing countries lessons from research* (Policy Research Working Paper 6036). Accessed from https://openknowledge.worldbank.org/bitstream/han dle/10986/6038/WPS6036.pdf

Becherer, R., & Helms, M. (2014). Green goals in organizations: Do small businesses engage in environmentally friendly strategies? *Journal of Small Business Strategy, 24*(1), 1–18.

Bocquet, R., et al. (2017). CSR, innovation, and firm performance in sluggish growth contexts: A firm-level empirical analysis. *Journal of Business Ethics, 146*(1), 241–254.

Burlea-Schiopoiu, A., & Mihai, L. S. (2019). An integrated framework on the sustainability of SMEs. *Sustainability, 11*(21), 6026.

Campbell, J. L. (2007). Why would corporations behave in socially responsible ways? An institutional theory of corporate social responsibility. *Academy of Management Review, 32*(3), 946–967.

Chen, A., Watson, R. T., Boudreau, M. C., & Karahanna, E. (2011). An institutional perspective on the adoption of Green IS & IT. *Australasian Journal of Information Systems, 17*(1).

Chendo, N. (2013). Manager's perception of environmental sustainability in small and medium scale enterprises (SMEs): Implication for competitive marketing advantages for sachet water manufacturers in Anambra state, Nigeria. *European Journal of Business and Management, 5*(7), 186–195.

Christmann, P. (2000). Effects of "best practices" of environmental management on cost advantage: The role of complementary assets. *Academy of Management Journal, 43*(4), 663–680.

Chu, S., et al. (2017). The impact of institutional pressures on green supply chain management and firm performance: Top management roles and social capital. *Sustainability, 9*(5), 764.

Dainty, A., Leiringer, R., Fernie, S., & Harty, C. et al. (2017). BIM and the small construction firm: A critical perspective. *Building Research and Information, 45*(6), 696–709.

Delmas, M. (2002). The diffusion of environmental management standards in Europe and in the United States: An institutional perspective. *Policy Sciences, 35*(1), 91–119.

Delmas, M. (2003) *In search of ISO: An institutional perspective on the adoption of international management standards.* Available at: https://papers.ssrn.com/sol3/papers.cfm?abstract_id=379800. Accessed 3 December 2022.

Dey, P. K., Malesios, C., De, D., Chowdhury, S., & Abdelaziz, F. B. (2020). The impact of lean management practices and sustainably-oriented innovation on sustainability performance of small and medium-sized enterprises: empirical evidence from the UK. *British Journal of Management, 31*(1), 141–161.

DiMaggio, P., & Powell, W. (1983). The iron cage revisited: Institutional isomorphism and collective rationality in organizational fields. *American Sociological Review*, 147–160.

Dodds, R., et al. (2013). What drives environmental sustainability in the New Zealand wine industry?: An examination of driving factors and practices. *International Journal of Wine Business Research, 25*(3), 164–184.

Dosi, G. (1988). Sources, procedures, and microeconomic effects of innovation. *Journal of Economic Literature*, 1120–1171.

El Baz, J., et al. (2016). on the corporate social responsibility practices of small- and medium-sized enterprises in the food-processing industry: Differences between France and Morocco. *Journal of Business Ethics, 134*(1), 117–133.

Eniola, A. (2014). The role of SME firm performance in Nigeria. *Oman Chapter of Arabian Journal of Business and Management Review, 3*(12), 1–15.

Eweje, G. (2020). Proactive environmental and social strategies in a small-to medium-sized company: A case study of a Japanese SME. *Business Strategy and the Environment, 29*(7), 2927–2938.

Famiola, M., & Wulansari, A. (2020). SMEs' social and environmental initiatives in Indonesia: An institutional and resource-based analysis. *Social Responsibility Journal, 16*(1), 15–27.

Famiyeh, S., & Kwarteng, A. (2018). Implementation of environmental management practices in the Ghanaian mining and manufacturing supply chains. *International Journal of Productivity and Performance Management, 67*(7), 1091–1112.

Gbandi, E., & Amissah, G. (2014). Financing options for small and medium enterprises (SMEs) in Nigeria. *European Scientific Journal January.* Available at: https://papers.ssrn.com/sol3/papers.cfm?abstract_id=3868198. Accessed 20 September 2022.

Ghazilla, R. A. R., et al. (2015). Drivers and barriers analysis for green manufacturing practices in Malaysian SMEs: A preliminary findings. *Procedia Cirp, 26*, 658–663.

Gholami, R., et al. (2013). Senior managers' perception on green information systems (IS) adoption and environmental performance: Results from a field survey. *Information & Management, 50*(7), 431–438.

Gibbons, P. T., & O'Connor, T. (2005). Influences on strategic planning processes among irish SMEs. *Journal of Small Business Management, 43*(2), 170–186.

Glover, J., et al. (2014). An Institutional Theory perspective on sustainable practices across the dairy supply chain. *International Journal of Production Economics, 152*, 102–111.

Grant, R. (1991). The resource-based theory of competitive advantage: Implications for strategy formulation. *California Management Review, 33*(3), 114–135.

Grewal, R., & Dharwadkar, R. (2002). The role of the institutional environment in marketing channels. *Journal of Marketing, 66*(3), 82–97.

Günergin, M., Penbek, Ş, & Zaptçıoğlu, D. (2012). Exploring the problems and advantages of Turkish SMEs for sustainability. *Procedia - Social and Behavioral Sciences, 58*, 244–251.

Halati, A., & He, Y. (2018). Intersection of economic and environmental goals of sustainable development initiatives. *Journal of Cleaner Production, 189*, 813–829.

INSTITUTIONAL PRESSURES, FIRM RESOURCE CONTEXT ... 145

Halme, M., & Korpela, M. (2014). Responsible innovation toward sustainable development in small and medium-sized enterprises: A resource perspective. *Business Strategy and the Environment, 23*(8), 547–566.

Hemingway, C. A. (2005). Personal values as a catalyst for corporate social entrepreneurship. *Journal of Business Ethics, 60*(3), 233–249. https://doi. org/10.1007/s10551-005-0132-5

Heras-Saizarbitoria, I., Landín, G. A., & Molina-Azorín, J. F. (2011). Do drivers matter for the benefits of ISO 14001? *International Journal of Operations and Production Management, 31*(2), 192–216.

Higgs, C. J., & Hill, T. (2019). The role that small and medium-sized enterprises play in sustainable development and the green economy in the waste sector, South Africa. *Business Strategy and Development, 2*(1), 25–31.

Hillary, R. (2004). Environmental management systems and the smaller enterprise. *Journal of cleaner production, 12*(6), 561–569.

Hsu, C. C., et al. (2013). Supply chain drivers that foster the development of green initiatives in an emerging economy. *International Journal of Operations and Production Management, 33*(6), 656–688.

Huq, F. A., Stevenson, M., & Zorzini, M. (2014). Social sustainability in developing country suppliers: An exploratory study in the ready made garments industry of Bangladesh. *International Journal of Operations and Production Management, 34*(5), 610–638. https://doi.org/10.1108/IJOPM-10-2012-0467/FULL/HTML

Idoko, E. C., Nkamnebe, A. D., & Amobi, D. S. C. (2013). Public policy and SMEs adoption of environmental sustainability orientation in Enugu, Nigeria. *African Journal of Business and Economic Research, 8*(1), 11–31.

Iorun, J. (2014). Evaluation of survival strategies of small and medium enterprises in Benue State, Nigeria. *International Journal of Academic Research in Accounting, Finance and Management Science, 4*(2), 259–267.

Journeault, M., Perron, A., & Vallières, L. (2021). The collaborative roles of stakeholders in supporting the adoption of sustainability in SMEs. *Journal of Environmental Management, 287*, 112349.

Kadiri, I. (2012). Small and medium scale enterprises and employment generation in Nigeria: The role of finance. *Kuwait Chapter of the Arabian Journal of Business and Management, 1*(9), 79.

Kilbourne, W., Beckmann, S., & Thelen, E. (2002). The role of the dominant social paradigm in environmental attitudes: A multinational examination. *Journal of Business Research, 55*(3), 193–204.

Klewitz, J., & Hansen, E. G. (2014). Sustainability-oriented innovation of SMEs: A systematic review. *Journal of Cleaner Production, 65*, 57–75.

Klewitz, J., Zeyen, A., & Hansen, E. G. (2012). Intermediaries driving eco-innovation in SMEs: A qualitative investigation. *European Journal of Innovation Management, 15*(4), 442–467.

Lamoureux, S. M., Scholar, F., & Lamoureux, S. M. (2019). The role of government support in SMEs' adoption of sustainability. *IEEE Engineering Management Review.* https://doi.org/10.1109/EMR.2019.2898635

Lee, K. H., Herold, D. M., & Yu, A. L. (2016). Small and medium enterprises and corporate social responsibility practice: A Swedish perspective. *Corporate Social Responsibility and Environmental Management, 23*(2), 88–99.

Lee, M. H., Mak, A. K., & Pang, A. (2012). Bridging the gap: An exploratory study of corporate social responsibility among SMEs in Singapore. *Journal of Public Relations Research, 24*(4), 299–317.

Leonidou, L. C., et al. (2017). Internal drivers and performance consequences of small firm green business strategy: The moderating role of external forces. *Journal of Business Ethics, 140*(3), 585–606.

Loucks, E. S., Martens, M. L., & Cho, C. H. (2010). Engaging small- and medium-sized businesses in sustainability. *Sustainability Accounting, Management and Policy Journal, 1*(2), 178–200.

Marques, C. S., & Ferreira, J. (2009). SME innovative capacity, competitive advantage and performance in a'traditional'industrial region of Portugal. *Journal of Technology Management & Innovation, 4*(4), 53–68.

Marquis, C., Glynn, M. A., & Davis, G. F. (2007). Community isomorphism and corporate social action. *Academy of Management Review, 32*(3), 925–945.

Martínez-Jurado, P. J., & Moyano-Fuentes, J. (2014). Lean management, supply chain management and sustainability: A literature review. *Journal of Cleaner Production, 85*, 134–150.

Masocha, R., & Fatoki, O. (2018). The impact of coercive pressures on sustainability practices of small businesses in South Africa. *Sustainability, 10*(9), 3032. https://doi.org/10.3390/su10093032

Masurel, E. (2007). Why SMEs invest in environmental measures: Sustainability evidence from small and medium-sized printing firms. *Business Strategy and the Environment, 16*(3), 190–201.

McKeiver, C., & Gadenne, D. (2005). Environmental management systems in small and medium businesses. *International Small Business Journal, 23*(5), 513–537.

Meyer, J. W., & Rowan, B. (1977). Institutionalized organizations: Formal structure as myth and ceremony. *American Journal of Sociology, 83*(2), 340–363.

Moyeen, A., & Courvisanos, J. (2012). Corporate social responsibility in regional small and medium-sized enterprises in Australia. *Australasian Journal of Regional, 18*(3), 364–391.

Muriithi, S. (2017). *African small and medium enterprises (SMEs) contributions, challenges and solutions.* Available at: http://repository.daystar.ac.ke/handle/123456789/3613. Accessed 20 September 2022.

Musa, H., & Chinniah, M. (2016). Malaysian SMEs development: future and challenges on going green. *Procedia-Social and Behavioral Sciences, 224,* 254–262. Available at: https://www.sciencedirect.com/science/article/pii/S1877042816305584. Accessed 14 January 2023.

National Bureau of Statistics Report. (2019). National survey of micro small & medium enterprises (MSMEs) 2017. Available at: https://nigerianstat.gov.ng/elibrary

Nnanna, O. J. (2001). Financial small-scale business under the new CBN directive and its likely impact on industrial growth of the Nigerian economy. *Bullion, 25*(3), 3.

Ogunmokun, O. C., Mafimisebi, O., & Obembe, D. (2022). Bank lending behaviour and small enterprise debt financing. *Journal of Entrepreneurship in Emerging Economies.* https://doi.org/10.1108/JEEE-02-2022-0043

Okpara, J. O. (2011). Factors constraining the growth and survival of SMEs in Nigeria: Implications for poverty alleviation. *Management Research Review, 34*(2), 156–171.

Oliver, C. (1997). Sustainable competitive advantage: Combining institutional and resource-based views. *Strategic Management Journal, 18*(9), 697–713.

Porter, M. E., & Kramer, M. R. (2019) *Creating shared value, managing sustainable business.* Springer. https://doi.org/10.1007/978-94-024-1144-7_16

Purvis, M., Drake, F., Hunt, J., & Millard, D. (2017). The manager, the business and the big wide world. In *The business of greening* (pp. 13–34). Routledge.

Revell, A., Stokes, D., & Chen, H. (2009). Small businesses and the environment: Turning over a new leaf? *Business Strategy and the Environment, 19*(5), 273–288.

Reyes-Rodríguez, J. F., Ulhøi, J. P., & Madsen, H. (2016). Corporate environmental sustainability in Danish SMEs: A longitudinal study of motivators, initiatives, and strategic effects. *Corporate Social Responsibility and Environmental Management, 23*(4), 193–212.

Roxas, B., & Chadee, D. (2012). Environmental sustainability orientation and financial resources of small manufacturing firms in the Philippines. *Social Responsibility Journal, 8*(2), 208–226.

Runde, D. F., Savoy, C. M., & Staguhn, J. (2021). Supporting small and medium enterprises in Sub-Saharan Africa through blended finance. Available at: https://www.csis.org/analysis/supporting-small-and-medium-enterprises-sub-saharan-africa-through-blended-finance. Accessed 5 June 2023.

Saka, A., Chan, D., & Siu, F. (2020). Drivers of sustainable adoption of building information modelling (BIM) in the Nigerian construction small and medium-sized enterprises (SMEs). *Sustainability, 12*(9), 3710.

148 K. W. BETA AND O. OGUNMOKUN

Sancho, M. P., et al. (2018). Understanding the link between socially responsible human resource management and competitive performance in SMEs. *Personnel Review, 47*(6), 1215–1247.

Schaper, M. (2002). The challenge of environmental responsibility and sustainable development: Implications for SME and entrepreneurship academics. In *Radical changing the world: Will SMEs soar or crash* (pp. 541–533).

Shibin, K. T., et al. (2020). Examining sustainable supply chain management of SMEs using resource based view and institutional theory. *Annals of Operations Research, 290*(1–2), 301–326.

Shields, J., & Shelleman, J. (2015). Integrating sustainability into SME strategy. *Journal of Small Business Strategy, 25*(2), 59–78.

Simpson, M., Taylor, N., & Barker, K. (2004). Environmental responsibility in SMEs: Does it deliver competitive advantage? *Business Strategy and the Environment, 13*(3), 156–171.

Songling, Y., et al. (2018). The role of government support in sustainable competitive position and firm performance. *Sustainability, 10*(10), 3495.

Soto-Simeone, A., Sirén, C., & Antretter, T. (2020). New venture survival: A review and extension. *International Journal of Management Reviews, 22*(4), 378–407.

Spence, L. J. (1999). Does size matter? The state of the art in small business ethics. *Business Ethics: A European Review, 8*(3), 163–174.

Upton, N., Teal, E. J., & Felan, J. T. (2001). Strategic and business planning practices of fast growth family firms. *Journal of Small Business Management, 39*(1), 60–72.

Vanguard News. (2013). *Eighty per cent of SMEs fail within 5 years—finance experts—Vanguard News*. Available at: https://www.vanguardngr.com/2013/10/eighty-per-cent-smes-fail-within-5-years-finance-experts/. Accessed 20 September 2022.

Viesi, D., et al. (2017). Energy efficiency and sustainability assessment of about 500 small and medium-sized enterprises in Central Europe region. *Energy Policy, 105*, 363–374.

Welford, R. (1996). Regional development and environmental management: new opportunities for cooperation. *Scandinavian Journal of Management, 12*(3), 347–357.

Welford, R., & Gouldson, A. (1993). *Environmental management & business strategy*. Pitman Publishing. Available at: https://www.cabdirect.org/cabdirect/abstract/19941904625. Accessed: 12 October 2022.

Westhead, P., & Storey, D. (1996). Management training and small firm performance: Why is the link so weak? *International Small Business Journal, 14*(4), 13–24.

Williamson, D., Lynch-Wood, G., & Ramsay, J. (2006). Drivers of environmental behaviour in manufacturing SMEs and the implications for CSR. *Journal of Business Ethics, 67*(3), 317–330.

Yang, C. S. (2016). Evaluating the use of alternative maritime power in Taiwan. *Maritime Business Review, 1*(3), 208–224.

Zailani, S. H. M., et al. (2012). The impact of external institutional drivers and internal strategy on environmental performance. *International Journal of Operations and Production Management, 32*(6), 721–745.

Zhu, Q., & Sarkis, J. (2006). An inter-sectoral comparison of green supply chain management in China: Drivers and practices. *Journal of Cleaner Production, 14*(5), 472–486.

WCED, S. W. S. (1987). World commission on environment and development. *Our Common Future, 17*(1), 1–91. Available at: https://idl-bnc-idrc.dspacedirect.org/bitstream/handle/10625/152/WCED_v17_doc149.pdf. Accessed 5 June 2023.

World Bank. (2018). *World governance indicators database.* World Bank.

Bribery, Corruption and Sustainability Activities in African Countries

Alessio Faccia and Zeenat Beebeejaun

1 Introduction

Corruption has attained dangerous levels throughout Africa. This condition is so ubiquitous that it has been dubbed the 'AIDS of democracy' (Kempe Ronald Hope, 2000). It ruins the fate of many civilisations in the region (Kempe Ronald Hope, 2000). Sub-Saharan Africa's Corruption Perception Index (CPI) reached an average score of 32 in 2022, placing the region the highest in the corruption and bribery ranking at the global level (Transparency.org, 2021). Moreover, the corruption crisis in Africa mirrors the continent's more widespread and infamous atmosphere of ethical failure and terrible government. The severely bad influence of corruption on socioeconomic development and poverty alleviation in the region has become a global issue; many foreign organisations are now concentrating on the core causes, repercussions, and efforts to contain this malignancy in society.

A. Faccia (✉) · Z. Beebeejaun
University of Birmingham Dubai, Dubai, UAE
e-mail: a.faccia@bham.ac.uk

Z. Beebeejaun
e-mail: z.beebeejaun@bham.ac.uk

© The Author(s), under exclusive license to Springer Nature Switzerland AG 2023
S. Adomako et al. (eds.), *Corporate Sustainability in Africa*,
Palgrave Studies in African Leadership,
https://doi.org/10.1007/978-3-031-29273-6_8

For clarification purposes, bribery has been defined by the state of Illinois and included in the United States Court of Appeals for the Seventh Circuit in the case of United States v. Isaacs as Bribery arises when material or personal gain is provided to a public official without the authority of law with the purpose that the public officials' acts advantageously to the offeror at any moment or in any manner in the service delivery of the public official's duties (Scott Turrow, 1985). The mainstream view on bribery is that it is wrong and unethical because it sabotages the institution where it is used.

The World Bank has defined corruption as the misuse of public authority for private gain, definition scholars like Bardhan (1997), Jain (2001), Olken (2007), and Rose-Ackerman (2011) adhered to. Moreover, Liu (2016) argued that to analyse corruption in a specific country or region, more experts are looking at the raw data rather than the perceptions of data. In the long term, micro factors studies on corruption will grow more common.

The ACFE manual of Fraud Examiner defines corruption as "*the term to describe various types of wrongful acts designed to cause some unfair advantage, which can take on many forms. Generally, corruption refers to the wrongful use of influence to procure a benefit for the actor or another person, contrary to the duty or rights of the others.*" The same manual defined bribery as the "*offering, giving, receiving, or soliciting anything of value to influence an official act or business decision.*" (ACFE, 2014, p.1.601).

Also, sustainable development has been defined as 'development that meets the needs of the present without compromising the ability of future generations to meet their own needs' by the United Nations General Assembly (World Commission on Environment & Development, 1987, p. 8). Later, Emas (2015) argued that this definition is ambiguous and implies an inevitable compromise, especially for developing countries, between economic development and the sustainability of the objectives to attain economic growth from an environmental sustainability perspective.

Other key aspects that must be considered in the discussion around the issues of corruption and bribery and their impact on sustainable development of the African continent include the particularities of the region, which result in the hybridisation of African countries from political, cultural, economic, and social perspectives, as well as the fight against poverty. These will be considered in this chapter, which provides a theoretical background and highlights the practical effects of implementing anti-corruption and anti-bribery measures, their impact on the issue of corruption and bribery, and how they influence the economic development of African countries. Also, this chapter examined the case studies of three African countries that have addressed the issues of bribery and corruption and have progressed in this direction.

2 THEORETICAL FOUNDATIONS

This subsection discusses how economic growth and sustainable development theories are linked to the situation in African countries and how their principles can help understand the profound impact of corruption and bribery on the perpetuation of poverty in the region. Also, newer perspectives have been added that propose a paradigm shift, specifically 'new' growth models and models of degrowth in the context of the Global South, which will be discussed.

Bribery and Corruption Theories

When referring to bribery and corruption, many theories have been formulated so far. Among them, the most relevant and well-known are:

Agency theory: This theory suggests that bribery and corruption occur when there is a principal–agent relationship, and the agent (the person who is entrusted with power or authority) uses that power to benefit themselves at the expense of the principal (the person who has given the agent the power) (Yukins, 2010). In this scenario, the agent may be more likely to engage in bribery or corruption to maximise their gains. In sustainability, agency theory can help explain how bribery and corruption undermine sustainable development (Monteiro et al., 2018). When agents use their power or authority to benefit themselves at the principal's expense, they may engage in practices that harm the environment, violate human rights, or contribute to social inequalities. For example, in the case of corporate sustainability, managers may engage in bribery and corruption to secure contracts or approvals for projects that are harmful to the environment or local communities. It can result in the degradation of natural resources, loss of biodiversity, or negative impacts on public health. Such practices can ultimately undermine the long-term sustainability of the business and the communities in which it operates. To address these challenges, companies can adopt policies and practices that promote transparency, accountability and ethical behaviour. It can include implementing anti-bribery and anti-corruption policies, conducting due diligence on business partners and suppliers, and engaging in stakeholder dialogue and consultation. By doing so, companies can reduce the risks of engaging in practices detrimental to sustainable development and help promote a more sustainable future. In Africa, agency theory can help explain how corruption and bribery undermine sustainable development. When agents abuse their power or authority for personal gain, it can lead to the exploitation of natural resources and social inequalities (Monteiro et al., 2018). For example, in the extractive industry, bribes may be paid to obtain licenses or permits to extract resources, resulting in environmental degradation and loss of biodiversity. Corruption can also lead to poor governance and inadequate service delivery, hindering sustainable development. African companies can adopt policies and practices that promote transparency, accountability, and ethical behaviour to address these challenges. It can include implementing anti-bribery and anti-corruption policies, conducting due diligence, and engaging in stakeholder dialogue and consultation to promote sustainable development.

Rational choice theory: According to this theory, individuals engage in bribery and corruption because they believe the benefits outweigh the costs (Carson, 2014). It means that if the benefits of engaging in bribery or corruption (such as financial gain or career advancement) are greater than the potential consequences (such as legal or reputational risks), individuals are more likely to engage in such behaviours. In sustainability, rational choice theory can help explain why individuals and organisations may engage in bribery and corruption despite the negative impacts on the environment and society (Dimant & Schulte, 2016). For example, a company may engage in corrupt practices, such as paying bribes to government officials to obtain permits or licenses for activities that harm the environment, such as mining or logging. The company may see this as a necessary cost of doing business and believe that the financial benefits of obtaining the permit outweigh the potential costs of being caught or facing reputational damage. However, such practices can severely impact sustainability, including environmental degradation, social inequality, and economic instability. Bribes paid to officials may be used to fund illegal activities or perpetuate corrupt systems, contributing to political instability and undermining the rule of law. To address these challenges, governments can adopt policies and regulations that increase the costs of engaging in corrupt practices, such as stronger enforcement mechanisms and penalties. Companies can also adopt sustainability frameworks and engage in sustainable business practices prioritising ethical behaviour and responsible stewardship of natural resources. By doing so, they can help promote a more sustainable future for all. In Africa, rational choice theory can help explain why individuals and organisations engage in corruption despite the negative impacts on sustainability (Ostrom, 1998). In some countries, corrupt practices may be seen as a necessary cost of doing business, and individuals may feel that the financial benefits of engaging in such behaviour outweigh the potential costs of legal or reputational risks. It can lead to environmental degradation, social inequality and economic instability, all undermining sustainable development. To address these challenges, governments can implement policies and regulations that increase the costs of engaging in corrupt practices, such as stronger enforcement mechanisms and penalties. Companies can also adopt sustainable business practices that prioritise ethical behaviour, responsible stewardship of natural resources, and transparency. It can help promote a more sustainable future for Africa (Utting, 2000).

Cultural theory: posits that bribery and corruption occur because of cultural factors, such as social norms, values, and beliefs. In some cultures, for example, it may be more acceptable to engage in bribery or corruption than in others (Banuri & Eckel, 2012). Cultural theory suggests that cultural factors significantly influence bribery and corruption. In some cultures, bribery and corruption may be seen as a way to get things done or as a normal part of doing business, while in others, it is strictly prohibited and carries severe penalties. It can have significant implications for sustainability, particularly in industries that significantly impact the environment or society. For example, in cultures where bribery and corruption are more accepted, companies may engage in unethical practices that harm the environment or communities in which they operate. It can include illegal logging, mining in protected areas, or engaging in activities that violate labour laws or human rights. Such practices can seriously impact sustainability, contributing to environmental degradation, social inequality, and economic instability. To address these challenges, policymakers and companies can work to shift cultural norms and values around bribery and corruption. It can include education and awareness-raising campaigns and developing stronger legal and regulatory frameworks that promote transparency and accountability. Promoting a culture of integrity and ethical behaviour can help create a more sustainable future for all (Joseph et al., 2019). Cultural theory can explain

156   A. FACCIA AND Z. BEEBEEJAUN

the prevalence of bribery and corruption in African societies. In some African cultures, bribery and corruption may be seen as necessary to achieve business objectives or obtain services from government officials (Luiz & Stewart, 2014). It can lead to unethical practices, such as illegal logging, mining in protected areas, or engaging in activities that violate labour laws or human rights, significantly impacting sustainability. To address these challenges, policymakers and companies can work to shift cultural norms and values around bribery and corruption through education and awareness-raising campaigns, promoting ethical behaviour, and developing stronger legal and regulatory frameworks that promote transparency and accountability. Doing so can promote a culture of integrity and ethical behaviour and help create a more sustainable future for Africa (Armstrong, 2005).

Institutional theory: This theory suggests that bribery and corruption occur because of weaknesses in the institutional framework of society. It can include inadequate legal and regulatory frameworks, weak law enforcement, and a lack of transparency and accountability (Chadee et al., 2021). Institutional theory suggests that weaknesses in the institutional framework of society can contribute to bribery and corruption. It can be particularly problematic in industries that significantly impact sustainability, such as those that exploit natural resources or rely on labour exploitation. For example, weak legal and regulatory frameworks can make it easier for companies to engage in unethical practices, such as illegal logging or exploiting vulnerable workers. Weak law enforcement can also contribute to a lack of accountability, allowing companies to act with impunity (Coumans, 2010). To address these challenges, policymakers and companies can work to strengthen the institutional framework for sustainability. It can include developing and enforcing stronger legal and regulatory frameworks that promote transparency and accountability and increasing funding for law enforcement and regulatory agencies (Stern & Holder, 1999). By doing so, we can help create an institutional framework that supports sustainable development and prevents bribery and corruption from undermining our efforts to build a more sustainable future. In Africa, institutional theory suggests that bribery and corruption occur because of weaknesses in the institutional framework of society (Pillay & Kluvers, 2014). Inadequate legal and regulatory frameworks, weak law enforcement, and a lack of transparency and accountability can contribute to unethical practices, particularly in industries that significantly impact sustainability, such as natural resource extraction and labour-intensive industries. For example, illegal logging and exploitation of vulnerable workers are prevalent in some African countries, and weak institutional frameworks contribute to the persistence of these unethical practices. To address these challenges, policymakers and companies can work to strengthen the institutional framework for sustainability by implementing and enforcing stronger legal and regulatory frameworks that promote transparency and accountability, increasing funding for law enforcement and regulatory agencies, and engaging in multi-stakeholder collaborations. By doing so, we can create an institutional framework that supports sustainable development and prevents bribery and corruption from undermining our efforts to build a more sustainable future for Africa (Mackey et al., 2018).

Political economy theory: argues that bribery and corruption are inevitable outcomes of the interaction between politics and economics. In this view, individuals and organisations may engage in bribery and corruption to gain political or economic power and influence. Political economy theory argues that bribery and corruption are inevitable outcomes of the interaction between politics and economics. It can be particularly problematic in industries that significantly impact sustainability, such as those that exploit natural resources or labour. For example, political and economic elites may use their power and influence to gain control over natural resources or exploit labour for personal gain. It can lead to environmental degradation, social inequality, and economic instability, all undermining sustainability. To address these challenges, policymakers and companies can work to reduce the influence of political and economic elites on sustainability. It can include developing and implementing policies that promote transparency, accountability, and ethical behaviour and increasing civic engagement and community participation in decision-making. By doing so, we can help ensure that sustainability is prioritised over individual gain and prevent bribery and corruption from undermining our efforts to build a more sustainable future. In Africa, political economy theory suggests that bribery and corruption are inevitable outcomes of the interaction between politics and economics. Exploiting natural resources and labour for personal gain by political and economic elites has contributed to environmental degradation, social inequality, and economic instability, all undermining sustainability. For example, some African countries with vast natural resources have suffered from corruption, with political and economic elites using their power and

158   A. FACCIA AND Z. BEEBEEJAUN

influence to control and exploit these resources. To address these challenges, policymakers and companies can work to reduce the influence of political and economic elites on sustainability by developing and implementing policies that promote transparency, accountability, and ethical behaviour. Civic engagement and community participation in decision-making can also help to prioritise sustainability over individual gain and prevent bribery and corruption from undermining efforts to build a more sustainable future for Africa.

Theory	Theory description	Implication for African countries
Agency theory	Bribery and corruption occur when agents use their power or authority to benefit themselves at the principal's expense	Agents abuse their power or authority for personal gain, leading to the exploitation of natural resources and social inequalities. Policymakers and companies can implement anti-bribery and anti-corruption policies, conduct due diligence, and engage in stakeholder dialogue to promote sustainable development
Rational choice theory	Individuals engage in bribery and corruption because they believe the benefits outweigh the costs	Corrupt practices may be considered a necessary business cost, leading to environmental degradation, social inequality, and economic instability. Policymakers can implement policies and regulations that increase the costs of engaging in corrupt practices, and companies can adopt sustainable business practices that prioritise ethical behaviour, responsible stewardship of natural resources, and transparency
Cultural theory	Bribery and corruption occur because of cultural factors such as social norms, values, and beliefs	In some cultures, bribery and corruption may be more accepted, leading to unethical practices that harm the environment or communities. Policymakers and companies can work to shift cultural norms and values around bribery and corruption by implementing education and awareness-raising campaigns and developing stronger legal and regulatory frameworks that promote transparency and accountability

(continued)

BRIBERY, CORRUPTION AND SUSTAINABILITY ACTIVITIES ... 159

(continued)

Theory	Theory description	Implication for African countries
Institutional theory	Bribery and corruption occur because of weaknesses in the institutional framework of society	Inadequate legal and regulatory frameworks, weak law enforcement, and a lack of transparency and accountability can contribute to unethical practices, particularly in industries that significantly impact sustainability. Policymakers and companies can work to strengthen the institutional framework for sustainability by implementing and enforcing stronger legal and regulatory frameworks, increasing funding for law enforcement and regulatory agencies, and engaging in multi-stakeholder collaborations
Political economy theory	Bribery and corruption are inevitable outcomes of the interaction between politics and economics	Exploiting natural resources and labour for personal gain by political and economic elites has contributed to environmental degradation, social inequality, and economic instability. Policymakers and companies can work to reduce the influence of political and economic elites on sustainability by developing and implementing policies that promote transparency, accountability, and ethical behaviour. Civic engagement and community participation in decision-making can also help prioritise sustainability over individual gain

Theories of Economic Growth and Sustainable Development

Economic growth—its causes, forms, and effects—has been high on economists' agenda from the start of systematic financial analysis in the era of the classical economists from William Petty to David Ricardo. However, economic development issues and reality are far older (Kurz & Salvadori, 2003). Central to the classical theories of economic growth developed by Torrens (1821) from Adam Smith's and David Ricardo's classical economic principles was the notion of surplus product, which derived the surplus rate, understood as the ratio of the surplus product to the necessary input. From this, there was only a minor conceptual step but a big historical milestone for the growth rate (Kurz & Salvadori, 2003).

Following this, the 'neoclassical' growth models emerged, also called exogenous growth models, belonging to Alfred Marshall (1890), Gustav Cassel (1932), Knut Wicksell (1901), Robert Solow (1956), Trevor Swan (1956) and Lars Waldén (1961). Taking a broad approach to understand the neoclassical growth models, they argued that if the marginal inclination to save is positive, output grows as the exogenous causes cause it to grow in steady-state equilibrium (Kurz & Salvadori, 2003). Outside of the steady-state equilibrium, the growth rate may be demonstrated to rely on the system's behavioural parameter, that is, the inclination to save (and invest), yet the parameter has no bearing on the long-term expansion rate.

The more recent literature includes 'new' growth models (NGMs), which were classified into three main schools of thought, namely the class of constant returns to capital whereby there are no decreasing returns to the capital since no noncumulative element, such as unskilled work, is used in the creation of the accumulable factors, investment products, and human capital (Rebelo, 1991). The second school of thought assumes the return to capital is bounded from below, taking convex technology whereby the marginal product of money is a decreasing function (Jones & Manuelli, 1990). Finally, the third class of NGM includes models where several variables are working to counterbalance any trend for diminishing capital returns, such as models focusing on human capital formation (Rebelo, 1991) and knowledge accumulation (Romer, 1986).

More recently, post-Keynesians have begun investigating the evolution of advanced economies' growth models before and after the 2008 crisis, prompted by Baccaro and Pontusson (2016). Specifically, post-Keynesian economics (Baccaro & Pontusson, 2016; Blecker & Setterfield, 2019; Hein, 2014; Lavoie, 2014) has a long history of demand-led growth theories. Recent occurrences, such as the 2008 financial crisis, the eurozone crisis, and the economic crisis created by the COVID-19 epidemic, have demonstrated that these models are more suited to dealing with modern supply-side challenges.

A theoretical mapping of these models and how they impact African countries have been summarised in Table 1.

Table 1 Theoretical and empirical mapping and implications

Author	Theory	Description of the theory	Implications for African countries
Torrens (1821)	The classical theory of economic growth	The concept of surplus product, from which the surplus rate was formed, is the stepping stone for the growth rate	The classical theory has profound policy implications for international trade in 'underdeveloped countries. (Myint, 1958)
Marshall (1890) Cassel (1932) Wicksell (1934) Solow (1956) Swan (1956) Waldén (1961)	Neoclassical growth model	In steady-state equilibrium, if the marginal tendency to save is positive, output rises as the exogenous factors force it to expand	The neoclassical economic paradigm transformed the institutional dynamics and the implications of reorganising African countries' economic departments and government organisations (Stein, 2021)
Rebelo (1991)	'New' growth model (NGM): Constant returns to capital	There are no declining capital returns since no fixed-interest factor, such as unskilled labour, produces accumulable elements, investment goods, or human capital	With constant returns to scale, the contribution of education to economic growth is limited in developing countries (Pritchett, 2001)
Jones and Manuelli (1990)	'New' growth model (NGM): Bounded return to capital	The return on capital is constrained from below, using convex technology and assuming that the marginal product of money is a critical function	African authorities must avoid declining marginal productivity of major production inputs (Atta-Mensah, 2017)
Rebelo (1991) Romer (1986)	'New' growth model (NGM): multivariate models	Numerous factors work together to counteract any trend of declining capital returns, such as models concentrating on human capital creation and knowledge accumulation	

(continued)

Table 1 (continued)

Author	Theory	Description of the theory	Implications for African countries
Bonaiuti (2012) Schwartzman (2012) Escobar (2015)	Degrowth and the Global South	Several perspectives of post-development, including political, economic, social, etc., suggest that prosperity can be attained without economic growth in Global South countries	The dialogue between degrowth and post-development has great implications for decolonial prosperity in developing African countries
Lavoie (2014) Hein (2014) Baccaro and Pontusson (2016) Blecker and Setterfield (2019)	Demand-led growth theories in post-Keynesian economics	The evolution of advanced economic growth models before and after the 2008 crisis highlights some in-demand components and financial balances	The macroeconomic policies resulting from such demand-led growth models have repercussions for African countries globally
Savvides (1995)	Endogenous-growth model in African countries	Initial endowment, investment, population growth, trade flow, inflation, financial sector development, government growth, and political freedom are important predictors of Africa's GDP per capita growth rates	Countries such as Cameroon, Burkina Faso, and Ivory Coast are worse off than other African countries, mainly due to their inclusion in the CFA Franc Zone
Gyimah-Brempong (2002 Anoruo and Braha (2005) Podobnik et al. (2008) d'Agostino et al. (2016)	Corruption impact on economic growth	Corruption suppresses economic growth both directly and indirectly by reducing productivity and limiting investment	Specifically, a unit increase in corruption reduces GDP and the income growth rate per capita by 0.75 to 0.9 percentage points and 0.39 to 0.41 percentage points per year, respectively (Gyimah-Brempong, 2002)
Qafa (2017)	Degrowth and its impact on the economy of Sub-Saharan Africa	Sub-Saharan Africa is split between the unrealistic aim of "sustainable economic expansion" and the Degrowth ideology	The Global North must help Africa confront poverty rates and inequality that fast growth cannot address

Author	Theory	Description of the theory	Implications for African countries
Blundo et al. (2008)	Corruption and bribery in Sub-Saharan Africa in the paradigm of degrowth	In the degrowth paradigm, corruption and bribery complicate the struggle against corruption because of interactions between native and foreign elements	Rational bureaucracy versus native politics in various African countries propagates the controversy between the colonial power and the independent nation
Jacquemot (2012)	The implementation of Western democratic models in African countries to curb corruption	The Western models cannot be successfully implemented to eliminate corruption due to African countries' particularities and fragmentation, making them difficult to reform at once	'The African state' is a 'proto-state' distinguished by scattered and rudimentary populations. We must no longer regard the African state as a temporary framework for developing a modern state
MacKay (2021)	The need for development strategies in the Global South	The Global South's absolute economic and political independence from the Global North's economic and political structure is the only long-term solution to global climate and inequality challenges	This approach offers a sustainable solution to African countries' global economic, cultural, political, and environmental concerns
Gründler and Potrafke (2019)	The long-term impact of corruption on economic growth	Data analysis from 175 countries between 2012 and 2018 indicates that corruption is linked with a 17% reduction in real GDP per capita	The impact of corruption is even deeper in autocracies since it decreases FDIs and increases inflation
Olamide and Maredza (2021)	Pre-COVID-19 impact of corruption on economic growth in South Africa	Corruption, inflation, and foreign debt payments all hurt economic development, but investment has a favourable one	The findings from South Africa could be of significant importance for other African countries since they can limit the impact of corruption and external debt on economic growth by improving and strengthening public institutions and pursuing tax evaders and avoiders to enhance government income

(continued)

Table 1   (continued)

Author	Theory	Description of the theory	Implications for African countries
de Villiers et al. (2020)	The COVID-19 pandemic worsened an already low economic growth in South Africa	The shutdown wreaked havoc on an already shaky economy, resulting in devastating societal effects. The government has had to raise its borrowings, while future tax receipts are expected to be drastically cut, resulting in a severely limited public budget for many upcoming years	The example of South Africa and how its government dealt with the COVID-19 pandemic in an already suffering economy can be used by other African countries as a lesson of how not to act, although a real-time reaction is impossible since all countries faced the pandemic almost at once

Empirical Analysis of Bribery, Corruption, and Economic Growth in African Countries

The economic growth of the African continent has been studied by Savvides, who used an endogenous-growth model to examine the determinants of the various growth rates in GDP per capita across Africa (Savvides, 1995). The researcher found that initial endowment, investment, population increase, trade direction, inflation, financial development, and government sector expansion are vital in economic growth (Baccaro & Pontusson, 2016). In addition to economic determinants, the author found that political freedom is a key contributor to economic growth. Finally, Savvides identified inclusion in the CFA Franc Zone as a key determinant since Cameroon, Burkina Faso, and Ivory Coast scored worse than other African countries.

Researchers who studied the issue of corruption and its impact on economic growth are numerous, including Gyimah-Brempong (2002), Anoruo and Braha (2005), and Podobnik et al. (2008). Moreover, d'Agostino and others (D'Agostino et al., 2016). The main findings indicate that corruption, directly and indirectly, stifles economic progress by decreasing productivity and limiting investment (Anoruo & Braha, 2005). Specifically, a unit rise in corruption lowers GDP and the rate of income growth per capita by 0.75–0.9% points and 0.39–0.41% per year, respectively (Gyimah-Brempong, 2002). Gyimah-Brempong (2002) has also found a positive correlation between corruption in African countries and income inequality, implying that corruption harms the poor more than the wealthy. Later, d'Agostino and others (D'Agostino et al., 2016). Used an endogenous growth model and demonstrated that corruption correlates with military burden via indirect and additive effects to amplify its detrimental impact. The political ramifications are that the impact of remittances on economic growth in nations with high military costs is worse than previously anticipated (Podobnik et al., 2008). Moreover, Podobnik and others found that the corruption perception index (CPI) increase was negatively and significantly linked with a decrease in foreign direct investments per capita (FDIs) and GDP per capita growth rate in the continent.

Nevertheless, the core of the corruption issue has been explained by Pandjo Boumba (1991) at the microeconomic level rather than utilising the macro-perspective of the economic growth theories above. The author explained that the man in power must satisfy four basic utility functions: a demand function for pure economic goods; a function indicating its demand for luxury; a function rebuilding the demand for family solidarity; and a function rebuilding a process of personal power concentration. Also, the researcher examines the dynamics of political elites and economic progress in Sub-Saharan Africa, concluding that development and modernity occur concurrently with liberation and rendering economic sub-systems autonomous. It is worth noting that while elites are frequently regarded as a precondition for growth because they demonstrate the degree of hegemony in the region, poverty is interpreted as hegemonic inefficiency.

Newer empirical evidence on corruption and economic growth has been put forward by Gründler and Potrafke (2019), who highlighted that most previous empirical research used the inverted CPI to quantify corruption, ignoring the fact that the CPI was not comparable across time. Since 2012, the CPI has been similar over time. The authors use recent data from 175 nations from 2012 to 2018 to re-examine the relationship between corruption and economic development. When the inverted CPI increases by one standard deviation, the aggregate long-run effect of corruption on growth are that real GDP per capita decreases by roughly 17%. Corruption negatively impacts economic growth in autocracies, reducing FDI and raising inflation.

In the current context of the COVID-19 pandemic, the effects of corruption on economic growth are amplified. Before the pandemic, an empirical study of South Africa revealed that corruption, inflation, and foreign debt payments all harm economic development, but investment has a favourable impact (Gbenga Olamide & Maredza, 2021). External debt has a beneficial short-run influence on growth but a negative long-run effect. The importance of improving and strengthening public institutions and pursuing tax evaders and avoiders to enhance government income was underlined.

Amid the COVID-19 pandemic, also focusing on the case of South Africa, de Villiers et al. (2020) showed that starting from the early lockdown and rigorous testing program, the world community commended South Africa's first health response. The shutdown wreaked havoc on an already shaky economy, resulting in devastating societal effects. The first shutdown postponed the outbreak, but the infection rate gradually increased, necessitating more restrictions and perhaps causing significant economic damage (de Villiers et al., 2020). The government was forced to raise its borrowings, while future tax receipts are expected to be drastically cut, resulting in a severely limited taxpayer fund for many years (de Villiers et al., 2020). This aspect limits the government's capacity to meet basic socioeconomic needs prior to the COVID-19 issue.

Degrowth and the Global South

The degrowth theory defines the concept as a deliberate slowing of energy and resource consumption to restore the economy's balance with the living environment, eliminating inequality and promoting human well-being. By studying the social constraints to economic development imposed by capital multiplication, Bonaiuti (2012) invented the idea of degrowth in the Global South. Schwartzman approached degrowth and anthropogenic emissions change from a global political viewpoint. On the other hand, Escobar enlarged the debate on degrowth (DG) and post-development (PD) models by situating them within a broader field of ecological and generational transition paradigms and merging concepts from the North and the Global South (Escobar, 2015).

Qafa recently examined whether the practices anchored in the idea of degrowth can help the economy of Sub-Saharan Africa, starting from the observation that, for a long time, our planet has exhibited symptoms that it has reached the stage when it can no longer replenish itself at the same pace that it is being exploited (Qafa, 2017). The author also notices that Sub-Saharan Africa is torn between the unattainable' sustainable economic growth' agenda and the Degrowth paradigm (Qafa, 2017). Since turning points usually give the finest possibilities, now may be the chance for the Global North to assist Africa in addressing poverty rates and disparities that rapid growth cannot (Qafa, 2017). Also, while growth appears incompatible with environmental protection, degrowth ensures this forced compatibility. Realising the truth behind the 'growth' rhetoric and socioeconomic inequality can assist in addressing global issues without the need for economic expansion (Qafa, 2017).

However, the issue of corruption and bribery in Africa, especially in Sub-Saharan Africa, together with the aspect of hybridisation of African countries, renders more complex the fight against corruption more, even in the paradigm of degrowth, since the interaction between native and non-native elements such as the rational bureaucracy versus the native politics in various countries of the continent perpetuate the conflict

168   A. FACCIA AND Z. BEEBEEJAUN

between the colonial state and the independent state (Blundo et al., 2008).

Lastly, Jacquemot analyses whether Western democratic models could be successfully implemented in African countries to eradicate corruption but concludes the contrary. The scholar argues that 'The African state', as he calls the entire region, is a 'proto-state' characterised by its fragmented and primitive communities, disintegrated by its inherent ethnic differences and chronic and pathological corruption (Blundo et al., 2008). At the same time, the author contends that we must cease viewing the African state as a transitory structure in developing a modern state (Blundo et al., 2008). In his view, the state is "captured" by its holders. Specifically, it is 'privatised' in that each owner of a fraction of public power controls it for his own and the advantage of his network (Blundo et al., 2008).

Therefore, MacKay proposes that the total economic and political autonomy of the South from the Western economic and political system is the only answer to global climate and inequality concerns, which should be viewed as a long-term vision via degrowth (MacKay, 2021). This strategy would consider the disparities in economic and political systems between the South and North, but it would also give an efficient solution for global concerns that go beyond behavioural or national tactics and are systemic at the global level (MacKay, 2021).

Table 1 below includes a mapping of the economic growth theories and main results of the empirical findings discussed above with their implications or outcomes in African countries.

3   Practical Considerations on Anti-Corruption Measures and Their Impact on Sustainable Development

According to an African Union assessment of Illegal Financial Flows (IFFs) from Africa, money leaving the continent through criminal routes surged from over $20 billion in 2001 to $60 billion in 2010 (African Union, 2021).[1] Last year, the United Nations estimated the IFFs level at approximately $88.6 billion, representing around 3.7% of the African

---

[1] African Union, 'Illicit financial flows' Report of the High-Level Panel on Illicit Financial Flows from Africa' (2021) https://au.int/sites/default/files/documents/40545-doc-IFFs_REPORT.pdf (accessed 15 January 2022).

continent's gross domestic product (GDP) (UN.org, 2021).[2] This aspect is especially important since combating corruption, particularly illicit financial flows (IFFs), is a matter of life and death for Africa's development and must be addressed immediately. There is widespread agreement that if the cash being drained from Africa is effectively held, it might be diverted towards the continent's development (UN.org, 2021).

The IFFs are mostly associated with business transactions, tax evasion, and criminal activity, including money laundering, drug, weapons, people trafficking, bribery, corruption, and abuse of power (African Union, 2021). Countries with abundant natural resources and insufficient or non-existent institutional architecture are the most vulnerable to illicit cash flows. These illegal flows have a severe influence on Africa's development efforts. The most serious implications are the loss of investment capital and income that could have been utilised to fund development programs, the weakening of state institutions, and the erosion of the rule of law.

Sustainable Development Goals (SDGs) in African Countries

As the issues of bribery and corruption have been discussed above in light of the extant literature that sheds some light on the impact of these issues on economic growth and development of the global economy and particularly of African countries, this section adds the element of sustainability. This helps determine how bribery and corruption affect sustainable development and economic growth and how sustainable development goals can limit corrupted behaviours and contribute to economic growth in African countries.

The Sustainable Development Goals (SDGs), sometimes called the Global Goals, were approved in 2015 by all United Nations Member States as a global call to eradicate poverty, safeguard the environment, and guarantee that all people live in peace and prosperity in 2030 (UNDP, 2021). The 17 SDGs are interconnected because they acknowledge that actions in one area will impact the results in others and that growth must balance social, economic, and environmental sustainability (UNDP, 2021). The SDGs include no poverty, zero hunger, good health and well-being, quality education, gender equality, clean water and sanitation,

---

[2] UN.org, 'Tackling illicit financial flows, a matter of survival for Africa's development' (July 2021) https://www.un.org/africarenewal/magazine/july-2021/tackling-illicit-financ ial-flows-matter-survival-africas-development (accessed 15 January 2022).

170   A. FACCIA AND Z. BEEBEEJAUN

affordable clean energy, decent work and economic growth, industry, innovation and infrastructure, reduced inequalities, sustainable cities and communities, responsible consumption and production, climate action, life below water, life on land, peace, justice and strong institutions, and partnerships for the goals (UNDP, 2021).

As shown by the reports on the CPI in Sub-Saharan Africa, bribery continues to obstruct access to essential services. According to the 2019 Global Corruption Barometer in Africa, more than one out of every four persons—or over 130 million residents in the 35 African nations questioned—paid a bribe to access key public services such as health care. Unless these corruption issues are addressed, several Sub-Saharan African nations risk falling short of their Sustainable Development Goal (SDG) objectives by 2030.

Furthermore, the 10th edition of the Global Corruption Barometer (GCB) for Africa shows that whereas most Africans believe corruption has worsened in their nation, they also think that, as citizens, they can significantly contribute to the battle against corruption (UNDP, 2021). Some countries in Sub-Saharan Africa experienced significant improvement in the CPI thanks to the lowering of the corruption and bribery levels which, in turn, contributed to the progress towards the SDGs, including Angola, Ivory Coast, Ethiopia, Senegal, and Tanzania (UN.org, 2021). Instead of making new guarantees, governments must execute multiple existing anti-corruption agreements, notably Agenda 2063, the African Union's transformative plan for equitable prosperity and sustainable development (UNDP, 2021).

Learning from the Legislation Changes in OECD Countries to Eradicate Corruption

In 1997, the Organization for Economic Co-operation and Development (OECD) adopted the Convention against Bribery of Foreign Public Officials in International Business Transactions; in short, the OECD Anti-Bribery Convention, which built a new coercive arsenal in response to the challenge posed by the widespread corruption in international marketplaces (OECD, 2021).[3] This aspect was updated in 2009 with the

---

[3] OECD, '2021 OECD Anti-Bribery recommendation' (2021) https://www.oecd.org/daf/anti-bribery/2021-oecd-anti-bribery-recommendation.htm (accessed 15 January 2022).

Recommendation of the Council for Further Combating Bribery and the Recommendation on the Tax Deductibility of Bribes to Foreign Public Officials.

A report that examines the extent to which various countries have progressed in terms of implementing the OECD anti-corruption legislation reveals success stories such as Columbia, which has been collaborating closely with the OECD to strengthen the integrity of its public procurement system by strengthening the institutional framework and establishing a National Agency for Public Procurement (OECD, 2016).[4]

Nevertheless, for anti-corruption regulations to be successful, penalties must be appropriate and deterrent, and bribes and the revenues of bribes must be confiscated. Furthermore, bribery investigations and prosecutions should be conducted independently of concerns of national economic benefit, the possible impact on ties with another nation, and the identification of the persons or firms implicated (OECD, 2021). Moreover, in the effort to make international bribery a crime, the OECD report shows that 24 countries that have adhered to the OECD Anti-Bribery Convention were still due to conclude their foreign bribery enforcement policies as of 2016 (OECD, 2021).

In 2021, the Anti-Bribery recommendation by the OECD created legally enforceable norms to criminalise payments to foreign public officials in international economic transactions, as well as a slew of other steps to make this happen. This aspect is the first and unique worldwide anti-corruption tool focusing on the 'supply side' of bribery transactions (Atta-Mensah, 2017). The 2021 Recommendation for Further Combating Bribery of Foreign Public Officials in International Business Transactions strengthens and supports the Anti-Bribery Convention's implementation (Atta-Mensah, 2017). Today, 44 countries signed the OECD Anti-Bribery Convention, including the 37 OECD countries and Argentina, Brazil, Bulgaria, Costa Rica, Russia and South Africa (Atta-Mensah, 2017).

---

[4] OECD, 'Putting an end to corruption' (2016) https://www.oecd.org/corruption/putting-an-end-to-corruption.pdf (accessed 5 February 2022).

4 CASE STUDIES OF AFRICAN COUNTRIES FIGHTING BRIBERY, CORRUPTION, AND WORKING TOWARDS SUSTAINABILITY GOALS

The following examples of African economies show the particularities of three selected countries fighting bribery and corruption issues to support their growth and sustainable development. They include success stories like Seychelles and less successful like South Africa, for instance, still fighting long-lasting corruption in the fishing industry with major consequences for implementing environmental regulations.

Seychelles and Its Progress as the Least Corrupt Country in Africa

In 2020, the CPI of Seychelles was 66 out of 100, significantly improving from the score of 40 in 2005 (Knoema.com, 2020).[5] Ellis (1996)[6] noted that as Britain ended its colonial dominance in the Indian Ocean in 1971, the British government endowed the islands with an international airport to alter their economic and geopolitical position by giving simple physical access to the rest of the globe. Within a few years after gaining independence in 1976, Seychelles had become a strategic priority for the two superpowers and several minor powers—France, South Africa, and others—all of which aspired to exert influence in the islands (Ellis, 1996). The country was particularly vulnerable to the pressures that larger governments could exert, owing to its small size and tiny army, and possibly also because its tourist industry relied on Seychelles' ability to sustain an image of calmness and untarnished beauty to attract tourists (Ellis, 1996).

The archipelagos caused the issue of corruption and bribery, comprised a hundred islands in the western Indian Ocean, and became a haven for fraudsters and tax evaders (Shaer et al., 2014).[7] Like other minor tax

---

[5] Knoema.com, 'Seychelles—Corruption perception index' (2020) https://knoema.com/atlas/Seychelles/Corruption-perceptions-index (accessed 16 January 2022).

[6] Stephen Ellis, 'Africa and international corruption: The strange case of South Africa and Seychelles' (1996) 95 African Affairs 165.

[7] Matthew Shaer, Michael Hudson and Margot Williams, 'Sun and shadows: How an island paradise became a haven for dirty money' (3 June 2014) International Consortium of Investigative Journalists (ICIJ) https://www.icij.org/investigations/offshore/sun-and-shadows-how-island-paradise-became-haven-dirty-money/ (accessed 16 January 2022).

havens, Seychelles has an outsized influence that belies its limited market share (Shaer et al., 2014). An event from 2012 states that two African journalists acting as affluent Zimbabweans looking to invest in Seychelles were blatantly offered shady secrecy services, quickly becoming a classic example of offshore covert inquiry.[8]

However, in recent years, the country managed to lower its corruption by investigating the issue on a case-by-case approach and running awareness sessions for workers in the public and private sectors through the Anti-Corruption Commission of Seychelles (ACCS) with financial support from the EU of Rs 6.7 million (Seychelles News Agency, 2021).[9] The legal framework has also been improved in the past year, and the governance offered by the ACCS will continue for at least seven years (Seychelles News Agency, 2021).

In 2020, Seychelles had the highest GDP per capita in Africa, raising {the highest GDP per capita in Africa in 2020, at $12,323, despite a considerable reduction from the previous year's figure of USD 17,448 (Van Nieuwkerk, 2021).[10] Nevertheless, concerns persist about the continuation of shared prosperity. Climate change has continued to pose long-term sustainability threats to this 115-island archipelago in the Western Indian Ocean (Van Nieuwkerk, 2021). Wavel Ramkalawan, the newly elected leader of Seychelles, was elected as the country's fifth president in October. The government's first aim was to limit Covid-19 and recover from the country's economic and social consequences (Van Nieuwkerk, 2021).

Rwanda: The Anti-Corruption Efforts Do Produce Remarkable Results

In Rwanda, the Office of the Ombudsman was implemented to lead the fight against corruption, have investigative and prosecutorial powers, and specialist chambers handling corruption at the Intermediate Court

---

[8] Nicholas Shaxson, 'How Seychelles became a paradise for dirty money and corruption' (10 June 2014) *Tax Justice Network* https://taxjustice.net/2014/06/10/corrupt-little-seychelles-became-paradise-dirty-money/ (accessed 16 January 2022).

[9] Seychelles News Agency, 'Seychelles marks the World Anti-Corruption Day with historical breakthrough' (9 December 2021) http://www.seychellesnewsagency.com/art icles/15954/Seychelles+marks+the+World+Anti-Corruption+Day+with+historical+breakt hrough (accessed 16 January 2022).

[10] Anthoni Van Nieuwkerk, Seychelles In *Africa Yearbook*, Volume 17 (2021) 365.

(Bizimana, 2019).[11] Rwanda is also a member of the East African Association of Anti-Corruption Authorities, its accounts receivable division, the Commonwealth Africa Anti-Corruption Centre, the African Union Advisory Board on Corruption, the United Nations Office on Drugs and Crime, and others (Bizimana, 2019).

According to the Rwanda Governance Board's 2018 Rwanda Governance Scorecard, 83% of residents support the government's anti-corruption, openness, and accountability measures (Bizimana, 2019). Also, based on the World Bank rankings, Rwanda has improved significantly, from 26% in 1996 to 71% in 2017 (Bizimana, 2019). Rwanda placed 48 on Transparency International's 2018 Corruption Perceptions Index, up from 83 in 2005 and 121 in 2006 (Bizimana, 2019).

Moreover, Rwanda passed a new anti-corruption law in September 2018, which broadened the definition of corruption to include bribery, sexual corruption, embezzlement, making choices based on partiality, friendship, or enmity, influence peddling, illegal enrichment, inappropriate use of public property, misuse of power, and demanding or receiving undue or excessive money (Bizimana, 2019).

These changes had significantly contributed to the country's economic growth since its GDP per capita growth reached 7.2% in 2019, amid an economic boom right before the COVID-19 pandemic started (World Bank, 2021).[12] This aspect was possible as Rwanda implemented significant economic and structural changes and maintained its economic growth rates over the last decade with the International Monetary Fund and the World Bank (World Bank, 2021). Moreover, the country's rapid economic growth has been matched by significant gains in living conditions, including a two-thirds reduction in childhood mortality and near-universal elementary school attendance (World Bank, 2021). With increased flexibility in the private sector, which will aid in maintaining strong investment rates and accelerate development, Rwanda's improved living conditions and education will help advance the country towards reaching the SDGs 2030.

---

[11] Patrick Bizimana, 'An Africa success story: Anti-corruption efforts in Rwanda produce results' (2019) FCPA Blog. https://fcpablog.com/2019/03/13/an-africa-success-story-anti-corruption-efforts-in-rwanda-pr/ (accessed 16 January 2022).

[12] World Bank, 'The World Bank in Rwanda' (2021) https://www.worldbank.org/en/country/rwanda/overview#1 (accessed 16 January 2022).

BRIBERY, CORRUPTION AND SUSTAINABILITY ACTIVITIES ... 175

South Africa and How Bribery Hinders Environmental Regulation on Fisheries

Since the extant literature does not include many studies on how and why corruption impedes environmental standards on a microeconomic scale, Sundström (2013)[13] examined the link between corruption and regulatory requirements through private, in-depth interviews with small-scale farmers in South African fishers. Respondents highlighted how inspectors' and other resource users' expected behaviour in soliciting or accepting bribes was critical in meeting the regulatory requirements (Sundström, 2013). The interviews also provided insights into the perplexing role of public leaders' integrity since resource users usually know inspectors personally and maintain the discretion required for bribes to continue, yet they portray them as dishonest and describe how corrupt activities reduce their credibility (Sundström, 2013). Moreover, the South African case results highlight the need to combat major and local corruption to improve the efficiency of natural resource management legislation (Sundström, 2013).

In recent years, South Africa intensified its fight against corruption and bribery, notably through the adherence to the OECD Anti-Bribery Convention as of 2007, yet progress still needs to be made. However, an important change in the fisheries' corruption was made by viewing illegal fishing as a fisheries management issue and as 'fisheries crime,' situated within the South African and wider African context (de Coning & Witbooi, 2015).[14] This aspect explains the new fisheries crime paradigm, describing the causes for its creation and outlining the legal obstacles and opportunities it brings to combat illegal fishing. South Africa is an example of an African country (de Coning & Witbooi, 2015).

Comparing Rwanda and South Africa, Khan and Pillay showed that they both have painful histories, including a wide range of cultural and political battles, profound divides, institutional brutality, and genocide

---

[13] Aksel Sundström, 'Corruption in the commons: Why bribery hampers enforcement of environmental regulations in South African fisheries' (2013) 7 International Journal of the Commons 454.

[14] Eva de Coning and Emma Witbooi, 'Towards a new'fisheries crime'paradigm: South Africa as an illustrative example' (2015) 60 Marine Policy 208.

176   A. FACCIA AND Z. BEEBEEJAUN

(Khan & Pillay, 2019).[15] South Africa's most recent decades of its journey of fighting corruption and bribery were marked by the agreements reached during the democratic transition that significantly impacted the adoption of conventional neoliberal economic policy. On the other hand, Rwanda's path was shaped by the bloody civil war in 1994. According to senior United Nations officials, '800,000 Tutsis and moderate Hutus have killed in roughly a hundred days' a 'genocide.' (Miser, 2019)[16] Moreover, The Rwandan Patriotic Front (RPF), led by Paul Kagame, has controlled the country since 2004. The RPF's dominance is based on military superiority, the achievement of certain developmental objectives, and the repression of dissent in a framework of just two major ethnic groupings (Goodfellow, 2017).[17]

However, both nations share a similar theme and common ground: the different ruling parties' political ambition to reform their communities and political economy (Khan & Pillay, 2019). Given the disastrous effects of corruption on the polity and economy, a significant portion of this political will is devoted to arresting and battling corruption, necessitating negotiating and navigating contentious social connections (Khan & Pillay, 2019). As a result, success in combating corruption is frequently projected as critical for delivering equitable, democratic, open, empowering, and ultimately 'sustainable' development routes (Khan & Pillay, 2019). Also, the authors demonstrated that tackling corruption cannot be divorced from power, political economics, the mechanics of public policy design, and policy execution mechanisms. This article proposes a link between clientelism, economic growth, and service delivery, with implications for job creation and alleviating poverty and inequality decrease (Khan & Pillay, 2019).

---

[15] Firoz Khan and Pregala Pillay, 'Corruption and its repercussions on employment, poverty and inequality: Rwanda and South Africa Compared' (2019) 8 Journal of Reviews on Global Economics 1203.

[16] Miser, 'The facts are stubborn. Africa in Fact' (2019) 51 The Journal of Good Governance in Africa 70.

[17] Tom Goodfellow, 'Seeing political settlements through the city' (2017) 49 Development & Change 1.

5 Summary of the Chapter

To conclude, this chapter addresses the issues of corruption, bribery, and sustainable development that have been put into perspective in the African context, especially the Sub-Saharan African context, where they are still at peak levels, through measures such as the CPI and the SGDs.

In the second section of the chapter, some theoretical underpinnings for the discussion on sustainable development have been provided, marked by an incursion into the theories on bribery and corruption (agency, rational choice, cultural, institutional, and political economy) and those on economic growth (classical growth models, neoclassical growth, and new growth) and how these were applied to the African countries and finishing with new proposals of degrowth theories formulated for the Global South context which Africa is part of.

The third section considers some measures against corruption and bribery in the continent, focusing on the SDGs 2030, the Global Corruption Barometer for Africa and the lessons learned from the OECD Anti-Bribery Convention, which laws and penalties against corruption and bribery.

The last section comprises three case studies focusing on Seychelles, Botswana and South Africa, selected as countries with major corruption and bribery problems but which made great efforts and registered significant progress in overcoming these issues in their sustainable development path.

References

ACFE. (2014). *Fraud examiner Manual*. International Edition.

African Union. (2021). *Illicit financial flows*. Report of the High-Level Panel on Illicit Financial Flows from Africa. https://au.int/sites/default/files/docume nts/40545-doc-IFFs_REPORT.pdf. Accessed 15 January 2022.

Anoruo, E., & Braha, H. (2005). Corruption and economic growth: the African experience. *Journal of Sustainable Development in Africa, 7*(1), 43–55.

Armstrong, E. (2005). Integrity, transparency and accountability in public administration: Recent trends, regional and international developments and emerging issues. *United Nations, Department of Economic and Social Affairs, 1*(10), 1–10.

Atta-Mensah, J. (2017). Theoretical foundations of Africa's economic transformation and growth. *Theoretical Economics Letters, 7*, 1150.

Baccaro, L., & Pontusson, J. (2016). Rethinking comparative political economy: The growth model perspective. *Politics & Society, 44*(2), 175–207.

Banuri, S., & Eckel, C. (2012). *Experiments in culture and corruption: A review.* Emerald Group Publishing Limited.

Bardhan, P. (1997). Corruption and development: A review of issues. *Journal of Economic Literature, 35*, 1320.

Bizimana, P. (2019). *An Africa success story: Anti-corruption efforts in Rwanda produce results.* FCPA Blog. https://fcpablog.com/2019/03/13/an-afr ica-success-story-anti-corruption-efforts-in-rwanda-pr/. Accessed 16 January 2022.

Blecker, R. A., & Setterfield, M. (2019). *Heterodox macroeconomics: Models of demand, distribution and growth.* Edward Elgar.

Blundo, G., de-Sardan, J. P. O., Arifari, N. B., & Alou, M. T. (2008). *Everyday corruption and the state: Citizens and public officials in Africa.* Bloomsbury Publishing.

Bonaiuti, M. (2012). Growth and democracy: Trade-offs and paradoxes. *Futures, 44*(6), 524–534.

Carson, L. D. (2014). *Deterring corruption: Beyond rational choice theory.* Available at SSRN 2520280.

Cassel, G. (1932). *The theory of social economy* (1st German ed., 1918). Harcourt Brace.

Chadee, D., Roxas, B., & Kouznetsov, A. (2021). Corruption, bribery and innovation in cee: Where is the link? *Journal of Business Ethics, 174*(4), 747–762.

Coumans, C. (2010). Alternative accountability mechanisms and mining: The problems of effective impunity, human rights, and agency. *Canadian Journal of Development Studies/revue Canadienne D'études Du Développement, 30*(1–2), 27–48.

d'Agostino, G., Dunne, J. P., & Pieroni, L. (2016). Corruption and growth in Africa. *European Journal of Political Economy, 43*, 71–88.

De Coning, E., & Witbooi, E. (2015). Towards a new'fisheries crime' paradigm: South Africa as an illustrative example. *Marine Policy, 60*, 208–215.

De Villiers, C., Cerbone, D., & Van Zijl, W. (2020). The South African government's response to COVID-19. *Journal of Public Budgeting, Accounting & Financial Management, 32*(5), 797–811.

Dimant, E., & Schulte, T. (2016). The nature of corruption: An interdisciplinary perspective. *German Law Journal, 17*(1), 53–72.

Ellis, S. (1996). Africa and international corruption: The strange case of South Africa and Seychelles. *African Affairs, 95*, 165.

Emas, R. (2015). *The concept of sustainable development: Definition and defining principles* (Brief for GSDR).

Escobar, A. (2015). Degrowth, postdevelopment, and transitions: A preliminary conversation. *Sustainability Science, 10,* 451.

Goodfellow, T. (2017). Seeing political settlements through the city. *Development & Change, 49,* 1.

Gründler, K., & Potrafke, N. (2019). Corruption and economic growth: New empirical evidence. *European Journal of Political Economy, 60,* 101810.

Gyimah-Brempong, K. (2002). Corruption, economic growth, and income inequality in Africa. *Economics of Governance, 3,* 183–209.

Hein, E. (2014). *Distribution and growth after Keynes: A Post-Keynesian guide.* Edward Elgar Publishing.

Kurz, H. D., & Salvadori, N. (2003). Theories of economic growth: Old and new. In *The theory of economic growth: A 'classical' perspective* (pp. 1–22). Edward Elgar.

Hope, K. R. (Sr.). (2000). Corruption and development in Africa. In *Corruption and development in Africa* (pp. 17–39). Palgrave Macmillan.

Jain, A. K. (2001). Corruption: A review. *Journal of Economic Surveys, 15*(1), 71–121.

Jones, L. E., & Manuelli, R. (1990). A convex model of equilibrium growth: Theory and policy implications. *Journal of political Economy, 98*(5, Part 1), 1008–1038.

Joseph, C., Gunawan, J., Madi, N., Janggu, T., Rahmat, M., & Mohamed, N. (2019). Realising sustainable development goals via online integrity framework disclosure: Evidence from Malaysian and Indonesian local authorities. *Journal of Cleaner Production, 215,* 112–122.

Khan, F., & Pillay, P. (2019). Corruption and its repercussions on employment, poverty and inequality: Rwanda and South Africa compared. *Journal of Reviews on Global Economics, 8,* 1203.

Knoema.com. (2020). *Seychelles—Corruption perception index.* https://knoema.com/atlas/Seychelles/Corruption-perceptions-index. Accessed 16 January 2022.

Lavoie, M. (2014). *Post-Keynesian economics: New foundations.* Edward Elgar.

Liu, X. (2016). A literature review on the definition of corruption and factors affecting the risk of corruption. *Open Journal of Social Sciences, 4*(6), 171–177.

Luiz, J. M., & Stewart, C. (2014). Corruption, South African multinational enterprises and institutions in Africa. *Journal of Business Ethics, 124,* 383–398.

MacKay, S. (2021). The global South, degrowth and The Simpler Way movement: the need for structural solutions at the global level. *Globalisations, 19*(5), 828–835.

Mackey, T. K., Vian, T., & Kohler, J. (2018). The sustainable development goals as a framework to combat health-sector corruption. *Bulletin of the World Health Organization, 96*(9), 634.

180 A. FACCIA AND Z. BEEBEEJAUN

Marshall, A. (1890). *Principles of economics* (8th ed., 1920). Macmillan.
Miser. (2019). The facts are stubborn. Africa in Fact. *The Journal of Good Governance in Africa, 51,* 70.
Monteiro, M. D. S., Viana, F. L. E., & Sousa-Filho, J. M. D. (2018). Corruption and supply chain management toward the sustainable development goals era. *Corporate Governance: THe International Journal of Business in Society, 18*(6), 1207–1219.
Myint, H. (1958). The "classical theory" of international trade and the underdeveloped countries. *The Economic Journal, 68*(270), 317–337.
OECD. (2016). *Putting an end to corruption.* https://www.oecd.org/corruption/putting-an-end-to-corruption.pdf. Accessed 5 February 2022.
OECD. (2021). *2021 OECD Anti-Bribery recommendation.* https://www.oecd.org/daf/anti-bribery/2021-oecd-anti-bribery-recommendation.htm. Accessed 15 January 2022.
Olamide, E. G., & Maredza, A. (2021). Pre-COVID-19 evaluation of external debt, corruption and economic growth in South Africa. *Review of Economics and Political Science* (forthcoming).
Olken, B. A. (2007). Monitoring corruption: Evidence from a field experiment in Indonesia. *Journal of Political Economy, 115,* 200.
Ostrom, E. (1998). A behavioral approach to the rational choice theory of collective action: Presidential address, American Political Science Association, 1997. *American Political Science Review, 92*(1), 1–22.
Pandjo Boumba, L. (1991). *Analyse économique de l'élite dans le développement.* Doctoral dissertation, Paris 2.
Pillay, S., & Kluvers, R. (2014). An institutional theory perspective on corruption: The case of a developing democracy. *Financial Accountability & Management, 30*(1), 95–119.
Podobnik, B., Shao, J., Njavro, D., Ivanov, P. C., & Stanley, H. E. (2008). Influence of corruption on economic growth rate and foreign investment. *The European Physical Journal B, 63,* 547–550.
Pritchett, L. (2001). Where has all the education gone? *The World Bank Economic Review, 15*(3), 367–391.
Rebelo, S. (1991). Long run policy analysis and long run growth. *Journal of Political Economy, 99,* 500.
Romer, P. M. (1986). Increasing returns and long-run growth. *Journal of Political Economy, 94,* 1002.
Rose-Ackerman, S. (2011). *Anti-corruption policy: Can international actors play a constructive role?* (Yale Law & Economics Research Paper No. 440).
Savvides, A. (1995). Economic growth in Africa. *World Development, 23,* 449.
Schwartzman, D. (2012). A critique of degrowth and its politics. *Capitalism Nature Socialism, 23*(1), 119–125.

BRIBERY, CORRUPTION AND SUSTAINABILITY ACTIVITIES ... 181

Seychelles News Agency. (2021, December 9). *Seychelles marks the World Anti-Corruption Day with historical breakthrough.* http://www.seychellesne wsagency.com/articles/15954/Seychelles+marks+the+World+Anti-Corrup tion+Day+with+historical+breakthrough. Accessed 16 January 2022.

Shaer, M., Hudson, M., & Williams, M. (2014, June 3). Sun and shadows: How an island paradise became a haven for dirty money. *International Consortium of Investigative Journalists (ICIJ).* https://www.icij.org/investigations/off shore/sun-and-shadows-how-island-paradise-became-haven-dirty-money/. Accessed 16 January 2022.

Shaxson, N. (2014, June 10). *How Seychelles became a paradise for dirty money and corruption.* Tax Justice Network. https://taxjustice.net/2014/06/10/ corrupt-little-seychelles-became-paradise-dirty-money/. Accessed 16 January 2022.

Solow, R. M. (1956). A contribution to the theory of economic growth. *Quarterly Journal of Economics, 70,* 65.

Stein, H. (2021). Institutionalizing neoclassical economics in Africa: Instruments, ideology and implications. *Economy and Society, 50*(1), 120–147.

Stern, J., & Holder, S. (1999). Regulatory governance: Criteria for assessing the performance of regulatory systems: An application to infrastructure industries in the developing countries of Asia. *Utilities Policy, 8*(1), 33–50.

Sundström, A. (2013). Corruption in the commons: Why bribery hampers enforcement of environmental regulations in South African fisheries'. *International Journal of the Commons, 7,* 454.

Swan, T. W. (1956). Economic growth and capital accumulation. *Economic Record, 32,* 334.

Torrens, R. (1821). *An essay on the production of wealth.* Longman, Hurst, Rees, Orme, and Brown.

Transparency.org. (2021, January 28). CPI 2020: Sub-Saharan Africa. *Transparency International. The global coalition against corruption.* https://www. transparency.org/en/news/cpi-2020-sub-saharan-africa. Accessed 15 January 2022.

Turrow, S. (1985). What's wrong with bribery. *Journal of Business Ethics, 4,* 249.

UN.org. (2021, July). *Tackling illicit financial flows, a matter of survival for Africa's development.* https://www.un.org/africarenewal/magazine/ july-2021/tackling-illicit-financial-flows-matter-survival-africas-development. Accessed 15 January 2022.

United Nations General Assembly. (1987). *Report of the world commission on environment and development: Our common future.* United Nations General Assembly, Development and International Co-operation: Environment.

Utting, P. (2000). *Business responsibility for sustainable development* (No. 2). Geneva 2000 Occasional Paper.

Van Nieuwkerk, A. (2021). Seychelles. In *Africa Yearbook* (Vol. 17, p. 365).

182   A. FACCIA AND Z. BEEBEEJAUN

Waldén, L. J. (1961). *A neoclassical theory of economic growth*. Allen and Unwin.

Wicksell, K. (1934). *Lectures on political economy* (1st Swedish ed., 1901). Routledge.

World Bank. (2021). *The World Bank in Rwanda*. https://www.worldbank.org/en/country/rwanda/overview#1. Accessed 16 January 2022.

World Commission on Environment and Development. (1987). *Brundtland Report to the UN* (p. 8).

Yukins, C. R. (2010). A versatile prism: Assessing procurement law through the principal-agent model. *Public Contract Law Journal, 40*, 63.

BIBLIOGRAPHY

African Union. (2021). *Illicit financial flows*. Report of the High-Level Panel on Illicit Financial Flows from Africa [Online]. Available at: https://au.int/sites/default/files/documents/40545-doc-IFFs_REPORT.pdf. Accessed 15 January 2022.

Anoruo, E., & Braha, H. (2005). Corruption and economic growth: The African experience. *Journal of Sustainable Development in Africa, 7*(1), 43–55.

Atta-Mensah, J. (2017). Theoretical foundations of Africa's economic transformation and growth. *Theoretical Economics Letters, 7*(5), 1150–1178.

Baccaro, L., & Pontusson, J. (2016). Rethinking comparative political economy: The growth model perspective. *Politics and Society, 44*(2), 175–207.

Bardhan, P. (1997). Corruption and development: A review of issues. *Journal of Economic Literature, 35*, 1320–1346.

Bizimana, P. (2019). *An African success story: Anti-corruption efforts in Rwanda produce results*. FCPA Blog [Online]. Available at: https://fcpablog.com/2019/03/13/an-africa-success-story-anti-corruption-efforts-in-rwanda-pr/. Accessed 16 January 2022.

Blecker, R. A., & Setterfield, M. (2019). *Heterodox Macroeconomics: Models of demand, distribution and growth*. Edward Elgar.

Blundo, G., de-Sardan, J. P. O., Arifari, N. B., & Alou, M. T. (2008). *Everyday corruption and the state: Citizens and public officials in Africa*. Bloomsbury Publishing.

Bonaiuti, M. (2012). Growth and democracy: Trade-offs and paradoxes. *Futures, 44*, 524–534.

Cassel, G. (1932). *The theory of social economy* (1st German ed., 1918). Harcourt Brace.

de Coning, E., & Witbooi, E. (2015). Towards a new'fisheries crime' paradigm: South Africa as an illustrative example. *Marine Policy, 60*, 208–2015.

d'Agostino, G., Dunne, J. P., & Pieroni, L. (2016). Corruption and growth in Africa. *European Journal of Political Economy, 43*, 71–88.

Ellis, S. (1996). Africa and international corruption: The strange case of South Africa and Seychelles. *African Affairs, 95*, 165–196.

Emas, R. (2015). *The concept of sustainable development: Definition and defining principles* (Brief for GSDR).

Escobar, A. (2015). Degrowth, post-development, and transitions: A preliminary conversation. *Sustainability Science, 10*(3), 451–462.

Goodfellow, T. (2017). Seeing political settlements through the city. *Development & Change, 49*(1), 1–24.

Gründler, K., & Potrafke, N. (2019). Corruption and economic growth: New empirical evidence. *European Journal of Political Economy, 60*, 1–38.

Gyimah-Brempong, K. (2002). Corruption, economic growth, and income inequality in Africa. *Economics of Governance, 3*(3), 183–209.

Hein, E. (2014). *Distribution and growth after Keynes: A Post-Keynesian guide.* Edward Elgar Publishing.

Hope, K. R. (2000). Corruption and development in Africa. In *Corruption and development in Africa* (pp. 17–39). Palgrave Macmillan.

Jacquemot, P. (2012). Understanding corruption mechanisms within Sub-Saharan Africa's elites. *Revue internationale et stratégique, 1*, 125–130.

Jain, A. K. (2001). Corruption: A review. *Journal of Economic Surveys, 15*(1), 71–121.

Jones, L. E., & Manuelli, R. (1990). A convex model of equilibrium growth: Theory and policy implications. *Journal of Political Economy, 98*, 1008–1038.

Khan, F., & Pillay, P. (2019). Corruption and its repercussions on employment, poverty and inequality: Rwanda and South Africa compared. *Journal of Reviews on Global Economics, 8*, 1203–1212.

King, R. G., & Rebelo, S. (1990). Public policy and economic growth: Developing neoclassical implications. *Journal of Political Economy, 98*, 126–150.

Knoema.com. (2020). *Seychelles—Corruption perception index* [Online]. Available at: https://knoema.com/atlas/Seychelles/Corruption-perceptions-index. Accessed 16 January 2022.

Kurz, H. D., & Salvadori, N. (2003). Theories of economic growth: Old and new. *The theory of economic growth: A 'classical' perspective* (pp. 1–22). Edward Elgar.

Lavoie, M. (2014). *Post-Keynesian economics: New foundations.* Edward Elgar.

Liu, X. (2016). A literature review on the definition of corruption and factors affecting the risk of corruption. *Open Journal of Social Sciences, 4*(6), 171–177.

MacKay, S. (2021). The global South, degrowth and The Simpler Way movement: the need for structural solutions at the global level. *Globalisations*, 1–8.

Marshall, A. (1890). *Principles of Economics* (8th ed., 1920). Reprint, reset (1977). Macmillan.

Miser, F. (2019, October–December). The facts are stubborn. Africa in fact. *The Journal of Good Governance in Africa, 51*, 70–79.

Myint, H. (1958). The "classical theory" of international trade and the underdeveloped countries. *The Economic Journal, 68*(270), 317–337.

OECD. (2016). *Putting an end to corruption* [Online]. Available at: https://www.oecd.org/corruption/putting-an-end-to-corruption.pdf. Accessed 5 February 2022.

OECD. (2021). *2021 OECD Anti-Bribery recommendation* [Online]. Available at: https://www.oecd.org/daf/anti-bribery/2021-oecd-anti-bribery-recommendation.htm. Accessed 15 January 2022.

Olamide, E. G., & Maredza, A. (2021). Pre-COVID-19 evaluation of external debt, corruption and economic growth in South Africa. *Review of Economics and Political Science* (forthcoming).

Olken, B. A. (2007). Monitoring corruption: Evidence from a field experiment in Indonesia. *Journal of Political Economy, 115*(2), 200–249.

Pandjo Boumba, L. (1991). *Analyse économique de l'élite dans le développement.* Doctoral dissertation, Paris 2.

Podobnik, B., Shao, J., Njavro, D., Ivanov, P. C., & Stanley, H. E. (2008). Influence of corruption on economic growth rate and foreign investment. *The European Physical Journal B, 63*(4), 547–550.

Pritchett, L. (2001). Where has all the education gone? *The World Bank Economic Review, 15*(3), 367–391.

Qafa, M. F. (2017). Can degrowth rescue Sub-Saharan Africa? *International Journal of Technology, 16*(2), 191–200.

Rebelo, S. (1991). Long run policy analysis and long run growth. *Journal of Political Economy, 99*, 500–521.

Romer, P. M. (1986). Increasing returns and long-run growth. *Journal of Political Economy, 94*, 1002–1037.

Rose-Ackerman, S. (2011). *Anti-corruption policy: Can international actors play a constructive role?* (Yale Law & Economics Research Paper No. 440).

Savvides, A. (1995). Economic growth in Africa. *World Development, 23*(3), 449–458.

Seychelles News Agency. (2021, December 9). *Seychelles marks the World Anti-Corruption Day with historical breakthrough* [Online]. Available at: http://www.seychellesnewsagency.com/articles/15954/Seychelles+marks+the+World+Anti-Corruption+Day+with+historical+breakthrough. Accessed 16 January 2022.

Shaer, M., Hudson, M., & Williams, M. (2014, June 3). Sun and shadows: How an island paradise became a haven for dirty money. *International Consortium of Investigative Journalists (ICIJ)* [Online]. Available at: https://www.icij.org/investigations/offshore/sun-and-shadows-how-island-paradise-became-haven-dirty-money/. Accessed 16 January 2022.

Shaxson, N. (2014, June 10). *How Seychelles became a paradise for dirty money and corruption.* Tax Justice Network [Online]. Available at: https://taxjustice.net/2014/06/10/corrupt-little-seychelles-became-par adise-dirty-money/. Accessed 16 January 2022.

Schwartzman, D. (2012). A critique of degrowth and its politics. *Capitalism Nature Socialism, 23*(1), 119–125.

Solow, R. M. (1956). A contribution to the theory of economic growth. *Quarterly Journal of Economics, 70,* 65–94.

Stein, H. (2021). Institutionalising neoclassical economics in Africa: Instruments, ideology and implications. *Economy and Society, 50*(1), 120–147.

Sundström, A. (2013). Corruption in the commons: Why bribery hampers enforcement of environmental regulations in South African fisheries. *International Journal of the Commons, 7*(2), 454–472.

Swan, T. W. (1956). Economic growth and capital accumulation. *Economic Record, 32,* 334–361.

Torrens, R. (1821). *An essay on the production of wealth.* Longman, Hurst, Rees, Orme, and Brown. Reprint edited by J. Dorfman (1965). Kelley.

Transparency.org. (2021, January 28). CPI 2020: Sub-Saharan Africa. *Transparency International. The global coalition against corruption* [Online]. Available at: https://www.transparency.org/en/news/cpi-2020-sub-saharan-africa. Accessed 15 January 2022.

Turrow, S. (1985). What's wrong with bribery. *Journal of Business Ethics, 4*(4), 249–251.

UNDP. (2021). *Sustainable Development Goals* [Online]. Available at: https://www.africa.undp.org/content/rba/en/home/sustainable-development-goals. Accessed 16 January 2022.

United Nations General Assembly. (1987). *Report of the world commission on environment and development: Our common future.* United Nations General Assembly, Development and International Co-operation: Environment.

UN.org. (2021, July). *Tackling illicit financial flows, a matter of survival for Africa's development.* [Online]. Available at: https://www.un.org/africaren ewal/magazine/july-2021/tackling-illicit-financial-flows-matter-survival-afr icas-development. Accessed 15 January 2022.

Van Nieuwkerk, A. (2021). Seychelles. In *Africa Yearbook* (Vol. 17, pp. 365–372). Brill.

de Villiers, C., Cerbone, D., & Van Zijl, W. (2020). The South African government's response to COVID-19. *Journal of Public Budgeting, Accounting & Financial Management, 32*(5), 797–811.

Waldén, L. J. (1961). *A neo-classical theory of economic growth.* Allen and Unwin.

Wei, S.-J. (1999). *Corruption in economic development. Beneficial grease, minor annoyance, or major obstacle?* (World Bank Policy Research Working Paper No.

2048) [Online]. Available at: https://documents1.worldbank.org/curated/en/175291468765621959/pdf/multi-page.pdf. Accessed 15 January 2022.

Wicksell, K. (1934). *Lectures on political economy* (1st Swedish ed., 1901). Routledge.

World Bank. (2021). *The World Bank in Rwanda* [Online]. Available at: https://www.worldbank.org/en/country/rwanda/overview#1. Accessed 16 January 2022.

Organizational Culture and Corporate Sustainability in Africa

Dhawal Sharad Jadhav

1 Introduction

Sustainability discussions are sempiternal, like old wine in a new bottle; it is always on the global agenda. The debate on sustainability has been amaranthine since the late 1970s and has never faded. The sustainability journey, initiated from discussions on oil, forest, and production, has brought us to the present scenario of sustainable development goals (SDGs), which were always in search of peace, people, and the planet. It has been almost a half-century since humans discussed the same with too little to achieve. However, sustainability debates and the role of stakeholders in others, with their duties and responsibilities being considered accountable might lead us to the desired goal. The contribution of each stakeholder, small or large, can never be overlooked (Amankwah-Amoah et al., 2019). Government, legal regulations, political programs, Non-Governmental Organizations (NGOs), Corporates, or even for that matter a single individual, make considerable contributions toward sustainability. Varied modern terminologies like Sustainable

D. S. Jadhav (✉)
MICA, Ahmedabad, Ahmedabad, India
e-mail: dhawaljadhav.fpm21@micamail.in

© The Author(s), under exclusive license to Springer Nature
Switzerland AG 2023
S. Adomako et al. (eds.), *Corporate Sustainability in Africa*,
Palgrave Studies in African Leadership,
https://doi.org/10.1007/978-3-031-29273-6_9

Entrepreneurship (Adomako et al., 2021), Corporate Sustainability (CS), Sustainable Corporate Venturing, Sustainable intrapreneurship, Sustainability innovations, and Sustainability Strategies (Danso et al., 2019) revolve around stakeholders and their respective deeds and action.

A critical stakeholder besides individual entrepreneurs who made its mark is the Corporate (firm) in sustainability issues (Adomako & Tran, 2022). In an era of failures by governing authorities in developed, developing, and underdeveloped economies, corporates have been in the driving seat for welfare and prosperity. Nevertheless, the capitalist approach of corporates is one of the root causes behind social and environmental imbalances, which indirectly leads to a lack of sustainability in society. However, marginalizing corporate's creative and innovative approaches in modern corporate culture to solve sustainability issues is also incorrect. Talking about creativity and innovation, which boomeranged in various dimensions in the past decade, also developed reciprocal relationships between cultures. Culture is the pivotal point around which creativity and innovation revolve, and on the contrary, transforms the culture itself, eventually. Cultural norms and values with different ideologies influence entrepreneur and corporates to move toward a more sustainable solution for the survival of human civilization.

The research in sustainability will develop further understanding of the concept. It is argued that additional academic research would derive a better understanding, but lack of research in the least developed countries results in the concept lagging. The inclination toward CS in the least developed and developing countries is on the rise but is not rapid enough to match the pace of change. A gradual increase in research on CS in Africa would help increase the depth of knowledge in the overall concept. Policymaking and implementation of policies to achieve CS can be encouraged in such countries by establishing the connection between cultural values and moral standards rather than the economic outcome.

Talking about the cultural values of African countries, it has a lot to contribute to the conscious behavior of the world towards sustainability. Misunderstanding and inaccessibility of the African continent led to an altogether different image of Africa. Few failures of a political leader cannot overtake the glory of great leaders like Nelson Mandela and Martin Luther King. As the inaccessible rich traditional culture is more in oral than written, it has left gems of cultural thoughts that need to be unearthed. African cultural values, environmental beauties, hardworking and robust individuals, and much more need to be understood and cannot be studied from a distance. The African social philosophy "Ubuntu" can be the torchbearer of the world at large in the Sustainability dilemma. "Ubuntu is the capacity in African culture to express compassion, reciprocity, dignity, harmony, and humanity in the interests of building and maintaining a community with justice and mutual caring." (Nussbaum, 2003). Bishop Dandala (South Africa) views "Ubuntu is not a concept easily distilled into a methodological procedure. Rather, it is the bedrock of a specific lifestyle or culture that seeks to honor human relationships as primary in any social, communal, or corporate activity." Clubbing the social philosophy of Ubuntu with environmental and economic aspects would lead us to the modern concept of CS. Moreover, good leaders with good values craft the best world. "Umuntu ngumuntu ngabantu" (a person is a person because of others) (Nussbaum, 2003). Further, good leaders create good corporates, bringing sustainable development (social, environmental, and economic) that make a corporate a sustainable corporate.

2 Sustainability and Its Importance in the African Continent

Brundtland Commission has drawn the basic principle of sustainability, "meeting the needs of the present without compromising the ability of future generations to meet their own needs (WCED, 1987)." A large consensus developed around the fundamental understanding of sustainability, a combination of social, environmental, and economic concepts that bring sustainability (Bansal, 2005; Elkington, 1998). The balance between the urge to prosper and the preservation of social and environmental needs to be achieved (Nations, 2015). Talking about the commitment of the African continent toward sustainability can be ascertained from the interest shown by all African countries at the Paris climate conference in 2015 to act in the direction of environmental protection. The Greenhouse gas emissions of Africa are merely 3.6% of global greenhouse gas emissions, far less than the Asian and Pacific developing economies (Hubacek et al., 2021). The story would likely change; the big picture of rapid urbanization to achieve economic growth would undoubtedly change the above-mentioned figures. The African continent has shown rigor in fighting against various problems that would drastically change its ecosystem. Current figures are showing minimal changes and a long way to go ahead. Out of 17 goals under SDG, only two goals (i.e., Goal 12—Responsible Consumption and Production & Goal 13—Climate Action) have shown progress in Africa, as reported (IISD, 2021). The continent faces significant problems of financial inadequacy for healthcare, infrastructure development, poor governance, and bad leadership (Kyambalesa, 2004). Sustainable development is the demand of the day for the African continent. One needs to focus on various SDG goals (SDG 3— Good Health and well-being, SDG 9—Industry, innovation, and infrastructure, SDG 16—Peace and Justice), which need immediate attention (IISD, 2021). The above figures bring an enormous scope for development and improvement if seen through a different lens—higher scope of development, the initial stage of the growth cycle, and high hopes for a better future. Positive signs of development are coming out in reports. Africa has seven out of ten countries having the fastest economic growth in the world (Asongu & Rangan, 2016). United Nations, in its report of 2018, predicted a 75% urbanization rate by 2050 for Africa, against the current rate of urbanization of 50% (currently, half of the population of Africa lives in Urban areas).

Development is inevitable, and everyone deserves the right to develop; even mother nature allows every species to evolve as per the required needs. The only accountability we as a human species must keep in mind while developing is to be more and more sustainable on all three fronts of sustainability (Social, Environment, and Economic). The rule applies to all the world economies, and the same applies to the African continent. The African continent's benefit is that it can refer to the experiences of developed and developing economies to sketch their path to sustainable development. Sustainability and sustainable development is not a single actor's game; instead, it is a game of a team, and all the stakeholders play a vital role in the game. Restricting the scope of the article to one single stakeholder, we have selected corporations (firms) as change agents moving economies to sustainability and sustainable development. There has been disagreement for decades that the question of social and environmental problems is the responsibility of corporations in the quest for sustainability (Bansal, 2002).

On the other hand, various literature reflects the importance of sustainability and its linkage with positive corporate performance (Podsakoff & Macjenzie, 1997; Waddock & Graves, 1997). Embedding sustainability into day-to-day business functions and culture gives organizations an upper hand in fighting against environmental hazards and the negative impact of globalization, helping in economic contribution and poverty alleviation (Haugh & Talwar, 2010). This chapter will examine the academic and theoretical relevance of organizational culture (OC) in CS in the African context through web communication and qualitative content analysis.

3   Evolution of Corporate Sustainability

Before understanding the cultural connection of an organization with CS, it is essential to understand the concept of CS. Exploring the concept leads us to the evolution of the concept. The origin of CS goes back to the 1980s, which talks about incorporating environmental responsibility, social equity, and economic prosperity into the day-to-day activities of corporates. Brundtland's report (Brundtland, 1987) tokened CS. CS is all about long-term economic, social, environmental, and organizational goals. The acceptance of CS worldwide is due to its connections with the World Commission on Environment and Development (WCED, 1987). The report mentions the vital role of sustainability and future benefits to the current generations and the generations to come. The need of the present generation is to cater without hampering the ability of future generations to enjoy the same is the central idea.

Various definition of CS was mentioned in the past. We can observe the effect of various disciplines on the definition of CS (Kidd, 1992). Shrivstava (1995) brought ecological concerns to the table by proposing the effects of economic activities on non-users. The benefits of developed economies have transferred the cost onto the developing and developed economies (Shrivstava, 1995). Whereas the academic work of Carroll (1999) on Corporate social responsibility serves as a crucial concept through which the concept of CS flourished. Philanthropic activities and corporate citizenship (Carroll, 1999) were the outcomes that provided a new dimension to CS. In their definitions of CS, numerous authors revealed concern about natural and social development and depletion (Sharma & Aragon-Correa, 2005). The overall outcome of all definitions directed the concept of CS to an assemblage of Social, Economic, Environmental, Cultural, Operational, and Decision-making activities.

The future relies on corporates to navigate toward sustainable approaches and policies. Not only do corporates derive wealth maximization, but along with it, by following CS, they also develop better relations, reputation, and reliability with stakeholders. The Implementation of CS policies have a competitive advantage for corporates (Daily & Huang,

2001). Academic literature suggests various theories at the root, which has led the CS concept to maturity. Stakeholder Theory, Triple Bottom Line (TBL) Theory, and Institutional Theory are some of the significant theories nurturing the concept of CS. Effective policy framing is one side of the coin, but without its appropriate implementation, it need not be of any use. Transforming policy to action-oriented implementation is the crux of all stories (Ahmed et al., 2021).

The major drawback of CS is implementing the policy drafted for a problem-solving activity. More emphasis on academic research to increase the effective implementation of policies becomes the day's demand in the field of CS. Corporates and their culture were under the scanner for CS; more surprisingly, the organization itself was under the "black box" ideology (Howard-Grenville, 2006.). Rather than looking inside the organization, all research studied the external dimension of corporates. The culture of an organization becomes essential for bringing the imbalance to par (Wilkinson et al., 2001). Implementation of CS policies combines society with self-regulation, dynamic leadership, and stakeholders (Crane, Corporate greening as amoralization, 2000). The "Triple I" framework can analyse policy practices of corporate (Schaltegger et al., 2013). The "Triple I" approach consists of understanding corporate motivation for sustainability, which connects it with the core business, and finally, implementation of the same considering all stakeholders. The construct of "Triple I" has been explained in Fig. 1. Key components of the constructs are (a) Intention "why do companies manage sustainability?" (b) Integration "To what extent is corporate sustainability embedded in core business and organization?" and (c) Implementation "How is corporate sustainability operationalized?" which analyses (d) Practice of Corporate Sustainability. The usage of "Triple I" helps to draw the significant characteristics that affect sustainability. Sustainability concept being two dimensional is subjective on the individual ground for the corporate and general on the global ground for sustainable solutions. "Triple I" analysis considers other factors such as "Sectoral structure, Company Size, Annual Revenue, Number of employees" at the company level, and "Spread of National Average, Common global Pattern, and Intensity of Corporate practice" at the country-specific level. Implementing CS policies is not the only drawback; CS being a multifaceted concept requires changes from the top to bottom, including cultural values.

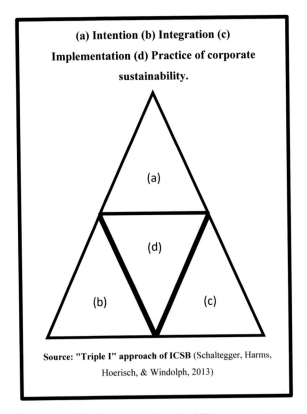

Fig. 1 Triple I approach of corporate sustainability

4 Evolution of Organizational Culture

The predictable behavior of humans leads us to the social system. Human behavior reflects values and culture. Moreover, culture not only affects humans but organizations as well. The Distribution of power, Organizational goals, Organizational Objectives, Decision-making process, Organization structure, and even reward systems are affected by culture. Culture and organizational theories have been discussed since the late 1970s and early 1980s (Hofstede, 1980; Schwartz & Davis, 1981). It proposes that OC can achieve sustainable business development, as it is a vital element. OC will help understand environmental, social, and

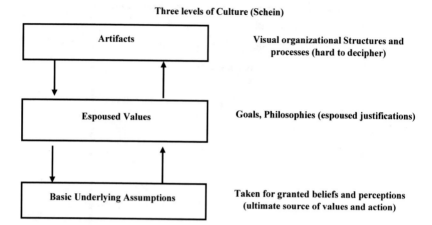

Fig. 2   Three levels of culture

economic beliefs. Though important, it continues to be a controversial concept in academic research (Crane, 1995; Jarnagin & Slocum, 2007). The controversy that hovers around the concepts of OC is based on diversity and varied perspectives. Consumer perspective, employee perspective, value congruence of the employee, and gender discrimination drive OC to various controversies. Varied definitions of culture prevail, but the primarily accepted definition amongst all is the one given by Edgar H. Schein in his book (Organizational Culture and Leadership).

> Culture is both a dynamic phenomenon that surrounds us at all times, being constantly enacted and created by our interactions with others and shaped by leadership behavior, and a set of structures, routines, rules, and norms that guide and constrain behavior.

Further, Schein states that the introduction of culture to an organization evolves into the concept of OC. In the words of Schein in his book (Organizational Culture and Leadership)

> When one brings culture to the level of the organization and even down to groups within the organization, one can see clearly how culture is created, embedded, evolved, and ultimately manipulated, and, at the same time, how culture constrains, stabilizes, and provides structure and meaning to the group members.

The study of OC continues to be highlighted due to various factors, but the critical factor that should draw our attention is "Failure in implementing change" (Linnenluecke & Griffiths, 2010). It says that Unique corporate cultures should be developed and appropriately managed for the steady performance of the firm. Developing and managing firms included "change" and its "practical implementation." Change in the external environment needs an exact reflection in the firm's internal environment. The strategy for growth with no change in OC would result in failure when implementing change. Without inculcating a change in OC, it would not be easy to achieve goals. The irony in the concept of OC is that people do not understand the culture unless and until the firm's culture is under test by new demands. People are unaware of their OC, and by the time they come to know it, it has become the organization's practice. This in turn resists the implementation of new strategies. The varied levels of cultures suggested by authors affect the organization and the stakeholders' behavior. The highest level of culture would be global level culture which talks about trends and technology globally. It is the broadest of all cultures and, includes the whole ecosystem of the globe—for example, sustainability practices. The lesser level of culture would be a national-level culture which would expand at the country level—further moving toward lesser-level cultures of the individual's, ethnic group, business, and occupation, and ultimately to gender-specific cultures. These cultures have various factors, such as language, values, and feelings. The least broad cultural level of all is a single OC. Management values, leadership styles, day-to-day activities, and routines depict OC and its uniqueness. There can be subcultures in an organization based on its production cycle, supply chain management system, and various functional departments. To inculcate change in a culture, looking at organizational goals does not constantly introduce a new culture. Change can come by modifying existing culture by establishing traditional management values and philosophies.

The three levels of culture explained by Edger Schein in his books talk about Artifacts, Espoused beliefs and Values, and Underlying Assumptions. Schein defines artifacts as visible organizational structures and processes that an observer from outside the organization observes (Schein, 2010). It is an OC that one perceives at the initial interaction with an organization, be it a recruit to the organization, a consultant, or a stakeholder. Actions that can be felt and observed, be it tangible or intangible, like environment, the pattern of Communication and language, observable values, and activities which are taken together in an organization. This level of culture is easy to notice and register but challenging to understand and decode. Schein draws the characteristics of this level as "difficult to decipher."

The second level of OC talks about individual values and actions drawn at initial levels of initiation of the activity. Individuals' beliefs and values are the distinguishing factors that create cultural differences. The leader or founder injects beliefs and values into the organizations. Beliefs and values reaching the level of no discussion become the organization's philosophy and come into practice during times of uncertainty. Beliefs at this level can be helpful to predict the behavior at the level of the artifact. Beliefs not based on previous learning will turn out to be "espoused theories," which can help understand what people say but would be way different from their actions. There was seen a higher level of contradiction at this level of OC.

The third level of the basic underlying assumption comes to action when repeated action comes into practice in a problem situation. This level transforms educated guess into the predominant line of action due to repeated usage. The level of acceptance reaches a point where any other premise suggested would not be accepted. Any action against accepted values and beliefs would disrupt mental stability and lead to anxiety and defensiveness.

"Organizational Cultural" and "Corporate Sustainability": Qualitative Content Analysis of African corporates.

The concepts mentioned CS and OC would be challenging to understand if not related to any African corporate. As the African continent is the second largest besides Asia, it would be challenging to select one corporate for all. Corporate selection is based on the company's sustainability practices and hence, it would be easier to relate the concept of CS and OC to the same. The African continent's sustainability issues need discussion before moving to a selection of the corporate. As discussed earlier, sustainability issues are subjective at different levels, be it global, continental, or national. Here we discuss sustainability issues in Africa rather than any specific country or region. The African continent faces several environmental-related challenges including "land degradation, biodiversity loss, deforestation, extreme vulnerability to climate change,

Carbon emission and water." The African continent has enormous potential for sustainability (Quartey & Oguntoye, 2020). "Africa is home to all nature's gifts that one can imagine, like the land being the second-largest continent, having arable land for agriculture and, around 12% of the world's oil reserves. It has almost 8% of natural gas amongst the world's natural gases reserves in addition to forest and wildlife." With the high usage of resources, considerable attention should be drawn to human well-being, as 15% of the world's population reside in Africa. It becomes the responsibility of the stakeholders to nurture, preserve, and utilize the same through a sensible approach. Talking about the corporate as a stakeholder towards the same should focus not only on economic and social environmental aspects but also on the social and human aspects.

We have selected the top three African corporates (having headquarters in Africa) from a list of the top 250 companies espoused by the African Business magazine[1] to study CS and OC in this chapter. The intention is to draw attention as to how sustainability and culture go hand in hand in an organization (corporate).

The companies selected were Naspers Limited, Anglo American Platinum, and First Rand Limited, all public companies listed on the National or Regional Stock Exchanges (Table 1). No second-ranked company with its headquarters outside South Africa was selected. This chapter tries to draw attention to cultural values and beliefs. Company headquarters located outside the African continent would affect OC. The other selected companies have their headquarters in Africa.

Let us analyse the selected companies' web communication with the help of qualitative content analysis to try and understand the concepts of Edger Schein's three levels of OC and "Triple I" of ICSB to understand CS. For analysis, we will rely on the reports and data provided by the organizations in their annual reports and official websites. First, let us understand the three levels of OC in all organizations by highlighting the content available. To understand the first level, "Artifacts," we consider the organization's published strategy statements. Schnier provides various examples of phenomena to artifacts in his book with, "published lists of values, myth, and stories" being some of them.

---

[1] https://african.business/dossiers/africas-top-companies/.

198 D. S. JADHAV

Table 1 Top 5 companies in 2021

Sr. No	Ranking 2021	Ranking 2020	Company name	Sector	Country	Market cap 2021($m)	Head quarter
1	1	2	Naspers	Consumer non-cyclicals	South Africa	104,163	Cape Town
2	2	4	Anglo American	Metals and Mining	United Kingdom	53,182	London
3	3	5	Anglo American Platinum	Non-energy materials	South Africa	38,666	Johannesburg
4	4	6	First rand	Finance	South Africa	19,610	Johannesburg
5	5	7	Vodacom Group	Telecommunications	South Africa	15,698	Midrand

We believe in the power of local backed by global scale, and we look for opportunities to address big societal needs in markets where we see the greatest growth potential. (**Naspers Limited**)[2]

We have moved from a growth-driven to a value-driven strategy. Implementing this value-driven strategy will deliver a stable, competitive, and profitable business that will be sustainable in the long-term and will deliver value to all stakeholders. (**Anglo American Platinum**)[3]

FirstRand commits to building a future of SHARED PROSPERITY through enriching the lives of its customers, employees, and the societies it serves. This is the foundation to a sustainable future and will preserve the group's enduring promise to create long-term value and superior returns for its shareholders. (**First Rand Limited**)[4]

We observe here that corporates interact with stakeholders by presenting strategies. If we consider the language in the paragraphs, it represents a dialogue between the corporate and stakeholders, introducing them to organization strategies. These strategies are present on

---

[2] https://www.naspers.com/about/strategy.

[3] https://www.angloamericanplatinum.com/about-us/our-approach.

[4] https://www.firstrand.co.za/the-group/about-firstrand/.

the website of the company. The company delivers a strong message to all stakeholders. Web communication, the virtual interface in a pandemic, will be the only communication medium.

To understand the second level, "Espoused beliefs and value," & third level, "Basic Underlying Assumptions," we consider the philosophies of all organizations.

We believe in the power of local backed by global scale. We continue to back new business models to fuel our growth and increasingly look for opportunities to address significant societal needs in markets with tremendous growth potential. These include all significant markets in the world. When we see a company with promise, we move quickly to expand and scale it.

We believe we are the best global growth partner for founders, startups, and other investors with the ambition to scale in our markets. Our operating model is different from many other companies. We both invest in and run leading companies, and we add value at all life stages. We create our businesses or invest in early-stage companies, take promising models and grow them quickly to scale, evolve and grow companies already at scale, and hold investments in listed companies with significant upside. **(Naspers Limited)**[5]

Our work spans every kind of challenge. However, whatever we are doing, we remember our values. These six values from the blueprint for our way of working: Innovation, Safety, Care and Respect, Integrity, accountability, and collaboration. **(Anglo American Platinum)**[6]

FirstRand is known for delivering on its promises – a reputation stemming from its unique owner-management philosophy. The foundations of the philosophy are created by the group's founders, entrepreneurs who understood the value of treating their employees like owners so that every employee, regardless of their position, is fully empowered to make a real contribution to the group's success. With empowerment comes commitment and accountability, which has been the cornerstone to FirstRand's sustained outperformance. This philosophy guides how the group's people need to behave to deliver the best results for customers, society, shareholders, and others. It currently captures in a set of promises. **(First Rand Limited)**[7]

---

[5] https://www.naspers.com/about/strategy.

[6] https://www.angloamericanplatinum.com/about-us/our-approach.

[7] https://www.firstrand.co.za/the-group/firstrand-philosophy/.

The above discloses the philosophies of how the leaders, founders, and promoters have presented their thought processes which in the short run become the espoused beliefs of the organization. Using the same beliefs and values turns them into basic underlying assumptions which due to repeated usage solves the organizations' problems. This chapter relies on secondary research for the empirical testing of concepts using qualitative content analysis. The "Triple I" concept analysis is conducted similarly in the above manner. Identifying the content of Intention, Integration, and implementation will help derive CS practices. The content of the Organization's Intention, Integration, and implementation of "Naspers Limited"[8] and "Anglo American Platinum"[9] is as follows.

Using technology to catalyze positive change and find solutions for shared global challenges. (**Naspers Limited**)

Pursuing excellence in sustainability is a fundamental part of our business strategy, and one of our five primary business levers. (**Anglo American Platinum**)

The above statements depict the corporate's apparent motivation to bring solutions to global challenges. The statements used by the corporates are their intentions to be sustainable (Perks et al., 2022). Intentions need to be integrated into the organization's goals at the second stage of the "Triple I" approach. The content on the website proves the fulfillment of the second stage of the approach—a refined integration of the Intention.

We create sustainable value by building consumer internet companies that address big societal needs – they improve people's everyday lives and enrich the communities they serve. We back local entrepreneurs, providing the funds and support they need to help them grow and achieve their dreams. Our local focus combined with our global scale means the companies we operate and invest in can deliver far-reaching impact. (**Naspers Limited**)

We deliver excellence in sustainability through (a) Improved employee health and safety and striving towards zero harm (b) Effective environmental management, maintaining ISO 14001 certification and pursuing environmental best practices (c) Creating sustainable value for communities

---

[8] https://www.naspers.com/sustainability/overview.

[9] https://www.angloamericanplatinum.com/about-us/our-approach.

and achieving this by engaging regularly, transparently and meaningfully. (**Anglo American Platinum**)

In the above paragraphs, organizations accept integrating sustainability intention into their day-to-day activity. Implementing the same sustainable goal will lead the organization to develop a better CS (Frempong et al., 2022).

> Sustainability is at the core of what we do. Our focus on digital platforms helps keep our environmental impact light while enabling newer, more innovative, and greener ways to serve the world's everyday needs. (**Naspers Limited**)
> We make a positive contribution through job creation; skills development; education; health provision; local economic development; procurement opportunities; payment of royalties and taxes; and infrastructure development and housing. (**Anglo American Platinum**)

The above statements make it clear how the organization can establish sustainability, considering all levels in an organization.

In this chapter, we have tried to run with preliminary qualitative content analysis to get an idea of web communication (Karyotakis & Antonopoulos, 2021). Qualitative content analysis is one of the better options available to analyse the media available from the corporate. Qualitative content analysis of website communication helps us understand the discourse behind the text. It can be a small effort to club web communication with well-established OC and CS concepts and develop an analysis for conceptual understanding.

5 Managerial Implication

Communication by corporates is a day-in, day-out process, with never-ending effort. Post-pandemic, the importance of virtual platforms and online Communication has increased. The world moved into the metaverse half a century back, but post-pandemic, the whole process of going virtual is the new normal worldwide, and hence corporates have to understand the importance of virtual platforms. First, the organization cannot risk overlooking active virtual platforms such as social media handles and passive virtual platforms like corporate websites, which are static but have become the new interface of Communication for such companies. Second, the online platform is the only medium left for corporates during the pandemic which started bringing about a gradual shift in the digital culture of the corporates and their stakeholders. Corporate websites became the only source of communication during the pandemic which organizations could manage. So due care and consideration are required when updating the same.

Third, if appropriately communicated, the concept of CS would be more effective than when being merely presented on a static virtual platform. Effective communication of efforts toward sustainability will be highly appreciated and acknowledged by stakeholders. Corporates claiming to be green fail at some point to explain to their stakeholders how effective the product is and what remarkable contribution takes place through such a small initiative. Finally, Web communication and content analysis will increase due to changing media consumption habits. Merely claiming CS would be challenged in years to come will not be accepted. Integration of sustainability intentions in OC and communicating it to all stakeholders effectively will be the unannounced mission of corporates leaders and management.

6 Conclusion

This chapter discusses the evolution of CS and changes required in the OC to collaborate with modern concepts. The chapter also highlights the importance of web communication and data content being created by the corporate. Virtual actions, be they active or static in the post-pandemic era, would be scanned and analysed for information on the culture, beliefs and values, practices, and the claims of corporates. Whether physical or virtual, corporates need to continuously analyse their cultural growth in sustainability parameters. Various maturity models on OC and CS are available in literature; utilizing them for continuous evaluation should be strongly recommended. The cultural alignment maturity model[10] and the business sustainability maturity model (Cagnin et al., 2005) are examples of maturity models considered on subjective grounds.

---

[10] https://hroutsider.wordpress.com/2012/04/09/organizational-culture-are-you-taking-it-to-the-next-level/

References

Adomako, S., & Tran, M. (2022). Sustainable environmental strategy, firm competitiveness, and financial performance: Evidence from the mining industry. *Resources Policy, 75*, 102515.

Adomako, S., Amankwah-Amoah, J., Danso, A., & Dankwah, G. (2021). Chief executive officers' sustainability orientation and firm environmental performance: Networking and resource contingencies. *Business Strategy and the Environment, 30*(4), 2184–2193.

Ahmed, M., Mubarik, M., & Shahbaz, M. (2021). Factors affecting the outcome of corporate sustainability policy: A review paper. *Environmental Science and Pollution Research, 28*(9), 10335–10356.

Amankwah-Amoah, J., Danso, A., & Adomako, S. (2019). Entrepreneurial orientation, environmental sustainability and new venture performance: Does stakeholder integration matter? *Business Strategy and the Environment, 28*(1), 79–87.

Asongu, S., & Rangan, G. (2016). Trust and quality of growth. *Economics Bulletin, 36*(3), 1854–1867.

Bansal, P. (2005). Evolving sustainably: A longitudinal study of corporate sustainable development. *Strategic Management Journal, 26*(3), 197–218.

Brundtland, G. H. (1987). *Report of the World Commission on environment and development: "Our common future."* UN.

Cagnin, C., Loveridge, D., & Buttler, J. (2005). Business sustainability maturity model. *Business Strategy and the Environment Conference, 2005*, 4–6.

Carroll, A. (1999). Corporate social responsibility: Evolution of a definitional construct. *Business & Society, 38*(3), 268–295.

Crane, A. (1995.). Rhetoric and reality in the greening of organizational culture. *Greener Management International, 12*, 49–62.

Crane, A. (2000). Corporate greening as amoralization. *Organization Studies, 21*(4), 673–696.

Daily, B., & Huang, S. (2001). Achieving sustainability through attention to human resource factors in environmental management. *International Journal of Operations & Production Management.*

Danso, A., Adomako, S., Amankwah-Amoah, J., Owusu-Agyei, S., & Konadu, R. (2019). Environmental sustainability orientation, competitive strategy and financial performance. *Business Strategy and the Environment, 28*(5), 885–895.

Elkington, J. (1998). Partnerships from cannibals with forks: The triple bottom line of 21st-century business. *Environmental Quality Management, 8*(1), 37–51.

Frempong, M., Mu, Y., Adu-Yeboah, S., Hossin, M., & Amoako, R. (2022). Corporate sustainability and customer loyalty: The role of firm's green image. *Journal of Psychology in Africa*, 1–7.

204   D. S. JADHAV

Haugh, H., & Talwar, A. (2010). How do corporations embed sustainability across the organization? *Academy of Management Learning & Education, 9*(3), 384–396.

Hofstede, G. (1980). Culture and organizations. *International Studies of Management & Organization, 10*(4), 15–41.

Howard-Grenville, J. (2006). Inside the "black box" how organizational culture and subcultures inform interpretations and actions on environmental issues. *Organization & Environment, 19*(1), 46–73.

Hubacek, K., Chen, X., Feng, K., Wiedmann, T., & Shan, Y. (2021). Evidence of decoupling consumption-based CO_2 emissions from economic growth. *Advances in Applied Energy, 4*, 100074.

IISD. (2021). *IISD (8th February 2021) 2020 Africa SDG index and dashboards report-leaving no one*. IISD.

Jarnagin, C., & Slocum, J. (2007). Creating corporate cultures through mythopoetic leadership. *SMU cox school of business research paper series* (07-004).

Karyotakis, M., & Antonopoulos, N. (2021). Web communication: A content analysis of green hosting companies. *Sustainability, 13*(2), 495.

Khizar, H., Iqbal, M., Khalid, J., & Adomako, S. (2022). Addressing the conceptualization and measurement challenges of sustainability orientation: A systematic review and research agenda. *Journal of Business Research, 142*, 718–743.

Kidd, C. (1992). The evolution of sustainability. *Journal of Agricultural and Environmental Ethics*, 1–26.

Kyambalesa, H. (2004). *Socio-economic challenges: The African context*. Africa World Press.

Linnenluecke, M., & Griffiths, A. (2010). Corporate sustainability and organizational culture. *Journal of World Business, 45*(4), 357–366.

Nations, U. (2015). *Transforming our world: The 2030 Agenda for Sustainable Development*. United Nation.

Nussbaum, B. (2003). Perspectives. *African culture and Ubuntu, 17*(1), 1-12.

Perks, C., Mudd, G., & Currell, M. (2022). Using corporate sustainability reporting to assess the environmental footprint of titanium and zirconium mining. *The Extractive Industries and Society, 9*, 101034.

Podsakoff, P., & Macjenzie, S. (1997). Impact of organizational citizenship behavior on organizational performance: A review and suggestion for future research. *Human Performance, 10*(2), 133–151.

Quartey, S., & Oguntoye, O. (2020). Promoting corporate sustainability in small and medium-sized enterprises: Key determinants of intermediary performance in Africa. *Business Strategy and the Environment, 29*(3), 1160–1172.

ORGANIZATIONAL CULTURE AND CORPORATE ...   205

Schaltegger, S., Harms, D., Hoerisch, J., & Windolph, S. (2013). *International corporate sustainability barometer.* CSM (Center for Sustainability Management).

Schein, E. (2010). *Organizational culture and leadership.* John Wiley & Sons.

Schwartz, H., & Davis, S. (1981). Matching corporate culture and business strategy. *Organizational Dynamics, 10*(1), 30–48.

Sharma, S., & Aragon-Correa, J. (2005). Corporate environmental strategy and competitive advantage: A review from the past to the future. In *Corporate environmental strategy and competitive advantage* (pp. 1–26). Edward Elgar.

Shrivstava, P. (1995). The role of corporations in achieving ecological sustainability. *Academy of Management Review, 20*(4), 936–960.

Trice, H., & Beyer, J. (1984). Studying organizational cultures through rites and ceremonials. *Academy of Management Review, 9*(4), 653–669.

Waddock, S., & Graves, S. (1997). The corporate social performance-financial performance link. *Strategic Management Journal, 18*(4), 303–319.

WCED, S. (1987). Our common future. *World Commission on Environment and Development, 17*, 1–91.

Wilkinson, A., Hill, M., & Gollan, P. (2001). The sustainability debate. *International Journal of Operations & Production Management.*

Entrepreneurship and Sustainability

Sustainability Activities and Business Model Innovation

Alessio Faccia⑩, Zeenat Beebeejaun⑩, and Narcisa Roxana Mosteanu⑩

1 INTRODUCTION

Innovation Taxonomy and Technology Paradigms

The innovation taxonomy classifies incremental innovation, radical innovation and new technological systems (Ettlie et al., 1984). It helps evaluate the economic importance of new technologies. A technological shift took place in the 1980s and 1990s to a more flexible, information-intensive and computerised technology (Soskice, 1999). This shift falls into the fourth type of innovation, which deals with changes in the

---

A. Faccia (✉) · Z. Beebeejaun
University of Birmingham Dubai, Dubai, United Arab Emirates
e-mail: a.faccia@bham.ac.uk

Z. Beebeejaun
e-mail: z.beebeejaun@bham.ac.uk

N. R. Mosteanu
Finance and Business Management, American University of Malta, Cospicua, Malta
e-mail: narcisa.mosteanu@aum.edu.mt

© The Author(s), under exclusive license to Springer Nature Switzerland AG 2023
S. Adomako et al. (eds.), *Corporate Sustainability in Africa*, Palgrave Studies in African Leadership,
https://doi.org/10.1007/978-3-031-29273-6_10

technical–economic paradigm matching technological revolutions (Perez, 2004, 2010).

This chapter focuses only on the last type of innovation, namely the innovation paradigm shift (Sanyang et al., 2016). Sometimes changes in the technological system have such far-reaching effects that their influence is decisive not only on certain sectors but also on the general trend of the economy: those 'waves of creative destruction' (Stein, 1997) pivot the Schumpeterian theory (Shumpeter, 1942) on long-lasting cycles in economic development.

Examples of these profound transformations, called '*techno-economic paradigm changes*' or '*technological revolutions*', are the spread of the steam engine and electric energy or the set of innovations associated with the electronic computer. The term 'paradigm' identifies a process of economic choice within the range of technically possible combinations of innovations (Cantwell & Santangelo, 2000). Therefore, it takes a relatively long time (at least a decade) for a new paradigm to stabilise (Stiglitz, 2002) and even longer for it to spread through the system through a complex interaction between technological, economic and political factors. A new paradigm affects the structure and conditions of production and distribution in almost all sectors of the economy (Bartez-zaghi, 1999); it enhances the perception of the existing paradigm's limits on the further development of productivity, profitability and the market.

The new technical–economic paradigm induced by information and communication technology is based on multiple innovations affecting some of the fastest developing sectors in all major industrialised countries (hardware, electronic components, telecommunications); in addition to notable improvements in technical performance, it has already produced a sharp fall in costs and an anti-inflationary trend in prices in these sectors.

Thanks to its potential economic advantages, the current technological revolution affects all other sectors, albeit in very different ways. It is necessary to consider individual products and processes and the changes that information and communication technology induce in the organisation and structure of companies and industries.

The spread of information and communication technology has numerous side effects on the economy (Stiroh, 2002)and produces radical changes in factory layouts, robotics, computer control, mindset, management structure (Gunasekaran & Yusuf, 2002) and procedures of large companies. Products and processes can be changed more efficiently and quickly; company functions (design, production, procurement) are much more closely integrated, helped by using the ERPs (Enterprise Resource Planning systems) (Carton & Adam, 2009). The importance of economies of scale (Woudstra, 2010) based on specialised techniques of capital-intensive mass production diminishes; the number and weight of the mechanical components of many products are reduced; networks of component suppliers and finished product fitters can be better integrated, resulting in capital savings; new 'business as a services' (BaaSs) (Theobaldt & Vervest, 2012) satisfy the growing demand for software, projects, information and technical consultancy on the part of manufacturing companies. Many innovative small businesses are developing rapidly, providing these services and introducing new hardware and components. These shifts are far beyond single radical innovations and justify using the term 'paradigm shift'.

Several research programs implemented in Europe, America and Japan have identified the success factors in industrial innovation (Evanschitzky et al., 2012). One of the main success factors is the relationship with the potential users of the innovation (Blindenbach-Driessen & Van Den Ende, 2006). The failures concerned the lack of interest in future users and the presumption that the innovating company knew their needs better than anyone else. In some cases, which proved to be commercially disastrous, the new products had never been tested to the conditions they would have been used before being placed on the market.

Another factor that proves to be very important is the extent and intensity of engagement with external scientific and technical advice sources (Klevorick et al., 1995). Successful innovations usually depended on a good level of research and development within the company, but this was almost always complemented by information, suggestions and advice provided by external researchers and technicians, active in universities and public laboratories or as consultants.

2 OPEN INNOVATION IN AFRICA

Innovation arises from the chaos (Quinn, 1985a) generated by relationships, comparisons and ideas that can emerge at any moment, and it is also born thanks to a leadership capable of managing this chaos and directing it towards a shared purpose (Quinn, 1985b). Open Innovation is a paradigm where companies can and must use external ideas and internal ones and access markets with internal and external paths if they want to progress in their technological skills. The idea of 'open innovation' was introduced by the American economist Henry Chesbrough in the essay 'The era of open innovation' (Chesbrough, 2003) as opposed to 'closed innovation', where the innovation is generated within the companies' boundaries—using their sole resources—which according to Chesbrough, could no longer be enough, despite the fears of the companies that they are no longer the only 'owners' of the inventions. The new knowledge and business models introduced by startups not engaging with existing potentially more digitally advanced companies can prove a disadvantage. Indeed, the risk is always at the root of progress and success.

Among the concrete, open innovation approach is inter-company agreements, economic support for startup competitions, hackathons, acquisition by large corporations of innovative startups, corporate accelerators for startups, and partnerships with universities, research centres and incubators to innovate in specific sectors.

In the collective imagination, Africa is bent by poverty. From an economic perspective, it remains the poorest continent on the planet. However, it is becoming a model even for the richest countries searching for sustainable solutions. African countries are rich in natural resources that can be exploited to generate clean energy. A successful example is given by Kenya, which produces 70% of its energy needs from renewable sources and could reach 100% in the next ten years (Takase et al., 2021). In addition to using alternative energies, Africa has become a destination chosen by many companies to test green devices (Sabban, 2021) and give the African people a better life. In short, if absolute poverty remains today, it seems the starting point for a cleaner world.

Thanks to the climate and the variety of natural resources, several multinationals have experimented with products to be launched in Africa. In Kenya, Alphabet, Google's holding, tested Project Loon, an autonomous balloon technology with mobile towers inside for internet connection powered by solar panels (4G LTE connection speeds are up to 18.9 Mbps in download and 4.74 in upload).

In addition to Kenya, other countries are moving towards Sustainable and Open Innovation. Egypt is planning a solar-powered greenhouse (Sagheer et al., 2021) for lettuce that will be fully automatic. The Dutch firm that owns the patent, Vander Hoeven, confirmed that it would place some in other African states if the greenhouse works.

Indeed, since 1999, Africa has experienced an unstoppable pace of growth (Zhao et al., 2021): it has reached a level of education that guarantees six years of schooling (Atilola et al., 2021) on average compared to four in the 1990s (the global average is eight years), it has registered an exponential increase in population (Atoyebi & Anuodo, 2018), bringing about one million Africans to the labour market every month and has become a hub of technological innovation with 400 million dollar local companies, more profitable than their counterparts in the rest of the world.

The expansion of local businesses has made the African continent a test laboratory for global innovation. This context has favoured corporate experimentation in different fields, such as high-tech, low-tech, agricultural, transportation, micro-credit and banking services.

In addition, seven African countries, with Uganda and Egypt in the lead, have been included by Harvard University's Center for International Development (Bowles et al., 2020) among the 15 growing economies by 2027, thanks to an improving education system, an ambitious effort to lower trade barriers and the progressive democratisation of the continent.

In 2017, the G20 Global Compact (Mabera, 2019) with Africa was launched, which today counts 12 African countries, together with some international organisations and bilateral partners of the G20, to promote private investment in Africa.

In October 2019, Ethiopian Prime Minister Abiy Ahmed Ali was awarded the Nobel Peace Prize for a historic agreement with Eritrea, and in July 2019, the African Continental Free Trade Treaty (AfCFTA) was signed by 54 countries. Regulates the opening of borders and creates a Pan-African area of commercial exchange, the largest in the world. This agreement is crucial for adopting Open Innovation strategies that can improve the growth and integration of innovative approaches. The evolution of African countries is highly uneven, and it is creating opportunity gaps. The main factors that should be considered to face the innovation challenges are an extremely young population, good access to the web and great social challenges to overcome.

3 Sustainability Issues in Africa

For several reasons, sustainability is critical for business model innovation in the African context. Firstly, Africa is highly dependent on natural resources and ecosystems, which are vulnerable to degradation and depletion. It makes it important for African businesses to adopt sustainable practices to preserve these resources for future generations.

Secondly, Africa has a rapidly growing population and lacks infrastructure and resources. It means businesses must be mindful of their impact on the environment and society and work to minimise negative impacts and promote sustainable development.

Finally, the African continent is at risk of being left behind in transitioning to a low-carbon economy. Sustainable business models can help African businesses stay competitive and attract investment while contributing to the fight against climate change.

Furthermore, sustainability is critical for business model innovation in Africa because it helps protect natural resources, promote sustainable development and stay competitive in a rapidly changing global economy.

Another reason sustainability is critical for business model innovation in the African context is that it can help improve local communities livelihoods. Many African communities rely on natural resources for their livelihoods, and businesses that operate in these areas are responsible for ensuring that their activities do not harm local communities or their ability to make a living. By adopting sustainable business models, businesses can work to improve the livelihoods of local communities and promote sustainable development.

In addition, many African countries face serious socio-economic challenges such as poverty, unemployment and inequality. Businesses that adopt sustainable business models can help to address these challenges by creating jobs, improving access to goods and services and promoting economic growth. It can help to reduce poverty, improve living standards and promote more equitable and inclusive economic development.

Finally, sustainability is critical for business model innovation in Africa because it can help attract and retain customers and talent. Increasingly, consumers and employees are looking for socially and environmentally responsible businesses. By adopting sustainable business models, African businesses can demonstrate their commitment to these values, which can help to attract and retain customers and talent.

In summary, sustainability is critical for business model innovation in the African context because it can help to protect natural resources, promote sustainable development, improve the livelihoods of local communities, address socio-economic challenges and attract and retain customers and talent.

- **The indications that global warming is causing major upheavals are becoming more and more evident.**

An example of an African country whose sustainability issues have been severely impacted is the Cocoa Republic, which has a population of nearly 28 million and is projected to increase soon. The country faces various challenges regarding demographic and economic growth—including the necessity for implementing sustainable development practices while preserving its fragile ecosystem. The Cocoa Republic committed itself to reduce greenhouse gas emissions by 30.41% by 2030 at COP26 in Glasgow, Scotland. It is a major and indispensable endeavour as the country's wealth, whose economy largely revolves around agriculture, relies on its fertile land. To sustain progress and meet targets set for 2030, a transition to green growth is vital; many aspects need attention.

- **Climate change realities**

The average temperature is already increasing, thus causing harm to the environment. The African desert wind, called the Harmattan, now blows for almost three months compared to a decade ago when it only lasted two weeks. Sea levels are also rising, which may have serious consequences, especially in coastal African countries.

Climate change could harm one of Africa's most important crops, cocoa. The continent is the world's largest exporter of this product, producing around 2 million tonnes per year. Rising temperatures could make the land drier and less fertile, causing a decline in production since plantations need to be moved to higher altitudes where temperatures are more favourable.

- **Forest preservation**

On 17 November 2021, the European Commission proposed a new law to close the EU market to any product implicated in deforestation. It would include soya, timber, cocoa, coffee, palm oil and beef,

216   A. FACCIA ET AL.

as well as some of their derivative products, such as leather and furniture. The closure of the EU market could help reduce global warming by reducing the amount of rainforest destroyed yearly. It would also protect endangered animal species and improve biodiversity levels.

- **The plastic waste epidemic is a serious problem that needs to be addressed.**

s.

As the population of a continent continues to grow, there is an increase in the overall generation of waste. Of this waste, 95% ends up in well-managed landfills or the wild, accumulates, threatens aquatic life in Africa's lagoons and flows into streams and rivers to coastal mouths.

Plastic waste is a major environmental problem across the continent, with a significant proportion of plastic waste ending up in the oceans, rivers and on land, where it can harm wildlife, damage ecosystems and negatively impact human health.

In Africa, the problem is exacerbated by a lack of effective waste management systems, limited public awareness about the impacts of plastic waste, and the fact that many African countries have weak regulations and enforcement mechanisms to control the use and disposal of plastic. It has led to plastic waste accumulating in many African cities, towns, and rural areas, causing environmental and public health problems.

It is important to take a multi-faceted approach that includes reducing the amount of plastic produced and used, improving waste management systems, raising public awareness about the impacts of plastic waste and implementing regulations and enforcement mechanisms to control the use and disposal of plastic.

In addition, businesses operating in Africa can play a key role in addressing the plastic waste epidemic by adopting sustainable business models that reduce plastic use and promote environmentally-friendly alternatives. It can include using more biodegradable materials, investing in recycling and waste management infrastructure, and promoting circular economy principles.

In summary, the plastic waste epidemic is a serious problem that needs to be addressed in Africa. A multi-faceted approach is needed, including reducing the amount of plastic produced, improving waste management systems, raising public awareness and implementing regulations and enforcement mechanisms. Businesses operating in Africa can play a key role by adopting sustainable business models that reduce the use of plastic and promote environmentally-friendly alternatives.

- **Saving the mangroves**

Mangrove forests are coastal ecosystems that grow on land between the water and the atmosphere. They are rich in biodiversity, with mangroves dominating their landscape. These trees have a high tolerance to salt air and can absorb large amounts of CO_2 from the environment. As an important part of local economies, these forests play an important role in mitigating global warming by absorbing carbon dioxide emissions from human activities. Mangrove forests also provide marine life with crucial habitats, helping to sustain fisheries and tourism industries. Africa's mangroves are a key part of stability and diversity in ecosystems, yet they face constant threats of extinction.

4 SUSTAINABILITY AND INNOVATION IN AFRICA

This section focuses on the renewal of development challenges in Africa concerning the increase in inequalities, climate change, food insecurity, population growth and political conflicts to challenge the effectiveness of public policies. In this context, it questions how to adapt a systemic and interactive analysis framework of innovation to strengthen the societal capacities that drive new technological, economic and social trajectories. This proposal thus highlights how the analytical framework of the National Innovation System (SNI) remains incomplete in understanding the different structures of governance of innovation. Finally, for innovation to be a vector for the inclusive and sustainable development of the most fragile economies, it is necessary to renew the priority indicators that steer research and technology. Three axes structure our special issue and relate to the need to strengthen Capacities while improving the mechanisms of innovation governance.

- **Propaedeutic to the theory of National Systems of Innovation applied to economic development**

Widely used and disseminated as a key concept within international organisations, as well as a current instrument of economic policy, the

218 A. FACCIA ET AL.

National Innovation System (SNI) makes it possible to identify the actors participating in the innovation process in a national framework, while putting highlights the learning relationships between these actors. In this article, we will present in a didactic and synoptic way the concept's genesis, its evolution from a theoretical point of view and its application within the framework of a developing economy.

- **The determinants of innovation in an African middle-income economy, a reassessment of innovation models**

Research on innovation in African economies is scarce. We contribute to the literature on the determinants of innovation in several ways. First, we assume that African economies are very diverse and that, consequently, the complex set of drivers on innovation behaviour must be assessed according to the type of economy. We distinguish several categories of African economies and focus our research on middle-income African economies, particularly Cameroon. Secondly, we take innovation behaviour in its diversity (product/process; simple/complex). Based on World Bank data for 2016, econometric estimates tend to show that R&D expenditure does not explain the decision to innovate. This hardly neo-Schumpeterian result could be explained by three factors: an atypical innovator model of the market pull type, the presence of so-called below-the-radar innovation and the importance of frugal innovation.

- **The National Innovation System applied to agriculture: a methodological proposal for diagnosis in Africa**

Appropriate methodologies have not always guided policy interventions in the agricultural sector to reduce the risk of failure. In Africa, interventions in the agriculture sector have long relied on two main approaches. First is the linear (top-down) approach to development, then the participatory (top-down-bottom-up) or systemic approach. However, linear models of innovation diffusion have become obsolete. Also, within the interactional models, some stand out from the others. It is the case with the National Innovation System (NIS) framework, a policy analysis and governance tool in many African countries, including Burkina Faso. In the latter case, the (SIN) framework has been tested since the early 2000s. Nowadays, it is very popular in policy and research. Agriculture is a key sector in African countries like Burkina Faso. The current challenge is to develop a practical methodological guide for diagnosing African agricultural innovation systems. It brings us to the contextualisation of the tools provided by the model. This article is a contribution based on the authors' research results. The first part of the article presents the approach used. Then, it reviews the approaches to agricultural innovation in Burkina Faso and Africa in general and their theoretical foundations. Finally, it makes a methodological proposal for diagnosing agricultural innovation systems in Burkina Faso and Africa.

- **Digital innovation and structural transformation of African economies, risky opportunities for development?**

Due to the speed and scale of the changes it brings about in sub-Saharan Africa, digital technology is transforming traditional political, economic, social and cultural models. Nevertheless, who benefits from these changes? Do these technologies contribute to a profound structural transformation of West African economies and societies, breaking with the previous development models? This section summarises the state of knowledge that can be mobilised on the nature of the relationship between digital technology and the structural transformation of African economies (pooling of resources, industrialisation of services, risks of globalised governance) and the emergence at several levels of regulatory frameworks for this technological sector. To do this, we mobilise different empirical experiences in the governance of the French-speaking part of Africa in support of national research and innovation policies and the analysis of the conditions for developing digital technology in the agricultural sector. We thus document the range of opportunities and risks posed by exploiting these technologies in the context of the development of Africa.

5   Leapfrogging Technology Shifts

In the African case, where technological progress has been interrupted or discontinued in many countries, the innovative process occurs through the direct (not gradual) introduction of new technologies. This process is identified as 'leapfrogging' (Adeleye, N., & Eboagu, 2019). In many African countries, until recently classified somewhat improperly as the

Third World, an extraordinary acceleration of development can be witnessed, achieved by skipping less efficient, more expensive or polluting technologies and moving directly to the more advanced ones. A classic example of technology leapfrog is mobile communication technology. Many developing countries have skipped twentieth-century landline technology to shift to twenty-first century mobile technology directly.

Technological and entrepreneurial hubs have been concentrated near the coasts and ports (Hönke, 2018). It is here that most of the hubs being researched are concentrated. Most tech hubs have partnerships with Orange, MTN and Vodafone (Curwen & Whalley, 2018), the major players on the TLC market in the continent, and with tech companies such as Microsoft, Amazon, Apple and Facebook (Heston & Zwetsloot, 2020).

6 Innovation and Sharing Economy in Africa

Many examples of innovative technologies (listed in Table 1 below) served the purpose of the so-called 'sharing economy'.

7 African Innovation and Economy During and Post COVID-19

Africa is focusing on technology for its recovery. The COVID-19 pandemic has accelerated the digitisation process in various countries due to the necessary use of smart solutions to guarantee people's safety.

Africa is particularly struggling from the coronavirus pandemic in terms of human and economic lives but is nevertheless benefiting from innovation during this period. Moreover, the impact of COVID-19 is significant not only on individual lives but also on business, society and businesses, with the result that—where the epidemic hinders human interaction - technology has been used. Due to COVID-19, there was a generalised drop in the Gross Domestic Production (GDP) (Ataguba, 2020). The impact is even more serious in the economies of countries with a strong growth rate and those linked to oil exports, such as Nigeria (Andam et al., 2020; Farayibi & Asongu, 2020). Despite these direct consequences, African states appear to be positive about the prospects of resilience and growth, thanks to new technologies.

SUSTAINABILITY ACTIVITIES AND BUSINESS MODEL ... 221

Table 1 Innovative African solutions and sharing economy

ARED (McDaveand Hackman-Aidoo, 2021)	It is a Hardware-as-a-Service company based in Rwanda and Uganda. Its product is Shiriki Hub (https://startsomegood.com/shiriki-hub), a mobile solar kiosk for charging phones and accessing the Internet
Diylaw (Laver, 2019) https://diylaw.ng/	It allows for simplifying the creation of legal documents avoiding costly consultations for entrepreneurs
Envyl (Lanz, 2021) https://www.envyl.com/	The startup allows African users to buy goods in US online stores and receive them directly in Africa. This success is made possible by creating a community of people who regularly travel to and from the United States and play as 'couriers' by filling their luggage space in exchange for a fee. Therefore, the goods arrive based on those who make their luggage space available and postal transit times once they arrive in Africa
Malaria No More (Turner & Robinson, 2014) https://www.malarianomore.org/	It is a non-profit project that uses Mobile technology that has allowed an impressive leap forward: the organisation uses SMS to educate on the use of mosquito nets and the recognition of malaria symptoms
Meltwater https://www.meltwater.com/en	It promotes the training of future technology startuppers by providing coaching and mentorship
Mlouma (Ndour & Gueye, 2016) https://www.mlouma.com/	The Senegalese platform offers users an overview of the agricultural products available in each production area and market. With Mlouma, sellers or buyers can report the products they want to sell or book a product of their interest. All via SMS
Shuttlers (Junaid, 2019) https://www.shuttlers.ng/	Nigerian startup simplifies the movements of commuters who work in Lagos (with over 16 million inhabitants, it is the largest city in Africa). The Shuttlers app allows users to reserve seats onboard shuttle buses at a competitive price

In 2019, digitisation created 1.7 million direct jobs in Africa (Ndung'u & Signe, 2020) and around 15.6 billion in tax revenues for the various African governments (Mehboob, 2021). During lockdown and social distancing, many businesses revolutionised their services. Despite millions of job losses due to the pandemic due to the depreciation of oil prices and the reduction of tourism, the increased use of digital services is creating new jobs. The growth and spread of apps (i.e., Glovo, Uber and Jumia) and the creation of jobs that they directly and indirectly entail (including the sale of smartphones and tablets) have substantially proved resilient. Even where investments do not require large sums, the lack of funds to support the development of the services is somehow mitigated by international organisations that try to make up for it by granting financial contributions (Clifton et al., 2018).

Therefore, African countries are determined to improve their future growth chances through technological innovation. Even if digitisation is not uniformly developed, its rise is strong in all states. Through technology, Africa can ensure its resilience and create a sustainable economy for its inhabitants.

According to the International Monetary Fund, by 2025, almost half a billion Africans living in sub-Saharan air will connect via smartphones (Alper & Miktus, 2019): the growth potential is to predict a bright future.

8 Innovation and Regulatory Framework in Africa

Thanks to regulatory reforms and digital innovations, African governments use public resources more efficiently and provide more social services. They are also working to improve the quality of the business environment to attract investment from the private sector.

However, many more economic opportunities are expected. Governments must extend access to electricity and finance and improve competition policies to support economic activities and encourage innovation (Jamasb et al., 2018). Broadband infrastructure is essential to ensure the implementation (Ndemo, 2020) of the leapfrogged introduction of new technologies. Furthermore, the commitment to accountability within the main institutions responsible for formulating policies and public administration performance remains below citizens' expectations (de la Cuesta et al., 2019).

With renewed momentum and vigour, industrialisation support is part of Africa's economic policy agenda. Industrialisation in twenty-first-century Africa requires innovative strategies that encompass the full potential of African countries (OECD, 2017). Above all, innovative industrialisation strategies should go beyond the manufacturing industry's sectoral logic. Africa can promote economic sectors with high growth and job creation potential. The strategies should also include leadership skills for entrepreneurs with great potential.

Innovation should not be feared. Furthermore, governments should prepare ad hoc legislation and interventions to train students and workers. Politics and institutions can govern change and development and harmonise it with their growth objectives. There is no lack of ideas, visions and suggestions to cooperate internationally.

Some models can be obtained according to national or macro-regional specificities. Starting from the concept that innovation is never a negative factor in itself and that it is possible to apply in time the measures that make it possible to govern this new transition towards the Fourth Industrial Revolution, the first step consists in supporting the phase of R&D. The states that innovate the most are also those that spend the most on research and development, on average around 3% of the public budget (Maroto et al., 2016) (e.g., South Korea, Israel, Japan, Germany, USA).

Moreover, it is necessary to facilitate knowledge dissemination, reduce barriers to exchanging know-how and facilitate partnerships between institutions and the private sector. Greater circulation and competition in terms of innovation prevent SMEs from being isolated from player sizes. In this sense, it is necessary to consider ad hoc international legislation that facilitates more and more data, especially cross-border flows and commercial agreements.

Education remains a fundamental factor that should not be seen as merely pursuing market trends. Training students and workers to operate with digital tools must be functional to make knowledge more flexible and find future changes in the labour market and goods and services. Estimates of skill mismatches vary depending on who supplies them, but it emerged that even the most advanced and technologically advanced countries encounter difficulties to be faced with difficulty in order to avoid a total disconnect between the world of work and school and university education.

9 Conclusions

Africa has already embarked on a path of technological, IT and digital innovation for years that has attracted the attention of analysts and scholars, as well as investors from all over the world, and now several countries of the continent are aiming to invest even more in technologies to accelerate the post-COVID restart.

The African continent is witnessing the blossoming of new startups with high technological potential, and the most representative examples can be spotted in Nigeria, which in 2015 equalled Germany for new businesses, and in Kenya, where more and more hubs are used to host innovators and investors from all over the world. Silicon Savannah has become the expression used to depict how Kenyans are innovating. It expresses, also from a narrative and evocative point of view, a place and a space, which, like others in Africa, is exploited to impress and project a repositioning of the continent on the international chessboard.

Many startups founded by African women have sprung up recently, especially in Nigeria, South Africa and Uganda. All to improve people's lives, simplify bureaucratic processes and live more sustainably. Still, the African continent is often underestimated. The approach and vision men and women can have given the backwardness in the technological and digital fields are underestimated.

African states are looking ahead, creating new technological hubs and reducing the digital divide. With COVID-19 pushing global economies to a breaking point, technology in Africa has allowed some companies to thrive amid unprecedented challenges, putting the continent on a par with other markets in highly innovative sectors.

The African economy looks forward to concluding developments with the European Union and the United States. In this regard, in 2021, the European Parliament developed a strategy for sustainable development between European Union and Africa. Thus, because Africa offers a new labour force, 1 million new employees come from Africa every month.

Africa represents a particular interest both for the opportunities it offers and the desire to develop and collaborate for the social and business environment, with a special openness to entrepreneurship, education and equal access to work and education for all citizens, regardless of gender or religious affiliation. For the future, the EU's added value to its partnership with Africa is expected to be substantial, but it depends on both's ability to combine intercontinental dialogue with local and regional specificities, partner countries' sensitivities and existing social structures, and its desire to build with Africa a long-term vision based on common values, mutual interests and a renewed commitment to multilateralism.

REFERENCES

Adeleye, N., & Eboagu, C. (2019). Evaluation of ICT development and economic growth in Africa. *Netnomics*, 1–25.

Alper, M. E., & Miktus, M. (2019). *Bridging the mobile digital divide in Sub-Saharan Africa: Costing under demographic change and urbanisation.* International Monetary Fund.

Andam, K. S., Edeh, H., Oboh, V., Pauw, K., & Thurlow, J. (2020). *Estimating the economic costs of COVID-19 in Nigeria* (Vol. 63). International Food Policy Research Institute.

Ataguba, J. E. (2020). COVID-19 pandemic, a war to be won: Understanding its economic implications for Africa. *Applied Health Economics and Health Policy, 18*(3), 325–328.

Atilola, O., Abiri, G., Adebanjo, E., & Ola, B. (2021). The cross-cutting psychosocial and systemic barriers to holistic rehabilitation, including educational re-engagement, of incarcerated adolescents: Realities in and perspectives from Africa. *International Journal of Educational Development, 81*, 102335.

Atoyebi, T. A., & Anuodo, O. (2018). Demography and the future of Africa. In *The Palgrave handbook of African politics, governance and development* (pp. 803–813). Palgrave Macmillan.

Bartezzaghi, E. (1999). The evolution of production models: Is a new paradigm emerging? *International Journal of Operations & Production Management, 19*(2), 229–250.

Bassanini, A., & Scarpetta, S. (2002). Growth, technological change, and ICT diffusion: Recent evidence from OECD countries. *Oxford Review of Economic Policy, 18*(3), 324–344.

Blindenbach-Driessen, F., & Van Den Ende, J. (2006). Innovation in project-based firms: The context dependency of success factors. *Research Policy, 35*(4), 545–561.

Bowles, J., Larreguy, H., & Liu, S. (2020). Center for International Development.

Cantwell, J., & Santangelo, G. D. (2000). Capitalism, profits and innovation in the new techno-economic paradigm. *Journal of Evolutionary Economics, 10*(1), 131–157.

Carton, F., & Adam, F. (2009). Towards a model for determining the scope of ICT integration in the enterprise: The case of Enterprise Resource Planning (ERP) systems. *Electronic Journal of Information Systems Evaluation, 13*(1), 17–26.

Chesbrough, H. W. (2003). *Open innovation: The new imperative for creating and profiting from technology.* Harvard Business Press.

Clifton, J., Díaz-Fuentes, D., & Gómez, A. L. (2018). The European Investment Bank: Development, integration, investment?. *JCMS: Journal of Common Market Studies, 56*(4), 733–750.

Curwen, P., & Whalley, J. (2018). High-speed data in Africa: an assessment of provision via mobile networks. *Digital Policy, Regulation and Governance, 20*(3).

de la Cuesta, B., Martin, L., Milner, H. V., & Nielson, D. L. (2019). Owning it: Accountability and citizens' ownership over aid, oil, and taxes. *Journal of Politics, 84*(1).

Ekeocha, D. O., Ogbuabor, J. E., Orji, A., & Kalu, U. I. (2021). International tourism and economic growth in Africa: A post-global financial crisis analysis. *Tourism Management Perspectives, 40*, 100896.

Ettlie, J. E., Bridges, W. P., & O'keefe, R. D. (1984). Organisation strategy and structural differences for radical versus incremental innovation. *Management Science, 30*(6), 682–695.

Evanschitzky, H., Eisend, M., Calantone, R. J., & Jiang, Y. (2012). Success factors of product innovation: An updated meta-analysis. *Journal of Product Innovation Management, 29*, 21–37.

Farayibi, A., & Asongu, S. (2020). The economic consequences of the COVID-19 pandemic in Nigeria. *European Xtramile Centre of African Studies*, WP/20/042 (2020).

Gunasekaran, A., & Yusuf, Y. Y. (2002). Agile manufacturing: A taxonomy of strategic and technological imperatives. *International Journal of Production Research, 40*(6), 1357–1385.

Heston, R., & Zwetsloot, R. (2020, December). *Mapping US multinationals' global AI R&D activity.* CSET.

Hönke, J. (2018). Beyond the gatekeeper state: African infrastructure hubs as sites of experimentation. *Third World Thematics: A TWQ Journal, 3*(3), 347–363.

Jamasb, T., Thakur, T., & Bag, B. (2018). Smart electricity distribution networks, business models, and application for developing countries. *Energy Policy, 114*, 22–29.

Junaid, O. (2019). *The sharing economy, African style: A comparative assessment of the Kenyan and Nigerian digital sharing economies* (Doctoral dissertation).

Klevorick, A. K., Levin, R. C., Nelson, R. R., & Winter, S. G. (1995). On the sources and significance of interindustry differences in technological opportunities. *Research Policy, 24*(2), 185–205.

Lanz, D. (2021). Envoy Envy? Competition in African mediation processes and ways to overcome it. *International Negotiation, 1*(aop), 1–28.

Laver, N. (2019). Minding the legal access gap. *Solicitors Journal, 162*, 22.

Mabera, F. (2019). Africa and the G20: A relational view of African agency in global governance. *South African Journal of International Affairs, 26*(4), 583–599.

Maroto, A., Gallego, J., & Rubalcaba, L. (2016). Publicly funded R&D for public sector performance and efficiency: Evidence from Europe. *R&D Management, 46*(S2), 564–578.

McDave, K. E., & Hackman-Aidoo, A. (2021). Africa and SDG 9: Toward a framework for development through intellectual property. *US-China Law Review, 18*, 12.

Mehboob, D. (2021). *OECD 2021 corporate tax report makes the case for pillar two.* International Tax Review.

Ndemo, B. (2020). *The role of mobile technologies and inclusive innovation policies in SME development in Sub Saharan Africa.* Edward Elgar Publishing.

Ndour, M., & Gueye, B. (2016). Mlouma: To connect the agricultural products market players. *Emerald Emerging Markets Case Studies, 6*(3), 1–18.

Ndung'u, N., & Signe, L. (2020). *The fourth industrial revolution and digitisation will transform Africa into a global powerhouse.* Foresight Africa Report.

OECD. (2017). *African Economic Outlook 2017: Entrepreneurship and industrialisation,* OECD Publishing.

Perez, C. (2004). Technological revolutions, paradigm shifts and socio-institutional change. *Globalisation, economic development and inequality: An alternative perspective,* 217–242

Perez, C. (2010). Technological revolutions and techno-economic paradigms. *Cambridge Journal of Economics, 34*(1), 185–202.

Quinn, J. B. (1985a). *Managing innovation: Controlled chaos.* University of Illinois at Urbana-Champaign's Academy for Entrepreneurial Leadership Historical Research Reference in Entrepreneurship.

Quinn, J. B. (1985b). Innovation and corporate strategy: Managed chaos. *Technology in Society, 7*(2–3), 263–279.

Sabban, A. (2021). Introductory Chapter: Green computing technologies and industry in 2021. In *Green computing technologies and computing industry in 2021.* IntechOpen.

Sagheer, A., Mohammed, M., Riad, K., & Alhajhoj, M. (2021). A cloud-based IoT platform for precision control of soilless greenhouse cultivation. *Sensors, 21*(1), 223.

Sanyang, S., Taonda, S. J. B., Kuiseu, J., Coulibaly, N. T., & Konaté, L. (2016). A paradigm shift in African agricultural research for development: The role of innovation platforms. *International Journal of Agricultural Sustainability, 14*(2), 187–213.

Shumpeter, J. A. (1942). Capitalism. Socialism and democracy, Harper.

Soskice, D. (1999). Divergent production regimes: Coordinated and uncoordinated market economies in the 1980s and 1990s. *Continuity and Change in Contemporary Capitalism, 38*, 101–134.

Stein, J. C. (1997). Waves of creative destruction: Firm-specific learning-by-doing and the dynamics of innovation. *The Review of Economic Studies, 64*(2), 265–288.

228   A. FACCIA ET AL.

Stiglitz, J. E. (2002). *Towards a new paradigm for development: Strategies, policies and processes*, 116–122. Columbia Academic Commons. https://doi.org/10.7916/D8MC98VB

Stiroh, K. J. (2002). Are ICT spillovers driving the new economy? *Review of Income and Wealth, 48*(1), 33–57.

Takase, M., Kipkoech, R., & Essandoh, P. K. (2021). A comprehensive review of energy scenario and sustainable energy in Kenya. *Fuel Communications, 7*, 100015.

Theobaldt, L., & Vervest, P. (2012). Making business smart: How to position for business as a service. In *Globalization of professional services* (pp. 53–61). Springer.

Turner, J. W., & Robinson, J. D. (2014). Malaria no more: Nothing but nets. *Health Communication, 29*(10), 1067–1068.

Woudstra, U. A. (2010). Economies of scale in ICT: How to balance infrastructure and applications for economies of scale in ICT and business. Universiteit van Amsterdam [Host]

Zhao, X., Ni, Y., Zhao, H., Liu, X., He, B., Shi, B., ... & Liu, H. (2021). Plant growth-promoting ability and control efficacy of Penicillium aurantiogriseum 44M-3 against sesame Fusarium wilt disease. *Biocontrol Science and Technology, 31*(12), 1314–1329.

Understanding the Impact of the Entrepreneurial Ecosystem on Sustainability in Africa

Joseph Kwadwo Danquah, Mavis Serwah Benneh Mensah, William Yamoah, and Qazi Moinuddin Mahmud

1 Introduction

The global economy has undoubtedly been struck by Covid-19 leading to a very deep but mercifully short recession. With the pressure induced by Covid-19 on all major sources of development, both developed and developing countries may struggle. In this challenging moment, how can countries avoid a reversal of what has been achieved? Arguably, entrepreneurial

---

J. K. Danquah (✉)
School of Management, The University of Bradford, Bradford, UK
e-mail: j.k.danquah1@bradford.ac.uk

M. S. B. Mensah
Centre for Entrepreneurship and Small Enterprise Development (CESED), School of Business, The University of Cape Coast, Cape Coast, Ghana
e-mail: mmensah@ucc.edu.gh

W. Yamoah
Public Administration and Policy Management, The University of Ghana, Accra, Ghana

© The Author(s), under exclusive license to Springer Nature Switzerland AG 2023
S. Adomako et al. (eds.), *Corporate Sustainability in Africa*, Palgrave Studies in African Leadership, https://doi.org/10.1007/978-3-031-29273-6_11

229

activities contribute to sustainability, but over the years many countries have become successful while others are struggling to navigate the social, national and international obstacles facing them (Pobee & Mphela, 2021). The United Nations (UN) have argued that entrepreneurship contributes to sustainability through job creation, economic growth, innovation and improving social conditions (UN, 2020).

Countries recognise the need for a comprehensive and holistic approach to entrepreneurship that includes establishing the unique factors for the entrepreneurial ecosystem (EE) and long-term strategies that seek to address the recovery. Promoting entrepreneurship and strengthening competitiveness is vital for all; the Covid-19 pandemic has caused a significant adverse impact on the progress of and deepened the fragilities in Africa's economies. This has provided an unprecedented opportunity to emerge with a better and more efficient set of policies and measures to promote entrepreneurship with a view to building EE that leads to sustainability (UN, 2020).

The contribution of entrepreneurship to sustainable economic development dates back 300 years. The Schumpeterian perspective considers entrepreneurs as 'agents of creative destruction' (Bate, 2021); for example, entrepreneurs create new businesses and these bring jobs, intensify competition with innovative goods and increase productiveness by changing technology. According to Carvalho et al. (2010), being an entrepreneur is not inherited but can be learned through educational institutions. Entrepreneurs seek opportunities by taking the risk to create value. However, entrepreneurs require a favourable environment to innovate and enable their business to prosper, which is termed an ecosystem (Maroufkhani et al., 2017). Both researchers and policymakers argue that the EE is a community of multiple coevolving stakeholders that provides a supportive environment for new and existing businesses within a country or region (Cao & Shi, 2021). What are the multiple factors that exist in Africa? According to Cao and Shi (2021), developing countries have a

---

e-mail: wyamoah022@st.ug.edu.gh

Q. M. Mahmud
Department of Management, Faculty of Business Studies, The University of Ghana, Bangladesh, India
e-mail: q.m.mahmud@bradford.ac.uk; Dr.qmmahmud@du.ac.bd

phenomenal EE, but what are the factors that drive the sustainability of countries in Africa?

To address the above questions, this study provides a systemic review of the various EEs that prevail in Africa. The paper provides a clearer understanding of the unique ecosystem in Africa and provides insights into the distinctive characteristics of Africas' EE, thus highlighting the implications for sustainability. Previous studies have focused merely on individual countries; for example, Sheriff and Muffatto (2015) studied Botswana, Egypt, Ghana and Uganda; Mwantimwa et al. (2021) analysed the case of Tanzania; Bate (2021) focused on EE of BRICS club countries; and Pobee and Mphela (2021) studied Malawi. Our study focused on a broader context, especially concerning regions that require development.

Over the past few decades, researchers have made significant strides in improving the quality of synthesising research in a systematic, transparent and reproducible manner to inform both policymakers and governments about the delivery of quality services. To answer the research question outlined below, this study employed a systematic review to reduce biasness through thorough literature searches of academic and non-academic materials (Tranfield et al., 2003). This process plays a significant role in evidence-based practice and adopting this strategy enabled the researchers to summarise, integrate and, where possible, cumulate the findings from different perspectives (Menezes & Kelliher, 2011).

2 Methodology

As a qualitative study, this literature review is guided by the research question, from which we defined keywords for the database searches. The study question is what are the multi factors that constitute developing countries' EE sustainable enterprise development? First, we defined EE as a different set of actors and factors that are interlinked to create conducive and productive entrepreneurship (Mensah & Amarteifio, 2021). However, this paper focused on EE factors. We, therefore, included the dynamic, institutional, social, cultural and local processes that promote business development. Given that we were concerned with geographical or regional dimensions to explain social and economic performance and sustainability of enterprises, it was important to understand that environments affect entrepreneurial activities; therefore, we included studies from different perspectives—developed economies.

For this purpose, we considered studies that make up the central body of the review that were identified, classified and analysed (Marino et al., 2019). In selecting studies, we focused on the keywords; entrepreneurship, entrepreneurs, EE and sustainability in Africa; however, we used studies conducted in developed countries as a benchmark to help understand different perspectives on EE in a different context. To achieve our aim, we searched using keywords in different databases (e.g., University of Bradford Canvas, Scopus, Wiley, Google Scholar, ScienceDirect, JSTOR). We selected journal articles and other scientific papers published in respected conferences, and on government websites, and non-governmental organisations' websites. We initially included studies that contained the words entrepreneurs, sustainability, entrepreneurial, entrepreneurship and EE.

The purpose was related to analysing the factors that constitute EE in Africa for sustainable enterprise development. To maintain homogeneity for the review, EE in developed countries was excluded from the study. According to Marino et al. (2019), the year of publication is significant in a literature review; this review focused on studies published between 2010 and 2022.

Due to the objectives of the study, we narrowed our selection to Africa; this procedure of searching and analysing the documents turned up a total of 46 publications that make up the study (25 qualitative studies, 18 quantitative papers and three mixed-method studies). Entrepreneurship was captured by different authors; for example, Sherriff and Muffatto (2015) consider entrepreneurship as polysemous and multidimensional without a common consensus. Different definitions have been proposed but all these, according to Sherriff and Muffatto (2015), focus on self-employment and uncertainty, managerial talents, managerial competencies, identifying opportunities, minimising organisation inefficiencies and identification and exploitation of market arbitrage opportunities. These descriptions reflect on the six schools of thought of entrepreneurship based on internal and external locus of control. Moreover, EE can be described as autotrophic or heterotrophic.

Different authors have addressed variables that correspond to different dimensions or types of EE and entrepreneurship. We decided to incorporate into the central body of the review a higher level of detail only the first time that each paper is referred to; furthermore, we monitored studies that were published in 2022. The review was treated in a narrow but broadly chronological way and emphasis is placed on studies there were carried out in Africa. We compile and discuss EE factors for sustainable development in Africa. The EE dimension presented by different authors has been described in the following sections.

3 THE CONCEPT OF SUSTAINABILITY

The term 'sustainability' has a primeval and universal origin (Gomis et al., 2011) that generally implies the capability of something to sustain itself over a period. It has become an integral element of social science and is not confined to managing only natural or environmental resources sustainably (Ballestar et al., 2020). Gomis et al., (2011, p. 176) defined sustainability provisionally as 'a moral way of acting, and ideally habitual, in which the person or group intends to avoid deleterious effects on the environmental, social, and economic domains, and which is consistent with a harmonious relationship with those domains that is conducive to a flourishing life.' This statement fundamentally presents sustainability as an ethical concept, although in the literature it has been observed that scholars have defined and interpreted sustainability from diverse perspectives that, however, have sometimes made it problematic to conceptualise this popular buzzword with clarity (Salas-Zapata & Ortiz-Muñoz, 2018).

Analysing and synthesising the various meanings of the term, Salas-Zapata and Ortiz-Muñoz (2018) explored four fundamental ways to theorize sustainability. Firstly, this term can be employed to imply a set of social-ecological criteria for guiding human actions or their results. Secondly, can be used to refer to a vision or goal of humankind that is accomplished through the convergence of environmental, social and economic purposes of a certain reference system. Thirdly, the term sustainability might refer to an empirical object or entity that can be understood and followed in a particular social-ecological system. Finally, sustainability can also be used to indicate an approach entailing the inclusion of social, economic and ecological dimensions in the study of system, human activity, or output.

Based on these four different conceptualisations, sustainability can thus be construed as embracing three core dimensions such as social, economic and ecological or environmental, although it was initially concerned with the friction between human aspirations towards a better life and the restraints inflicted by nature (Kuhlman & Farrington, 2010). Sustainability is fundamentally embedded in the three pillars of society, economy and ecology. Thus, it can be stated that sustainability is founded on the 'triple bottom line' consisting of people, profit and planet having an interdependent relationship (Thiele, 2016). However, the existing literature asserts that, in steering sustainability by addressing this triple bottom line robustly, entrepreneurship plays a significantly critical role (Auerswald, 2015; Naude, 2017; Opute, 2020). The next section presents a theoretical framework of EE that has a deep connection with sustainability.

4 Theoretical Framework of the Entrepreneurial Ecosystem

The term ecosystem is primarily a multidimensional and complex ecological concept, which is about a community of living organisms and its associated physical environment. The process-functional approach of the ecosystem has three major dimensions (meaning, metaphor and model), which permit the use of the concept in different fields—economics, management, policymaking and social science (Sheriff & Mffatto, 2015). According to Sheriff and Mffatto (2015), the meaning has a neutral connotation; that is, the transformation of the concept into practical use requires the building of models, for example, the ecological economics model. The metaphor aspect of the ecosystem is not technical; it allows the use of the concept in a different situation where there is a need to link a phenomenon being studied that is its initial stage. A particular phenomenon in its infancy is the EE (Tracey & Phillips, 2011; Sheriff & Mffatto, 2015; Maroufkhani et al., 2017; Mukiza & Kansheba, 2020; Kang et al., 2021). The concept may be applicable in the study of social ecology—behavioural science (understanding the interaction between individuals and their environment).

The reality is that the ecosystem concept is complex and adaptive, which require, collaborative planning and consensus building for a community to respond to changes. There is an absolute difference between a machine and an organism, thus, a machine can perform certain assigned tasks but the organism may adapt due to the environmental changes. System theory has therefore caused management scholars to consider institutions as an organism. This is relevant because institutions function in an environment that is dynamic, and understanding the complexity model builds on fuzzy, multivalent and multidisciplinary representations of reality. Complex adaptive systems are the same as social systems, ecologies, economies, cultures, politics, technologies and institutions. These examples are from the foundation of the entrepreneurship environment in societies (Sheriff & Mffatto, 2015). The sustainability concept is linked to an ecosystem.

Entrepreneurship

The fourth industrial revolution places much premium on human capital, agility, resilience and innovation. As pointed out by Schwab (2019), economic growth remains a critical pathway for developing countries to reduce poverty and increase human capital. Goal 2 (zero hunger) of the UN's sustainable development goals (SDGs) is likely to be missed and growth has been subdued in Africa.

Researchers like Kansheba (2020), and Audretsch and Belitski (2017) have acknowledged the contribution of entrepreneurship to economic growth; specifically, entrepreneurship creates jobs, provides decent livelihoods and contributes to GDP. For developing countries to achieve some economic growth, entrepreneurship should be central to all development policies (Atiase et al., 2017). Entrepreneurship is being referred to as the fourth production factor in the macroeconomic production function. Economic growth helps society to develop; however, according to Sheriff and Muffatto (2015), not all entrepreneurship contributes to economic development. Entrepreneurship is considered productive when it contributes to a society's welfare, while unproductive entrepreneurship focuses on rent-seeking or violence. Destructive entrepreneurship is when resources are expended to capture rents or expropriate wealth (Lucas & Fuller, 2017).

One of the objectives of this study is to understand the EE; therefore, we focus on productive entrepreneurship because the other two types of entrepreneurships that contribute to economic growth are questionable. A conducive environment for entrepreneurship to thrive is important for countries in Africa because productive entrepreneurship activity depicts the significance of economic growth (Lucas & Fuller, 2017). Entrepreneurship is less developed in Africa, and because of these, developing countries are confronted with low living standards, high-income disparities, unemployment, health problems, inflation and macroeconomic instability (Lafuente et al., 2018). However, in developed countries, there is a common public venture capital that seeks to promote (productive) entrepreneurship, and this provides new and small businesses with opportunities to grow.

Entrepreneurship has been conceptualised by different authors, for example, Ricard Cantillon (1730) considered it in terms of self-employment and risk-taking activities; Jean Say (1810) described entrepreneurship consisting of managerial talents accompanied by uncertainty and obstacle; whereas Joseph Schumpeter (1910) defined it as promoting new factors for socio-economic development; and Harvey Leibenstein (1970) described it as minimising organisational inefficiencies. From the above definitions, six main taxonomies of entrepreneurship theories can be espoused. Entrepreneurship theories have been applied in different disciplines such as economics, management, psychology, sociology, business and anthropology. Table 1 explains the six schools of thought of entrepreneurship based on the extant literature.

These schools of thought are critical to entrepreneurial theory and understanding these will help entrepreneurship development. However, this study focuses on the environmental school of thought, which focuses on the natural world in which entrepreneurship activities are done as this form part of an EE. This physical environment exacts either a positive or a negative influence on the decision-making process. Indeed, the entrepreneurship environment can be defined as conditions like economic, socio-culture, trade, political, physical and virtual infrastructure, and institutions that prevail or influence the decision or willingness to venture into entrepreneurship. A supportive environment promotes a positive activity unleashing and fostering entrepreneurial desire.

According to Sheriff and Muffatto (2015), the main theory related to the entrepreneurship environment is the institution theory. Institutions are complex, covering many fields like sociology, history, economics, ecology and political science, and these explain factors that an entrepreneur must encounter to achieve their main goals. Moreover, these are responsible for the provision of stability and incentives that either promote or hinder social behaviour (Sheriff & Muffatto, 2015; Kang et al., 2021; Lee, 2021).

A conducive EE promotes entrepreneurship development; many studies argue that institutional theory provides an opportunity to examine how different institutional settings affect behaviours. Moreover, this theory has been used to assess how environmental influences on entrepreneurship, specifically, relate to start-ups. A country's rules or laws are important for understanding entrepreneurship growth (Atiase et al., 2017; Lee, 2021). Institutional theory can be used to determine the role of environmental factors in the creation, management and design

UNDERSTANDING THE IMPACT ... 237

Table 1 The six schools of thought on entrepreneurship

Entrepreneurial schools of thought	*Characteristics*
Environmental School of Thought (Kuratko & Hodgetts, 2007)	1. Both external and internal factors affect entrepreneurs' desires 2. Focus on institutions, values and influence of society forms the environmental framework that affects entrepreneurs 3. Freedom and support within the environment determine a manager's desire to pursue an entrepreneurial career
Financial/Capital School of Thought (Van de Ven, 1993)	1. This is based on the capital-seeking process 2. Entrepreneur's development is dependent on venture capital 3. An entrepreneurial venture is dependent on financial management
Displacement School of Thought (Schjoedt & Shaver, 2007)	1. Entrepreneurial desire is dependent on someone's frustration and based on the frustration, the motivation to succeed. There are three major types of displacement—political, cultural and economic displacement
Trait School of Thought (Bird, 1992)	1. Entrepreneurs have similar characteristics like creativity, determination, achievement, technical knowledge, etc 2. Family development is considered very important in the creation of entrepreneurs
Venture Opportunity School of Thought (Kuratko, 2007)	1. Entrepreneurs look for opportunities to create new businesses 2. Entrepreneurs' succeed depends on market awareness and creativity
Strategic Formulation School of Thought (Hitt et al., 2001)	1. The planning process is vital – effective planning and formulation help businesses to survive

Source Compiled by Authors (2022)

of business; thus, the attitudes, beliefs and values of a society predict the entrepreneurial behaviour of people in that setting. An environment that promotes an entrepreneurial spirit within a region allows innovativeness to flourish. The ability of people and businesses to exploit entrepreneurial opportunities in a society depends on various institutional factors. We now turn our attention to the importance of entrepreneurship to sustainability.

Entrepreneurship and Sustainability

Entrepreneurship offers sustainability, but its roles and nature are ambiguous; however, entrepreneurship permits the achievement of a more sustainable economy (Hall et al., 2010). The entrepreneurship literature advocates that innovation serves as a catalyst for change allowing sustainable development. A society that adopts innovative solutions can withstand current sustainability challenges (Youssef et al., 2017). Evidence from the literature suggests that an increase in the number of entrepreneurships in Africa has led to marginal growth rates and promoting entrepreneurship is fundamental for economic sustainability.

Sustainable entrepreneurship is a business creation process that links entrepreneurial activities to the achievement of economic, environmental and societal goals (Kang et al., 2021). Entrepreneurial activities could be a solution to numerous social and environmental issues. Current entrepreneurship encompasses features like sociability, competitiveness, innovativeness, dynamism and progressiveness (Hall et al., 2010). Sustainable entrepreneurship is about innovation, market orientation and a personality-driven form of value creation based on the strategic decision. The global challenges are multifaceted, dynamic and cross-cutting, and require theoretical and disciplinary perspectives which are sufficient to produce adequate and durable solutions. Knowledge has become an important factor in determining the standard of living more than labour, land and tools (Iyigun, 2015).

There is a positive correlation between small-medium-scale enterprises (SMEs) involved in sustainable development and entrepreneurial activities. Many researchers have acknowledged that entrepreneurs contribute significantly to economic sustainability through product innovation, job creation and utilisation of business opportunities (Iyigun, 2015). Moreover, entrepreneurs who move further from financial performance engage in ethical and social behaviour and practices that are acceptable, leading to holistic and equal contributions to economic, social and environmental sustainability. Entrepreneurs act like a catalyst in transforming economies into sustainable economies by providing critical social and environmental goods and services. Entrepreneurs' activities are utilised to solve problems, and making profits becomes a means, not an end. Understanding entrepreneurship and sustainability provides an opportunity to understand the EE.

5 The Impact of the Entrepreneurial Ecosystem on Sustainability in Africa

Complexity science is the pillar of the EE. The EE approach is built around a complex perspective where the design of the components is significant in determining territorial economic outcomes (Lafuente et al., 2018). According to Spigel (2017), EE represents the types of political, cultural, economic and social environment within a specific region that supports high-growth entrepreneurship. This explains the dynamic and institutional interactions connected to stakeholders which support resource mobilisation and entrepreneurial action.

The EE construct is independent but interlinked number of themes. Our analysis shows hundreds of specific elements, for example, Isenberg (2011) argues that for convenience purposes the EE can be grouped into six domains; infrastructure support, culture, human capital, enabling policies and leadership, finance and market. Contributing to the debate, Maroukhani et al., (2017) expanded Isenberg's (2011) framework by adding two more domains—crowdsourcing and industrial dynamics.

Although EEs can be viewed using the same eight domains, each EE is the result of hundreds of elements interacting in highly complex and idiosyncratic ways. Developing a country's EE evolved due to societal norms and values (Tracey & Phillips, 2011); however, Castillo et al. (2015) state that these practices do not embrace entrepreneurial behaviour. Mukiza and Kansheba (2020), using panel regression in their research, concluded that financial capital, institutional capital, knowledge capital and the market have no direct influence on productive entrepreneurship in developing countries. Social capital has a negative and significant direct influence on productive entrepreneurship.

The entrepreneurial environment determines how entrepreneurship occurs, and EE influences entrepreneur's behaviour. From the traditional perspective of EE—*the interconnected set of entrepreneurial stakeholders in a regional entrepreneurial environment that fosters engagement in entrepreneurship to contribute to a prosperous regional economy* (Pita et al., 2021, p. 6). EE is connected to local economic development and promotes start-ups especially, organisations, institutions, actors and process formally and informally mingle to mediate, control and links the performance within the local setting. Governments and policymakers hence should not ignore the interconnection of elements and should focus on how these elements or circumstances lead to a better outcome.

However, EE might have profound impacts on sustainability in Africa as has been observed in many Asian countries (Lafuente et al., 2018). To realise a sustainable growth in Africa, the ecosystem needs to function vigorously to expedite the innovative activities of entrepreneurs. The sustainable development of least developed and developing countries essentially relies on the survival of the ventures formed by entrepreneurs, for which the presence of an inclusive and healthy EE is a fundamental precondition. EE as a collaborative network of actors can persuade each other in mobilising entrepreneurship and thereby boosting economic growth. EE can facilitate entrepreneurship at the country level to contribute to a more efficient directing of resources to the economy, which in turn leads to superior economic performance of the country (Lafuente et al., 2018).

The existing literature indicates that, in comparison to the developing countries of Asia and South America, the entrepreneurial performance in Africa is moderate (Rodrik, 2016). Poor institutional growth and a dearth of opportunities for productive entrepreneurship are found to be crucial constraints in African countries (Beugré, 2016; Gomes et al., 2011, 2018). Improving the EE can be a great way to resolve these issues and subsequently achieve sustainable development in Africa through promoting productive entrepreneurship (Beugré, 2016; Mwatsika, 2018).

The biggest advantage of EE is that this approach emphasises the interconnection between environmental factors, in particular the country perspective, inducing high-impact entrepreneurship (Lafuente et al., 2018). Lafuente et al. (2018) thus argued that what African countries now require is a robust policy stimulating EE to achieve sustainability. The significance of EE in fostering economic prosperity or sustained development in Africa as well as other geographic settings is quite evident in the extant literature (Lafuente et al., 2018). However, the success of EE depends on both the quality and quantity of interactions between the various actors mentioned earlier.

6   Entrepreneurial Ecosystem in Africa—The New Narrative

Research on EE in Africa is scarce; however, the reality is that entrepreneurship development in Africa is only feasible in an efficient EE that is dynamic, and resource endowed. All EE is believed to have self-organisation, scalability and sustainability (Atiase et al., 2017). There should be an interaction between the entrepreneur's abilities, aspirations and attitude, which could push resources via the creation and operation of new businesses. Therefore, EE is made up of institutions, systems, ecosystem management services, entrepreneurs and subsystems. A sound EE will push resource allocation and sharing towards productivity. For example, research by Sheriff and Muffatto (2015) using four countries in Africa (Ghana, Botswana, Uganda and Egypt) concludes that institutional factors account for the quality of EE.

EE encompasses various elements such as institutions, organisations and individuals, which can either inhibit or promote entrepreneurship. The development of the constituent of EE can be an expensive process, as it requires the development of absorptive capacities in industries, firms and the government. Arguably, EE design, construction and implementation is a linear process or a one-size-fits-all process. Therefore, there is a need to understand the dynamics of culture and behavioural characteristics (Ngongoni et al., 2017).

According to Kang et al. (2021), the inductive functional characteristics of EE focus on knowledge spill-over, innovation, incubator and sustainable development function. The ecological elements of the entrepreneurial region can be used to measure the indicators of the region's health assessment of EE. The key element of the EE can be identified in Africa's economies through system element recognition, key technologies and future market users, such as capital, skilled workers and entrepreneurial knowledge (Kang et al., 2021). The dynamic function of a system or region promotes the sustainable development of EE.

Several factors exist in determining the EE in a region, given the conceptualisation and physical boundaries of the EE, researchers advocate the local level appears to be an appropriate aggregate level for many entrepreneurial decisions. Figure 1 shows the matrix structure of Isenberg (2011) and Maroufkhani et al. (2017). The following section will explain how each domain supports the analysis of EE.

Culture

Within the specific region, the effectiveness of entrepreneurial activities is not only revealed by the type of entrepreneurs but also by the ecosystem. Research has established that the success of EE relates to the entrepreneurial spirit embedded within societies. EE among cities posits that entrepreneurs within a region that considers failure and success

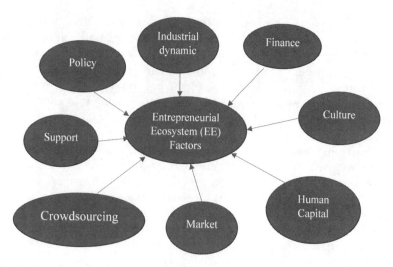

Fig. 1 Entrepreneurial Ecosystem (EE) factors for sustainability in developing countries (*Source* Compiled by Authors 2022)

stories are likely to develop and grow faster than those that see failure as misfortune (Wald & Kansheba, 2020). An entrepreneurial culture promotes the exhibition of values, behaviour, attributes and beliefs which foster an entrepreneurial spirit among members of society. Moreover, entrepreneurial culture brings actors together within the ecosystem by ensuring trust and confidence among various players. However, bureaucratic and corrupt societies inhibit entrepreneurial development within an ecosystem. For example, a study by Kshetri (2014) shows that positive changes in social values and norms specifically entrepreneurship, have a significant positive impact on EE.

In a region or society, the lack of an entrepreneurial culture inhibits the growth of an EE, but a supportive entrepreneurial culture promotes success, openness and a positive attitude. If the culture of a region or society is dynamic it leads to changes in social interaction, and a successful entrepreneur influences society's dynamism, by providing useful information and skills on how to manage start-ups or businesses (Wald & Kansheba, 2020).

The culture of a region or society can tolerate the honest mistakes of entrepreneurs and create opportunities for failures (Maroufkhani et al.,

2017). The culture at large needs to appreciate entrepreneurship as an occupation. An entrepreneur's success story inspires potential youth and proves to ordinary people to venture into business by creating employment opportunities and economic development. However, different countries have different cultures and clearly and clearly, the environment differs in terms of culture.

Market

As well-functioning financial market facilitates entrepreneurship; for example, developed countries with higher levels of financial development facilitate faster industrial sector development (Nir, 2014). Lack of access to finance in Africa inhibits latent entrepreneurs. In South Korea, support for the chaebol has created an unfavourable environment for earlier start-ups. Market accessibility is an important factor in driving entrepreneurial activities. For example, Estonia has a well-developed antitrust law and competition, which makes it easy for youths or start-ups to enter the domestic market. Moreover, their government helps entrepreneurs access the European Union market.

Research has demonstrated that entrepreneur's benefit from agglomeration economies and bigger market potentials. The market size determines economic growth and employment, for example, high labour costs may dissuade start-ups due to higher opportunity costs. Developed economies offer incentives to innovate and develop new business ideas (Audretsch & Belitski, 2017). Developing economies, arguably, tend to exhibit relatively underdeveloped market mechanisms. According to Isenberg (2011), market accessibility is a contributing factor for productive entrepreneurship. A market without barriers supports new firm development and stimulates new start-ups.

Entrepreneurship within the ecosystem shows three phases; first is the conceptual stage, in which the entrepreneur needs access to market opportunities and resources. In the second phase, the development phase, the entrepreneur will develop by testing new ideas and improving existing ones. In the final phase, the maturity stage; the entrepreneur implants their business more strongly within the ecosystem while establishing a competitive advantage (Kansheba, 2020). Government programmes and policies that support market mechanisms create an enabling environment for entrepreneurs or start-ups to go through the various phases sustainably.

Human Capital

Human capital is considered the most relevant competitive pillar among all the EE factors. In the model developed by Isenberg (2011), the availability of labour and educational institutions induces EE. Adequate human resources are needed to promote and achieve the human capital objective. Moreover, sufficient and high-quality educational institutions are critical in the development of human capital within a successful ecosystem. A study by Coa and Shi (2021) indicates that the lack of human capital inhibits entrepreneurial activities within a region. Evidence suggests that human capital in developing countries prefers to work for someone else instead of starting a new business.

According to the human capital theory, knowledge acquired through entrepreneurial training and development and education increases entrepreneurs' cognitive abilities, leading to more recognition and exploitation of entrepreneurial opportunities (Coa & Shi, 2021). The quality of education within regions demonstrates entrepreneurial disparities. The human capital of a nation is an important factor for EE as it is the pool of human capital that supplies potential entrepreneurs. Evidence suggests that education promotes human capital, which is a relevant ingredient for the development of EE (Sheriff & Muffatto, 2012). Industrialisation linked to local entrepreneurship improves productivity and increases employment. Most developing countries operate within sectors with low or easy entry and human capital is not relevant, however, governments of such countries should make technology and innovation part of the economy's DNA to enable change through human capital investment, which is critical of EE for and productivity.

Policy

Entrepreneurial policy is significant in creating an enabling EE; evidence suggests that developed countries' policies are ineffective in solving market failures but waste resources only to generate a low-growth business. The appropriateness of EE is not only influenced by the type of entrepreneurs but also by policies and programmes (Bate, 2021). The policy is a critical determinant of entrepreneurship; for example, policy-specific is important—it must fit into the specific regional context rather than taking a one-size-fits-all approach.

EE is a complex system of interaction; however, the conceptual understanding of these interactions is important. An entrepreneurship policy that targets more support of an EE might inhibit an EE in another region. Therefore, it is important to appreciate regional differences and similarities in the implementation of EE policies. According to Bate (2021), developing countries should implement entrepreneurial policies and programmes that seek to support EE rather than increasing the size of new firms. To endorse an effective entrepreneurial policy, evaluating both the quantity and quality of entrepreneurship is important for policy implementation.

The global entrepreneurship monitor (GEM) opines that countries in Africa do not have policies that support effective productive entrepreneurship. Therefore, weak policy formulation hurts entrepreneurship development (Atiase et al., 2017). An EE policy should focus on players like entrepreneurial actors, entrepreneurial culture/attitude, resource providers and entrepreneurial connectors because they serve as a catalyst in promoting sustainable enterprise development. The African region's EE is arguable, deterred by the bureaucracy of government and administrative procedures. Corruption inhibits entrepreneurial activities. Bate (2021) argues that a country's policy on entrepreneurship has two ends—the positive (reaping the fruits of productive entrepreneurship) and the negative.

Finance

From the microeconomic perspective, finance is a factor of production, and it is used for capital investment, for either growth or start-up. Financial capital is a critical component of entrepreneurial capital. It is argued that a region's financial soundness promotes regional growth. However, in Africa, access to credit is limited and the magnitude of this challenge inhibits entrepreneurial activities (Atiase et al., 2017).

An advanced financial market enables entrepreneurship to develop, and evidence suggests that a lack of access to capital is one of the biggest impediments for the development of latent entrepreneurs (Kshetri, 2014). Finance is a relevant resource for entrepreneurs, in both the start-up and scale-up phases, and according to Kansheba (2020), there are various indicators of reliable financial capital within an ecosystem—reliable financial systems with entrepreneur-friendly debt, availability of venture capital and angel capitals. Lack of finance is one of the key factors that inhibit entrepreneurial activities. Resource scarcities for start-ups in developing countries are reflected in resource provision and, access as well as mobilization. Moreover, start-up failures in developing countries are attributed to the financial resource gap (Kansheba, 2020). Due to a lack of finance access, high-skilled individuals tend to engage in employment rather than high-risk entrepreneurial careers.

Crowdfunding

An alternative to the traditional form of funding, crowdfunding is another novel funding source by which external capital can be acquired through an online communication mechanism (Maroufkhani et al., 2017). This mechanism allows businesses to collect necessary funds in the form of either investment or donation from diverse sources to fulfil financial requirements. Normally, this process is conducted through the internet and this concept is derived from the notion of crowdfunding, which is the use of the creativity and expertise of a great number of individuals (World Bank, 2013).

Crowdfunding innovation is largely attributed to the financial crisis in 2008 where many entrepreneurs, start-ups and artisans faced difficulty in raising funds. This innovative strategy provided an avenue for transactions between funders and creators through the internet (Hoque et al., 2018). This platform is gradually increasing because of its multidimensional benefits. According to the World Bank (2013), 45 countries of the world had active crowdfunding platforms and these are only in developed countries.

The crowdfunding market was $5.1 billion in 2013 and it has been growing exponentially but this growth is limited to developed countries. However, Hoque et al. (2018) note that this crowdfunding has potential in developing countries because projects lack sufficient funding and developing countries have the prospect of manage growth and entrepreneurship through this initiative. Moreover, crowdfunding is for the smooth development of social enterprises and thereby their development can be enhanced.

Industrial Dynamic

The industrial dynamic concept promotes sectoral innovation; thus, different innovation strategies are pursued to leverage technological regimes, which creates an opportunity for complex knowledge distribution. According to Maroufkhani et al. (2017), the industrial dynamic can be aggregated as the magnitude, frequency and changes in customers' preferences within the boundaries of the industry. This can be considered a multidimensional concept.

The industrial dynamic determines the changes and the important environmental elements for the survival of firms in a highly competitive economy. Evidence suggests that the industrial dynamic is driven by technology, however, technology advancement in developing countries is a fundamental issue (Miah & Omar, 2012). Countries with technological advancement have increased their capital income and improved the quality of their citizens' lives.

Innovation influences industrial dynamics, which in the long run affects the growth and survival of firms and the rate of entry. It is important to understand that innovation permits the collaboration of various sectors such as financial institutions, universities, entrepreneurs and government. Industrial dynamic is about transformation process, evolutionary theory, dynamism, technologies and dynamic efficiency. These are the driving force of industrial development and economic growth (Maroufkhani et al., 2017). Industrial changes help enterprises to have productive entrepreneurs.

Support

Support comes in different forms; EE is a set of interconnected elements such as human skills, market, culture, leadership and support (Mukiza & Kansheba, 2020). Access to public support designed for start-ups and ventures in an ecosystem motivates citizen, especially new talent, and produces diverse culture expression. Encouraging EE comes as a strategy to nurture a region's economy by fostering entrepreneurial processes and activities that seek the growth of businesses.

Unfavourable support can be inimical to entrepreneurship. Arguably, government support has been driving entrepreneurship in many developing countries; however, the support can have a negative impact as well. According to Kshetri (2014), it is also important to look at the differential rate of development of institutions to support entrepreneurship within a region. For example, the South Korean government's strong favouritism and support for the chaebol have created an unfavourable environment for SMEs in the country and in Estonia, insufficient collateral hindered SMEs' ability to access bank lending. In South Korean, the government's excessive support for the venture capital industry created a moral hazard problem. Some argue that government support for the venture capital sector inhibits the development of a self-sustaining investment ecosystem (Lee, 2021).

Many African countries are challenged by inherent risky environments and political instabilities. Moreover, factors such as finance, managerial skills and infrastructure, unaffordable services, lack of incubators and unsupportive culture inhibit entrepreneurial growth (Mukiza & Kansheba, 2020). Furthermore, support structures such as public or private organisations that help the start-up and growth of ventures are important for their sustainability.

7 Conclusions and Limitations

This study aimed to understand the various factors that constitute EE in Africa, as undoubtedly, African countries need to appreciate the emerging concept to help in achieving sustainability. The concept has captured the attention of scholars and governments. We systematically scrutinised the extant literature on EE, and our findings show eight factors that constitute EE that can help countries in Africa achieve sustainability. The factors are crowdsourcing, support, industry dynamic, finance, culture, human capital, market and policy. Our study summarises the literature on the EE from developing countries' perspectives. These factors are interlinked and countries in Africa should not consider each as a standalone; programmes directed at addressing them should be holistic. We contribute to the literature on entrepreneurship and sustainability by identifying EE factors that can be found in all developing countries. We fill the gap by improving our understanding of the issues and challenges affecting the sustainability of enterprises. This provided the potential to expand the theoretical perspectives of EE. We recommend that countries in Africa should focus on these variables to develop their economies in a sustainable manner and policymakers should provide an enabling environment that fosters new business opportunities.

UNDERSTANDING THE IMPACT ...   249

Our study encountered some limitations. The analysis is based on different studies with different objectives. This may suffer inherent bias due to subjectivity among the various studies. Moreover, our focus was on Africa, and we only reviewed studies carried out in developing countries from 2010 to 2022. There may be studies that were conducted before 2010 which might recognise important factor/s of EE, but our study ignored them. Future research should expand the scope of our study. A precise review is required.

REFERENCES

Atiase, V. Y., Mahmood, S., Wang, Y., & Botchie, D. (2017). Developing entrepreneurship in Africa: Investigating critical resource challenges. *Journal of Small Business and Enterprise Development, 25*(4), 644–666.

Audretsch, D. B. & Belitski, M. (2017). Entrepreneurial ecosystem in cities. Establishing the framework conditions. *Journal of Technology Transfer, 42*(5), 1030–1051. https://doi.org/10.1007/s10961-016-9473-8.

Auerswald, P. P. (2015) *Enabling entrepreneurial ecosystems.* Ewing Marion Kauffman Foundation.

Ballestar, M. T., Cuerdo-Mir, M., & Freire-Rubio, M. T. (2020). The concept of sustainability on social media: A social listening approach. *Sustainability, 12*(5), 1–19. https://doi.org/10.3390/su12052122

Bate, A. F. (2021). A comparative analysis on the entrepreneurial ecosystem of BRICS club countries: Practical emphasis on South Africa. *SN Business Economics, 1*(121), 1–20. https://doi.org/10.1007/s43546-021-00120-2

Beugré, C. D. (2016). *Building entrepreneurial ecosystems in sub-Saharan Africa: A quintuple helix model.* Springer.

Bird, B. J. (1992). The operation of intentions in time: The emergence of the new venture. *Entrepreneurship Theory and Practice, 17*(1), 11–20.

Castillo, M.A.S., Peris-Ortiz, M., and Del Valle, I.D. (2015) What is different about the profile of the social entrepreneur. *Nonprofit Management and Leadership, 25*(4), 349–369.

Cao, Z., & Shi, X. (2021). A systematic literature review of entrepreneurial ecosystem in advanced and emerging economies. *Small Business Economy, 57*, 75–110.

Carvalho, L., Dominguinhos, P., & Costa, T. (2010). Creating an entrepreneurship in ecosystem in higher education. In Soomro, S. (Ed.), *New achievement in technology education and development,* INTECH Open Access Publisher.

Gomes, E., Cohen, M., & Mellahi, K. (2011). When two African cultures collide: A study of interactions between managers in a strategic alliance between two African organizations. *Journal of World Business, 46*(1), 5–12.

Gomes, E., Vendrell-Herrero, F., Mellahi, K., Angwin, D., & Sousa, C. M. P. (2018). Testing the self-selection theory in high corruption environments: Evidence from African SMEs. *International Marketing Review*. https://doi.org/10.1108/IMR-03-2017-0054

Gomis, A. J. B., Parra, M. G., Hoffman, W. M., & Mcnulty, R. E. (2011). Rethinking the concept of sustainability. *Business and Society Review*, 116(2), 171–191.

Hall, J. K., Daneke, G. A., & Lenox, M. J. (2010). Sustainable development and entrepreneurship: Past contributions and future directions. *Journal of Business Venturing*, 25(5), 439–448.

Hitt, M. A., Ireland, R. D., Camp, S. M., & Sexton, D. I. (2001). Guest editors' introduction to the special issue strategic entrepreneurship: Entrepreneurial strategies for wealth creation. *Strategic Management Journal*, 22, 497–491.

Hoque, N., Ali, M. H., Arefeen, S., Mowla, M., & Mamun, A. (2018). Use of crowdfunding for developing social enterprises: An Islamic approach. *International Journal of Business and Management*, 13(6), 156–164.

Iyigun, N.O. (2015). What could entrepreneurship do for sustainable development? A corporate social responsibility-based approach. *Procedia—Social and Behavioural Sciences*, 195, 1226–1231.

Isenbeng, D. (2011). The entrepreneurship ecosystem strategy as a new paradigm for economic policy: Principles for cultivating entrepreneurship. *Open Journal of Business and Management*, 8(8).

Kang, Q., Hongbo, L., Cheng, Y., & Kraus, S. (2021). Entrepreneurial ecosystems: Analysing the status quo. *Knowledge Management Research and Practice*, 19(1), 8–20.

Kansheba, J. M. P. (2020). Small business and entrepreneurship in Africa: The nexus of entrepreneurial ecosystems and productive entrepreneurship. *Small Enterprise Research*, 27(2), 110–124.

Kansheba, J. M. P., & Wald, A. E. (2020). Entrepreneurial ecosystems: A systematic literature review and research agenda. *Journal of Small Business and Enterprise Development*, 27(1), 943–964.

Kshetri, N. (2014). Developing successful entrepreneurial ecosystems lessons from a comparison of an Asian tiger and Baltic tiger. *Baltic Journal of Management*, 9(3), 330–256.

Kuhlman, T., & Farrington, J. (2010). What is sustainability? *Sustainability*, 2, 3436–3448. https://doi.org/10.3390/su2113436

Kuratko, D. F. (2007). Entrepreneurship leadership in the 21st century: Guest editor's perspective. *Journal of Leadership and Organisation Studies*, 13, 1–11.

Kuratko, D. F., & Hodgetts, R. M. (2007). *Entrepreneurship: Theory, process, practice* (7th ed.). Thomson and Southwestern Publishing.

Lafuente, E., Szerb, L., & Acs, Z. J. (2018). *The entrepreneurship paradox: More entrepreneurs are not always good for the economy—The role of the entrepreneurial ecosystem on economic performance in Africa*.https://doi.org/10.2139/ssrn.3307617.

Lee, H. (2021). Supporting the cultural industrial using venture capital: A policy experiment from South Korea. *Cultural Trend*. https://doi.org/10.1080/09548963.2021.1926931

Lucas, D. S., & Fuller, C. S. (2017). Entrepreneurship: Productive, unproductive, and destructive—relative to what? *Journal of Business Venturing Insights, 7*, 45–49. https://doi.org/10.1016/j.jbvi.2017.03.001

Marino, J., Rivero, A. G., & Dabos, G. E. (2019). MBAs and career development: A literature review from the human capital perspective. *Journal of Management, 35*(64), 109–126.

Maroufkhani, P., Wagner, R., & Ismail, W. K. W. (2017). Entrepreneurial ecosystems: A systematic review. *Journal of Enterprising Communities: People and Places in the Global Economy, 12*(4), 545–564.

Menezes, L. M., & Kelliher, C. (2011). Flexible working and performance: A systematic review of the evidence for a business case. *International Journal Management Reviews, 13*, 452–474.

Mensah, M. S. B., & Amarteifio, E. N. A. (2021). *Exploratory study of the entrepreneurial ecosystem in Central Region, Ghana*. International Conference, Universities, Entrepreneurship, and Enterprise Development in Africa. Sankt Augustin, 19–20 February 2020.

Miah, M., & Omar, A. (2012). Technology advancement in developing countries during digital age. *International Journal of Science and Applied Information Technology, 1*(1), 30–38.

Mukiza, J., & Kansheba, P. (2020). Small business and entrepreneurship in Africa: The nexus of entrepreneurial ecosystems and productive entrepreneurship. *Small Enterprise Research, 27*(2), 110–124.

Mwatsika, C. (2018). The ecosystem perspective of entrepreneurship in local economic development. *Journal of Economics and Sustainable Development, 9*(12), 94–114.

Mwantimwa, K., Ndege, N., Atela, J., & Hall, A. (2021). Scaling innovation hubs: Impact on knowledge, innovation and entrepreneurial ecosystems in Tanzania. *Journal of Innovation Management, 9*(2), 39–63.

Naude, W. (2017). *Entrepreneurship, education and the fourth industrial revolution in Africa* [Discussion paper series, IZA DP No. 10855]. IZA Institute of Labor Economics.

Ngongoni, C. N., Grobbelaar, S. S. & Schutte, C. S. L. (2017). The role of open innovation intermediaries in entrepreneurial ecosystems design. *South Africa Journal of Industrial Engineering, 28*(3), special edition, 56–65.

Nir, K. (2014) Developing success entrepreneurial ecosystems: Lessons from a comparison of an Asian tiger and Baltic tiger. *Baltic Journal of Management, 9*(3), 330–356.

Opute, A. P. (2020). Small and medium enterprises marketing: Innovation and sustainable economic growth perspective. In Nwankwo, S., and Gbadamosi, A. (Eds.), *Entrepreneurship marketing: Principles and practice of SME Marketing*. Routledge Publishers.

Pita, M., Costa, J., & Moreira, C. (2021). Entrepreneurial ecosystem and entrepreneurial initiative: Building a multi-country taxonomy. *Sustainability, 13*, 40–65.

Pobee, F. and Mphela, T. (2021). An analysis of the entrepreneurship ecosystem of Malawi: The global entrepreneurship index (FEI) approach. *Journal of Development and Communication Studies, 8*(1), 224–238.

Rodrik, D. (2016). An African growth miracle? *Journal of African Economies, 27*, 10–27.

Salas-Zapata, W. A., & Ortiz-Muñoz, S. M. (2018). Analysis of meanings of the concept of sustainability. *Sustainable Development, 1–9.* https://doi.org/10.1002/sd.1885

Schjoedt, I., & Shaver, K. G. (2007). Deciding on an entrepreneurship career: A test of the pull and push hypotheses using the panel study of entrepreneurial dynamics data. *Entrepreneurship Theory and Practice, 31*(5), 733–752.

Schwab, K. (2019). *The global competitive report 2019.* World Economic Forum. https://www3.weforum.org/docs/WEF_TheGlobalCompetitiveness Report2019.pdf. Accessed: 28th February 2022.

Sheriff, M., & Muffatto, M. (2015). The present state of entrepreneurship ecosystem in selected countries in Africa. *African Journal of Economic and Management Studies, 6*(1), 17–54.

Spigel, B. (2017). The relational organisational of entrepreneurial ecosystems. *Entrepreneurship Theory and Practice, 41*(1), 49–72.

Thiele, L. P. (2016). *Sustainability.* 2nd edition.

Tracey, P., & Phillips, N. (2011). Entrepreneurship in emerging markets strategies for new venture creation in uncertain institutional contexts. *Management International Review, 51*, 23–39.

Tranfield, D., Denyer, D., & Smart, P. (2003). Towards a methodology for developing evidence-informed management knowledge by means of systematic review. *British Journal of Management, 14*, 207–222.

United Nations. (2020). *Entrepreneurship for sustainable development.* https://unctad.org/system/files/official-document/a75d257_en.pdf. Accessed: 21st February 2022.

Van de Ven, A. H. (1993). The development of an infrastructure for entrepreneurship. *Journal of Business Venturing, 8*, 211–230.

World Bank. (2013). *Crowdfunding's potential for the developing world*. https:/ /www.infodev.org/infodev-files/wb_crowdfundingreport-v12.pdf. Accessed 1st February 2022.

Youssef, A. B., Boubaker, S. & Omri, A. (2017). *Entrepreneurship and sustainability: The need for innovative and institutional solutions*. https://mpra.ub. uni-muenchen.de/84503/1/mpra_paper_84503.pdf. Accessed 21st February 2022.

Strategic Entrepreneurship Approach for a Sustainable African Ecosystem

Narcisa Roxana Moşteanu ⓘ
and Albert Dans Michael Ngame Mesue

1 INTRODUCTION

This chapter aims to present a strategic entrepreneurship design for Africa. The main challenge we want to address is to properly design a strategy for Entrepreneurs on the African continent that takes advantage of fast-developing world where Africa has its place. The objective of this chapter is a researchable one and will contribute to the body of knowledge by creating awareness to these start-ups and Small and Medium Size Enterprises that struggle to survive by laying emphasis on the opportunities in technological advancements, robotics, the internet of things, blockchain and artificial intelligence to grow smartly in a harsh environment. Related searches have been conducted on entrepreneurial efforts in Africa and the impact of the internet and technology. Relationships and correlations are presented as a possible solution for a strategic entrepreneurship design. Emphasis is laid on the understanding of how the general and specific environmental constraints faced by Entrepreneurs in Africa affect the growth and survival of entrepreneurial ventures. Entrepreneurship is

---

N. R. Moşteanu (✉) · A. D. M. N. Mesue
College of Business, American University of Malta, Cospicua, Malta
e-mail: narcisamosteau@yahoo.com

© The Author(s), under exclusive license to Springer Nature
Switzerland AG 2023
S. Adomako et al. (eds.), *Corporate Sustainability in Africa*,
Palgrave Studies in African Leadership,
https://doi.org/10.1007/978-3-031-29273-6_12

a critical driver of economic development, and Africa needs sustainable economic growth to address its challenges, including poverty, unemployment, and inequality. Developing a strategy for entrepreneurship can help create jobs, boost productivity, and generate wealth. African entrepreneurs have the potential to develop innovative solutions to local challenges and create products and services that can be scaled globally. Developing a strategy for entrepreneurship can help create an enabling environment for innovation and technology transfer. Finally, African entrepreneurship development has significant implications for sustainability, as it can contribute to creating long-term economic growth, social development, and environmental sustainability.

Present chapter includes seven parts—part 2 it starts by presenting the need of entrepreneurship in Africa and significant implications for sustainability; part 3 presents the external evaluation analysis using PESTELE tool; part 4 is conducting the SWOT analysis to establish the possible directions of entrepreneurship in Africa; part 5 is presenting the African entrepreneurship and ecosystem analysis through the lens of parts 3 and 4; part 6 introduces a possible Strategy for a sustainable entrepreneurial African ecosystem; and part 7 comes to conclude and underline the beneficial parts of entrepreneurship developments in Africa and the implications for sustainability.

2 THE NEED OF ENTREPRENEURSHIP IN AFRICA AND SIGNIFICANT IMPLICATIONS FOR SUSTAINABILITY

As people strive for survival daily on basis, starting up a business venture looks like a good opportunity for increasing their wealth, but is never an easy task especially in a continent like Africa where, despite the unique challenges that present themselves, prospects from the rich human, socio-cultural, ethnic, and natural resource diversity of 54 officially recognized countries tend to portray the continent as an emerging market. Africa has more than 130 ethnic groups and a minimum of 3000 languages thus confirming the forecast that by 2100 about one-third of the world's population will inhabit Africa. Thus, portraying the continent as an emerging market and the world's next big growth market. In the book *Africa's business revolution: how to succeed in the worlds next big growth market*, Leke (Leke et al., 2018) clearly specified that, Africa currently boasts of $1.4 trillion in consumer spending, which is more than India, that there are more than 400 companies with more than $1 billion as annual revenue and the continent is about 11.73 million square miles making it bigger than China, the USA and Europe combined in terms of surface area.

A report published by the Global Entrepreneurship Monitor (Global Entrepreneurship Monitor, 2020/2021) underlines that Sub-Saharan Africa has the highest number of people at the early stages of entrepreneurial activity with Nigeria and Zambia leading on the global scale. Nevertheless, businesses in this part of the continent struggle from the time when they initially start up throughout the growth process. As such local entrepreneurs find it very difficult to thrive in business. Some businesses wind up prematurely partly due to financial difficulties and also because of the presence of already existing bigger business structures that are currently enjoying more political and economic advantages. Despite, the challenges and difficulties faced by entrepreneurs in Africa, the underlying fact that the potency of this sector cannot be compromised.

It is worth noting that the fast-growing population of African markets and countries represent an opportunity for investors and entrepreneurs from all over the world. Though, there is a need to meet with greater innovation, infrastructural and institutional developments so that particular sectors of African economies that are known to be full of opportunities can be harnessed to grow, creating new jobs, increase economic well-being, and create wealth. In Global Entrepreneurship Monitor reports criticized the South African government and legislature solely for restrictions on employment and considered the enacted laws as bottlenecks for start-ups and their survival (Herrington et al., 2010). Therefore, the present chapter aims to underline and draw a possible strategic design with a clear mission and vision, intended to help entrepreneurs to create value from the opportunities of this era, while identifying and working on the general and specific challenges faced by their societies, in order to sustainably grow their businesses to interact on the global platform.

The essence is to create a blueprint for interested entrepreneurs, no matter the financial or general macroenvironmental challenges they are faced with. A blueprint that helps businesses to grow, over time when technology and efforts are directed toward meeting global demands in a bid to establish sustainably profitable business ventures, while reducing poverty and unemployment in African countries. Thus, demonstrating that businesses in Africa like in all other parts of the world, can yield societal benefits if these surrounding factors and forces influencing entrepreneurship are well defined and understood.

We cannot overstress the fact that, despite the challenges faced by entrepreneurs in Africa, entrepreneurship is a major factor in economic and regional development. It contributes significantly to economic growth, job creation, and business innovation (Mensah et al., 2019). There are a number of opportunities on the continent that if properly harnessed could reap many benefits for stakeholders from all over the world and Africa in particular. Most of the difficulties faced by entrepreneurs and start-ups in Africa are structural as well as institutional, and this cuts across almost all African countries. In order words, entrepreneurs in Africa, especially start-ups, SMEs find it very difficult to sustainably grow their businesses to the point of breakeven. Entrepreneurship can be defined as a way of thinking about solving problems by harnessing the available resources and opportunities socially, profitably, and sustainably in a bid to create wealth. Africa is a continent deeply rooted in entrepreneurship and many African households survive from entrepreneurship. In the views of previous researchers Quartey and Abor (Quartey et al., 2011) in Ghana, for instance, SMEs owned and managed by Ghanaian's account for about 90% of businesses, contributing to about 80% of the labor force, and 70% to the Ghanaian Gross Domestic Product and economic productivity. Despite the overconfidence in governance, legislature and even the whole educational paradigm characterizing the learning system in Africa do not train youths to be societal problem solvers in this rapidly evolving digital and technological age. Investment ventures need to be undertaken primarily by Africans before foreign investment. This is obvious because Africans constitute that vulnerable majority plagued by the harsh socio-economic, political, and cultural environment and systems. Thus, African Entrepreneurs (Afro-preneurs) are best positioned in tackling their day-to-day challenges.

The most challenging of situations faced by start-ups in Africa refers to the difficulty of raising capital. Access to financial resources has always been the main setback for SMEs in sub-Saharan Africa especially. Leke (Leke et al., 2018) confirmed that almost 75% of the SMEs surveyed were financed by internal funds and only 10% used traditional banking loans. Entrepreneurs and small business owners cannot easily access finance to expand their business, and they are usually faced with problems of collateral security, high-interest rates, extra bank charges, inability to evaluate financial proposals, and limited financial knowledge consequently making it difficult for small businesses to access finance according to Virk

(2019). This is further compounded by the fact that most African countries are lower-middle income economies. According to World Bank's classification (World Bank, 2020), lower-middle-income economies are those economies with a per capita Gross National Income within the range of $1,026 to $3,995. Emerging and developing economies like Ghana, Nigeria, Egypt, and Cameroon all fall within this category, and this puts their citizens in a position where thy cannot easily save to invest in entrepreneurial ventures.

Other than inaccessibility to finance, most entrepreneurs face the problem of power insufficiency, despite the natural ability of the continent to generate hydroelectric and solar energy, which can give way to an industrial Africa. The absence of electricity in rural settings and communities accounts for the limited amount of transformed and processed cash crops and agricultural produce. According to Vernet (Vernet et al., 2019), rural electrification is positively correlated to the creation of Microenterprises. Furthermore, rural electrification also leads to an increase in income, expenditure, and the proportion of customers from outside the rural setting. The Nigerian economy for example depends enormously on gasoline generators to supplement electricity for domestic use. According to Energy Institute Report of 2019 from the Access to Energy Institute,[1] Nigerians spend close to $12 billion annually on purchasing and running petroleum generators.

In addition to financial and electrical constraints, there is so much lacking and needed to be done in Africa in order to meet up with the infrastructural demands of the continent as a whole, although well-capitalized private sector infrastructure developers are gradually popping up from South Africa, Nigeria, and Egypt and there is still a very huge gap to fill in terms of infrastructure. According to the African Development Bank,[2] the continent is getting urbanized at a very fast rate, and this accounts for the fact that about $170 billion is needed every year in infrastructural investments in order for Africa to unleash its true economic potential. For SMEs and businesses, in general, to be conducted successfully and efficiently there is a need for basic infrastructures like constant power, good transportation, and internet networks and facilities,

[1] https://www.energyinst.org/ei-near-me/africa.
[2] https://www.afdb.org/en

and these are normally to be supplied by governments and public institutions in African countries. Unfortunately, governments in most African countries pay very little attention to this kind of challenge. This is in addition to the already highly corrupt existing business practices. This makes it difficult for Entrepreneurs and businesses that are dependent on these facilities to thrive.

Viewing the economy as a business recalls the macroeconomic concepts of Gross Domestic and National Products. In a scenario where all stakeholders; socio-economic and political have to be positively committed to meeting up with national and international objectives. Our strategic plan acknowledges the role of correct and efficient governance and accountability so that national resources are harnessed as opportunities to resolve global problems such as the Refugee crisis, wars, hunger, starvation, and unemployment, just to name a few. Entrepreneurship in Africa supplementing governments in resolving Unemployment for its growing populations.

Fortunately, a growing number of African leaders are taking action toward addressing these challenges. Virk (2019) confirms that countries like Rwanda, Ghana, South Africa, Nigeria, and Kenya, to name a few, have created a single location where entrepreneurs can find and file all necessary paperwork to legally register their businesses. However, more efforts are needed to make these processes digital in order to make them faster, more efficient, and less time-consuming. Virk (2019) further ascertains that a few African governments and entrepreneurs are making it possible for online business registration. This will help reduce the time spent processing and storing chunky manual data. In Cameroon for example, the operating cost for start-ups is high from the rents of the business facility to the acquisition of necessary machinery and technological input. During the last phase of 2019, Cameroon took the initiative to support and develop any entrepreneurial initiative by bringing together stakeholders in the Ministry of SMEs to come and debate the development of the entrepreneurial sector in Cameroon.[3] Therefore, despite the harsh business environment, that generally surrounds SMEs in most African countries, governments are gradually working on adopting better strategies and policies to enable the growth and survival of Entrepreneurship and SMEs in their economies.

---

[3] https://www.businessincameroon.com/economy/0709-10782-cameroon-over-14-200-new-smes-were-created-in-2019-minpmesa.

African entrepreneurship development has significant implications for sustainability, as it can contribute to creating long-term economic growth, social development, and environmental sustainability. Possible contributions of entrepreneurship developments to African economic sustainability may be in the area of job creation; inclusive growth; innovation; access to finance and social environment responsibilities.

3 External Environment Analysis

One of the most common tool to analyze the external environment is PESTELE—The Political, Economic, Social, technological, Environmental, and Legal. This is used as a tool to analyze the macro environment of an organization, and this includes factors that directly affect an organization. Entrepreneurship in Africa is to be looked like a joint venture that seeks to satisfy organizational stakeholders where the objective is the growth of sustainable and autonomous entrepreneurs.

This analysis will consider external factors and how they affect entrepreneurship and is used as our External Factor Evaluation Matrix African governments and the international community will be guided in decision-making based on findings from this analysis. Figure 1 represents the PESTEL evaluation chart.

4 The SWOT Analysis

Strengths

Strengths as African entrepreneurs are those innate attributes that give a comparative advantage in the world at large. This will include a growing African youthful population, the global market, the availability of land natural resources, and multicultural diversity. These attributes will help entrepreneurial efforts in achieving the objectives; those prior goals that initially brought together the involved stakeholders to tilt resources toward starting up businesses and SMEs. Ghana, Nigeria, South Africa, Angola, and Cameroon are just examples of how Sub-Saharan African countries can use entrepreneurship and business to help themselves escape poverty and live sustainably in a worthy manner. Figure 2 presents the SWOT analyze.

POLITICAL FACTORS	ECONOMIC FACTORS	SOCIO-CULTURAL FACTORS	TECHNOLOGICAL FACTORS	ENVIRONMENTAL FACTORS	LEGISLATIVE FACTORS
* The prevalence of poor governance in Africa. * Over reliance on the weak public sector. * General Political Instability. * Existence of bribery and corruption. * Partially free trade Area Agreement among African countries and consequent existing trade barriers among African nations. *African Policy and decision makers working on harmonized ways of overcoming trade restrictions.	* The African Development Bank (ADB) expects growth rates to rise by 4.01% in 2021. * Exchange rate stability as many African currencies are pegged to the Dollar and Euro. * Fluctuating interest rates. * Rising Inflation Rates * High Unemployment Rates. * Low GDP per capita * Low- and Middle-Income Economies	* Rapidly increasing population rates. According to Trading Economics, Nigeria's population alone is expected to from increase from 205.8million in 2020, to 210.87 in 2021 and 215.8 in 2022. * Africa enjoys a young age structure with about 2/5th of the population less than 14years. * General optimism towards job and career drive. * Poor health systems coupled with little health consciousness * Cultural diversity and barriers tend to hinder trade between African Nations.	* Limited technological incentives in Africa. * Emergence of a technological ecosystems with the proliferation of platforms for Android and iOS. * Ongoing research and Development in many African economies. * Noticeable growth in Africa's technological industry and technological business. * Slow but significant growth in computer engineering and technological hubs by over 50% in the last years.	* Existing climatic challenges such as global warming and fluctuation in weather and climate, which affects most especially entrepreneurs in the Agricultural sector with either excess rainfalls or most times with excess sunshine. * Organization of climate change conferences in 2020 in the USA, Asia, Europe and other places across the world for the sustainability of the planet as a whole.	* A series of anti-trust and competition laws enacted in South Africa particularly. In a bid to maximize competitor advantage. * Also, laws encouraging equality and discrediting discrimination are being enacted. Thus, nurturing an environment that promulgates business and consumer protection. * The African Union has been working with the Japan Patent Office in Senegal Dakar to design Intellectual Property rights in African artists, SMEs, and economies at large.

Fig. 1 PESTEL external evaluation chart

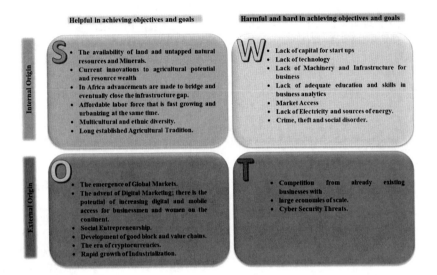

Fig. 2 SWOT analysis

Opportunities

There are several opportunities nowadays for all people over the world. First, because of rapidly advancing intelligence in data storage, processing and protection, information, and communication technologies. Second, financial technologies for business and financial analytics, can help SMEs analyze and process the information on their operations thus giving them accurate findings and results from software programs and applications are designed and updated on a rapid basis. Furthermore, the internet and the availability of digital markets where customers do not necessarily need to see their suppliers but are very sure of the reliability and consistency in business transactions and operations tend to be the featured characteristics of future global markets. Aspects of Entrepreneurial strengths will positively work with these external opportunities.

Strengths and Opportunities

This will bring us to a point of balance between our strengths and existing opportunities. Africa does not depend only on its innate natural endowment but also on intelligence and technology in this digital age. This ties in with what was said on CNBC Africa; a business platform, in 2019 by the Zimbabwean businessman and philanthropist, Strive Masiyiwa[4] who happens to be the founder and executive chairman of Econet Global; a company that deals with telecommunications, technology, and renewable energy.

Weaknesses

Talking about the weaknesses of entrepreneurs in Africa, there is much that has to be done with respect to ensuring that ethical and best practices are inculcated. These internal shortcomings can be avoided by African entrepreneurs specializing in what works for them. It is believed that weaknesses can always be overcome by working on them. In this digital age, afro-preneurs can always develop themselves and their businesses through the acquisition of necessary skills, know-how, and networks by interacting on digital platforms. The coming of social entrepreneurship will go a long way in giving everyone the opportunity to showcase their activity, product, or service to the world at large through blockchains, cryptocurrencies, and overall cyber security. It is also worth noting that the weakness of fluctuation in exchange rates, interest rates, and agricultural prices and be overcome by cryptocurrencies, digital and mobile money accounts (Moşteanu, 2020a). Financial transactions become a little more difficult to be conducted with cash, and online banking transactions are called to help the good development of economic activity (Moşteanu et al., 2020). Fortunately, over the years many countries in West Africa especially have been depending on these monetary tools such as Mobile Money locally known as (Momo) to facilitate transactions globally.

Threats (T)

Threats, refer to those external factors that are harmful to entrepreneurial efforts and have to be addressed with immediate effect. Usually in the guise of the associated risks surrounding opportunities or existing competition. Figure 3 represents the biggest obstacles to African entrepreneurship.

---

[4] https://cassavatechnologies.com/strive-masiyiwa/

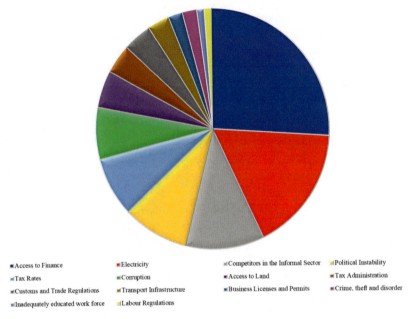

■ Access to Finance ■ Electricity ■ Competitors in the Informal Sector ■ Political Instability
■ Tax Rates ■ Corruption ■ Access to Land ■ Tax Administration
■ Customs and Trade Regulations ■ Transport Infrastructure ■ Business Licenses and Permits ■ Crime, theft and disorder
■ Inadequately educated work force ■ Labour Regulations

Fig. 3 Threats, weakness, and environmental challenges of entrepreneurs in Africa—biggest obstacles

5 THE AFRICAN ENTREPRENEURSHIP AND ECOSYSTEM ANALYSIS

Access to Financial Resources

Capital being one of the most important factors of production happens to be one of the most serious problems faced by entrepreneurs all around the continent. The financial ecosystem of Africa is traditional in nature and quite different from most parts of the world, making it difficult for most start-ups to acquire loans from commercial banks. In most cases when unable to acquire loans from banks they turn to Micro Finance institutions that intend to look at variables such as the gender of the applicant, turnover rate, financial statements, number of employees, and collateral security.

Whereas the Multicultural and ethnic diversity of most Sub-Saharan African countries which is deeply rooted in Agricultural traditions have reliable though rudimentary institutions that offer more helpful financial services at lower scales. Ethnic gatherings bring together farmers, retailers, and other business individuals with the common goal of creating wealth through savings, borrowing, individual and joint business investments. Experience proves that what some of these entrepreneurs really need is not the capital in itself but access to information, structures, and facilities such as warehousing, logistics, and international trade facilitators. This is because, the socio-political and economic environment may make the acquisition and accessibility of such relevant business information, facilities, and structures very expensive more than they really ought to be and such entrepreneurs diverting their financial resources to acquire these structures tend to reduce their capital for operations and business.

Financial institutions such as banks and micro finances are challenged to build technologies, mobile applications, and risk models that better appreciate the individuals at stake. In Cameroon, for example, Ovamba Solution[5]s, a TradeTech company that provides supply chain management services and investments to emerging market companies, has succeeded to pump in about $25 million into over 270 companies, ensuring that they make 7 times the amount of revenue and in some cases 4 times the amount of investment. Institutions like this are helpful because they are outliers to the normal traditional financial systems, models, and software and go a long way in incorporating algorithms that encompass if not all then most aspects of the humans such as their tradition, family status, and even their social standing in addition to the obvious financial procedures and risk models.

Restructuring the Informal Business Sector in Africa

The informal sector can be described to be that part of the economy in which businesses are either not registered or taxed. In Africa, most businesses and entrepreneurs operate in the informal sector, and this makes up a very significant portion of economic activity and plays a great role in the GDP of most African countries. However, despite the role of this sector on GDP, it is still considered to be problematic. This is not supposed to be the case because if more attention is directed to this sector, it could be better regulated and reorganized thus creating more

---

[5] https://www.ovamba.com/

value for the economy as a whole. The main problem in the informal sector in most African countries is caused by companies that evade tax and that are smugglers, not those SMEs, start-ups, or entrepreneurs that are not recorded, registered, or officially recognized by the government. The reason is that SMEs create employment for many people who intend to contribute cumulatively and actively to the economy.

Governments across African countries have as a duty to identify these two classes of companies and enterprises that operate in the Informal sector; those who evade taxes and deal with smuggled products and those whose operations are not recognized. Restructuring this sector by recognizing the skills, talents, and occupations of those entrepreneurs and SMEs that contribute positively to the economy will go a long way in supporting these businesses because they will merge with the formal and global sectors in a customized way particular only to them. This will further help governments to track down tax evaders and other exploitative businesses while instituting appropriate tax rates and regimes that are convenient for the success and sustainable growth of start-ups.

Overcoming Electricity and Power Shortages

According to Fig. 4, power shortages and the unavailability of electricity in many areas of the continent remain the major constraints to entrepreneurial efforts. Large and Small enterprises depend on electricity and electrically operated machines to perform their tasks. It is impossible to operate businesses, SMEs, companies, and industries nowadays without a steady supply of power and electricity. In Nigeria for example to meet up with operations people must use fuel-operated generators that are environmentally harmful to produce electricity for their businesses. All of this is at a cost that still affects the profitability of these businesses.

The availability of solar energy could go a long way to substitute hydro-electric power and other than governments, private individuals could invest in energy companies to supplement government supplies as well.

The Role of Government in Ensuring a Suitable Environment for Entrepreneurs and Businesses

Africa's multicultural diversity is one of the most remarkable features of the continent. With more than 2,000 tribes, ethnic groups, and dialects

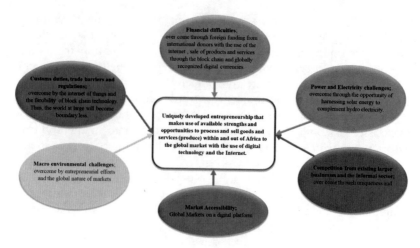

Fig. 4 Diagrammatic illustration of the decision stage

the continent can make use of diversity to create value for all its stakeholders. As of now, there are 8 regional economic blocks in Africa and despite the pressure on the leadership to integrate these blocks into one strong Union State as is the case with the European Union or the United States of America, there is still much to be done in this regard. The current situation can be seen as a trade barrier that still exists among different countries and economic areas. Nowadays, entrepreneurs have to pay tariffs and unnecessary customs duties for their products, in the trading process, on the same continent—Africa. Contrarily, the strength of African countries instead depends on the exchange of cultures and the interconnection of our economies. Governments can ensure that there are no duties for Intra-African trades and that there are good networks, infrastructures, and legislations guiding these integration attempts. The advent of online transactions will also go a long way in overcoming some of these barriers to trade.

Even though governments across the continent are working on closing the gap in infrastructure by envisioning strategies such as Vision 2035 for Cameroon and *Agenda 2063*; a blueprint aimed at transforming Africa into the global powerhouse of the future, much still has to be done to ensure that technological and other infrastructures are put in place to assist entrepreneurs produce, transport and transform products and services to other parts of the continent and the world at large. Public Laws can be revised and designed in a way that entrepreneurs and SMEs are given recognition for the role they play in economic growth and the productivity of the economy. Curriculum that equips the growing youthful population with entrepreneurial skills on how to conduct taxation exercises, business registration requirements, and procedures of their various communities and countries have to be instituted in educational institutions.

The Opportunities of the Digital Era

The challenges faced by most entrepreneurs in Africa are a result of a lack of machinery and technology. However, the coming of the internet as a catalyst for change and development is very vital and important in the sustainable growth of Africa SMEs because information and communication technologies go a long way to link African entrepreneurs with the global market. It is worth noting that according to estimates from the Global System for Mobile communications, in 2018, there were about 442 technology hubs across the continent in countries like South Africa, Nigeria, Cameroon, Ghana, Cote d'Ivoire, Morocco, Tunisia, Egypt, Kenya, Uganda, Zimbabwe, and Angola, and these hubs have been growing since then, expanding on ICT tools that are current with global trends. Moreover, these hubs are not only technology-inclined but incubators for the kind of SMEs that will characterize the African continent in the years to come. Teaching techniques are better to be updated to improve digital skills too (Moşteanu, 2021). After the COVID-19 pandemic, digital communication has become vital to all social and economic sectors. Today we are experiencing a transition from traditional learning to e-learning via digital means. Overnight, all of humanity is learning how to adapt to digital life and leaving traditional ways of doing things behind.

Companies like Ovamba Solutions Inc, already use up-to-date technologies like Artificial Intelligence and robotics to perform day-to-day operations and these have proven to be more reliable in management leadership. Also, the prevalence of mobile money accounts has gone a long way in overcoming time spent queuing at banks and time spent accessing money. These mobile money accounts have made money more accessible to its users and give many entrepreneurs up-to-date information on their financial and account situation. We cannot over-emphasize the role of these financial technologies in the follow-up, planning, and organization of SMEs on the continent.

Innovations in blockchain and Artificial Intelligence could also be a reliable way of linking African entrepreneurs to the global market. Nowadays blockchain ensures that sellers and providers of goods and services market their products internationally without having any contact with buyers while ensuring the reliability of business transactions through cryptocurrencies such as bitcoins. These advancements in artificial and digital intelligence (Moşteanu, 2020b) could go a long way in overcoming some of the weaknesses and shortcomings faced by African entrepreneurs (Moşteanu et al., 2020; Moşteanu, 2020c). However, much still must be done in this domain such as getting the necessary skill that is needed to set the digital era on its rails in Africa.

Sustainability of Entrepreneurship and Business Development

A recent study (Terán-Yépez et al., 2020) sustains that *entrepreneurship has been recognized as a mechanism with which to generate economic benefits. However, due to the emergence of the concept of sustainable development as a pressing issue that is affecting the current global system, it has been pointed out that entrepreneurship should not be based solely on generating wealth.* Entrepreneurship is better to meet the needs of consumers, using the optimal cost and new technologies at the required quality standards.

New technologies, strategies, and changes in human behavior, in conjunction, can drive innovative sustainability solutions. In general, entrepreneurs face a complex dilemma. How can entrepreneurship help create a post-pandemic reality where access to care is equitable, where all people's lives matter, and where the climate is balanced? how can entrepreneurship contribute to sustainable and balanced socio-economic development? Here we can say that entrepreneurs have the opportunity and responsibility to consider new technologies, the future ramifications of social innovation and business strategy, and to practice business ethics that prioritize the health of the long-term ecosystem and society at large.

To promote sustainable entrepreneurship, it is necessary to understand the sustainable entrepreneurial process. Entrepreneurs' previous experiences and skills, as well as knowledge of similar initiatives, are closely related to motivation and idea generation. Previous experiences and skills are generally related to a sensitivity to a social or environmental issue, or generated by extraordinary events or constraints, such as the COVID-19 pandemic. In most situations, both dimensions of sustainability can be integrated at the same time and before the venture is launched. One of the stimuli for sustainable entrepreneurship can be educational practices more aligned to the sustainability issues facing local communities, stronger dissemination of successful business cases related to sustainability in other countries and contexts, closer collaboration between universities and the business environment, and practice-based promotion learning in the curriculum (Matzembacher, 2019).

Most researchers have focused on sustainable entrepreneurship without considering the impact of mass media as a channel of achievement by changing consumer behavior toward the consumption of a particular product. The mass media also play an important role in promoting sustainable entrepreneurship with a direct impact on the purchasing behavior of consumers. A recent study of the food manufacturing sector in Nigeria revealed that customer satisfaction was the key dimension affecting sustainable entrepreneurship (Yakubu et al., 2022).

6 Possible Strategy for a Sustainable Entrepreneurial African Ecosystem

After conducting a pertinent external and internal environment analysis, and defining the opportunities, threats, strengths, and weaknesses, formulating a strategy for entrepreneurship in Africa requires consideration of the unique challenges and opportunities present on the continent. Possible key steps to follow: (1) Conduct market research: Before starting any business, it is essential to conduct market research to identify potential opportunities, target customers, and competition. In Africa, this research should consider factors such as local customs, cultural norms, and economic conditions; (2) Assess the legal and regulatory environment: Entrepreneurs in Africa need to be aware of the legal and regulatory framework that governs business operations in their country of operation. This includes understanding tax laws, registration requirements, and compliance with local labor laws; (3) Develop a business plan: A business plan serves as a roadmap for the entrepreneur to follow. It should include a detailed description of the business, financial projections, marketing strategy, and operational plan; (4) Build a network: Networking is essential for entrepreneurs in Africa. Building relationships with other entrepreneurs, investors, and mentors can provide valuable insights, advice, and support; (5) Consider local partnerships: In Africa, partnering with local businesses or individuals can be an effective way to navigate the local business environment and gain access to new markets; (6) Embrace innovation: Innovation is critical for success in any entrepreneurship venture. Entrepreneurs in Africa should embrace emerging technologies, such as mobile payment platforms, to gain a competitive advantage; (7) Secure funding: Funding is a critical factor in the success of any entrepreneurial venture. Entrepreneurs in Africa can seek funding from sources such as government grants, private investors, and crowdfunding platforms.

Strategy Formulation

Social entrepreneurship, characterized by social media marketing is one of the various ways through which entrepreneurs in Africa are encouraged to conduct businesses. This justifies the need for skills in graphic designing, coding, blogging, and ICT. Thus, building websites, secure blockchains, and networks. By so doing creating an enabling environment for secure and digitalized transactions. The evolution of cryptocurrency and digital currencies is another aspect of entrepreneurship in Africa today with increasing awareness growing in digital accounts and banks. More than three-fourths of Africans have mobile money accounts, possess smartphones and use either iOS or android operating systems and they use these devices for day-to-day business, as such giving them the possibility to by-pass unnecessary trade barriers (Moşteanu et al., 2020). The use of matrixes like Porter's Five Forces (Porter, 2012), the External Evaluation, and Internal Evaluation Matrices at each stage (external and internal) are essential in monitoring the strategies put in place to ensure that they meet expectations and if not adjust to suit reality (Fig. 5). Moreover, the international nature of African entrepreneurship calls for more effective audits internally and externally especially as the pressures in the macro environment could be very variable.

A balanced evaluation matrix will go a long to ensure a sure and steady strategic design for entrepreneurship in Africa while taking into consideration the changing world.

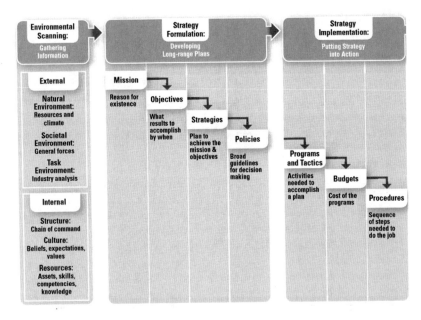

Fig. 5 Generic strategic plan digital entrepreneurship in Africa

Ethics, Civics, Social Responsibility, and Sustainability for Entrepreneurship in the African Context Vis a Vis the Changing World of This Era

The growing nature of competition in the world of today implies that businesses must work on gaining and sustaining competitive advantages. Therefore, African entrepreneurs better engage in international business with global operations, by so doing they will be safeguarding the prior-most aspect of effectiveness in today's world. The rich cultural and traditional heritage that is the foundation of civic and ethical consideration in Africa acts like an ethical foundation for doing business in Africa. However, the blending of home values and ethics with foreign and globally acknowledged values establishes the ethical standards for business in Africa in this era. As such, entrepreneurs in Africa are challenged to do more than is legally expected to be responsible by stakeholders and consumers. Environmental sustainability, civics, ethics, and social responsibility are vital aspects to be considered for business operations in Africa, and this will be characterized by organizational responsibility on the part of SMEs and entrepreneurs.

Justification for Intensive Strategies

Given the need to gain and sustain competitive advantages, entrepreneurship in Africa is recommended to take an intensive strategic approach which is normally characterized by product development, market penetration, and lastly market development. African entrepreneurs operate in products and services whose markets are comparatively not saturated and there is a need for specific products and services. In this way entrepreneurs have the advantage of economies of scale. This means that as African entrepreneurs gain more customers and increase their production, they can potentially lower their per-unit costs, which can give them a competitive advantage in the marketplace. In addition, operating in a less saturated market can also give African entrepreneurs the opportunity to differentiate themselves from their competitors and create a unique brand identity. This can help them attract more customers and establish a loyal customer base.

Transfer of technical know-how skills and machinery from foreign and related businesses could go a long way to develop the products and services offered by African Entrepreneurs at prices that reflect their comparative advantage and as such ensure the growth and expansion of entrepreneurial effort. Therefore, the internet will be used as a tool and catalyst to fasten the interconnection of global stakeholders while giving way to untapped markets abroad, increasing in the scope of operations and the capacity of production. Intensive strategies geared at increasing market share call for ample work in research and development. It is also important to note that operating in a less saturated market also comes with its own challenges. For example, there may be a lack of infrastructure or support systems, and entrepreneurs may need to invest more resources into building their businesses from the ground up. Nonetheless, with the right strategies and resources, African entrepreneurs can leverage the advantages of less saturated markets to achieve success.

7 Conclusions and Further Considerations

Entrepreneurs in Africa are left with options to embrace the opportunities of the digital era or on the other hand, continue to be frightened by the rapid advancements in technology and intelligence. The ideal strategic plan for entrepreneurs given their mission of overcoming the hard business environment they are faced with it is to use their strengths and the opportunities presented given by artificial intelligence and digitalization and access the global markets.

The potential of digitalization can go a long way in overcoming financial, power/electricity problems, competition from existing businesses in the informal sector, market penetration, trade restrictions, barriers, and the overall harsh macro environment. This will increase the quality of life and safe leaving conditions. Leke (Leke et al., 2018) said *real opportunity is based on how you perceive the risk as a half-full or half-empty glass. Understanding the local context will help to better realign actual and perceived risk.* In this case, the real opportunity (perceived risk) will be to embrace the rapidly moving global technological trade markets and financial systems whereas the actual risk is to see these rapidly advancing technologies as threats, whereas there is an expedient need for SME survival and growth on the African continent.

Dependence on the Internet

The Internet is a very inevitable aspect in the world of today and that of the future. This can be seen as goods and services being traded online, people can study and do all sorts of research online, connections are made from all angles of the globe and a global platform is created for everybody. Entrepreneurs in Africa are to recognize the value of this tool and use it for the achievement of their goals and objectives. Our study has demonstrated that despite the harsh general or macroeconomic environment of the continent, the internet and new technology can be used to overcome these challenges to a greater extent. Harnessing the potential on the internet is a smart move aimed at growth and stability in all aspects of the economy and consequently, the individuals involved.

Research and Development

The role and need for extensive Research and Development cannot be undermined because it provides the basis for an in-depth understanding of the problems faced and possible insights as to how to overcome these shortcomings. Future and current entrepreneurs have to equip themselves with trending concepts and their correlation with the past and future in a bid to attain their growth and development goals. The continent is expected to be inhabited by 2.3 billion people in 30 years' time and to host one-third of the global population by the year 2100. Therefore, all stakeholders are challenged to ensure a good quality of life and standard of living that is commensurate to current-day standards in developed parts of the world. Entrepreneurship can open doors for many skills and can tackle unemployment problems for everyone who is part of the value chain. Even the nature of jobs is changing with automation, robotics and artificial intelligence overtaking highly skilled traditional jobs. More than ever, dependence on ICT and the specializations therein are paramount for true growth and development. Current and future entrepreneurs in Africa need to equip themselves with these skills and see how to use them in the African context. Also, socio-political, economic, social, and financial institutions need to design financial products to further enhance development based on research.

The Utilization of Solar Energy as a Supplement to Hydroelectricity

Given the naturally endowed nature of the continent, the energy needed for the running of industrialization and production processes should be harnessed from the sun during the dry seasons, and from the hydroelectric dams during the rainy seasons. Countries like Nigeria which depend so much on diesel-run generators that usually cause a lot of air and sound pollution, can rely on the installation, utilization, import, and manufacturing of solar electricity panels in every segment or area of the value chains of businesses and economic activities. This will go a long way in encouraging entrepreneurial effort in a cost-efficient manner.

The Utilization of Appropriate Machinery to Ensure Efficient Products and Services

An entrepreneurial culture that is designed to suit consumer needs, while serving and patronizing them is a culture that guarantees success in business. Given the strategies of market penetration development and product development, African entrepreneurs are required to be market and customer protective. Businesses and customers are to be treated as stakeholders who deserve their right to utility and the duty to spend for this utility. The implementation of up-to-date financial recording, analysis, auditing, and suggestions should be taken into consideration by businesses, economic and financial stakeholders. An ecosystem characterized by financial literary, business analyses, consultants, artificial and business intelligence is to be nurtured and cherished to ensure a sustainable development. Software and machines such as mobile/digital banking, currency exchange services, and cash registers are necessities for African entrepreneurs in this era.

A Boom in Agricultural and Food Production and Processing

Africa has always been considered to be the breadbasket of the world as it has a variety of flora and fauna due to its geographic location. This gives the continent a comparative advantage in terms of soil quality and the products thereof. This clearly explains a significant majority of Africans are farmers compared to other regions of the world. The whole concept behind international trade among countries and nation states is to conveniently exchange goods and services that are mutually interactive and influenced by the forces of demand and supply. Therefore, the present state of poverty, in particular for Africans who depend on farming and agriculture for their subsistence, can be changed to a more desirable system where entrepreneurial farmers invest and get established for commercial purposes, for the establishment and legacy businesses that stood the test of time and the global market (Wechuli et al., 2018).

The emphasis on entrepreneurial learning and development toward sustainable development is highly increasing in order to cater to competent human capital as required by volatile, uncertain, complex, and ambiguous contemporary globalization. The emergence of volatile, uncertain, complex, and ambiguous has urged people to be ready for any possibilities that are out of their comfort zones1, including entrepreneurial education in a sustainable manner, as highlighted by the United Nations' Sustainable Development Goals (Chander et al., 2020; Johansen, 2012; Sachs, 2012).

Considering the volatile, uncertain, complex, and ambiguous landscape of global economic growth, future leaders are called to support and stimulate sustainable entrepreneurial initiatives.

Now, in the new global economy, sustainable entrepreneurship has become an important point in the business environment, as it tries to encourage innovation and create sustainable products in an attempt to achieve the goals of sustainable development by the year 2030.

Possible Contributions of Entrepreneurship for African Sustainability Developments

Entrepreneurship development can create jobs and reduce poverty in Africa, which is essential for social and economic sustainability. By creating new businesses and expanding existing ones, entrepreneurs can provide employment opportunities for the growing population of young people in Africa.

African entrepreneurship can promote inclusive growth, which is essential for sustainability. By creating opportunities for disadvantaged groups, such as women and marginalized communities, entrepreneurship can help reduce inequality and promote social cohesion.

Entrepreneurship development can drive innovation and technology transfer in Africa, which is crucial for economic and environmental sustainability. By developing new products, services, and business models, entrepreneurs can create sustainable solutions to local challenges and contribute to global sustainable development goals.

Access to finance is a critical challenge for African entrepreneurs, and developing sustainable funding mechanisms, such as venture capital, impact investing, and microfinance, can help support entrepreneurship development in Africa.

African entrepreneurs can promote sustainable business practices, such as social and environmental responsibility, which is essential for long-term sustainability. By incorporating sustainability principles into their business models, entrepreneurs can contribute to a more sustainable future.

REFERENCES

Chander, N., Siow, M. L., Ramachandran, S., Kunasekaran, P., & Rathakrishnan, T. (2020). Conceptualizing inclusive learning and development: A framework towards entrepreneurial competency practices for sustainability. *Sustainability, 12*, 6905. https://doi.org/10.3390/su12176905

Global Entrepreneurship Monitor. (2020/2021). https://www.gemconsortium.org/file/open?fileId=50691

Herrington, M., Kew, J., & Kew, P. (2010). Global entrepreneurship monitor, UCT centre for innovation and entrepreneurship.

Johansen B. (2012). Leaders make the future: Ten new leadership skills for an uncertain world; Berrett-Koehler Publishers, p. 112.

Leke, A., Chironga, M., & Desvaux, G. (2018). *Africas business revolution: how to succeed in the worlds next big growth market.* Harvard Business Review Press.

Matzembacher, D. E., Raudsaar, M., de Barcellos, M. D., & Mets, T. (2019). Sustainable entrepreneurial process: From idea generation to impact measurement. *Sustainability, 11*(21), 5892. https://doi.org/10.3390/su11215892

Mensah, A. O., Fobih, N., & Adom, Y. (2019). Entrepreneurship development and new business start-ups: Challenges and prospects for Ghanaian entrepreneurs. *African Research Review, 13*(3), 27. https://doi.org/10.4314/afrrev.v13i3.3

Moşteanu N. R. (2020a). Challenges for organizational structure and design as a result of digitalization and cybersecurity, *The Business and Management Review, 11*(1), 278–286. https://doi.org/10.24052/bmr/v11nu01/art-29

Moşteanu N. R. (2020b). Management of disaster and business continuity in a digital world, *International Journal of Management, 11*(4), 169–177. https://doi.org/10.34218/IJM.11.4.2020b.018

Moşteanu, N. R. (2020c). Artificial intelligence and cyber security—A shield against cyberattack as a risk business management tool—Case of European countries. *Quality-Access to Success Journal, 21*(175), 148–156.

Moşteanu N. R., Faccia A., Cavaliere L. P. L. & Bhatia S. (2020). Digital technologies' implementation within financial and banking system during socio distancing restrictions – back to the future, *International Journal of Advanced Research in Engineering and Technology, 11*(6), 307–315. https://doi.org/10.34218/IJARET.11.6.2020.027.

Moşteanu N. R. (2021). Teaching and learning techniques for the online environment. How to maintain students' attention and achieve learning outcomes in a virtual environment using new technology, *International Journal of Innovative Research and Scientific Studies, 4*(4). https://doi.org/10.53894/ijirss.v4i4.298

Moşteanu, N. R., & Faccia, A. (2021). Fintech frontiers in quantum computing, fractals, and blockchain distributed ledger: Paradigm shifts and open innovation. *Journal of Open Innovation: Technology, Market, and Complexity, 7*(1), 1–19. https://doi.org/10.3390/joitmc7010019

Porter, G. (2012). Mobile phones, livelihoods and the poor in Sub-Saharan Africa: Review and prospect. *Geography Compass, 6*(5), 241–259. https://doi.org/10.1111/j.1749-8198.2012.00484.x

Quartey, P., & Abor, J. (2011). Do Ghanaians prefer imported textiles to locally manufactured ones? *Modern Economy, 02*(01), 54–61. https://doi.org/10.4236/me.2011.21009

Sachs, J. D. (2012). From millennium development goals to sustainable development goals. *Lancet, 379*, 2206–2211.

Terán-Yépez, E., Marín-Carrillo, G. M., del Pilar Casado-Belmonte, M., & de las Mercedes Capobianco-Uriarte, M. (2020). Sustainable entrepreneurship: Review of its evolution and new trends. *Journal of Cleaner Production, 252*, 119742. https://doi.org/10.1016/j.jclepro.2019.119742

Vernet, A., Khayesi, J. N., George, V., George, G., & Bahaj, A. S. (2019). How does energy matter? Rural electrification, entrepreneurship, and community development in Kenya, *Energy Policy, 126*, 88–98. https://doi.org/10.1016/j.enpol.2018.11.012

Virk, P. (2019, March 6). *5 challenges that African start-ups face in business*. https://www.linkedin.com/pulse/5-challenges-african-start-ups-face-business-parminder-vir-obe Accessed on 18 March 2020.

Wechuli, C. O., & Kiriinya, S. N. (2018). Competitiveness in the telecommunication sector in Kenya using porters five forces model. *International Journal of Research in Finance and Marketing, 8*(7), 1–10.

World Bank. (2020). Country classification, https://datahelpdesk.worldbank.org/knowledgebase/articles/906519-world-bank-country-and-lending-groups Accessed on 18 March 2020.

Yakubu, B. N., Salamzadeh, A., Bouzari, P., Ebrahimi, P., & Fekete-Farkas, M. (2022). Identifying the key factors of sustainable entrepreneurship in the Nigerian food industry: The role of media availability. *Entrepreneurial Business and Economics Review, 10*(2), 147–162.

https://www.energyinst.org/ei-near-me/africa

https://www.afdb.org/en

https://www.businessincameroon.com/economy/0709-10782-cameroon-over-14-200-new-smes-were-created-in-2019-minpmesa

https://cassavatechnologies.com/strive-masiyiwa/

https://www.ovamba.com/

Promoting Sustainability in Africa Through Entrepreneurial Branding

Samuel Yaw Kusi , *Arinze Christian Nwoba, Adedapo Adebajo, and Osei Yaw Adjei*

1 Introduction

Governments, institutions, companies, and civil societies around the world have strengthened their interest in sustainability-related issues. Paris Agreement of 2015, COP26, and the Bonn 2022 meeting by the United Nations emphasize the urgency of the need to ensure sustainability as a daily focal point of discussion. Moreover, there is an increasing academic interest in sustainability initiatives (Nwoba et al., 2021). For instance, previous studies into green supply chains have investigated and shown the importance of institutional drivers in the perspective of regulations, markets, and suppliers, and organizational internal motivation and

---

S. Y. Kusi (✉)
Department of Marketing, Faculty of Management, Law, & Social Sciences, University of Bradford, Richmond Road, Bradford BP7 1DP, United Kingdom
e-mail: s.kusi2@bradford.ac.uk

A. C. Nwoba · A. Adebajo
Loughborough Business School, Loughborough University, Epinal Way, Loughborough LE11 3TU, United Kingdom
e-mail: a.c.nwoba@lboro.ac.uk

A. Adebajo
e-mail: adedapo.adebajo@lboro.ac.uk

© The Author(s), under exclusive license to Springer Nature Switzerland AG 2023
S. Adomako et al. (eds.), *Corporate Sustainability in Africa*, Palgrave Studies in African Leadership,
https://doi.org/10.1007/978-3-031-29273-6_13

managerial commitment in achieving environmental sustainability (e.g., Agarwal et al., 2018); Hsu et al. (2014) study into subsidiaries and their green purchase also highlighted the critical role of sustainability in multinational enterprises endevors. Besides, entrepreneurial brands such as Mukuru Clean Stoves by Charlot Magayi—a Kenyan entrepreneur with the main aim to promote clean cooking brands made from locally recycled materials (Kinyanjui, 2022) from the Eastern African country are examples of how entrepreneurship could help address sustainability challenges. Accordingly, the Kenyan government in 2016 reduced imported duties on such stoves by about 15%, thus 10% instead of 25% to encourage the sale and use of sustainable stoves (Njagi, 2018). Hence, African governments in collaboration with entrepreneurs could explore branding activities to achieve their sustainable goals. Nonetheless, such insight is limited in the literature, and this book chapter stands to close this important void.

Besides, there is a call to put much effort into psychological factors such as *tangibility*—that showcases one's actions relevant to addressing sustainability (Scannell & Gifford, 2013; White et al., 2019). The above examples of entrepreneurs and their branding activities and actions highlight those tangible aspects of sustainability as a step forward to reducing their carbon footprint. Thus, these entrepreneurs take proactive and timely actions by committing to innovative brands that demonstrate reduced carbon emissions. In turn, they have gained local and international recognition with institutions such as International Energy Agency (IEA)—emphasizing the need for such brands in dealing with sustainable cooking practices that could save the lives of about 2.8 million people globally out of the 2.8 billion people that use burning wood, coal, or kerosene indoors (Ngaji, 2018). Nonetheless, studies are lacking on this emotional response and other factors mentioned regarding sustainability (White et al., 2019). This further provides an avenue for this study to close this important vacuum in the literature most importantly, in the field of entrepreneurial sustainable branding.

Besides, sustainability orientation as a new paradigm has emerged and witnessed in strategic management and entrepreneurship scholarship (e.g., Adomako et al., 2021; Bartolacci et al., 2020; Khizar et al., 2022; Kuckertz & Wagner, 2010). Nonetheless, the overall emphasis on the

---

O. Y. Adjei
pesewa one PLC, ABAPA, Accra, Ghana

branding of entrepreneurial firms and how governments could partner with them in promoting sustainable practices have received little attention. Meeting up with sustainability-related issues aligns with the triple bottom line agenda propagated over two decades ago (Elkington, 1997). We see the cooperation of formal institutions (e.g., governments) and entrepreneurs will bring much attention to sustainability in the African context. Hence, our study is guided by institutional theory, sustainability orientation, and entrepreneurial branding literature.

2 INSTITUTIONS AND SUSTAINABLE ACTIONS

Institutional theory espouses social behavior to come into existence through a process established on structures to serve as a guide for a particular context (Scott, 2008). Moreover, over some time, organizations become isomorphic based on the set processes (DiMaggio & Powell, 1983). Hence, bodies assigned to regularize organizations in their operations apply some form of a burden on these organizations. Thus, regulatory bodies provide compliance guidelines—values, beliefs, systems of operation, culture, and standards of practices, which bring organizations in line with what the context required of them (DiMaggio & Powell, 1983; Scott, 1995). Fundamental to this is that, organizations will get recognition and legitimacy when found to align with the environmental requirements. In that regard, the legitimacy that "the actions of an entity are desirable, proper, or appropriate within some socially constructed system of norms, values, beliefs, and definitions" (Suchman, 1995, p. 574) will be beneficial to entrepreneurial brands. These brands especially small new ventures suffer from smallness, newness, and foreignness (Zahra, 2005), and require brand legitimacy for their continued survival and growth (Kusi et al., 2021). So, regularizing organizational operations by requiring them to comply with property rights regulations, appropriate licensing, and certifications such as ISO and standard brand systems are expected to generate the needed legitimacy for these brands (Odoom et al., 2017; Zhu et al., 2013). Gaining brand legitimacy also has the prospect to drive customers to the brand and then form acquaintance with its sustainable message.

Nonetheless, the need for cooperation is an important point to emphasize here rather than the regulatory bodies operating as kings over these organizations. Rather, the approach should emphasize firms to having responsibility for their shareholders and the general stakeholder cohort

(Bolton & Matilda, 2015; Chabowski et al., 2022; Elkington, 2018). Institutions enforce regulations to ensure consumers have expectations from the brand bought. However, largely in emerging markets, such as those in Sub-Saharan Africa, the lack of appropriate brand regulations has led to false advertising, cheating, and counterfeiting running contrary to the ethos of sustainable brand practices (Odoom et al., 2017; Sheth & Sinha, 2015). Earlier, we highlighted how proper regulation by the Kenyan government has encouraged the consumption of more sustainable stoves. Thus, due to the reduction of import—duties, the burden of higher prices considering the degree of the consumer purchasing power of the country has gone down, making it possible for those dealing in and consuming such products to increase (Njagi, 2018). These are the expectation of institutions and their bid to promote sustainable practices.

3   ENTREPRENEURIAL BRANDING

Emerging economies such as those in Africa have high rates of small and medium enterprises (SMEs). The entrepreneurial aspect prompts interest in understanding how their brands could help conscientize the consumer populace on how to become more sustainable consumers (Elkington, 2018). Central to entrepreneurial branding are the entrepreneurs who take much lead and control in promoting to create brand awareness (Kusi et al., 2021). Their decision-making becomes apparent in sustainable practices. Entrepreneurial branding is defined in this study to mean "brand management that places much prominence on co-creating the brand with relevant stakeholders in a complex environment deriving this from flexible, creative, utilization of existing resources, entrepreneurial experience, and the application of effectual decision-making logic" (Kusi et al., 2022, p. 2). Entrepreneurial branding covers four key aspects: *philosophy, cumulative experience, decision-making logic,* and *context* (Kusi et al., 2022) of which we hold a strong conviction that sustainable branding practices could yield a positive result for the African continent.

Brand *philosophy* underpinning an entrepreneur's actions and activities is important in brand development and growth (Egger et al., 2013; Kusi et al., 2021). Thus, brand management philosophy under effectual logic runs on the idea that brands management is not only in the hands of the entrepreneur/firm but rather in cooperation with relevant stakeholders who become partners in brand development (Heding et al., 2020, p. 11; Merz et al., 2009; Swaminathan et al., 2020; Törm älä &

Gryn-Jones, 2017). We believe this will further harness or strengthen entrepreneurs' emotional responses toward sustainable practices which we discuss in detail later. Moreover, this will be advanced by taking into cognizance entrepreneurial flexibility, creativity, and innovativeness that bring distinctive advantages (Kusi et al., 2021; Low & Fullerton, 1994).

Cumulative experience relates to entrepreneurial experiences that are needed to advance brands needing creative and experimental approaches (Politis et al., 2012). Because the entrepreneurial approach is flexible, it can adapt to different challenges when going through trials, and experimentations among others (Sarasvathy et al., 2014). This challenge is more critical in the African context whereby local entrepreneurs strive to pursue a brand development agenda that can highlight the need for more sustainable consumption through government interventions. This possibility is further elaborated on later in the book chapter.

Decision-making logic is based on two routes: a causal approach where decision-making to advance brand management is based on calculations, forecasting, planning, and goal-setting typical of traditional brand management. On the other hand, the effectual decision-making approach to branding incorporates co-creations, flexibility, creativity, and entrepreneurial experience (Kusi et al., 2022). In that respect, brand development goes beyond co-creation to embrace flexibility and entrepreneurial skills. Promoting sustainability in Africa will progress accordingly if effectual decision-making is adopted. Governments, business entities, corporate bodies, and society at large can join forces to achieve this common goal. The onus is not only on the government but a joint force to empower and promote this timely action.

Due to the complexity and dynamism of the operating environment, *context* becomes important in addressing sustainable-related issues. Therefore, *context*—in the entrepreneurial domain becomes imperative to understanding and promoting more sustainable consumption. Predicting tomorrow from today is not all that simple, for instance, the COVID-19 pandemic took the world by surprise and hence, our attention shifted significantly toward a healthy lifestyle, and consciousness about the environment to make it a better way. Entrepreneurs rose to this challenge through innovative brands that brought consumers and other stakeholders ever closer to sustainable consumption. Ambronite ignited this consciousness to provide consumers with more sustainable Keto products so they could stay healthier during the COVID-19 period (Kusi et al., 2021). Latex Foam, a leading rubber mattress producer in Ghana,

286   S. Y. KUSI ET AL.

West Africa contributed immensely toward the COVID-19 fight by donating 1,000 pieces of mattresses to the Ministry of Health, Ghana (Graphic.com, 2020).

4   ENTREPRENEURIAL BRANDING IN PROMOTING SUSTAINABILITY

The brand *philosophy* held by the entrepreneurs (Baumgarth et al., 2013) will be critical to sustainable actions and activities that will help advance efforts to address more sustainability (Adomako et al., 2021). What entrepreneurs represent or their core values carved into the brand values is hence meaningful here. Our view is based on the postulation of entrepreneur's means such that an individual could envisage a prospective course of action based on their available means that could be what they represent, network base, and accumulated knowledge (Sarasvathy, 2001). Drawing the *tangibility* of the entrepreneur into this line of discussion, we find a balance where these two concepts/lines of literature will endeavor to us much understanding into promoting sustainable practices through branding. Thus, what entrepreneurs represent could be their actions and passion for addressing sustainability-related issues through using branding practices. Hence, in our above example of Mukuru Clean Stoves, the entrepreneur stands for cleaner cooking through which numerous lives could be saved from smoke inhalation. The entrepreneur put in efforts to bring this into reality, and now we see the footprints. The stove's position in the eyes of the consuming public of cooking that used to use or still follow traditional wood has solace and a sense of urgency to shift toward a more sustainable way of cooking. The characteristics of the entrepreneurs are infused into the brand and customers' perceptions align with that so change through more sustainable consumption could be achieved. Previous studies have found that entrepreneurs' means available are a catalyst to brand identity development, thus, their zeal for quality, healthy lifestyle, and a green, stress-free life is expressed through their branding practices, the packing that communicates all these (Kusi et al., 2021). By this, we believe entrepreneurs through what they represent culminating in their tangibility could harness more sustainable practices.

Cumulative experiences of the entrepreneurs built into branding practice is another avenue we believe could help promote more sustainable practices and consumption on the African continent. We based this argument on the literature that showcases that a founder's experience is critical to a firm's growth and survival (Reuber & Fischer, 1999). Besides, the experience of the entrepreneur provides the grounds to reduce over-optimism (Ucbasaran et al., 2010); other studies report that with the presence of experience, firms stand to be exposed to the new set of knowledge (Freixanet & Renart, 2020). Moreover, a recent research study concluded that individual entrepreneurs' experiences motivate and drive their decision-making to engage in more sustainable related ventures and this also results in successful growth (Reynolds & Holt, 2021); experience from sustainable practices further strengthens engagement in more sustainable activities (Scarlata et al., 2016). Effectual decision-making literature posits that entrepreneurial experiences coupled with effectual logic of decision-making are a precursor to adopting a branding philosophy, that is, why the sources of competitiveness derive from the brand (Kusi et al., 2022). Accordingly, having a previous experience in brand development, and a strong tangibility—holding a passion for disseminating sustainable ideology will be ideal avenues for promoting and supporting sustainable practices and consumer behavior. Thus, experiences built over time become a source of wealth that can draw upon for future endeavors. Such experiences as sustainable packaging that depicts responsible behavior toward the environment will advance a good course of promoting sustainability. For instance, Dangote Cements, a Nigerian multinational industrial conglomerate, has enshrined sustainability across all its operations, procedures, and corporate culture and this has contributed to the conglomerate being the most successful multinational brand in Nigeria.

Decision-making about sustainability through branding practices could be another avenue to promote sustainability on the African continent. First, effectual decision-making logic entails co-creating activities with relevant stakeholders (Sarasvathy, 2001). The branding literature also holds the notion that consumers are no more passive recipients who take the brand as given but rather have become co-creators of it (e.g., Merz et al., 2009; Tajvidi et al., 2020; Törmälä & Gryn-Jones, 2017). Accordingly, a recent study has called for firms to relieve part of their brand-building activities into the hands of relevant stakeholders due to the dynamism and changing pattern of the consumer world (Heding et al., 2020; Ramaswamy & Ozcan, 2016; Swaminathan et al., 2020). Globally, the call for sustainable practices is not an individual affair but a collective voice and action that is required. Various institutions entrusted with regulations such as copyright, dismantling counterfeiting, and cheating among others could rise to the challenge by collaborating with brand owners to streamline things, especially in emerging markets such as Africa. With such steps undertaking, false advertising that fails to demonstrate its sustainable footprints, cheating that will nullify any attempt to promote sustainable practices, and brand counterfeit—with the potential to contaminate original brands striving to be in accord with authorities to promote the agenda of sustainability could help address the lack of appropriate brands that fight a good cause on the continent (Odoom et al., 2017; Sheth & Sinha, 2015). With a conceited effort through brand co-creation, it is with the firm belief that the promotion of sustainable practices could achieve its goals.

In addition, a recent study established that branding goes beyond co-creation to incorporate affordable loss and leveraging contingencies (e.g., Kusi et al., 2022). The affordable loss principle thrives on inviting relevant stakeholders to join the venture (i.e., the brand) so they make commitments that otherwise could have been borne by the entrepreneur (Sarasvathy et al., 2014). In branding practices, time commitment by the consumer translates into resource commitment that ordinarily, the firms would have committed to branding activities such as promoting sustainability. In this vein, consumers become brand ambassadors—the highest point of commitment to a brand (Keller, 2016) and will communicate the sustainability aspects of the brand to their friends and family (Kusi et al., 2021). They could express the sustainable nature of the brand to others for free; such time enjoyed for free by the brand could use those resources to engage in more sustainable activities and actions. The authors' realized that crowdfunding is another avenue brands especially new ones explore for development (Kusi et al., 2021). Such avenues have been utilized by Dangote Cements—thus, when it started its brand development and had limited resources resorted to sourcing financial help from customers and other stakeholders who shared their brand values of bringing sustainability to build a cement brand. Since the brand was an innovative one and related well with customers' values, they bought into it and helped advance to develop rapidly. We see here that the sustainable message carried by the brand was able to spread to customers in domestic and foreign markets. Brands on African content could explore similar means to bring the attention of the citizenry in line with what governments are trying to achieve.

Further, contingencies and other arising co-creation opportunities are important avenues studies have reported entrepreneurs to explore and exploit to disseminate their branding-related activities for development in a particular *context*. Entrepreneurs engage with relevant partners through co-creation, and cooperative branding practices to develop their brands. For example, Dangote Cement leveraged stakeholders in Tema, Ghana to gain entrance into the Ghanaian market. Due to the continuously unstable and unpredictable business environment in Africa, it becomes critical to involve other stakeholders outsides of the firm to involve in brand development (Gabrielsson, 2005; Iglesias, et al., 2020; Törm älä & Gryn-Jones, 2017).

Accordingly, a recent study conceptualizes that the corporate social responsibility of the brand in question is not only an internal firm-level responsibility but rather, it should take a multistakeholder approach (Maon et al., 2021). This reflects MTN, South Africa's multinational mobile telecommunication provider's MTN Skills Acadewhichhat fronts its sustainability drive is fixated on multistakeholder partnerships from around the globe (Forum MTN, 2023). Sustainable practices should emanate from the manager who is flexible in his/her endeavors with these actions not based fully on planning but rather in an adaptive and emergent manner (e.g., Wickert & de Bakker, 2018). With this, the sustainable philosophy of the firm could be properly achieved and hence, other stakeholders will take it on board. Moreover, employees should be drafted into the sustainable actions and practices of the brand, and they should not be perceived as passive recipients of the message the firm wants to put across (Maon et al., 2021; Opoku-Dankwa & Rupp, 2019). We notice this in Access Bank, Ghana—West Africa during COVID-19 pandemic committed to addressing the challenge through a volunteering program by its 1,200 employees to educate the general public on good hygiene practices and others to help contain the virus (Graphic.com, 2020). This resonates with the following statement: *"Only partnerships can drive the inclusive implementation of Sustainable Development Goals. They have the strong potential to unlock progress across multiple SDGs, acting as the connective tissues that can ensure an integrated and holistic approach to sustainable development. All stakeholders, big or small, are development actors and have the power to transform the world collectively"* Anima J. Mohammed—Deputy Secretary-General, United Nations.

Bringing the whole stakeholder community under a single umbrella to pursue such an important course would be in its rightful direction. Once seen as being part of a bigger community would be obliged to commit to the course of action—more sustainable practices which the various conferences on sustainability seek to achieve. By this, it is believed that it might bring some sanity to the regulatory body in that each stakeholder would serve as a check on the others and could help address the lack of adequate overseeing responsible which results in negative consequences discussed earlier (Odoom et al., 2017). Showing their ability and responsibility toward employees and the environment at large propels them to support the agenda of more sustainable practices the world is calling for. The tangibility nature of the entrepreneur is envisaged here to bring into life through leadership by example, walking the talk. Education through the brands and branding practices and actions has a significant potential to help reduce our carbon footprint. Once, a formidable multistakeholder joins forces to pursue a common course of action the burden of proof lies on the general rather than the particular.

5 CONCLUSION

Sustainability-related issues have generated a lot of academic, governmental, and practitioner attention. Best describing this global agenda are recent meetings such as CoP27 and CoP27 among others highlighting the need for a cooperative pursuit of this agenda. Moreover, there has been significant research dedicated to sustainability from different spheres. Nonetheless, entrepreneurs and their brands and branding practices could be explored to advance the course of more sustainability has not had many focal points. This is surprising because entrepreneurs through their tangibility—inherent values tend to sphere-head sustainable practices and actions. Thus, their pursuit is not just about sustainability but how to become more sustainable consumers (Elkington, 2018). In that respect, this study investigates effectual decision-making logic and branding to push the agenda further on the African continent. The focus has been on four key pillars: *philosophy, cumulative international experience, decision-making logic,* and *context* (Kusi et al., 2022). Philosophy of the entrepreneur such as orienting toward sustainable practices through branding; prior experience in sustainable branding practices; branding decision-making aligning with effectual principles— whereby relevant stakeholders become integral to branding practices that promote sustainability; and exploring avenues to continually promote sustainability-related issues with a flexible approach to branding that mitigates against the unstable environment. Collaboration with institutions entrusted to regulate business operations and hence strengthen the case for sustainable practices through branding could be more focused in their pursuits. Due to the presence of multistakeholders, driving and ensuring sustainability prevails, such institutions especially from emerging markets such as Africa that mostly take a carefree perspective in safeguarding rules and regulations and hence result in negative consequences could now be streamlined.

Through this study, we have exhibited the importance of collaborative branding practices relevant to government interventions in entrepreneurial branding and how such actions promote sustainability. Accordingly, we harness effectuation theory in explaining branding practices that could help address sustainability challenges on the African content. Besides, tangibility from the emotional literature has been seen as an important component in promoting sustainability through branding.

REFERENCES

Agarwal, A., Giraud-Carrier, F. C., & Li, Y. (2018). A mediation model of green supply chain management adoption: The role of internal impetus. *International Journal of Production Economics, 205*, 342–358.

Altshuler, L., & Tarnovskaya, V. V. (2010). Branding capability of technology born globals. *Journal of Brand Management, 18*(3), 212–227.

Amankwah-Amoah, J., Danso, A., & Adomako, S. (2019). Entrepreneurial orientation, environmental sustainability, and new venture performance: Does stakeholder integration matter? *Business Strategy and the Environment, 28*(1), 79–87.

Bartolacci, F., Caputo, A., & Soverchia, M. (2020). Sustainability and financial performance of small and medium-sized enterprises: A bibliometric and systematic literature review. *Business Strategy and the Environment, 29*(3), 1297–1309.

Baumgarth, C., Merrilees, B., & Urde, M. (2013). Brand orientation: Past, present, and future. *Journal of Marketing Management, 29*(9–10), 973–980.

Bolton, L. E., & Mattila, A. S. (2015). How does corporate social responsibility affect consumer response to service failure in buyer-seller relationships? *Journal of Retailing, 91*(1), 140–153.

Casidy, R., & Yan, L. (2022). The effects of supplier B2B sustainability positioning on buyer performance: The role of trust. *Industrial Marketing Management, 102*, 311–323.

Chabowski, B. R., Gabrielsson, P., & Mena, J. A. (2022). Using bibliometric research to advance the business-to-business sustainability literature: Establishing an integrative conceptual framework for future application. *Industrial Marketing Management, 102*, 527–545.

DiMaggio, P. J., & Powell, W. W. (1983). The iron cage revisited: Institutional isomorphism and collective rationality in organizational fields. *American Sociological Review, 48*(2), 147–160.

Eggers, F., O'Dwyer, M., Kraus, S., Vallaster, C., & Guldenberg, S. (2013). The impact of brand authenticity on brand trust and SME growth: A CEO perspective. *Journal of World Business, 48*(3), 340–348.

Elkington, J. (2018). 25 years ago I coined the phrase "Triple bottom line." here's why it's time to rethink it. *Harvard Business Review.*

Elkington, J. (1997). The triple bottom line. *Environmental Management: Readings and Cases, 2,* 49–66.

Freixanet, J., & Renart, G. (2020). A capabilities perspective on the joint effects of internationalisation time, speed, geographic scope and managers' competencies on SME survival. *Journal of World Business, 55*(6), 101–110.

Gabrielsson, M. (2005). Branding strategies of born globals. *Journal of International Entrepreneurship, 3*(3), 199–222.

Heding, T., Knudtzen, C. F., & Bjerre, M. (2020). *Brand management: Mastering research, theory and practice* (3rd ed.). Routledge Taylor & Francis.

Hsu, P. F., Hu, P. J. H., Wei, C. P., & Huang, J. W. (2014). Green purchasing by MNC subsidiaries: The role of local tailoring in the presence of institutional duality. *Decision Sciences, 45*(4), 647–682.

Iglesias, O., Landgraf, P., Ind, N., Markovic, S., & Koporcic, N. (2020). Corporate brand identity co-creation in business-to-business contexts. *Industrial Marketing Management, 85,* 32–43.

Keller, K. L. (2016). *Reflections on customer-based brand equity: Perspectives, progress,and priorities. AMS Review, 6*(1), 1–6.

Khizar, H. M. U., Iqbal, M. J., Khalid, J., & Adomako, S. (2022). Addressing the conceptualization and measurement challenges of sustainability orientation: A systematic review and research agenda. *Journal of Business Research., 142,* 718–743.

Kinyanjui, M. (2022). *kenyan entrepreneur making environmental-friendly stoves wins ksh.150m.* https://www.citizen.digital/news/kenyan-entrepreneur-making-environmental-friendly-stoves-wins-ksh150m-n310528 (Accessed: 23/01/2023)

Kuckertz, A., & Wagner, M. (2010). The influence of sustainability orientation on entrepreneurial intentions—Investigating the role of business experience. *Journal of Business Venturing, 25*(5), 524–539.

Kusi, S. Y., Gabrielsson, P., & Baumgarth, C. (2022). How classical and entrepreneurial brand management increases the performance of internationalising SMEs? *Journal of World Business, 57*(5), 101311.

Kusi, S. Y., Gabrielsson, P., & Kontkanen, M. (2021). Developing brand identities for international new ventures under uncertainty: Decision-making logics and psychic distance. *International Business Review, 30*(6), 1–16.

Leite, E. (2022). Innovation networks for social impact: An empirical study on multi-actor collaboration in projects for smart cities. *Journal of Business Research, 139,* 325–337.

Low, G. S., & Fullerton, R. A. (1994). Brands, brand management and the brand manager system: A gritical historical evaluation. *Journal of Marketing Research, 14*(May), 173–190.

Maon, F., Swaen, V., & De Roeck, K. (2021). Coporate branding and corporate social responsibility: Toward a multi-stakeholder interpretive perspective. *Journal of Business Research, 126,* 64–77.

Merz, M. A., Yi, H., & Vargo, S. L. (2009). The evolving brand logic: A service-dominant logic perspective. *Journal of the Academy of Marketing Science, 37*(3), 328–344.

Njagi, K. (2018). *Efficient cookstoves take up a new task in Kenya: heating.* https://www.reuters.com/article/uk-kenya-health-climatechange-idUSKC N1M609B. (Accessed: 23/01/2023)

Nwoba, A. C., Boso, N., & Robson, M. J. (2021). Corporate sustainability strategies in institutional adversity: Antecedent, outcome, and contingency effects. *Business Strategy and the Environment, 30*(2), 787–807.

Odoom, R., Agbemabiese, G. C., Anning-Dorson, T., & Mensah, P. (2017). Branding capabilities and SME performance in an emerging market: The moderating effect of brand regulations. *Marketing Intelligence & Planning, 35*(4), 473–487.

Opoku-Dakwa, A., & Rupp, D. E. (2019). Corporate social responsibility and meaningful work. In A. McWilliams, D. E. Rupp, D. S. Siegel, G. K. Stahl, D.A. Waldman (Eds.), *The Oxford handbook of corporate social responsibility, psychological and organizational perspectives,* pp. 70–95. Oxford University Press.

Politis, D., Winborg, J., & Dahlstrand, A. L. (2012). Exploring the resource logic of student entrepreneurs. *International Small Business Journal, 30,* 659–683.

Ramaswamy, V., & Ozcan, K. (2016). Brand value co-creation in a digitalized world: An integrative framework and research implications. *International Journal of Research in Marketing, 33*(1), 93–106.

Reuber, A. R., & Fischer, E. M. (1999). Understanding the consequences of founders' experience. *Journal of Small Business Management, 37*(2), 30–45.

Reynolds, N. S., & Holt, D. (2021). Sustainable development and profit? A sensemaking perspective on hybrid organisations and their founders. *Business Strategy and the Environment, 30*(4), 2147–2159.

Sarasvathy, S., Kumar, K., York, J. G., & Bhagavatula, S. (2014). An effectual approach to international entrepreneurship: Overlaps, challenges, and provocative possibilities. *Entrepreneurship Theory and Practice, 38*(1), 71–93.

Sarasvathy, S. D. (2001). Causation and effectuation: Toward a theoretical shift from economic inevitability to entrepreneurial contingency. *Academy of Management Review, 26*(2), 243–263.

Scannell, L., & Gifford, R. (2013). Personally relevant climate change: The role of place attachment and local versus global message framing in engagement. *Environment and Behavior, 45*(1), 60–85.

Scarlata, M., Zacharakis, A., & Walske, J. (2016). The effect of founder experience on the performance of philanthropic venture capital firms. *International Small Business Journal, 34*(5), 618–636.

Scott, W. R. (2008). *Institutions and organizations: Ideas and Interests.* Sage Publications.

Scott, W. R. (1995). *Institutions and organizations.* Sage.

Sheth, J. N., & Sinha, M. (2015). B2B branding in emerging markets: A sustainability perspective. *Industrial Marketing Management, 51*(1), 79–88.

Suchman, M. C. (1995). Managing legitimacy: Strategic and institutional approaches. *Academy of Management Review, 20*(3), 571–610.

Swaminathan, V., Sorescu, A., Steenkamp, J. B. E., O'Guinn, T. C. G., & Schmitt, B. (2020). Branding in a hyperconnected world: Refocusing theories and rethinking boundaries. *Journal of Marketing, 84*(2), 24–46.

Tajvidi, M., Richard, M. O., Wang, Y., & Hajli, N. (2020). Brand co-creation through social commerce information sharing: The role of social media. *Journal of Business Research, 121*, 476–486.

Törm älä, M., & Gryn-Jones, R. I. (2017). Development of new B2B venture corporate brand identity: A narrative performance approach. *Industrial Marketing Management, 65*(August), 76–85.

Ucbasaran, D., Westhead, P., Wright, M., & Flores, M. (2010). The nature of entrepreneurial experience, business failure and comparative optimism. *Journal of Business Venturing, 25*, 541–555.

Wickert, C. M. J., & de Bakker, F. G. A (2018). Pitching for social change: Toward a relational approach to selling and buying social issues. *Academy of Management Discoveries, 4* (1) (2018), 50–73.

White, K., Habib, R., & Hardisty, D. J. (2019). How to SHIFT consumer behaviors to be more sustainable: A literature review and guiding framework. *Journal of Marketing, 83*(3), 22–49.

Zahra, A. S. (2005). A theory of international new ventures: A decade of research. *Journal of International Business Studies, 36*(1), 20–28.

Zhu, Q., Cordeiro, J., & Sarkis, J. (2013). Institutional pressures, dynamic capabilities and environmental management systems: Investigating the ISO 9000-environmental management system implementation linkage. *Journal of Environmental Management, 114*(23), 232–242.

Gender and Sustainability

Beyond Mere Rhetoric: Gender Diversity and Corporate Sustainability Policies

Priscilla Akua Vitoh

1 INTRODUCTION

Over the past decades, the sustainable development policies of corporations have been impacted significantly by the Environmental, Social, and Governance (ESG) principles (Cho et al., 2021; Dover et al., 2020; LeBaron & Rühmkorf, 2017; Utting, 2008;). Gender diversity and equality within corporations are considered an integral part of ESG measures that researchers link to corporations' overall financial performance and sustainability (Cho et al., 2021; Provasi & Harasheh, 2021). It has previously been observed that, to safeguard their reputations and demonstrate to stakeholders that they are ethical and socially conscious, firms actively participate in gender diversity as part of their ESG initiatives (Connolly & Kaisershot, 2015; Utting, 2008). Policies on gender diversity in the workforce implemented by private corporations as a means of promoting business sustainability are not stand-alone initiatives. Both nationally and internationally, ESG policies have been pushed as a means of fostering gender diversity in the workforce. Notably, Gender Equality

---

P. A. Vitoh (✉)
University of Warwick, Coventry, England
e-mail: Priscilla.vitoh@warwick.ac.uk

© The Author(s), under exclusive license to Springer Nature
Switzerland AG 2023
S. Adomako et al. (eds.), *Corporate Sustainability in Africa*,
Palgrave Studies in African Leadership,
https://doi.org/10.1007/978-3-031-29273-6_14

298 P. A. VITOH

is goal number 5 of the 17 Sustainable Development Goals set by the United Nations (United Nations, 2015). One of the targets of this goal is to "ensure women's full and effective participation and equal opportunities for leadership at all levels of decision-making in political, economic and public life"(United Nations, 2015, Goal 5). This target translates into granting women a proportion of seats in government and managerial positions. Gender diversity policies recognise that people are vital to every corporate sustainability strategy as the primary agents who will implement a corporation's response to environmental and social issues. According to population data, women constitute an average of 50% (CountryMeters, 2023) of African countries' population. Thus, if companies are committed to attracting, honing, and utilising the capabilities of all qualified persons within a country, gender diversity must be an integral aspect of their corporate sustainability management. However, the issue of gender and corporate sustainability is multilayered and are driven by complex factors involving cultural, societal, and social roles ascribed to women.

In Ghana, the legislative framework within the country, particularly the 1992 constitution, prevents any overt exclusion of women from work. Ghana's1992 Constitution[1] gives the Ghanaian parliament the power to enact reasonably necessary laws to implement policies and programmes to redress the social, economic, or educational imbalance in Ghanaian society. The National Gender policy[2] introduced by the Government of Ghana through the Ministry of Gender, Children, and Social Protection recognises the existing bottlenecks and barriers and critical issues associated with gender equality concerns. The policy aims at mainstreaming gender equality and women's empowerment into Ghana's development efforts. The rationale behind these policies is that equal participation of women in the labour force is a means for "reducing the broader political, socio-cultural and material disadvantages women face" (Fine et al., 2020, 13). It allows women to develop and contribute their expertise and participate in high-level decision-making. These policies also identify the private sector as one of the key stakeholders in driving workplace gender diversity. The Ghanaian private sector is thus tasked to support bridging the

---

[1] Constitution of the Republic of Ghana 1992 Article 17(4)(a).

[2] "National Gender Policy: Ministry of Gender, Children and Social Protection" https://www.mogcsp.gov.gh/mdocs-posts/national-gender-policy/, accessed 10 May 2022.

gender inequality gap, ensure that corporate policies and practices incorporate gender equality principles, and provide incentives and support to women within their workforce.

This chapter examines the multilayered issue of gender and corporate sustainability and the complex factors involving women's cultural, societal, and social roles that must be addressed to ensure effective gender diversity policies within private and public corporations. It focuses on workforce diversity, particularly the horizontal (among sectors and industries) and vertical (within top-decision-making roles) female participation in the workforce It adapts a socio-legal enquiry that draws on African feminist and feminist political economy debates. It uses a desk research method incorporating primary, secondary, and non-legal sources.

I ask whether governmental and private corporation initiatives encouraging workforce gender diversity are tangible enough to even the gender workforce ratio in Ghana. The chapter contributes to the literature on gender and corporate sustainability in Ghana by synthesizing the debates and arguments and setting them within the Ghanaian context. It contributes significantly to knowledge by examining gender diversity in the workforce and corporate sustainability in Ghana using an African feminist lens and insights from the feminist political economy. The African feminist lens provides a unique perspective on gender diversity in the workforce and corporate sustainability in Ghana. It considers the historical and cultural context of gender relations in Africa and recognises the intersectional nature of gender, race, and class. Feminist political economy provides insights into the structural barriers that hinder women's participation in the workforce and their ability to achieve sustainable livelihoods. It recognises the role of gender in shaping economic structures and processes and how these impact women's access to resources and opportunities. Feminist political economy also considers the role of power relations in shaping economic structures and how these power dynamics affect women's ability to participate in decision-making processes.

The first section curates some debates on the role and importance of women in the workforce, particularly in leadership positions. The second section focuses on the role of Ghana as a State in setting regulatory guidance for gender diversity and the example it has established within public corporations. Finally, the paper reviews the gender diversity policies private corporations in Ghana have implemented and their impact on closing the workforce gender gap. It concludes that women's participation is integral to corporate sustainability in two interconnected ways. First, because Ghanaian women predominantly take up the social reproductive roles in society, they are actively part of birthing, raising, and nurturing the workforce. Second, women actively contribute to the workforce by offering their knowledge and experience to businesses. The chapter argues that tangible steps to increase gender ratios within the workforce can only be achieved if the structural, historical, and gendered nature of women's discrimination from workforce participation is recognised and addressed. It argues further that, while the private sector is recognised as a key player in bridging the gender gap in workforce participation, the private sector alone can't lead this change. Consequently, the Ghanaian State, both as the country's largest employer and the policymaker, must support private-sector efforts through legislation, incentives, enforcement, and policy.

2 WOMEN AND CORPORATE SUSTAINABILITY

Researchers acknowledge the unequal gender ratios within the workforce both across industries (horizontally) and in leadership positions (vertically) (Fine et al., 2020, 13). Yet, the subject of workplace gender diversity is not straightforward and has been the subject of intense debate (Sojo et al., 2016; OECD, 2017; Fine et al., 2020; Nyeadi et al., 2021). According to some research, gender diversity in the workforce is a crucial factor in the sustainability and expansion of businesses (UN Statistics Division, 2006; Revenga & Sudhir n.d.; Pareek et al., 2023). According to studies of this nature, having women in leadership roles in a company results in enhanced supervision of the firms' activities and higher pressure on the firm to exhibit socially acceptable behaviour (Maxfield et al., 2010; Pareek et al., 2023). This approach that empowering women by improving women's participation in the workforce will improve the overall economy of a nation is termed by the UN as smart economics (UN Statistics Division, 2006; Revenga & Sudhir n.d.; Loayza & Trumbic, 2022). Boulouta (2013) has argued that, over the years, achieving gender balance in the management hierarchy of corporate firms has proven to be very advantageous to the board's effectiveness, especially regarding monitoring, strategic direction, and relational function. Similarly, Salzmann et al. (2005, 129) emphasise that women in the governance body of organisations bring a "style change", which is positive for organisational effectiveness. Other research (Adams et al., 2011; Pareek et al., 2023) also reports that compared to men, women's management styles are more stakeholder-oriented, cautious, and pay more attention to welfare programmes. The common trend in these arguments is that women bring on board certain aspects of leadership that complement the existing male experience and mostly neutralise the effects that the aggressive approach of men would have yielded. Thus, the different leadership styles that come with gender diversity directly impact board performance and good corporate governance in general (Gipson et al., 2017). Therefore, gender diversity in the corporate world positively impacts corporate performance. However, some authors have cautioned against focusing on 'business case' arguments regarding workplace gender diversity. Such authors assert that contrary to common assumptions, these arguments may not be as effective in advocating change (Dover et al., 2020; Eagly, 2016; Fine & Sojo, 2019; Fine et al., 2020). Researchers with this school of thought believe that business benefits projected for women's inclusion are often unrealistic or supported by evidence (Fine et al., 2020, 3). They argue further that affirmative action policies, based on the perceived benefit of women in corporate roles, devalue merit, resulting in the unjust treatment of members of dominant groups(Dover et al., 2020).

One side of the argument centres on whether expecting a gender-diverse workforce across all industries is realistic. According to some studies (e.g. Hoffman & Yoeli, 2013), there are inherent differences in the kinds of roles either sex is drawn to or is suited for. To these researchers, industries have an inevitable limit on achieving equal gender ratios. Focusing specifically on gender diversity in terms of sex classifications (male or female), Fine et al. (2020 warn against making broad assumptions based on gender. They argue that while average sex differences could undoubtedly play a role in sex-related discrepancies in occupational results, such claims must be made cautiously (Fine et al., 2020). Their findings showed that the tendency to assume male or female characteristics are essential for success in male-typical or female-typical roles, respectively (Uhlmann & Cohen, 2005), is flawed (Fine et al., 2020, 9). To them, a combination of different attributes that may be common in men and women contribute to success in roles (Fine et al., 2020, 9). In this vein, some researchers have argued that it is not sex differences that lead to gender segregation in some industries, but rather the "gender-typing of occupations" (Fine et al., 2020). As occupational choices may be a form of "identity construction" and "self-affirmation" (Charles 2011, 365; Cech 2013; Fine et al., 2020), people may choose their careers to match the social construction of males or females. Nevertheless, some studies have shown that a generalised association of gender and pre-conceived sex differences to productive capability is flawed and may not reflect industry-specific situations (Fine et al., 2020). Such studies have found that differences in behaviour between men and women are not permanently fixed but might be flexible to occasion and context (Kennedy et al., 2017; Fine et al., 2020).

This paper challenges the predominantly binary position in the ongoing debate that focuses solely on sex differences on the one hand and business case arguments on the other hand. It argues that such binary analysis does not sufficiently address the gendered and historical discrimination that has led to unequal gender ratios in the first place. The exclusion of women from the workforce has colonial antecedence and forms part of the systematic disempowerment of African women (Lovett, 1989; Oyewumi, 1997, 2005). Chazan (1989, 186) explains that "although African societies have a vibrant indigenous state tradition, the boundaries and institutional foundations of the contemporary state system [are] closely associated with the colonial intrusion into the continent". The establishment of the colonial government was associated with the development of classes and the penetration of the capitalist economy (Chazan, 1989, 186). Women were marginalised within colonial African states and left out of traditional economic development (J. L. Parpart & Staudt, 1989). Colonial governments developed social-control measures to limit women's physical and social mobility to maintain male exclusivity to the public realm and capitalist economy (Chazan, 1989, 186). Women's labour remained necessary for the family's survival to augment the inadequate wages the colonial government paid to men. Yet, there was a gender distinction because the wage economy rendered these women non-workers (Oyewumi, 1997, 150). The cultural codes meticulously crafted in the colonial era to reinforce male dominance and women's subordination arguably remain in the present African States. Researchers' findings show continuous discriminatory treatment of African women within the private sector despite African countries' supposed commitment to gender equality (Adesua Lincoln & Adedoyin, 2012; Augustine et al., 2016; Diop, 2015). Lincoln and Adedoyin (2012, 658) argue that within the Nigerian context, women constitute an underclass with unequal opportunities in contributing to economic progress and receiving benefits from it. Others argue further that women are, in most cases, confined to low-paid, insecure jobs within the African labour market with limited career progression opportunities (Augustine et al., 2016; Diop, 2015). Researchers have shown that such cultural codes also affect women's horizontal and vertical involvement within the workforce.

Within Africa, the social roles ascribed to women and socio-cultural norms have influenced the roles women are perceived to be capable of undertaking within the labour market (Augustine et al., 2016; Adesua Lincoln & Adedoyin, 2012; Harrison & Lynch, 2005). Societal norms continue to influence what is perceived as "man's work" or "women's work"(Elson, 1999, 611). Historically, women's productive potential is perceived along their social reproductive roles (Harrison & Lynch, 2005). Thus roles that seem to be in the line of social reproduction, such as teaching and nursing, are ascribed as female-oriented jobs. Conversely, men are attributed to leadership-focused roles or those that require physical strength (Fine et al., 2020). Elson (1999, 3) strongly asserts that, although labour markets seek to put on a cloak of neutrality, labour markets are, in reality, "bearers of gender". While the employee/employer relationship does not have the same gender connotations, such as husband and wife or father and daughter, social stereotypes implicitly affect how companies operate. An example is a social stereotype where masculinity is associated with authority. Employers routinely underestimate women's production potential, resulting in lower pay and relegation to lower level positions (Anku-Tsede & Gadegbeku, 2014; Augustine et al., 2016; Diop, 2015; Elson, 1999). Additionally, the lack of gender diversity in senior management and high-earning roles is generally attributable to socially pre-conceived "gender-type" for occupations seeping into the fabric of corporate culture (Augustine et al., 2016; Elson, 1999). Women are often impeded from decision-making and senior management positions within corporations because they are perceived as being less aggressive than men (Augustine et al., 2016; Adesua Lincoln & Adedoyin, 2012; Booysen & Nkomo, 2010; Carli & Eagly, 2001; Heilman, 2001). Even in cases where women are given high-ranking roles, these stereotypes may contribute to why women were deemed suitable for the position (Maxfield et al., 2010). For instance, when the Nordic island of Iceland declared bankruptcy in 2008, it turned to two women to take over and "clean up" its collapsed financial system (Maxfield et al., 2010, 586–87; O'Conner, 2008). The belief was that, women are more risk-averse and can manage financial resources more "safely" than their male counterparts (Ferrary, 2009; Maxfield et al., 2010, 587). Thus, although private companies project themselves as "gender neutral" spaces, these prejudices continue to seep into the workspace resulting in a glass ceiling" (Augustine et al., 2016; Provasi & Harasheh, 2021), which poses a significant barrier to going beyond the rhetoric of gender diversity in the workplace as a corporate sustainability goal.

Another critical factor often lost in the binary debate is that corporate sustainability does not only require the presence of an existing workforce that can perform the tasks currently needed by companies. It also includes ensuring a reproduction in the training of the future workforce. Women's role in this regard is on both sides of this sustainability need. Within the labour market or market-oriented space (the productive economy), women lend their qualifications to the company's economic growth. Conversely, within the "reproductive economy", women's unpaid care responsibilities such as childcare, eldercare, cooking, and cleaning add to producing the future workforce, replenishing the current workforce, and supporting the past workforce (Elson, 1998, 1999; Hoskyns & Rai, 2007). The labour market is also at the intersection of these two economies (Elson, 1999), benefiting from the dual role women play within these two intersecting economies. While women are 50% of the population and can be part of the current productive workforce, their reproductive roles ensure the continuous production and sustainability of the future workforce. Employment is an avenue for most public positions of power (Fine et al., 2020). Researchers mostly agree that excluding anyone from employment opportunities perpetuates the historical relic of concentrating privilege and public power on a few people (Gheaus & Herzog, 2016; Suk, 2017). As Gheaus and Herzog (2016, 80) argue, "justice in the labour market requires a fair distribution of people to realise [all the benefits associated with labour] within their paid labour". Although, State legislative framework, may prevent any form of overt exclusion of women from work, women may be implicitly excluded from employment opportunities because workplace policies and practices do not recognise African women's dual role within the labour economy. Policies such as extended maternity leaves, breastfeeding rooms, and flexible working hours must be incentivised by the Ghanaian State and implemented by companies to allow effective female participation in the workforce. These policies will remove the structural barriers that impede women's ability to equally compete in the labour market.

As discussed above, the debates on gender diversity as a vehicle for corporate sustainability centre predominantly around whether there is merit in making a business case for ensuring a diverse workforce. The arguments also consider whether expecting gender-diverse workforces is realistic, considering the perceived sex differences and social norms that impact people's career choices. The author has argued that a binary focus on a business case for gender diversity or sex differences does not consider the labour market's role at the intersection of African women's dual role within the reproductive and productive economies. It argues that gender diversity cannot be achieved without grasping the realities of historical discrimination and economic devaluation African women have experienced, leading to unequal gender ratios in the workforce. The following section focuses on the role of Ghana as a State in setting regulatory guidance for gender diversity and the example it has established within public corporations.

3 Is the Ghanaian State Leading by Example for Private Corporations in Ghana?

This section focuses on the Ghanaian State as the primary employer in Ghana in setting the national workforce gender diversity agenda through policy and action for private-sector corporations to follow. The role of the State in establishing the basic framework for gender diversity within companies cannot be disregarded. The State's role is to provide a framework to ensure uniformity in the gender diversity approaches of companies and to ensure that people are not inadvertently disadvantaged because they belong to an industry or work for a company that does not have a robust strategy. Notwithstanding this, it is essential to recognise that the role of the State is not just in legislation to render discrimination illegal.[3] Specific legislation enacted by the State on gender diversity within private and public corporations can also drive the agenda on gender and corporate sustainability and ensure that all corporations have a more gender-diverse workforce.

Italy serves as an example of a nation with a corporate diversity policy that aims to define the standards for gender diversity for corporate sustainability. In 2011, the Italian government passed the "*Legge Golfo – Mosca*" (Golfo-Mosco law) to reserve quotas for women to serve on the boards of directors of publicly traded enterprises "pink quotas") (Moresco, 2014).

---

[3] Article 12 of 1992 constitution of Ghana makes all forms of discrimination against all persons illegal.

The legislation also included fines as high as one million euros for non-compliance with the regulations (Moresco, 2014). In their analysis of the impact of this law on gender diversity in the Italian workforce, Provasi and Harasheh (2021, 136) assert that the.

> Golfo-Mosco law in the Italian legal system was instrumental in breaking down the notorious crystal ceiling, unlocking the rigid and backward Italian situation, and above all in initiating a change based on a new culture for a greater gender balance and inclusiveness in companies and the country.

Nonetheless, a study of the law's effects after ten years of its introduction shows that while the number of female directors has increased from 7% in 2011 to 37% in 2020, (Renda, 2021) the increased participation of women at the board level has not resulted in gender parity at lower levels of corporations (Reuters Renda, 2021; Staff, 2019). Hence, while legislation is essential for enshrining the principle of equality and the formation of norms and perceptions, they do not result in a practical change within companies (Elson, 1999; Provasi & Harasheh, 2021). As an employer and regulator, the Ghanaian State sets the requirements that private corporations must follow within its borders. However, as Provasi and Harasheh Golfo-Mosco (2021) show in the Legge-Mosco case, legislation alone may not be adequate to address gender diversity within all levels of corporations.

Ghana has taken an action-based women empowerment drive that has seen some results since 2020. These have been reflected in affirmative action by the Ghanaian government in the appointment of regulatory agency officers, the selection of administrative heads, and the participation of women in politics and the corporate world. Regulations enacted since 2020 have included a mandatory slot for women on the composition of boards, committees, and councils for women. Thus, in critical areas of the economy like insurance, public–private partnership, real estate management, cybersecurity, education, and entrepreneurship, the Ghanaian President or appointing government authority must select at least a woman within their reserved appointments quota. The Cybersecurity Act 2020 (Act 1038), for instance, reserves two of the President's three-person nomination quota for women. (*Cybersecurity* Act 2020, sec. 5). The appointment committee is still free to nominate a woman to fill the unreserved quota despite the spot being earmarked for a woman. Some governmental boards have thus constituted boards that have more women than the reserved quota. The National Insurance Commission Board, which regulates and supervises the Ghanaian insurance market (The Insurance Act, 2021), has two women members, including the chairperson.[4] Likewise, the Real Estate Agency Council, the governing body of real estate agency regulation and management (*Real Estate Agency* Act, 2020) comprises four women('Works, Housing Minister Inaugurates Ghana Real Estate Agency Council Board', 2021). Apart from the one mandatory quota, the Real Estate Agency Act, 2020 requires the Minister for Works and Housing to nominate (*Real Estate Agency* Act 2020, sec. 5) the appointing authority has appointed three additional women to the Board.

While these appointments and slot reservations seem to be a positive step towards gender diversity within the public sector, the question becomes whether these steps taken by the Ghanaian State are exemplary enough for companies operating in Ghana to emulate. Is public policy driving a paradigm shift and entrenching the beneficial interest of workforce diversity within the population? While gender quotas in laws do not prevent any of the other positions from being filled by a woman, the requirement for a minimum number of women on boards instead of an equal number demonstrates that there is still a long way to go in Ghana in the effort to diversify decision-making roles. For instance, a mandatory requirement of one or two women on a 13-member board, hardly speaks of gender diversity. For instance, on The Public–Private Partnership Committee, a committee for steering the development and implementation of public–private partnership arrangements between contracting authorities and private parties regarding infrastructure development and services provision, only 1 out of 13 members is required by law to be a woman (*Public Private Partnership* Act 2021, sec. 21(1)). The quota requirements in legislation also do not adequately address the diversity of people who engage in the activities the board is regulating. Ghana is acknowledged as one of the countries with the largest population of women engaging in small and medium-scale enterprises (SMEs).[5] Yet, the Board of Ghana Enterprise Agency, the State corporation mandated to

---

[4] ('NIC | About Us—Board Of Directors' n.d.).

[5] ('Africa Claims Top Three Spots in Mastercard Index for Highest Concentration of Women Businesses Owners in the World | Middle East/Africa Hub' n.d.).

308   P. A. VITOH

support Ghanaian SMEs, has only two mandatory quotas for women out of the 13 members(*Ghana Enterprise Agency* Act 2020, sec. 4). Again, although Ghana provides access to education regardless of gender, the composition of the Ghana Tertiary Education Commission, established to regulate tertiary education in Ghana, has only one mandated woman member(*Education Regulatory Bodies* Act 2020, sec. 11) out of the 13 members.

The wording of the legislation, which mandates the compulsory appointment of women to decision-making public sector bodies, may also lead to the appearance of tokenism. Instead of the wording of the State showing that it is leading by example with the belief that there are capable and qualified women to fit these roles, the language projects the State as just requiring a woman on the body for the sake of it. For instance, in the Securities Industry Act of 2016,[6] the requirement for the four other persons who can serve on the board include.

> lawyer qualified to be appointed a Justice of the Superior Court of Judicature nominated by the General Legal Council, a chartered accountant nominated by the Institute of Chartered Accountants, Ghana; and an academic researcher in a relevant field and a woman.[7]

While all the other members are stated based on the qualification and skillset they may bring to the Commission, a "woman" is vague. The wording implies that any woman may be appointed to fill the position, regardless of their skill set or suitability for the role. One could argue that the word woman" can be read in the context of the entire section to imply that a woman must meet the same requirements as the other board members. Therefore, nonetheless, to prevent ambiguity, it is more beneficial for gender diversity requirements in laws to state specifically the qualifications of the woman eligible for the role. A good example of an effectively worded legislation is the wording of the section on the Board composition of the Ghana Tertiary Education Commission, which provides for the appointment of a woman "with the relevant experience" (*Education Regulatory Bodies* Act 2020, sec. 11(1)(i)). The section ensures that the woman appointed to the role will have the required

---

[6] 'Securities Industry Act', Act 929 (2016).

[7] 'Securities Industry Act', Act 929 (2016),sec 4(f).

skill set to adequately contribute to the Committee's decision-making processes.

As discussed earlier, State legislation may not successfully ensure gender diversity in all ranks of the corporate ladder. Nonetheless, State legislation provides a governing framework for gender diversity in ESG measures. Ghana has made strides, particularly since 2020, in affirmative action legislation, which entrenches gender diversity on State boards. Yet, similar to what Provasi and Harasheh (Provasi & Harasheh, 2021) found in the Italian Golfo Moscow case, the minimal gains of women on State Boards have not translated into gender diversity in the composition of regulatory and decision-making bodies within the Ghanaian public sector. Top management and day-to-day decision-making roles such as Chief Executive officers and managing and deputy managing directors remain predominantly occupied by males. Currently, only 5 are headed by women out of the 118 Ghanaian public service organisations. Similarly, only 38 out of the 260 Metropolitan, Municipal, and District Assemblies Chief Executives (MMDCEs) are women (Ghana Web, 2022). These statistics demonstrate that the State's efforts to promote gender diversity to foster corporate sustainability have perhaps been fragmented and have not gone beyond rhetoric. Gender quotas, which are likely, at best tokenistic, do not address the decision-making responsibilities in public organisations.

4   Private Corporations and Gender Diversity

This section examines private companies' progress in driving a gender diversity agenda within their workforce. The previous section has discussed the important role the State plays in driving public policy and enacting legislation that entrenches gender diversity within public and private corporations. It also noted that while the Ghanaian State has made inroads in passing legislation that mandates a quota for women on State boards, the allocations are arguably tokenistic and inadequate to achieve gender diversity in these bodies. The State has also failed to appoint women into decision-making roles such as CEO and MMDCEs. The diminished progress of the Ghanaian State in driving policy and setting a firm example of gender diversity in the workforce cannot, however, excuse private companies operating in Ghana from driving their gender diversity agenda. Private companies operating within the country cannot

310   P. A. VITOH

ignore sustainability and social responsibility because of the societal expectations on these firms to grow sustainably and impact society positively (Amankwah-Amoah et al., 2019; Adomako et al., 2021).

Corporate Ghana boards or management teams have been male-dominant in the past decades. Where women were represented, most of these women were likely to be non-executives and were not likely to play leadership roles on such boards. Even though women's under-representation in the corporate world is a global problem, researchers concede that the gender gap in high-ranking posts in Ghana has been too significant (Munemo, 2017; Nyeadi et al., 2021). Munemo (2017) observes that women remain underrepresented in all leadership positions, specifically in Ghanaian corporations' senior roles (Munemo, 2017). A survey on female representation in Ghanaian private sector Boards by the International Finance Corporation (2018) amplifies this fact. It revealed thus:

> A majority (77.85%) of firms surveyed did not have policies on gender. Only 5.70% of organisations had policies on gender, and 16.46% did not respond. Notwithstanding the absence of policies, 72.15% of the boards had female representation, even though the ratio of females to males remained low, with diversity typically ranging from 20.00% to 30.00%. Furthermore, only 6.33% had minimum thresholds for women on their boards, 75.95% did not have minimum thresholds, and 17.72%s failed to provide valid responses. Only about 4.43% have a standard for female representation. (IFC 2018,13)

Private corporations such as Nestle, Guinness, and MTN run programs focusing on gender diversity within their workforce. Some of these projects target encouraging women to take up male-dominated roles and allow for a balanced workforce.[8] These projects have seen some success as Ghana's female labour participation rate has, since 2011, consistently been above 60%,(Trading Economics, 2023). However, research shows that female participation within senior management positions is lower than 20% (The Boardroom Africa, Ghana Stock Exchange, and Board Diversity Charter 2020, 6). Thus, it is debatable whether or not ESG strategies for gender diversity in Ghanaian firms have significantly improved the situation at the top management level. According to the

---

[8] ('Empowering Women' n.d.).

Board Diversity Index (The Boardroom Africa, Ghana Stock Exchange, and Board Diversity Charter 2020, 6), women make up 8% of CEOs or Managing Directors (MDs), 15% of chief operations officers (COOs), and 13% of chief finance officers (CFOs) on Ghana's listed Boards. Research on the Ghana Club 100 (GC100) companies[9] showed a significant gap in the number of female CEOs of large private companies compared to their male counterparts (Ghana Investment Promotion Centre, 2023). The 19th edition published in October 2022 (Federated Commodities Limited (FEDCO), 2022) showed no significant improvement in women in top management compared to the 18th edition (Dawson-Ahmoah, 2020). Only one of the CEOs of the top 10 GC100 companies is female.[10] A total of 13 out of the 100 GC100 companies in the 19th edition have female CEOs/chairpersons.[11] Although this is an improvement of the 8 female CEOs[12] in the 18th edition, the change is not remarkable. While the GC100 female CEOs represent a wide range of industries including technology, travel, and healthcare. They continue to be concentrated in the financial services industry. Access Bank Ghana,[13] which has no female CEO, employed its first female Executive Director in 2022 (Segbefia, 2022). Similarly, Guarantee Trust Bank (2023) and First Atlantic Bank (2023) have female Executive Directors or General Managers. However, the rural Bank sector is a part of the financial services sector that does not follow this trend. None of the 23 rural banks on

---

[9] The Ghana Club 100 (GC100) compiled by the Ghana Investment Promotion Centre (GIPC) has been is existence since 1998. It is an annual compilation of the top 100 companies in Ghana.

[10] IDS Consulting Services', IDS Consulting Services, accessed 16 March 2023, https://idsconsultingservices.com/ the new entrant at number 8 has a female founder.

[11] Express IDS Consult Consult Agency Limited (ranked 8th), Standard Chartered Bank Ghana Ltd. (ranked 28th), Priority Insurance (ranked 38th), Zonda Tee (ranked 40th), Enterprise Life (ranked 43rd), Starlife Assurance (ranked 47th), Guinness Ghana Breweries Ltd. (ranked 72nd, NMH Nationwide Medical Insurance Company Limited (ranked 74th), Star Assurance (ranked 78th), Riali Consult (ranked 81st), L'aine Services Limited (ranked 83rd), Country Links (ranked 91st) and Land Tours Ghana Limited (ranked 100 h).

[12] Barclays Bank Ghana Ltd. subsidiary of ABSA (ranked 18th), Enterprise Life Assurance (ranked 22nd), Standard Chartered Bank Ghana Ltd. (ranked 30th), Starlife Assurance (ranked 40th), Glico Healthcare Ltd (ranked 75th), Guinness Ghana

[13] Ranked 93rd on the 18th edition GC100.

the GC100 list has a female CEO or Managing Director. Familial relations may also contribute to the number of female CEOs on this list. Star Assurance and Starlife Assurance are part of the Star Assurance group, a private company founded by a family(Star Assurance Group, 2023).The two female CEOs are the company's founder's twin children and the Group CEO's sisters (Asare, 2021). Consequently, even though some improvements have been recorded in some sectors of private businesses, there is a lot of room for growth in gender diversity in the private sector workforce.

5 Conclusion

This chapter has curated some debates on gender diversity as a tool for corporate sustainability. The arguments have focused on sex differences in the choice of profession and whether the focus should be on the business case for gender diversity. The chapter has argued that gender diversity in ESG measures does not sufficiently account for the structural and historical discrimination that has led to unequal gender ratios. Additionally, it has been suggested that women interact with the labour market on both a direct and indirect level, serving as both providers of social reproductive care to the current and future workforces and active participants in the labour force. To increase women's workforce participation tangibly, the State must lead in establishing practical ESG guidelines for gender diversity. It must also lead by example by increasing female participation in decision-making positions in State-owned corporations. This requires the State regulatory policies to recognise the gendered nature of the workforce and the historical inequalities women face. Such recognition, for instance, of the dual roles women play within the economy's reproductive and productive sides will enable policies to address the root of the unequal ratios. Policies such as fair treatment of pregnant women, protection against workplace harassment, parental leave, and flexible hours will go towards closing the existing gender gap in the workforce. These factors must also be considered when private companies create internal gender diversity policies. Policies based on these factors will increase gender diversity in the workforce and provide firms with a larger pool of potential employees to fill all levels of their workforce. Increasing the number of women in the workforce while accommodating their societal reproductive obligations will result in a stable labour force, which is essential to corporate sustainability.

References

Adams, R. B., Licht, A. N., & Sagiv, L. (2011). Shareholders and stakeholders: How do directors decide? *Strategic Management Journal, 32*(12), 1331–1355.

Adesua Lincoln, A., & Adedoyin, O. (2012). Corporate governance and gender diversity in Nigerian boardrooms. *Corporate Governance and Gender Diversity in Nigerian Boardrooms (September 30, 2012). World Academy of Science, Engineering and Technology, 71*, 1853.

Adomako, S., Ning, E., & Adu-Ameyaw, E. (2021). Proactive environmental strategy and firm performance at the bottom of the pyramid. *Business Strategy and the Environment, 30*(1), 422–431. Wiley Online Library.

'Africa Claims Top Three Spots in Mastercard Index for Highest Concentration of Women Businesses Owners in the World | Middle East/Africa Hub'. n.d. Accessed 3 April 2021. https://newsroom.mastercard.com/mea/press-rel eases/africa-claims-top-three-spots-in-mastercard-index-for-highest-concentra tion-of-women-businesses-owners-in-the-world/.

Amankwah-Amoah, J., Danso, A., & Adomako, S. (2019). Entrepreneurial orientation, environmental sustainability and new venture performance: Does stakeholder integration matter? *Business Strategy and the Environment, 28*(1), 79–87. Wiley Online Library.

Anku-Tsede, O., & Gadegbeku, C. (2014). Regulation and gender equality and non-discrimination of women in top management positions in Ghana. *African Journal of Business Management, 8*(19), 913–921.

Asare, Edward Asare. (2021). Meet The Twin CEOs Of StarLife Assurance And Star Asurance Kakra Duffuor-Nyarko & Boatemaa Barfour-Awuah | EdwardAsare - Sincere Human Stories | News. 2021. https://edwardasare. com/meet-the-twin-ceos-of-starlife-assurance-and-star-asurance-kakra-duf fuor-nyarko-boatemaa-barfour-awuah/.

Augustine, D., Wheat, C. O., Jones, K. S., Baraldi, M., & Malgwi, C. A. (2016). Gender diversity within the workforce in the microfinance industry in Africa: Economic performance and sustainability. *Canadian Journal of Administrative Sciences/revue Canadienne Des Sciences De L'administration, 33*(3), 227–241.

Booysen, L. A., & Nkomo, S. M. (2010). Gender role stereotypes and requisite management characteristics: The case of South Africa. *Gender in Management: An International Journal.*

Boulouta, I. (2013). Hidden connections: The link between board gender diversity and corporate social performance. *Journal of business ethics, 113*(2), 185–197. Springer.

Carli, L. L., & Eagly, A. H. (2001). Gender, hierarchy, and leadership: An introduction. *Journal of Social Issues, 57*(4), 629–636.

314   P. A. VITOH

Ghana Investment Promotion Centre. (2023). 'Home'. 2023. https://gipc.gov.gh/.

Cech, E. A. (2013). The self-expressive edge of occupational sex segregation. *American Journal of Sociology, 119*(3), 747–789. University of Chicago Press.

Charles, M. (2011). A world of difference: International trends in women's economic status. *Annual Review of Sociology, 37*, 355–371. Annual Reviews.

Chazan, Naomi. (1989). Gender perspectives on African States. In L. Jane and Staudt Parpart (Eds.), *Women and the State In Africa*, pp. 185–201. Lynne Rienner Publishers.

Cho, Y., Kim, S., You, J., Moon, H., & Sung, H. (2021). Application of ESG measures for gender diversity and equality at the organizational level in a Korean context. *European Journal of Training and Development, 45*(4/5), 346–365.

Connolly, N., & Manette, K. (2015). Corporate power and human rights. *The International Journal of Human Rights.* Taylor & Francis.

Constitution of the Republic of Ghana. (1992). https://www.wipo.int/edocs/lexdocs/laws/en/gh/gh014en.pdf.

CountryMeters. 2023. 'Africa Population'. (2023). https://countrymeters.info/en/Africa.

Cybersecurity Act. (2020). *Act 1038.*

Dawson-Ahmoah, Augustine. (2020). 2019 Ghana Club 100 Awards: Full List of Winners'. Ghana Investment Promotion Centre - GIPC. 2020. https://gipc.gov.gh/2019-ghana-club-100-awards-full-list-of-winners/

Diop, Ngone. (2015). Gender equality and sustainable development: Achieving the twin development goals in Africa. Brief for GSDR 2015'.

Dover, T. L., Kaiser, C. R., & Major, B. (2020). Mixed signals: The unintended effects of diversity initiatives. *Social Issues and Policy Review, 14*(1), 152–181.

Eagly, Alice H. (2016). When passionate advocates meet research on diversity, does the honest broker stand a chance?: Erratum.

Education Regulatory Bodies Act. (2020). *Act 1023.*

Elson, D. (1998). The Economic, the political and the domestic: Businesses, states and households in the organisation of production. *New Political Economy, 3*(2), 189–208.

Elson, D. (1999). Labor markets as gendered institutions: Equality, efficiency and empowerment issues. *World Development, 27*(3), 611–627.

'Empowering Women'. n.d. Nestlé Global. Accessed 8 March 2023. https://www.nestle.com/sustainability/people-communities/women-empowerment.

Federated Commodities Limited (FEDCO). (2022). Complete winners list of the 19th edition of Ghana club 100 awards'. 18 October 2022. https://fedco.com.gh/complete-winners-list-of-the-19th-edition-of-ghana-club-100-awards/

Ferrary, Michel. (2009). Why women managers shine in a downturn. *Financial Times* 15.

Fine, C., Sojo, V., & Lawford-Smith, H. (2020). Why does workplace gender diversity matter? Justice, organizational benefits, and policy. *Social Issues and Policy Review, 14*(1), 36–7.

Fine, C., & Sojo, V. (2019). Women's value: Beyond the business case for diversity and inclusion. *The Lancet, 393*(10171), 515–516.

First Atlantic Bank. (2023). 'Management'. 2023. https://firstatlanticbank.com.gh/management.html.

Ghana Web. (2022). 5 Women leading top government Aaencies. GhanaWeb. 14 January 2022. https://www.ghanaweb.com/GhanaHomePage/business/5-women-leading-top-government-agencies-1444759

Ghana Enterprise Agency Act. (2020). *Act 1043.*

Gheaus, A., & Lisa, H. (2016). The goods of work (other than money!). *Journal of Social Philosophy, 47*(1).

Gipson, A. N., Pfaff, D. L., Mendelsohn, D. B., Catenacci, L. T., & Warner Burke, W. (2017). Women and leadership: Selection, development, leadership style, and performance. *The Journal of Applied Behavioral Science, 53*(1), 32–65.

GTBank Ghana. (2023). 'Our People'. GTBank Ghana. 2023. https://www.gtbghana.com/about/our-people.

Harrison, L. A., & Lynch, A. B. (2005). Social role theory and the perceived gender role orientation of athletes. *Sex Roles, 52*(3), 227–236.

Heilman, M. E. (2001). Description and prescription: How gender stereotypes prevent women's ascent up the organizational ladder. *Journal of Social Issues, 57*(4), 657–674.

Hoffman, M., & Yoeli, E. (2013). The risks of avoiding a debate on gender differences. *Rady Business Journal, 6*, 6–7.

Hoskyns, C., & Rai, S. M. (2007). Recasting the global political economy: Counting women's unpaid work. *New Political Economy, 12*(3), 297–317.

International Finance Corporation. (2018). *Gender Diversity in Ghanaian Boardrooms: An Abridged Report on Women on Boards of Corporate and Public Institutions in Ghana.* 1 May. World Bank. https://doi.org/10.1596/30177.

Kennedy, J. A., Kray, L. J., Ku., & Gillian. (2017). A social-cognitive approach to understanding gender differences in negotiator ethics: The role of moral identity. *Organizational Behavior and Human Decision Processes, 138*, 28–44.

LeBaron, G., & Rühmkorf, A. (2017). Steering CSR through home state regulation: A comparison of the impact of the UK Bribery Act and Modern Slavery Act on global supply chain governance. *Global Policy, 8*, 15–28.

Loayza, N., & Tea Trumbic. (2022). Gender equality is smart economics. Yet, its progress remains slow. 1 March 2022. https://blogs.worldbank.org/developmenttalk/gender-equality-smart-economics-yet-its-progress-remains-slow

316   P. A. VITOH

Lovett, Margot L. (1989). Gender relations class formation and the Colonial State in Africa'. In L. Jane and Staudt Parpart (Eds.), *Women and the State in Africa*, pp. 23–46. Lynne Rienner Publishers Inc.

Maxfield, S., Shapiro, M., Gupta, V., & Hass, S. (2010). Gender and risk: Women, risk taking and risk aversion. *Gender in Management: An International Journal.*

Moresco, Hogan Lovells-Vittorio. (2014). Women on boards - Italy'. Lexology. 13 March 2014. https://www.lexology.com/library/detail.aspx?g=a3b4cfb7-f9f0-45da-8a2f-ce6097c684d0.

Munemo, P. (2017). Women's participation in decision making in public and political spheres in Ghana: Constrains and strategies. *Journal of Culture, Society and Development, 37*, 47–52.

'NATIONAL GENDER POLICY : Ministry of Gender, Children and Social Protection'. n.d. Accessed 10 May 2022. https://www.mogcsp.gov.gh/mdocs-posts/national-gender-policy/.

'NIC | About Us – Board Of Directors'. n.d. Accessed 10 May 2022. https://nicgh.org/about-us/board-of-directors/.

Nyeadi, J. D., Kamasa, K., & Kpinpuo, S. (2021). Female in top management and firm performance nexus: Empirical evidence from Ghana. *Cogent Economics & Finance, 9*(1), 1921323.

O'Conner, S. (2008). Iceland calls in women to clean up "Young Men's Mess". *Woman Capital, Available at: Www. Womancapital. Nl/Ft1. Htm (Accessed 2 February 2010).*

OECD. (2017). Report on the implementation of the oecd gender recommendations—some progress on gender equality but much left to do. Paris, France: OECD. https://www.oecd.org/mcm/documents/C-MIN-2017-7-EN.pdf.

Oyěwùmí, O. (1997). Colonizing bodies and minds: Gender and colonialism. In *The Invention of Women: Making an African Sense of Western Gender Discourses.* U of Minnesota Press.

———. (2005). *African gender studies: A Reader.* Palgrave Macmillan.

Pareek, R., Sahu, T. N., & Gupta, A. (2023). Gender diversity and corporate sustainability performance: Empirical evidence from India. *Vilakshan-XIMB Journal of Management, 20*(1), 140–153.

Parpart, J. L., & Staudt, K. A. (1989). Women and the State in Africa. In L. Jane and Staudt Parpart (Eds.), *Women and the State in Africa*, pp. 1–22. Lynne Rienner Publishers Inc.

Provasi, R., & Harasheh, M. (2021). Gender diversity and corporate performance: emphasis on sustainability performance. *Corporate Social Responsibility and Environmental Management, 28*(1), 127–137.

Public Private Partnership Act. (2020). *Act 1039.*

Real Estate Agency Act. (2020). *Act 1047.*

Renda, Ezio. (2021). 'Gender equality in boards and companies ten years after the Golfo Mosca Law'. 2021. https://www.knowledge.unibocconi.eu/not izia.php?idArt=23050

Revenga, A., & Shetty Sudhir. n.d. Empowering women is smart economics. *International Monetary Fund (IMF)- Finance and Development* (blog). Accessed 6 February 2023. https://www.imf.org/external/pubs/ft/fandd/2012/03/revenga.htm

Salzmann, O., Ionescu-Somers, A., & Steger, U. (2005). The business case for corporate sustainability: Literature review and research options. *European management journal, 23*(1), 27–36. Elsevier.

Securities Industry Act. (2016). *Act 929.*

Segbefia, Sedem. (2022, February 23). Access bank appoints first female executive director. *The Business & Financial Times* (blog). https://thebftonline.com/2022/02/23/access-bank-appoints-first-female-executive-director/.

Sojo, V. E., Wood, R. E., & Genat, A. E. (2016). Harmful workplace experiences and women's occupational well-being: A meta-analysis. *Psychology of Women Quarterly, 40*(1), 10–40.

Reuters Staff. (2019). Italy aims to boost quotas for women on corporate boards. *Reuters*, 16 December 2019, sec. Aerospace & Defense. https://www.reuters.com/article/italy-women-idUSL8N28Q49S.

Star Assurance Group. (2023). 'Welcome'. 2023. https://www.starassurancegroup.com/.

Suk, Julie. (2017). Discrimination and affirmative action. In *The Routledge Handbook of the Ethics of Discrimination*, 394–406. Routledge.

The Boardroom Africa, Ghana Stock Exchange, and Board Diversity Charter. (2020). 'Board Diversity Index Ghana - Publicly Listed Companies'. https://theboardroomafrica.com/wp-content/uploads/2020/09/2020-Ghana-Listed-Companies_Report.pdf.

The Insurance Act. (2021). *Act 1061.*

Trading Economics. (2023). Ghana—Labor Force, Female—1990–2020 Data | 2021 Forecast. 2023. https://tradingeconomics.com/ghana/labor-force-female-percent-of-total-labor-force-wb-data.html.

Uhlmann, E. L., & Cohen, G. L. (2005). Constructed criteria: Redefining merit to justify discrimination. *Psychological Science, 16*(6), 474–480.

UN Statistics Division. (2006). 'Gender Equality as Smart Economics: A World Bank Group Gender Action Plan 2007–10'. World Bank Publications.

United Nations. (2015). 'Goal 5'. 2015. https://sdgs.un.org/goals/goal5.

———. (2015). 'THE 17 GOALS | Sustainable Development'. 2015. https://sdgs.un.org/goals.

Utting, P. (2008). The struggle for corporate accountability. *Development and Change, 39*(6), 959–975.

'Works, Housing Minister Inaugurates Ghana Real Estate Agency Council Board'. (2021). *CBC Properties* (blog). 10 November 2021. https://cbcghanaltd.com/works-housing-minister-inaugurates-ghana-real-estate-agency-council-board/.

Gender and Sustainability in Africa

Esther Aseidu, Afia Nyarko Boakye, George Kofi Amoako, and Ebenezer Malcalm

1 INTRODUCTION

According to Pandurangarao and Kumar (2016), including gender equality in economic, social, and environmental development programmes can promote human well-being, dignity, ecological integrity, and social justice. The United Nations outcome document clearly shows that achieving gender equality and sustainable development were imperatives (Odera & Mulusa, 2020). It states that we acknowledge that

E. Aseidu (✉) · A. N. Boakye · G. K. Amoako · E. Malcalm
Ghana Communication Technology University, Accra, Ghana
e-mail: easaiedu011@gctu.edu.gh

A. N. Boakye
e-mail: aboakye@gctu.edu.gh

G. K. Amoako
e-mail: gamoako@gctu.edu.gh; gkamoako@gmail.com

E. Malcalm
e-mail: emalcalm@gctu.edu.gh

G. K. Amoako
Durban University of Technology, Durban, South Africa

© The Author(s), under exclusive license to Springer Nature Switzerland AG 2023
S. Adomako et al. (eds.), *Corporate Sustainability in Africa*,
Palgrave Studies in African Leadership,
https://doi.org/10.1007/978-3-031-29273-6_15

319

gender equality and women's empowerment are crucial for sustainable development and our shared future, the statement reads. We reaffirm our dedication to ensuring women's equal rights, access, and opportunities for leadership in the political, social, and economic spheres. We stress the importance of women in achieving sustainable development. We commit to advancing gender equality and women's empowerment as well as ensuring their full and effective participation in sustainable development policies, programmes, and decision-making at all levels because we recognise the leadership role that women can play in society (Odera & Mulusa, 2020).

The literature on the connection between gender equality and sustainability in Africa frequently lacks adequate theoretical and policy direction, methodical accumulation of empirical evidence, and coherence (Bayeh, 2016; Doğan & Kirikkaleli, 2021; Lawal et al., 2016). At the centre of the gender–sustainability nexus debate in Africa is a rethinking of the role of businesses and the problems with underdevelopment in the continent. Studies on women and gender in Africa demonstrate how frequently women's political, social, and economic experiences are vastly different from those of men (Medie, 2022; Oyewumi, 2016). Both feminist and non-feminist academics have highlighted gender as a key component in the explanation of this phenomenon (Medie, 2022). Nevertheless, the concept is used in numerous research, including those that pay attention to economic, social, and political issues. Due to substantial political and social developments, which affect gender norms in African firms, gender relations are malleable (Oyewumi, 2016).

Despite having the highest rate of any continent in the world, African women still face institutional obstacles and social constraints that limit their ability to succeed throughout most of the continent. Female-owned businesses perform worse than their male-owned counterparts, according to an analysis of firm-level data from African nations (Chaudhuri et al., 2020). The performance gap is caused by the combined effect of gendered inequalities (Lemma et al., 2022).

According to Bayeh (2016), gender inequality continues to be a major issue on a global scale, and sustainable development cannot be attained without addressing it. Not only is gender equality a fundamental human right, in addition, but it also constitutes the foundation for a world that is peaceful, productive, and sustainable (Rieckmann, 2017). Of the 17 Sustainable Development Goals (SDGs) contained in the Sustainable Development Agenda, achieving gender parity is the fifth. Contextualising sustainable development is crucial to understand the complex, intersectional role that gender plays in social justice, demographics, and corporate social responsibility. Therefore, the main aim of this chapter is to jointly address gender inequality regarding sustainability in Africa and outline moral, ethical, and practical justifications.

The rest of the section chapter is organised as follows. The following section discussed the various concept of sustainability, where the relevant definitions and theoretical perspectives are reviewed. Discussions of gender inequality in Africa and drivers of gender inequality follow this sector. The next section is the review of inadequate female empowerment as well as the challenges, bottlenecks, and hurdles that currently exist in female empowerment. The chapter ends with a conclusion and some recommendations.

2 The Concept of Sustainability

To comprehend firm-level sustainability, one must consider the literature on the firm's competencies, such as its corporate strategy (Amankwah-Amoah et al., 2019; Roxas et al., 2017). An organisation's actions and policies are determined by its philosophy, concepts, and set of norms known as strategic orientation (SO), which is often regarded as a firm-level ability (Cadogan, 2012; Hakala, 2011). Wide ranges of academic topics have heavily used the idea of strategic orientation (e.g. marketing, entrepreneurship). The concept of sustainability states that present demands must be met without impairing the capacity of future generations to meet their requirements (Crane & Matten, 2010). This translates into adopting a new framework for corporate accountability, such as Elikington's (1997) triple bottom line idea. Instructively, corporations are becoming more aware of the need to create and implement a strategic orientation to pursue the triple bottom line of sustainability, namely economic, social, and environmental (Heikkurinen & Bonnedahl, 2013, Khizar & Iqbal, 2020). Available literature refers to a company's approach to the social and environmental aspects of sustainable development as strategic orientation (Amankwah-Amoah et al., 2019; Roxas & Chadee, 2012). Again, a firm's strategic resource is described as a fluid competency that contributes to competitive advantage and superior firm performance, comparable to other strategic orientations such as entrepreneurial, market, technology, and learning (Claudy et al., 2016).

Building sustainable management of enterprises on the African continent requires a detailed awareness of potential solutions to pervasive inequality, notably gender difference. It is vital to have a discussion on the importance of contextual gender-related issues and how sustainability management is affected. It highlights discrepancies at the conceptual, pragmatic, and linguistic levels between individuals who support gender equality for the sake of sustainable development and those who hold opposite views. Since the UN Sustainable Development Goals (SDGs) were revealed, there has been an upsurge in studies on corporate sustainability and business orientation towards sustainable development (Del Giudice et al., 20.21; Di Vaio et al., 2020). Corporate Social Responsibility (CSR) is a notion that is heavily debated and emphasises social issues while mostly ignoring environmental and economic matters (Alshehhi et al., 2018). The triple bottom line (TBL) approach, particularly involves considering the three main facets of sustainability (economic, social, and environmental) is, however, replacing conventional CSR in literature (Elkington, 2013).

3   THEORETICAL PERSPECTIVES OF GENDER AND SUSTAINABILITY IN AFRICA

Gender and Sustainability are two variables that are interconnected and have been studied extensively in recent years. Theories of gender and sustainability have been developed in order to understand the complexities of gender and sustainability and the ways in which they interact with each other.

The first theory that has been developed to explain gender and sustainability is the gender-ecological intersectionality theory. This theory states that gender is a system of power that is socially constructed and intersects with other social structures such as race, class, and ethnicity (Garcia, 2017). It also states that gender influences the way people interact with their environment and how they perceive and act upon the environment, which can have an effect on sustainability. This theory has been used to explain how gender roles and norms influence how people engage with the environment and how this can lead to unsustainable practices.

The second theory that has been developed to explain gender and sustainability is the gender–sustainability nexus theory (Loftus, 2019). This theory states that gender has an effect on sustainability because it affects the way people think about, use, and protect natural resources.

It also states that gender roles and norms can lead to unequal access to resources and unequal power dynamics that can result in unsustainable practices. This theory has been used to explain how gender-based discrimination and inequality can lead to environmental degradation. Finally, the third theory that has been developed to explain gender and sustainability is the gender–environmental justice theory (Monroe, 2017). This theory states that gender intersects with other social structures such as race and class, which can lead to environmental injustices. It also states that gender roles and norms can lead to unequal access to environmental protection and that this can have an effect on sustainability. This theory has been used to explain how gender discrimination and inequality can lead to unequal access to resources and environmental degradation.

Gender and sustainability are closely interlinked in Africa, with both concepts being rooted in the social and economic development of the continent. This link is based on the theory of gender equality, which posits that women and girls have the right to have access to the same resources as men and boys and should have equal opportunities for economic and social advancement (Kabeer, 2010). This theory is further supported by the idea that gender equality is necessary for long-term economic growth and sustainable development (Kabeer, 2010). In Africa, gender and sustainability are further intertwined by the fact that women are often the most affected by environmental degradation, especially in rural areas (UNEP, 2011). Women are often the primary users of natural resources, such as water, land, and forests, and are therefore, more likely to be affected by environmental degradation (UNEP, 2011). In addition, women are often the primary caretakers of family and community and are thus more likely to be impacted by environmental and social changes (UNEP, 2011). The theory of gender equality is further supported by the theory of human rights, which states that all individuals should have the right to participate in political, economic, and social decision-making processes (Kabeer, 2010). This theory asserts that gender equality is essential for ensuring that all individuals have access to basic human rights, such as the right to education, healthcare, and economic opportunities (Kabeer, 2010). In Africa, gender equality is further supported by the theory of social justice, which states that all individuals should have access to equal opportunities and resources (Kabeer, 2010). This theory is particularly relevant to the concept of sustainable development, as it asserts that all individuals should have access to resources needed for long-term economic growth and sustainable development (Kabeer, 2010).

The theoretical literature on gender and sustainability is growing rapidly, as scholars from various disciplines seek to understand the intersecting and complex relationship between gender and sustainable development. This literature has become increasingly interdisciplinary, as scholars from fields such as anthropology, sociology, economics, geography, psychology, and political science have all contributed to the analysis of gender and sustainability. According to Schiff (2013), this literature has been particularly fruitful in exploring the relationship between gender and sustainability, and in identifying the ways in which gender roles and identities shape, and are shaped by, sustainable development. Scholars have argued that gender is a crucial factor in understanding sustainable development, and that the inclusion of gender perspectives is essential for achieving sustainable development outcomes. For instance, Eckerberg (2017) argues that gender is an important determinant of environmental outcomes, and that gender-inclusive policies can lead to more sustainable development. Similarly, Agarwal (2013) has suggested that gender-sensitive policies are essential for achieving sustainable development, as they can enable more equitable access to resources and empower women to take part in decision-making processes.

The literature has also highlighted the importance of gender in the implementation of sustainability initiatives. For instance, Biermann (2009) contends that women often occupy important roles in the implementation of sustainability initiatives, and can be key actors in the development of sustainable solutions. Furthermore, Femke (2016) has argued that women are often disproportionately affected by environmental change, and can provide valuable insights into the development of sustainable solutions. The literature has also identified a range of gender-specific issues related to sustainability. For instance, Agarwal (2013) highlights the gender-based differences in access to resources and power, which are important considerations in the development of sustainable solutions. Similarly, Riberio (2018) has argued that gender-based violence and discrimination can impede progress towards sustainable development and that policies should address these issues in order to promote sustainability. Finally, the literature has also identified the importance of gender-inclusive approaches to sustainability. For instance, Biermann (2009) has argued that gender-sensitive policies are essential for achieving sustainable development and that initiatives should be designed to ensure that both men and women are included in decision-making processes. Similarly, Femke (2016) has suggested that policies should be tailored to address the specific needs of different genders, in order to promote sustainable development outcomes.

The addition of more females to the board enhances the financial performance of United Kingdom (UK) businesses, according to a study by Brahma et al. (2021). This presents an economic argument in favour of having gender-balanced boards, together with arguments for how it will boost business performance and advance women's equality. Consequently, increasing the number of women in board positions will contribute to long-term sustainable transformation in the workplace, responsible governance, and global marketplace competitiveness.

In conclusion, the literature on gender and sustainability is extensive and growing, and has provided valuable insights into the relationship between gender and sustainable development. Scholars have identified the importance of gender in understanding and achieving sustainable development outcomes, and have suggested that gender-inclusive policies and initiatives are essential for achieving sustainable development outcomes.

Ortner (1972) asserts that feminist scholars have been examining the gendered traits attributed to both men and women since the middle of the 1970s. They have noticed that traditionally, women have been seen as being more in tune with nature. Men, on the other hand, have a history of being more in tune with culture, which is seen to be in charge of nature. Some individuals believe that women act as a link between society and nature. It assumes universality and consistency in perceptions and definitions of nature, culture, females, and males. MacCormack's (1980) claims that women are naturally more attuned to nature than males endured despite extensive criticism. These connections were further developed in environmental studies in the 1980s when views regarding women's innate affinity for nature gained traction in discussions about environmental issues and development. Gender has been disregarded in development discourse for a long time. The women in development (WID) movement attacked conventional development theory in the 1970s by claiming that women were denied access to the resources that enabled the development and called for their increased participation in the process (Ray, 2007).

However, the WID argument, which was vigorously promoted by non-governmental organisations (NGOs) and which portrayed women as having a strong affinity for the environment, replaced the WID argument in the early 1980s because it ignored the complexities of gender relations (Jackson, 1993). These ecofeminist theorists believed that women are biologically more connected to nature than men, and this idea gave rise to stereotypes of women as Mothers of Earth.

As a result, women were perceived as both more likely to be hurt by environmental deterioration and more likely to be in charge of maintaining and conserving the environment. In her critique, Leach (2007) sums up that 'this is a timeless, perhaps even natural role; subsistence, domesticity, and environment are entwined as a female domain; women are victims of environmental degradation (walking ever farther for that wood), but are also environmental careers and key fixers of environmental problems'(p. 69).

Furthermore, the historical oppression of women under patriarchal institutions was connected to the exploitation and degradation of nature. The environment and women were both presented as victims of development. Thus, it was believed that women had a special motivation to stop environmental exploitation because doing so would lead to their freedom (Agarwal, 1992; Mies & Shiva, 1993).

4   Sustainability Issues in Africa

When the growth pattern of the African continent is examined, it becomes clear that it is not sustainable, inclusive, or egalitarian for some main reasons.

Depletion of Africa's Natural and Mineral Resources

First, growth results from overusing Africa's natural and mineral resources. The resources of Africa would be depleted because of this growth strategy, compromising the rights, future, and well-being of succeeding generations because the latter are non-renewable and the majority of the profit is made outside of African nations. Africa accounts for more than half of the world's deforestation, according to data from the International Union of Forest Research Organisations (IUFRO) (Lotz, 2017). The arable land on the continent may also lose two-thirds of its overall area. Evidence that the extractive industries harm the populous is still accumulating, starting with the exploration phase of the mineral commodity and commonly followed by population displacements because of resource extraction (Büscher & Davidov, 2016). Men, who are traditionally regarded as the heads of households, frequently receive pay. Due to the unequal intra-household interactions, women may not always participate in the allocation of resources, which may therefore be used for purposes other than those of the family (Main, 2019). Women's money tends to benefit the family and kids more than men's, who often prioritise their personal preferences, including alcohol.

Environmental Degradation

A significant issue on the continent is environmental degradation. According to Sexton (2020), oil, diamond, and gas drilling are all associated with severe pollution because of the hazardous consequences of the materials used. The radioactive substances produced by uranium mining significantly harm the environment and the public's health (Sexton, 2020). The significant water demand by mining companies has made the water constraints in Africa worse. Water pressure is lower in isolated areas. Estimates show that more than 90% of urban African households in the richest quintile have indoor plumbing and upgraded water sources. Less than 50% of individuals use any form of improved water source for crucial health needs, while the poorest 40% of rural families lack access to piped water (Codjoe et al., 2016).

Only 61% of Sub-Saharan Africa is covered in water, falling short of the region's stated aim of 75% (Mitchell, 2013). Environmental deterioration exacerbates poverty, particularly in rural areas where the disadvantaged rely on the ecological system for subsistence (food, energy, and medicine). Due to water scarcity and deforestation, women and girls must travel long distances to gather firewood and provide food, drink, and energy for their families (Van Huis, 2017). Research suggests that Sub-Saharan African women spend approximately 40 billion hours yearly getting water (Bain et al., 2013). In nations such as Guinea and Malawi, women pay three and eight times more than males for water, respectively. The majority of African families' lack of energy exacerbates the already enormous obligations on women of unpaid caring and environmental degradation (Sarkodie, 2018). According to the Africa Energy Outlook, 2014, up to 730 million people in Sub-Saharan Africa rely on dangerous, inefficient energy sources such as biomass, which hurts their health and the environment by emitting greenhouse gases.

In Sub-Saharan Africa, more than 620 million people live without electricity (Bishoge et al., 2020). A better and more sustainable future for everybody is what the SDGs are meant to be as a 'blueprint'. Only if women and girls are successful will the 2030 Agenda's Sustainable Development Goal number 17, which focuses on enforcing gender equality, be a viable future. The inclusion of gender equality as a target in the 2030 Agenda for Sustainable Development in 2015 was a recognition by the United Nations of the importance of advancing gender equality as well as the requirement of this objective for sustainability (Razavi, 2016). However, due to the COVID-19 epidemic and its disproportionately detrimental effects on women and girls, a 2022 report on SDG 5 (Achieve gender equality and empower all women and girls) reveals regression rather than growth, significantly slipping behind the rest of the world in reaching this objective.

Income Inequality

Another impact of Africa's growth pattern on population well-being is an unequal distribution of income across the continent is the second illustration of how unsustainable it is. Young people, the poor, and women and girls receive a disproportionate part of the continent's economic growth. Women are still mostly restricted to low-paying, dangerous jobs with few career options because of the persistent gender gap in the labour market. According to empirical research, women's presence in non-agricultural paid jobs in Africa has made minimal progress (Akter et al., 2017; Bonner et al., 2018). Women's incomes in many African markets are estimated to be 60–75% lower than men's (Razavi, 2016). Men also significantly outnumber women in a variety of occupations, particularly in management and technical fields, mining and industrial sectors, reflecting the low economic power of African women who do not earn the high earnings associated with these jobs. It has been suggested that women's representation in board and smaller boards as a strategy can help African firms to improve sustainability practices and reporting (Githaiga & Kosgei, 2022).

5   Gender Inequality in Africa

Varieties of development issues in Africa have followed the continent's rapid economic growth and sustainable development, endangering its progress towards structural change (Kazeroony, 2020). It is especially important to address the twin issues of endemic and persistent inequality, particularly gender inequality, and the inherent sustainability of the continent's natural and mineral resources. If a continent like Africa is to achieve the Sustainable Development Goals outlined in the 2030 Agenda for Sustainable Development, gender equality and sustainable development principles are essential. Gender equality and sustainable development must be conceptualised if Africa is to meet the 2030 Agenda for Sustainable Development aim. A greater understanding of the important links between gender equality and sustainable development is critical for the continent's socioeconomic transition to achieve the structural changes required to realise its 2063 goal (Royo et al., 2022).

The African Agenda 2063 will guide the socioeconomic development of Africa (Ndizera et al., 2018). It attempts to speed up existing and ongoing continental growth and sustainable development initiatives. It will also help with the approval of the sustainable development goals that the UN General Assembly endorsed during its session in September 2015 as well as the successful execution of the African Common Position and goals for the post-2015 period. This briefing underscores the strong link between gender equality and sustainable development as part of the 2015 Global Sustainable Development Report (GSDR). If the remaining half of the continent's population is excluded from development processes, sustainable development in Africa and around the world cannot be accomplished or sustained. Africa will move towards equitable, transformative, and sustainable development if women are encouraged to get involved productively in resource management (Holmberg & Sandbrook, 2019). This would help eliminate the resource curse.

Numerous data points indicate a close connection between the main causes of gender inequality and sustainability. The most recent World Survey on the Role of Women in Growth shows that gender imbalance and unsustainable development are caused by inadequate legislation and the pursuit of economic expansion, which are the cornerstones of the current development paradigm. The goal of gender equality is to treat men and women equally in terms of rights, opportunity, and respect. While this does not indicate that men and women are equally valuable over the entire African continent, it does imply that their lives and labour are valued equally.

Gender equality will take numerous forms, depending on local customs and beliefs (Schirch, 2012). These circumstances are continually changing the political and economic challenges that women in Sub-Saharan Africa face. The gender gap in formal education has a long history on the continent as well. This disparity may be caused by sexism, the long-term effects of colonialism, current economic challenges, and other factors (Ako-Nai, 2013). Women, on the other hand, face higher levels of violence during political instability or conflict in patriarchal nations such as the Democratic Republic of the Congo, Rwanda, and Kenya.

Women are said to account for more than 78% of the agricultural labour force in some African regions and 50% of agricultural output in Asia, even though African women face violence and prejudice regularly. According to UN Studies Institute for Social Development research, if women had equal access to agricultural resources as men, production would increase by 20–30%, potentially resulting in a 12–17% reduction in global hunger. Gender is a key aspect of how climate change and environmental degradation affect people. Natural disasters like drought and famine, in addition to fluctuating commodity prices, have such a disproportionately negative impact on women and children.

6 Drivers of Gender Inequality

One of the Sustainable Development Goals set forward by the United Nations is gender equality. Thus, according to experts, it is imperative to eliminate barriers for rural women to advance sustainability, thriving communities, healthy landscapes, and the fight against global warming. Simply put, rural women require the same access to resources, education, and opportunities as males if they are to have a future worth living. A study by Yin and Choi (2022) indicates that a high female labour force participation rate (FLFPR) can help to promote a nation's economic development by increasing labour supply and productivity.

Giving women the same resources as males would help save the planet, as evidenced by a plethora of facts, but several individual women's personal experiences serve as convincing evidence as well. Gender inequality is caused by a variety of factors. However, this book chapter addresses inadequate female empowerment, economic and societal concerns, and a lack of capacity-building arenas as key factors for gender and sustainability in Africa.

Inadequate Female Empowerment

The 2030 Agenda for Sustainable Development was set out to maintain, consolidate, and make the Millennium Development Goals (MDG) 2015 successes more sustainable once they were successfully implemented in 2015. At the United Nations Sustainable Development Summit in September 2015, 193 UN Member States endorsed the new global action plan, 'Transforming Our World: The 2030 Agenda for Sustainable Development'. The 169 Targets and 17 Goals of the 2030 Agenda for Sustainable Development are reducing poverty, protecting the environment, and raising everyone's standard of living are some of its 169 objectives. In addition, it aims to improve social inclusion, lessen climate change, and promote national productivity.

Global developments have not affected all women equally. Kavane (2014) argues that, in some cases, development has led to a widening of the economic and social gap between men and women. It is common for new values to contradict established ones, and this affects how men and women interact with one another (Falola & Amponsah, 2012). Throughout history, both in developed and developing countries, women have not always been treated equally to men in all respects. According to research, women produce 50% of the food and perform 66% of the labour worldwide, but they only own 1% of the property and receive 10% of the income.

The Sustainable Development Goals (SDGs) are designed to act as a 'blueprint' for a more sustainable and prosperous future for everybody. The 2030 Agenda comprises 17 goals for sustainable development. Inequality between men and women, or a lack of security and opportunity for women and girls, has long been a problem in African countries. Concern for the Middle East and North Africa (MENA) economies has grown significantly and widely. In the MENA region, sociological, anthropological, or political approaches are widely used to address gender equality challenges. However, the economic repercussions of inequality are felt. In several African countries, women are not authorised to own property. They also have no right to vote or share their parents' assets. Among other things, women lack the freedom to pick their employment (McGovern & Wallimann, 2012). Female dictatorship has largely passed in several places of the world. MENA has made comparable development to other regions in a multitude of categories related to women's well-being. Women's educational attainment, fertility rates, and life expectancy are just a few pieces of evidence indicating the MENA region has made strides in these areas in recent decades. Indicators of womens political and economic empowerment lag far behind in the Middle East and North Africa (MENA) (Yousef, 2004). Taking into account the region's fertility rates, educational levels, and the age distribution of its female population, the Middle East and North Africa (MENA) have a substantially lower rate of female labour force participation than the rest of the world. It is also lower than expected (McGovern & Wallimann, 2012).

Women's rights in Africa are important indicators of how well the world is doing. Several gender difficulties continue to afflict African women in all parts of their lives, even though the majority of African and other countries adopted a comprehensive international convention on women's rights a few decades ago. Only a few women's empowerment successes can be attributed to the African continent (Dibie & Dibie, 2012). Women frequently make less money despite working greater hours than males, for instance (UN Human Development Index, 2013). Throughout their lives, gender inequality has had an impact on girls and women, and in Sub-Saharan Africa, they frequently experience the highest levels of poverty (Falola & Amponsah, 2012; Smee & Woodroffe, 2013). Despite this, a lot of people outside of the African continent think that women's rights are only a problem in Sub-Saharan African nations where religion is the law, like when Sharia law is in effect (Adomako-Ampofo et al., 2009; Ako-Nai, 2013; Falola & Amponsah, 2012). Consequently, the interaction of law with culture and religion is a crucial factor determining women's empowerment in Africa.

A growing number of Sub-Saharan African nations are debating whether to ratify or effectively implement the treaty in their nation, according to the United Nations Women Treaty (2013) report. All members of society benefit when women are empowered and treated equally, as this advances the causes of child survival and sustainable development. Thus, it is crucial to acknowledge the importance of women's rights and gender equality, especially in light of Africa's current situation. Throughout recorded history, women in Africa have traditionally held lesser status, even though their roles and relationships shift through time and among societies. In addition, there are gendered ethnic groups in many African countries, with men frequently claiming to have greater power, prestige, and wealth than women (Sam-Okere, 2013).

In the same way, that race can be used to categorise and evaluate people, gender is a physical and biological trait. To prepare boys and girls for adult responsibilities and to divide adult employment obligations by gender, African cultures frequently raise boys and girls differently. For instance, in rural locations, men are taught blacksmithing, building, and hunting skills, while women are taught how to increase the availability of vegetables, fruit, and other necessities. Additionally, girls are taught how to maintain their homes (Ako-Nia, 2013; Dibie & Offiong, 2009; Healry, 1998). It is a key priority and item on the work agenda to achieve Sustainable Development Goal (SDG) 5 (Gender equality and empowering women), which has been designated as a requirement for the accomplishment and sustainability of development.

As a result, the empowerment of women in Africa is a key focus for the Egyptian Agency of Partnership for Growth (EAPD), which thinks that women are crucial to the development of African nations. In collaboration with a variety of prestigious centres and organisations, the Agency provided training courses for female participants in this respect. In general, the Agency's programme must have 20% female involvement, and for the current fiscal year, the Agency is trying to increase this percentage. One of the areas of collaborating with the Egyptian National Council for Women to develop and provide training courses exclusively for women from the continent is the Empowerment of African Rural Women in Vocational Education or Small Business. Women in most economies only have around three-fourth of the rights that males do. Studies indicate that if there were greater gender parity in the workplace, it would favourably cascade into other industries that are prone to gender imbalance.

Women had only 24.3% of seats in African national parliaments at the start of 2019. Despite years of improvement in this area, women continue to be underrepresented in politics and administration. As a result, topics like gender-based violence, maternity leave, childcare, pensions, and laws supporting gender equality are frequently overlooked. Female politicians frequently raise these. A World Development Report (2019) study found that more than a billion women are not legally protected from interpersonal, financial, or sexual assault. Both significantly affect how well-off and independent women can be. Furthermore, there aren't frequently legal safeguards against harassment at work, school, or in public. Women are frequently compelled to make choices that compromise and restrict their goals when they lack safety in these risky circumstances.

In Ghana, the Ministry of Gender, Children, and Social Protection promote gender matters. Strategies for decreasing poverty and socioeconomic inequality between men and women, fostering health, and enhancing the efficiency of domestic financing and investments across the public and private sectors encompass gender equality and women's empowerment. Consequently, ensuring gender equality is thought to be crucial to protecting human rights and promoting sustainable development. Ghana's commitments to international accords, the 1992 Constitution, and national development frameworks determine the country's aspirations towards gender equality. In particular, Articles 17(1) and (2) of the 1992 Constitution ensure gender equality and prohibit discrimination based on social or economic status.

Ghana has made significant progress which is reflected in the Human Development Index (HDI) score of 0.558, the Gender Inequality Index (GII) score of 0.565, and the Social Institutions and Gender Index (SIGI), all of which show that the nation is actively promoting gender equality and the empowerment of women, men, girls, and boys (0.262). This policy's main goal is to mainstream issues of gender equality into national development processes by improving Ghanaians' social, legal, civic, political, economic, and sociocultural conditions, especially those of women, girls, children, the weak, and those with special needs, as well as those who are disabled and marginalised.

Despite substantial progress, there are still many areas of society where disparities exist, including those related to access to justice, health, economics, education, security, politics, energy, agricultural practices, and environmental management practices, among others. Patriarchal tendencies that have continually influenced society and the socialisation that people gain from their homes to public settings are linked to these factors, according to assessments.

Ghana's successive governments have made conscious efforts to address the challenges caused by these inequities by promoting girl-child education, social development, and protection initiatives, including the distribution of free school uniforms, free exercise books, skilled training for young women, and access to credit through initiatives like the Livelihood Empowerment against poverty, among others. The government has also enhanced the legal environment by passing laws, such as the Domestic Violence Act of 2007, to vehemently battle gender inequality and advance the welfare of women and girls (Act 732). The elimination of systemic social–cultural norms that limit women's empowerment must engage men and boys. It is obvious that stopping violence against women and girls and improving gender relations in both private and public areas are crucial policy problems.

7 Economic Factors for Gender Inequality

The division of labour exacerbates gender disparities in the workplace. In most civilisations, there is a common belief that men are innately more adequately informed to accomplish specific tasks than women do. These are often the highest paying positions. This discrimination has an impact on women's earnings. One of the things that cause gender inequality at work is the division of labour. There is a widespread belief that men are simply better equipped to perform specific tasks than women. The pay for those positions is often the highest. Women make less money because of this disparity.

As they participate in the paid workforce and perform additional work that is never compensated financially, women also shoulder the majority of the obligation for unpaid labour. The International Monetary Fund's structural adjustment programmes conducted in the 1980s and 1990s resulted in a continuous drop in formal sector employment, particularly in the civil service. As a result, more women were compelled to work in the unorganised sector in order to support their families and themselves (UN Human Development Report, 2013). Political and economic reasons have allegedly made the continent's already severe economic woes worse, according to Sam-Okere (2013). The worst political crises have affected several countries on the continent, including Liberia, Sierra Leone, Nigeria, The Democratic Republic of the Congo, Libya, Tunisia, Egypt, and Zimbabwe (UN Human Development Report) (2013). They have, however, also played a role in the rise of human trafficking, sex trafficking, and brain drain. Problems on the continent have been made worse by political, economic, and globalisation concerns (UN Human Development Report, 2013). As a result of migration and refugee status, the number of poor women in various African countries has increased. Armed conflict has recently murdered women in Africa, including Sudan, South Sudan, Libya, Liberia, Sierra Leone, Eritrea, Ethiopia, Angola, and Mozambique. According to Falola and Amponsah (2012) and Khakpoya (2006), the age group of men is a ubiquitous social component in traditional African communities.

8 Societal Factors for Gender Inequality

The general mentality of a society has a significant impact on gender difference, even though it may not be as visible as some of the other elements on this list. Men and women are valued differently and differently in society in every aspect, including jobs, the legal system, and healthcare. Legislation and institutional improvements can promote equality, but because gender stereotypes are entrenched, opposition often arises when significant changes are made. Additionally, it is simple for both men and women to overlook other examples of gender inequality when progress is made, such as the increased presence of women in leadership roles. These mental models promote gender inequity. Several communities, like the Tiriki ethnic group in Kenya and the Afikpo people in Nigeria, adopt this social organisation model (Ottenberg, 1965; Sangree, 1965). A group of males that are roughly the same age and reside in the same neighbourhood constitutes an age group, according to Khakpoya (2006). They were either born close to one another or they were both admitted into the same act at ceremonies.

9 Capacity-Building Factors for Gender Inequality and Sustainable Development

Gendered meanings, behaviours, and institutions that comprise and shape Africa's socioeconomic structure serve as a driving factor in the development of women's skills. According to scholarly studies and the media, women in Africa have experienced and still experience several injustices. According to Bayer (2016), 'women's rights are not properly being protected for women to participate in various the issues of their country but are subjected to abysmal violations'. The lengthy history of gender-based discrimination has been made worse by cultural connotations, colonial compromises, and a general lack of focused effort to solve the problem. Cases of gender-based discrimination, including rape, servitude, and wife beating, which are commonly reported in the local media, are hardly ever addressed and frequently go unpunished. Abuse of women's human rights and gender-based discrimination, however, has recently gained importance in development programmes as a result of the expansion of social movements on a local and international level. NGOs and the government, via its institutions, are giving gender equality and women's rights more priority on a national scale.

Gender-based discrimination cases, such as wife beating, rape, and servitude, are rarely addressed and frequently go unpunished, despite being widely publicised in the local media. Abuse of women's human rights and gender-based discrimination, however, has recently gained prominence in development programmes as a result of the expansion of social movements both locally and globally. On a national level, non-governmental organisations (NGOs) and the state, through its institutions, are emphasising gender equality and women's rights. The overall lack of gender statistics, according to the 37th Session of the United Nations Statistical Commission (UNSC), is a significant obstacle to the formulation of gender-inclusive plans, policies, and programmes for well-informed decision-making in many countries. A few issues suggested as obstacles to countries' capacities to gather, assess, and disseminate gender statistics include a lack of statistical aptitude, insufficient gender mainstreaming, and inadequate concepts and procedures.

The domestication of Agenda 2063 and the recent capacity-building workshop held by the Africa Union (AU) on Africa's voluntary National Review for the HLPF 2022 represents a significant effort to combat gender inequality and advance sustainable development.

10 PRACTICAL SOLUTIONS TO GENDER INEQUALITY AND SUSTAINABILITY DEVELOPMENT

1. Since women make up the majority of marginalised gender identities, fostering their development is one of our top goals. All genders, whether cisgender or transgender, should be treated equally and inclusively, including the many non-binary farmers and agricultural workers as well as anyone whose gender does not strictly fall into the categories of man or woman. Making farms and companies, more gender inclusive is essential if we want to guarantee that everyone involved in agricultural supply chains has access to equal opportunities and rights.

2. Resolving the underlying causes of gender inequality. By improving their access to school, developing their leadership skills, and increasing their presence in local decision-making bodies, families and community leaders may help women and girls advance their careers. Everyone, not just women, is affected by this, regardless of gender. We collaborate with men, women, young people,

and children to change the systems and practices that perpetuate inequality.

3. Getting back on track to a more egalitarian and sustainable future is by persistently stepping up joint efforts. All actors can contribute significantly by rethinking or bolstering their policies, methods of operation, and sourcing strategies to become more inclusive. We succeed as a community when we cooperate to give women and girls more agency and better chances.

4. Gender relations are founded on power dynamics that are social constructs. They are not static and can and should be exploited to alter Africa's social, economic, and environmental landscape. Because of changing political, economic, social, and cultural situations, gender negotiations continue at the local, national, and worldwide levels.

5. There is an urgent need for enacting laws to abolish cultural practices that discriminate against women. It is important to protect women's rights and realise their full potential, in addition to emphasising the critical role of women in guaranteeing Africa's sustainable development, as stated in various normative documents. It is critical to maintain their right to participate in public resource decision-making and profit from the methods employed to manage economic, social, and environmental policies.

6. The issue of sustainability has been exacerbated by a lack of uniformity in measuring sustainability. Peter et al. (2014) suggest that gender and sustainability should be addressed through:

- *Governance:* Sustainability needs to be dealt with at the corporate level, where management implements steps to ensure responsibility and openness about sustainability rather than just expressing concern on the surface. One of the primary obstacles, according to Dunphy et al. (2007), is guaranteeing accountability while fostering the innovation needed for the growth of a strategy rather than a compliance-based approach to sustainability.

- *Leadership:* Leadership, according to Louw and Venter (2014), is the capacity for strategic thought. They state that to be effective, strategic leaders must cultivate their absorptive capacity—the capacity to learn adaptive capacity, which is the capacity to embrace change, and managerial wisdom the capacity to see inequalities in the environment and take appropriate action. Wilson and Holton (2003) push people to adopt novel working methods while questioning the status quo by being receptive to new ideas. Creating mental representations and constructing cognitive models can help managers think more clearly.

- *Measure and report*: As corporate sustainability is a complicated issue, Searcy (2009) outlines a sustainability performance measurement system (SPMS) to help organisations at the beginning of the process.
- *Culture:* A sustainable vision and sustainable culture initiatives must be supported by and reflected in the prevailing organisational norms, according to Stead and Stead (2004). To address social and environmental issues related to gender and sustainability, organisations must impose a sustainability-centred culture.

11 Conclusion

Africa has a long way to ensure gender sustainability despite government and policy measures. A concerted effort and strong sensitisation are required to curb this menace in the continent and enterprises also can contribute immensely to reducing its prevalence. Any sustainable development must make a clear commitment to gender concerns in the leadership of African businesses and society. The linkages between gender equality and sustainability must be achieved as well as the inevitable tensions and trade-offs between the three elements of sustainability, to achieve sustainable development in Africa.

References

Agarwal, B. (1992). The gender and environment debate: Lessons from India. *Feminist Studies, 18*(1), 119–158.

Agarwal, B. (2013). Gender and sustainable development: Exploring the links. In B. Agarwal & A. Kabeer (Eds.), *Gender and sustainable development* (pp. 1–38). Routledge.

Ako-Nai, R. I. (2013). Western feminist theories. *Gender and power relations in Nigeria, 1.*

Akter, S., Rutsaert, P., Luis, J., Htwe, N. M., San, S. S., Raharjo, B., & Pustika, A. (2017). Women's empowerment and gender equity in agriculture: A different perspective from Southeast Asia. *Food Policy, 69*, 270–279.

Ali, S., Saleem, S., Imran, M., Rizwan, M., Iqbal, K., Qadir, G., & Neubauer, H. (2020). Detection of Brucella antibodies in selected wild animals and avian species in Pakistan. *Indian Journal of Animal Research, 54*(4), 478–481.

Alshehhi, A., Nobanee, H., & Khare, N. (2018). The impact of sustainability practices on corporate financial performance: Literature trends and future research potential. *Sustainability, 10*(2), 494.

Arnfred, S., & Adomako Ampofo, A. (2010). *African feminist politics of knowledge: Tensions, challenges, possibilities.* Nordiska Afrikainstitutet.

Bain, L. E., Awah, P. K., Geraldine, N., Kindong, N. P., Siga, Y., Bernard, N., & Tanjeko, A. T. (2013). Malnutrition in Sub-Saharan Africa: Burden, causes and prospects. *Pan African Medical Journal, 15*(1).

Bayeh, E. (2016). The role of empowering women and achieving gender equality to the sustainable development of Ethiopia. *Pacific Science Review b: Humanities and Social Sciences, 2*(1), 37–42.

Biermann, F. (2009). Gender and Sustainable Development: A Comprehensive Perspective. In M. Betsill & E. Corell (Eds.), *Global Environmental Politics* (pp. 437–459). MIT Press.

Bishoge, O. K., Kombe, G. G., & Mvile, B. N. (2020). Renewable energy for sustainable development in sub-Saharan African countries: Challenges and way forward. *Journal of Renewable and Sustainable Energy, 12*(5), 052702.

Bonner, C., Horn, P., & Jhabvala, R. (2018). Informal women workers open ILO doors through transnational organizing, 1980s–2010s. In *Women's ILO* (pp. 176–201). Brill.

Brahma, S., Boateng, A., & Nwafor, C. (2021). Board Gender Diversity and Firm Performance: The UK evidence. *International Journal of Finance and Economics, 26*(4), 5704–5719.

Büscher, B., & Davidov, V. (2016). Environmentally induced displacements in the ecotourism–extraction nexus. *Area, 48*(2), 161–167.

Cadogan, J. W. (2012). International marketing, strategic orientations and business success: Reflections on the path ahead. *International Marketing Review.*

Chaudhuri, K., Sasidharan, S., & Raj, R. S. N. (2020). Gender, small firm owner-ship, and credit access: Some insights from India. *Small Business Economics, 54*, 1165–1181.

Claudy, M. C., Peterson, M., & andf Pagell, M. (2016). The roles of sustainability orientation and market knowledge competence in new product development success. *Journal of Product Innovation Management, 33*, 72–85.

GENDER AND SUSTAINABILITY IN AFRICA   341

Codjoe, S. N. A., Okutu, D., & Abu, M. (2016). Urban household characteristics and dietary diversity: An analysis of food security in Accra. *Ghana. Food and Nutrition Bulletin, 37*(2), 202–218.

Crane, A., & Matten, D. (2010). *Business ethics: Managing corporate citizenship and sustainability in the age of lobalization* (3rd ed.). Oxford University Press.

Danso, A., Adomako, S., Amankwah-Amoah, J., Owusu-Agyei, S., & Konadu, R. (2019). Environmental sustainability orientation, competitive strategy, and financial performance. *Business Strategy and the Environment, 28*(5), 885–895.

Del Giudice, M., Chierici, R., Mazzucchelli, A., & Fiano, F. (2021). Supply chain management in the era of circular economy: The moderating effect of big data. *The International Journal of Logistics Management, 32*(2), 337–356.

Di Vaio, A., Palladino, R., Hassan, R., & Escobar, O. (2020). Artificial intelligence and business models in the sustainable development goals perspective: A systematic literature review. *Journal of Business Research, 121*, 283–314.

Dibie, R. (2018).Women's empowerment for sustainability in Africa.

Dibie, R. (2019). Chapter one overview of gender issues in Africa. *women's empowerment for sustainability in Africa*, 1.

Dibie, R., and Sam-Okere (2019). Chapter four government, NGOs, performance and women's empowerment in Nigeria. *women's empowerment for sustainability in Africa*, 102.

Doğan, N., & Kirikkaleli, D. (2021). Does gender equality in education matter for environmental sustainability in sub-Saharan Africa? *Environmental Science and Pollution Research, 28*(29), 39853–39865.

Eckerberg, K. (2017). *Gender, Environment and Sustainability*. Edward Elgar Publishing.

Elkington, J. (1997). The triple bottom line. *Environmental Management: Readings and Cases, 2*, 49–66.

Elkington, J. (2013). Enter the triple bottom line. In *The triple bottom line: Does it all add up?* (pp. 1–16). Routledge.

Falola, T., & Amponsah, N. A. (2012). *Women's roles in sub-Saharan Africa*. ABC-CLIO.

Femke, S. (2016). Gender and sustainability: A review of the literature. *Global Environmental Change, 38*, 1–12.

Fineman, M., & Dougherty, T. (Eds.). (2018). *Feminism confronts homo economicus: gender, law, and society*. Cornell University Press.

Garcia, C. (2017). Gender-ecological intersectionality theory: A critical review. *Gender, Place & Culture, 24*(4), 463–480.

Githaiga, P. N., & Kosgei, J. K. (2022). Board characteristics and sustainability reporting. A case of listed firms in East Africa. Corporate Governance: *The International Journal of Business in Society*, (ahead-of-print).

Hakala, H. (2011). Strategic orientations in management literature: Three approaches to understanding the interaction between market, technology, entrepreneurial and learning orientations. *International Journal of Management Reviews, 13*(2), 199–217.

Heikkurinen, P., & Bonnedahl, K. J. (2013). Corporate responsibility for sustainable development: A review and conceptual comparison of the market and stakeholder-oriented strategies. *Journal of Cleaner Production, 43,* 191–198.

Holmberg, J., & Sandbrook, R. (2019). Sustainable development: what is to be done?. In *Policies for a small planet* (pp. 19–38). Routledge.

Jackson, C. (1993). Doing what comes naturally? Women and environment in resources of small manufacturing firms in the Philippines. *Social Responsibility Journal, 8*(2), 208–226.

Kabeer, N. (2010). Gender equality and sustainable development. *Development in Practice, 20*(2), 208–219.

Kazeroony, H. H. (2020). Book review: *The Philosophy of Management Research.*

Keating, P. D. B., & Wilson, D. J. H. 2003. *Managerial economics 2nd ed.(Biztantra).* Dreamtech Press.

Khizar, H. M. U., Iqbal, M. J., Khalid, J., & Adomako, S. (2022). Addressing the conceptualization and measurement challenges of sustainability orientation: A systematic review and research agenda. *Journal of Business Research, 142,* 718–743.

Lawal, F. A., Ayoade, O. E., & Taiwo, A. A. (2016). Promoting gender equality and women's empowerment for sustainable development in Africa.

Leach, (2007). Earth Mother Myths and Other Ecofeminist Fables: How a Strategic Notion Rose and Fell. Development and Change. https://doi.org/10.1111/j.1467-7660.2007.00403

Lemma, T.T., Gwatidzo, T., & Mlilo, M. (2022). Gender differences in business performance: Evidence from Kenya and South Africa. *Small Business Economics*, pp.1–24.

Loftus, A. (2019). Gender and sustainability: A critical review of the gender-sustainability nexus. *Environment and Planning e: Nature and Space, 2*(1), 30–54.

Lotz, C. (2017). The International Union of Forest Research Organizations (IUFRO) and debates about forest-water relations during the late 19th century. *History Research, 7*(1), 1–19.

Lourens, A., Esterhuizen, E., Spoelstra, H., Vos, L., Venter, L., & Coetzee, S. (2014). *InfoForum: 12* (1), June 2014.

Lundahl, M., & Wadensjo, E. 2015. *Unequal treatment (Routledge Revivals): A Study in the Neo-Classical Theory of Discrimination.* Routledge.

MacCormack, C., & Strathern, M. (Eds). (1980). *Nature, culture and gender.* Cambridge

GENDER AND SUSTAINABILITY IN AFRICA   343

Main, G. (2019). Child poverty and subjective well-being: The impact of children's perceptions of fairness and involvement in intra-household sharing. *Children and Youth Services Review, 97*, 49–58.

McGovern, L., & Wallimann, I. (2012). Globalization and third world women.

Medie, P. A. (2022). Introduction: Women, gender, and change in Africa. *African Affairs, 121*(485), e67–e73.

Mies, M., & Shiva, V. (1993). *Ecofeminism.* Fernwood Publication.

Miles, K. (2011). Embedding gender in sustainability reports. *Sustainability Accounting, Management and Policy Journal, 2*(1), 139–146. https://doi.org/10.1108/20408021111162164

Mitchell, S. A. (2013). The status of wetlands, threats and the predicted effect of global climate change: The situation in Sub-Saharan Africa. *Aquatic Sciences, 75*(1), 95–112.

Monroe, C. (2017). Gender and environmental justice: Toward a gender-environmental justice theory. *Gender, Place & Culture, 24*(6), 824–846.

Ndizera, V., & Muzee, H. (2018). A critical review of Agenda 2063: Business as usual? *African Journal of Political Science and International Relations, 12*(8), 142–154.

Odera, J. A., & Mulusa, J. (2020). SDGs, gender equality and women's empowerment: what prospects for delivery. *Sustainable development goals and human rights: springer*, 95–118.

Ortner, S. B. (1972). Is female to male as nature is to culture? *Feminist Studies, 1*(2), 5–31.

Ottenberg, P. (1965). The Afikpo Ibo of Eastern Nigeria. *peoples of Africa.*

Outlook, A. E. (2014). A focus on energy prospects in Sub-Saharan Africa. *International Energy Agency IEA.*

Oyewumi, O. (Ed.). (2016). *African gender studies: A reader.* Springer.

Pandurangarao, J., & Kumar, K. N. (2016). Gender equality and sustainable sevelopment. *PARIDNYA-the MIBM Research Journal, 4*(1), 1–11.

Peter, C., & Swilling, M. (2014). Linking complexity and sustainability theories: Implications for modelling sustainability transitions. *Sustainability, 6*(3), 1594–1622.

Qureshi, S. (2013). The recognition of violence against women as a violation of human rights in the United Nations system. *South Asian Studies (1026–678X), 28*(1).

Ray, I. (2007). Women, water, and development. *Annual Review of Environment and Resources, 32*, 421–449.

Razavi, S. (2016). The 2030 Agenda: Challenges of implementation to attain gender equality and women's rights. *Gender & Development, 24*(1), 25–41.

Riberio, R. (2018). Gender issues and sustainable development. In B. Agarwal and S. A. Kabeer (Eds.), *Gender and Sustainable Development* (pp. 113–128). Routledge.

Rieckmann, M. (2017). *Education for sustainable development goals: Learning objectives.* UNESCO publishing.

Roxas, B., Ashill, N., & Chadee, D. (2017). Effects of entrepreneurial and environmental sustainability orientations on firm performance: A study of small businesses in the Philippines. *Journal of Small Business Management, 55,* 163–178.

Roxas, B., & Chadee, D. (2012). Environmental sustainability orientation and financial resources of small manufacturing firms in the Philippines, *Social Responsibility Journal, 8*(2), 208–226. https://doi.org/10.1108/174711112 11234842

Royo, M. G., Diep, L., Mulligan, J., Mukanga, P., & Parikh, P. (2022). Linking the UN Sustainable Development Goals and African Agenda 2063: Understanding overlaps and gaps between the global goals and continental priorities for Africa. *World Development Sustainability, 1,* 100010.

Sam Okere, J. (2013). Faith-Based NGOs and women empowerment in Nigeria. *Journal of International Politics and Development, 11*(1–2), 73–102.

Sangree, W. (1965). *The Bantu Tiriki of Western Africa.*

Sarkodie, S. A. (2018). The invisible hand and EKC hypothesis: What are the drivers of environmental degradation and pollution in Africa? *Environmental Science and Pollution Research, 25*(22), 21993–22022.

Schiff, M. (2013). Gender and sustainability: A critical review of the literature. *Sustainable Development, 21*(4), 268–277.

Schirch, L., Tabyshalieva, A., & Schnabel, A. (2012). Frameworks for understanding women as victims and peacebuilders. *In Defying victimhood: women and post-conflict peacebuilding,* 48–76.

Searcy, C. (2009). Setting a course in corporate sustainability performance measurement. *Measuring Business Excellence.*

Sexton, R. (2020). Unpacking the local resource curse: How externalities and governance shape social conflict. *Journal of Conflict Resolution, 64*(4), 640–673.

Silagy, C., Lancaster, T., Stead, L. F., Mant, D., & Fowler, G. (2004). Nicotine replacement therapy for smoking cessation. *Cochrane database of systematic reviews,* (3).

Smee, S., & Woodroffe, J. (2013). Achieving gender equality and women's empowerment in the post-2015 framework. *The Gender and Development Network. Retrieved from* http://www.gadnetwork.org.UK

Tracey, S., & Anne, B. (2008). *OECD insights sustainable development linking economy, society, environment: Linking economy, society, environment.* OECD Publishing.

UN Human Development Report (2013). *United nations human development report.* United Nations. UNDP.

UNEP (2011). Gender and environment. https://www.unenvironment.org/explore-topics/gender-and-environment

Van Huis, A. (2017). Cultural significance of termites in sub-Saharan Africa. *Journal of Ethnobiology and Ethnomedicine, 13*(1), 1–12.

Windolph, S. E., Harms, D., & Schaltegger, S. (2014). Motivations for corporate sustainability management: Contrasting survey results and implementation. *Corporate Social Responsibility and Environmental Management, 21*(5), 272–285.

World Bank. (2012). *World development report 2013: Jobs*. The World Bank.

World Development Report. (2019). *The changing nature of work*. World Bank. https://doi.org/10.1596/978-1-4648-1328-3

Yin, Z. H. & Choi, C. H. (2022). The effect of trade on the gender gap in labour markets: The moderating role of information and communication technologies. *Economic Research-Ekonomska Istraživanja*, pp.1–20.

Yousef, T. M. (2004). Development, growth and policy reform in the Middle East and North Africa since 1950. *Journal of Economic Perspectives, 18*(3), 91–116.

Corporate Governance and Sustainability

The Role of Accountability in Corporate Environmental Sustainability Framework

Mfon S. Jeremiah and Kassa Woldesenbet Beta⬤

1 INTRODUCTION

The chapter discusses the environmental sustainability framework which highlights what could prompt stakeholders' demand for environmental accountability system (EAS) and how being environmentally accountable translates into corporate environmentally sustainable behaviour. As the impact of climate change and green gas emissions deepens, many firms in pollution-intensive industries face conflicts and business operation resistance from the host communities in many parts of the world. It is well-documented that the negative impacts of corporate activities trigger community reactions against corporate business operations. For instance, the residents of the district of Kitimat in Northwest British Columbia successfully resisted the Enbridge Northern Gateway pipeline project designed to transport bitumen from Canada's oil sand to the

---

M. S. Jeremiah
Department of Accounting, University of Uyo, Uyo, Nigeria
e-mail: mfon.jerry@gmail.com

K. W. Beta (✉)
De Montfort University, Leicester, England
e-mail: kwoldesenbet@dmu.ac.uk

© The Author(s), under exclusive license to Springer Nature Switzerland AG 2023
S. Adomako et al. (eds.), *Corporate Sustainability in Africa*,
Palgrave Studies in African Leadership,
https://doi.org/10.1007/978-3-031-29273-6_16

west coast for onward export to Asia (Bowles & MacPhail, 2017). The common resistance strategies include, among others, diffusion activities, protests, blockades of project sites and violence (Conde, 2017).

The resistance is an indicator of the stakeholders' perception of real or potential social and environmental risks associated with business operation (Palma-Oliveira et al., 2018; Özkaynak et al., 2021). The resistance threatens corporate environmental legitimacy (Alrazi et al., 2015) and signals stakeholders' demand for a resilient EAS. EAS consists of rules, processes and procedures to mitigate environmental risks of business and improves environmental performance (Carman, 2010). Of course, unmitigated risks and the resultant resistance can negatively impact on the financial performance of firms in the form of a significant business cost (Franks et al., 2014). This is the cost of environmental negligence to business (Jeremiah et al., 2023).

Environmental accountability system (EAS) serves as means of involving stakeholders on environmental issues. It enables a collaborative assessment of observed and potential corporate activities that could generate environmental risks. It acts as a platform for corporations to disclose information on these activities and related environmental performance to the stakeholders. The system allows recording and analysing of stakeholders' reaction to environmental risks, their expectations and demands. Based on this process, a firm can be more environmentally accountable than others in similar industry if it engages with the stakeholders on environmental issues, provides relevant information on activities with environmental impact or if it is more responsive to an environmental legitimacy threats and stakeholders' expectations and demands.

Previous studies identified factors that drive the environmentally sustainable behaviour of firms. These salient factors include regulatory pressure (Christman, 2004; López-Gamero et al., 2010), corporate self-regulatory pressure (Anton et al., 2004; Graham & Woods, 2006), stakeholder pressure (Sarkis et al., 2008; Kassinis & Vafaes, 2006) and environmental visibility (Bowen, 2000). However, these factors do not have equal level of direct impacts on corporate environmental performance in all the industries and all places. For instance, state regulatory pressures have little influence on the environmental behaviour of firms in most less developed countries (LDCs) because of institutional capacity weakness (Graham & Woods, 2006; Strange, 1996; Tsikata, 1997). Corporate self-regulatory pressure is also found to be less effective in driving responsible environmental behaviour of firms in most pollution-intensive industries (Kolk et al., 2002) because many of the codes of conduct are very vague and 'this renders monitoring and sanctions useless if they exist at all' (p. 179).

Some industries are prone to generating significant social and environmental impacts on the host communities than others because of the nature of their business operations. Companies in such industries may exhibit relatively poor performance in terms of sustainability elements such as consumption of natural resources, emissions and health risk of their products or services compared to companies operating in other industries (Epstein & Roy, 2001, p. 590). This makes them environmentally visible, at least, at the operational level (Bowen, 2000). The visibility creates diverse environmental risk perceptions among the stakeholders. This invariably, instigates business resistance, corporate-community conflicts, displacement, distrust and the need for stakeholders' participation in environmental decision-making (Conde & Billon, 2017).

For several decades firms in extractive industries have used various strategies to respond to community reaction to environmental risks of business and legitimacy threats. These include, but are not limited to, public relations strategies (Öge, 2016; Zeithaml & Zeithaml, 1984), counter-reaction, blame-shifting and buck-passing (Ciupa & Zalik, 2020), attention diversion (Idemudia, 2009a, 2009b), covert corporate responses strategy, which is monitoring and containing firm's related environmental issue raised by the stakeholders (Uldam & Hansen, 2017) and defensive communicative strategy (Egbon & Mgbame, 2020). None of these corporate responsive strategies addresses the environmental concern of the affected stakeholders. For example, Shell uses laudable corporate social responsibility (CSR) initiatives such as awarding of scholarships to youths in Niger Delta to divert attention of the host communities, NGOs and the media from the huge environmental pollution associated with their business activities in the region. As argued in Jeremiah et al. (2023), a strategic responsiveness to business resistance that does not address the real problem neither creates a peaceful business environment nor leads to an improvement in corporate environmental performance (CEP). The manipulative approaches that involve distraction and impression management strategies have also failed to genuinely reduce business resistance, improve the environmental condition and the well-being of the host communities in extractive industries (Hooghiemstra, 2000; Ikelegbe, 2005; Johnston & Pongatichat, 2008; Obi, 2000). Such manipulative approach has led to a strained corporate-stakeholder relationship, stakeholder dissatisfaction and conflicts escalation (Edoho, 2008; Fagbohun, 2007; Ikelegbe, 2005; Obi, 2000). So, what alternative approaches and management strategies are available to deal with these pressing social and environmental problems? We draw on the environmental accountability perspective, stakeholder theory and Gidden's (1994) reflexive theory to find potential solution to these problems.

There is no universally accepted definition of environmental accountability. Burritt and Welch (1997) describe it as 'the actions made on behalf of the organisations and the impacts of resulting activities on the ecological systems' (p. 354). For O'Riordan (1989, 141), environmental accountability is 'a metaphor for socially responsible management practice, sanctioned by regular reporting and by demonstrating responsiveness to public interest'. But what roles EAS could play in enforcing environmental obligations is underexplored. Benner et al. (2004) examined this role in terms of global governance in multi-sectoral public policy networks. They concluded that without strong societal backing and involvement, the global governance will remain a failure. de Silva et al. (2020) analysed the role of accountability system on the public sectors environmental performance in Sri Lanka and found the limitations in public sector accountability as one of the main reasons for the mediocre environmental sustainability.

This chapter thus seeks to address the research question: *How does the environmental accountability system enable firms to deal with stakeholders' business resistance because of the firms' observed and potential risks to environment and society?*

Hence, this chapter develops a framework that lays out an informed approach a firm can adopt when responding to the stakeholders' reactions to observed or potential environmental risks of business and how it can improve firms' environmentally sustainable behaviour. The framework provides insight into the factors that trigger stakeholders' demand for environmental accountability system, what makes up such a system and how the system could influence CEP. The framework is important, particularly in less developed countries where the absence of strong regulatory system has invigorated the role of stakeholder in corporate sustainable programme (Boele et al., 2001a, 2001b; Idemudia, 2014). We argue that it is a robust system of environmental accountability embedded in corporate environmental sustainability framework that will sustain the effort of the stakeholders and make engagement strategy worthwhile. The model also portrays how participation concept in EAS could lead to genuine corporate socio-environmental responsiveness.

The remaining chapter is organised as follows. Section two develops and analyses the environmental sustainability system framework based on the relevant literature. Section three applies the developed framework in the context of Nigeria Oil and Gas Industry to show its relevance. The last section makes conclusion and recommendations.

2   ACCOUNTABILITY-BASED CORPORATE ENVIRONMENTAL SUSTAINABILITY FRAMEWORK

The framework draws from the work of Francis Bowen: 'Environmental visibility: a trigger of green organisational response' (Bowen, 2000), stakeholder theory and Giddens' modern reflexivity theory. The chapter thus adopts an integrated approach to develop a model/framework which incorporates factors that could work together to enhance environmental sustainability practices of firms. A system of accountability is a combination of three components of accountability: actors, processes and the outcomes (Benner et al., 2004). The role of the first component (actors) is crucial in any meaningful system of accountability. In terms of EAS the actors are the public, local community, environmental activists or the constituent of environmental stakeholders and the firms. These actors are the public (principal) and the firm (agent) in a simple principal–agent relationship. They form a critical component of a strategic environmental accountability system (Paddock, 2004). The *process* component relates to compliance-based accountability, which is concerned with laying down rules, processes and procedures which guide future performance, while *outcome* component, which is performance-based accountability focuses on the outcomes or results of the past activities (Carman, 2010). These two components can also be viewed as prospective (future) and retrospective (past) accountability (Gray et al., 1996). The former establishes the environmental requirements which firms must comply with, while the latter is concerned with examining and relating firms' actual environmental performance with the established requirements.

Corporate accountability redirects our attention to the question of *corporate environmental obligations* towards stakeholders, the role of public policy, and the imposition of sanctions in cases of non-compliance (Utting, 2008). EAS repositions the affected stakeholders at the centre of every decision concerning environmental issue. Whether in evaluating the environmental risk of prospective business, or setting acceptable environmental standards, or evaluating subsequent corporate environmental performance, or enforcing compliance, stakeholders have vital roles to play. EAS takes accountability beyond a mere abstract to a powerful factor that can drive corporate environmentally sustainable behaviour. Certain factors often drive firm's environmental accountability practice. Some of these are institutional factors and the firm's initiatives (Amoako et al., 2021). That is, firms may intentionally be environmentally accountable to avert certain unpleasant actions from external actors such as regulatory agencies, NGOs and environmental activists.

Stakeholder theory, according to Gray et al. (1996), is an explicit system-based view of organisation and its environment which recognises the dynamic and complex nature of interplay between them. stakeholder theory provides the theoretical support needed to effectively evaluate socio-environmental performance of firms and to understand the relationship between a firm and its stakeholders (Clarkson, 1995; Mitchell et al., 1997; Wood & Jones, 1995). Stakeholders are 'groups and individuals who benefit from or disadvantaged by, and whose rights are violated or respected by, corporate actions' (Evans & Freeman, 1993, p. 254). Freeman (1984, p. 46) broadly defines stakeholders as 'any group or individual who can affect or is affected by the achievement of the organization's objectives. Crucial issues in these definitions are those harmed by the activities of corporations and their tendency to affect the achievement of the corporate objectives. From the environmental perspectives, stakeholders are classified into three major groups: business, society and government (Mutti et al., 2012; Vazquez-Brust et al., 2010). The focus of this chapter is on the society. We draw on the stakeholder theory as it helps to explain the *role of accountability* in the relationship between the stakeholders and the organisation (Gray et al., 1996). Viewing through the lens of the agency theory, the community-firm relationship could be seen as principal–agent relationship (Alrazi et al., 2015). The local community (stakeholder) is the principal, while firm is the agent.

In Bowen's framework, four types of environmental visibility factors are identified: organisational visibility at the corporate level, organisational visibility at the operating level, issue visibility at the operating unit level and issue visibility at the corporate level. His brief qualitative test of this framework suggests a positive relationship between environmental visibility and green organisational response. In the present study, the framework is extended by capturing EAS as an intermediate factor between external factors and organisational socio-environmental responsiveness.

The starting point is Bowen's (2000) organisational visibility from the operating unit level. Most pollution-intensive firms are visible at their operating units. Environmental issues are also visible at this level. This visibility makes firms in pollution-intensive industry to be exposed to external pressure and negative reaction from the native communities (Wakefield et al., 2001). The model (Fig. 1) portrays an interplay of the outcomes of environmental stakeholder behaviour in a typical pollution-intensive industry. The framework explains four basic steps to improve corporate environmental sustainability practices.

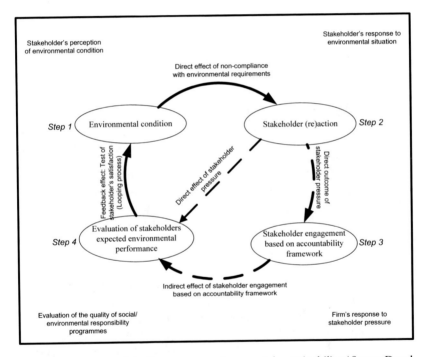

Fig. 1 Four-step model of corporate environmental sustainability (*Source* Developed by the researchers from literature reviewed)

356 M. S. JEREMIAH AND K. W. BETA

- Analyse the environmental condition and the associated risks
- Consider community reactions to business environmental risks
- Adopt an inclusive environmental accountability system
- Evaluate and manage stakeholders' environmental expectations

These four steps are discussed in detail sequentially with reference to Fig. 1.

Analyse the Environmental Condition and the Associated Risks

Firms' environmental friendliness is judged by the condition of the visible environment at the operating unit. Unacceptable environmental condition and the associated risks drive local community (external stakeholder) into taking action against polluting firm (see Fig. 1). Therefore, environmental visibility triggers actions not only from organisations as suggested by Bowen (2000) but also from the affected stakeholders. Such actions are based on the perceived environmental risks associated with business activities. Poor environmental conditions create stakeholders' risk perception, distrust in the corporate socio-environmental programmes and subsequent reactions. Stakeholders often respond to undesired outcomes of continuous environmental degradation and exert pressure for environmental accountability.

The *real* and *speculative* risks of the environmental pollution, most of the times, appear in pages of the media. When this happens, environmental stakeholders, firms, government and the community or society (Eweje, 2007) will be attracted to the scene, and awareness will be raised. The ways in which the risks are perceived, interpreted and investigated by stakeholders may lead them to take actions that result in changes in corporates' environmental policy and practice (Wakefield et al., 2001).

Giddens (1994) opined that stakeholders reaction depends on the reflexively developed awareness of the risks inherent in environmental pollution of an industry and that the stakeholders are likely to take actions that influence corporate environmental behaviour. Giddens (1994) further argues that as technology grows and information about previously unknown risks emerges, the stakeholders will exert new pressure for improved environmental quality.

Giddens' modern reflexivity theory explains the interconnection between reflexivity, risk and trust, which the modern age place on expert systems (Giddens, 1994, p. 83). Expert systems could be broadly defined

THE ROLE OF ACCOUNTABILITY IN CORPORATE ... 357

as any systems which rely upon the specialist knowledge and expertise of individuals for their effective operation (Unerman & O'Dwyer, 2007). These individuals are considered as experts, whereas anyone who has not acquired this expert knowledge and ability is considered as a non-expert. These non-experts, while placing their trust in the operation of expert systems, will expect the risks attributed to failure of such systems to remain within the acceptable boundaries (Giddens, 1990). In a situation where events occur, which *reflexively raise awareness* that the risks associated with the operation of any expert system are beyond the limits of risk considered acceptable, non-expert outsider is likely to withdraw the trust they have implicitly placed in the system (Unerman & O'Dwyer, 2007).

Beyond withdrawal of trust, the stakeholders in such a system will build a vocal and well-organised civil society that demands a firm, to at least, comply with the minimum environmental requirements to improve their environmental performance. Where corporation fails in these obligations, environmental risk awareness is bound to increase and the community will resist and pressure for accountability and improved environmental performance (Fig. 1). To rebuild the trust, the experts representing the stakeholders need to be involved in a viable EAS.

Community Reactions to Business Environmental Risks

Some studies suggest that in the absence of strict environmental regulation and strong enforcement, communities have emerged as informal environmental regulators (Hettige, et al., 1996; Phuong & Mol, 2004; World Bank, 2000). Most often, the affected communities and their alliances initiate actions that could lead to a change in the firm's planned projects and/or environmental behaviour (Wakefield et al., 2001). For example, because of the risk of displacement and pollution, the residents of the district of Kitimat in Northwest British Columbia successfully resisted the Enbridge Northern Gateway pipeline project designed to transport bitumen from Canada's oil sand to the West coast for onward export to Asia (Bowles & MacPhail, 2017; Jeremiah et al., 2023).

The trend of reactions sometimes follows certain stages ranging from tolerance to peaceful protest, outright resistance and insurgency (Jeremiah et al., 2023). Edino et al. (2010) used Ubeji town, a community in Niger Delta, where gas flaring takes place, as a case study to examine people's perceptions on gas flaring. It was found that though the residents perceive gas flaring as hazardous to health, development and general well-being of the community, they resolved to tolerate the flaring and live with it, but some migrated elsewhere. Albert et al. (2018) link people's migration in the region to oil spills as they no longer have cultivable lands.

Adopt an Inclusive Environmental Accountability System

The framework we develop makes the case for adopting an inclusive environmental sustainability system (EAS) as shown in Fig. 2. The model specifies three stages of EAS.

During retrospective accountability, firm reports its environmental performance to the stakeholders, and we call this answerability. Two decisions await stakeholders: either they offer support and trust if satisfied with real positive environmental performance of the firm or engage in resistance and conflict if the firm fails to adhere to environmental obligations.

One of the ways of reducing such conflict is by allowing stakeholders to participate in *prospective accountability* process as shown by double-headed arrows in Fig. 2. Prospective accountability involves defining rules and procedures and employing various means to ensure compliance with these expectations (Jos & Tompkins, 2004) to achieve the desired level of environmental performance/sustainability. Performance of environmental decisions made at this stage will be assessed using environmental auditing subsequently at retrospective accountability stage. At retrospective accountability stage, the compliance is evaluated through environmental audits, investigations and reviews of past performance

Fig. 2 The model of stakeholder's engagement in environmental accountability system (*Source* Developed by the researchers)

THE ROLE OF ACCOUNTABILITY IN CORPORATE ... 359

with aim of establishing whether rules have been broken. Environmental auditing is a key component of a resilient environmental management system (Melnyk et al., 2003). Auditing can lead to imposing punishments for the rules broken and/or deter future non-compliance with a set minimum level of performance; while acceptable level of compliance may attract rewards from the local community in the form of support and trust. This chapter argues that these dual accountability procedures have the tendency to drive environmental sustainability all things being equal.

Basis for Environmental Accountability System
Broadly, the concept of accountability is assumed in every given relationship; however, its demand is determined by the manner in which the economic, social and moral context of that relationship is managed. The demand stems from the existence of an unfavourable condition attributable to person(s') discretionary conducts that violate applicable moral principle in a relationship. Often, there are expectations from parties in any meaningful relationship. The condition upon which the relationship grows should be fair to all parties. The fairness theory holds that where the unfavourable condition exists (i.e., a negative state of events relative to a given frame of reference), and such negative event is due to someone's intentional or discretionary conducts that violate ethical principle of interpersonal conduct in a relationship, then the need for accountability arises (Folger & Cropanzano, 2001). It is natural for an aggrieved person in a relationship to react, no matter how.

As it is shown in Fig. 1, accountability is the function of external stakeholders' reaction to unfavourable environmental condition and corporate social and environmental responsiveness. In other words, unfavourable environmental condition, and environmental risks awareness prompt stakeholders' demand for a system of accountability. Thus, EAS requires stakeholders' involvement on environmental decisions that affect them. Having in place a well-coordinated robust EAS will influence an organisation's responsiveness to environmental issues.

360 M. S. JEREMIAH AND K. W. BETA

Stakeholder's Role in a Resilient EAS

'Stakeholder engagement is understood as practices the organisation undertakes to involve stakeholders in a positive manner in organisational activities' (Greenwood, 2007, p. 318). It allows stakeholders to participate in firm's activities (Greenwood, 2007). Such participation goes beyond the role of a watchdog to active involvement in socio-environmental decision of firms. 'One critical element of a strategic environmental accountability system is public participation in environmental decision-making' (Paddock, 2004, p. 249). Such participation enhances corporate accountability to the stakeholders (Gray et al., 1996). Therefore, *stakeholder participation is an inseparable component* of a system of accountability.

Environmental accountability has two faces, namely: 'accountability for environmental obligations' and 'mechanics of better environmental accountability' (Gray et al., 1996; Schedler, 1999). While the first aspect relates to retrospective *accountability,* the second focuses on the *prospective accountability* (Gray et al., 1996). Retrospective being performance-based accountability focuses on the facts about previous environmental sustainability programmes, while prospective which is compliance-based accountability is concerned with *laying down rules, processes* and *procedures* which could guide future performance (Carman, 2010).

From environmental obligation perspective, neglected environmental responsibility could mean that corporations undermine the terms of their implied social contract with the society. The basic moral and ethical obligations enshrined in such contract are also undermined. The observed deficient corporate social and environmental performance could lead to unpleasant reactions from stakeholders. To address this deficiency, the stakeholders, whose rights are trampled on, are expected to participate in setting prospective accountability procedure. The procedure/ environmental standards start with establishing the expected level of environmental performance. So, participation of stakeholders in decision-making and CSR programmes that help mitigate or ameliorate the environmental and social impact of business is vitally important. Besides, stakeholders should also be involved in monitoring the level of performance to ensure that corporations implement the plans and comply with the set standards. The system makes room for deployment of engagement strategy along with other basic concept of accountability such as answerability and enforceability (Schedler, 1999). It also involves dialoguing with the stakeholders (Gray et al., 2014). The guidance for such dialogue with stakeholders is provided in AccountAbility (1999). AccountAbility sets standards as benchmarks for such engagement and dialogue in AA1000.

In this chapter it is argued that a well-managed organisation will listen to the stakeholders, understand them and respond to their concern as suggested in Gray et al. (2014). The later edition of AccountAbility, which presents *AA1000 Stakeholders Engagement Standard,* emphasises that such engagement should be bound by the principle of materiality, completeness and responsiveness (AccountAbility, 2008). *Materiality* implies understanding the stakeholders' material concerns; *completeness* focus on understanding stakeholder concerns in terms of views, needs, performance expectations and perceptions associated with material issues; while *responsiveness* is concerned with coherently responding to stakeholders' material concerns (Gray et al., 2014). This type of accountability goes beyond the subjective judgement of actions or inactions of organisations. To a considerable extent, it revolves around reengineering of environmental management system to accommodate the views and concerns of the stakeholders. It calls for corporate social and environmental responsiveness that meets the need of the stakeholders. It is therefore proposed that involvement of stakeholders in a system of accountability will likely improve environmental performance to the satisfaction of the stakeholders.

Indeed, in environmental management decision-making, engagement strategy is increasingly encouraged from local to international scales (Stringer et al., 2007). However, in practice, the strategy fails because it is primarily corporate driven (Idemudia, 2009a). Although many benefits have been claimed for engagement with stakeholders, disillusionment has grown among practitioners and stakeholders who often felt let down when these claims are not realised (Reed, 2008).

Consequently, the need for a new kind of engagement has emerged. This includes the need to embed engagement in a broader concept of EAS. Since accountability is an *instrument* used in assessing responsibility (Crane & Matten, 2007), engagement is an honest means of inviting stakeholders for assessment of corporate social and environmental responsibility. Whenever organisation invites the affected stakeholders to participate in the process of finding solution to social and environmental problems created by the organisation, the indication is that the organisation is willing to be transparent and accountable. In that case, responsible engagement strategy helps firms to achieve their accountability to stakeholders, build trust and improve environmental sustainability.

The Strength and Limitation of a System of Accountability

The notion of 'accountability envisages the relationship between an organisation and the society in a principal-agent setting' (Alrazi et al., 2015, p. 45). But the principal–agent framework does not guarantee effective operation of system of corporate environmental accountability. Its main limitation is asymmetries of power relationship between the principal and the agent (Eisenhardt, 1989) that could distort information rights (Parker, 2005). An agent may opt giving out to the principal a kind of information that safeguards its interest.

Corporations play the role of an agent in a corporate–stakeholder relationship (Alrazi et al., 2015). In such a relationship, environmental accountability can be seen as 'a metaphor for socially responsible management practice, sanctioned by regular reporting and by demonstrating responsiveness to public interest' (O'Riordan, 1989, p. 141). A stakeholder is the principal; therefore, corporations as agents are responsible to disclose to them information on issues that affect them. We argue that the report made by an agent (corporation) is not always in the interest of the principal (stakeholder). Of course, agents often build various forms of operational structures to undermine accountability and transparency in such reports (Agyenim-Boateng et al., 2017). This informs the need for stakeholder engagement in firms' issues that concern them, rather than waiting for undermined reports.

In the context of stakeholder management, information asymmetry may explain the conflicts of interest, strategic organisational behaviour and the need for regulatory agencies to police such behaviour (Swift, 2001). Stakeholders need information to take informed decisions; however, information, or access to it, is a proxy for power (Swift, 2001). Multinational corporations possess such enormous power, which they often use in manipulating stakeholders' interest away from issues of material concern (Frynas, 2012; Idemudia, 2009b).

This chapter argues that although a system of accountability could not remove power imbalance, it attempts to redress it by institutionalising legal rights to information in a democratic and participative society (Gray et al., 1997). The most obvious manifestation of these rights can be found in statute laws (e.g., companies' acts, equal opportunities legislation) and standards established by statutory bodies (e.g., an environmental protection agency, health and safety at work inspectorate). Stakeholders can draw on these foundations to demand environmental accountability and resist corporate projects that would deny them these rights (Bowles &

MacPhail, 2017). Their right to resist business projects that could create social and environmental damage is captured in the concept of enforceability embedded in a system of accountability (Schedler, 1999). Peaceful protest is the most acceptable enforceability weapon in the hand of the stakeholder. Corporations, on the other hand, could willingly engage the stakeholders in a robust system of accountability and thus reduce the resistance, which could translate into huge business costs (Franks et al., 2014).

Evaluate and Manage Stakeholders' Environmental Expectations

In the fourth stage, corporates are expected to respond positively to business pollution threats and stakeholders' reaction to it (Schwartz & Carroll, 2003). From instrumental perspective of stakeholder theory, firms would do something to avoid stakeholders' actions that could threaten their legitimacy, business performance and reputation. One of the ways firms could respond positively to stakeholder's demand for accountability, as mentioned earlier, is through engagement with them in a resilient EAS.

Specifically, improvement in environmental conduct is often expected when external stakeholders demonstrate their dissatisfaction on firms' level of pollution. Stakeholders should be able to evaluate the extent to which the proposed change in the environmental management system and the improvement in the environmental sustainability indicators are achieved. Improvement could be observed in firms' *commitment* to the physical environmental sustainability management strategies of pollution prevention, product stewardship, and sustainable development (Hart, 1995). Strategies of managing legitimacy threats due to non-compliance with environmental obligations and project resistance differ from *distraction* and *impression* management strategies (Jenkins, 2004, p. 30) such as:

- informing stakeholders about intended improvements in performance
- seeking to change stakeholders' perceptions of the event
- distracting attention away from the issue, and
- changing external expectations about its performance.

Specifically, commitment demonstrates corporate practical concern with environmental wellbeing of a wider constituent of stakeholders. They need to demonstrate this concern by 'integrating the "voice of environment," that is, external stakeholder perspectives, into product design and development processes' (Hart, 1995, p. 993). Firms should proactively engage with stakeholders' social and environmental concern and satisfy them by developing appropriate environmental management strategies and, social and environmental programmes. Involvement of stakeholders in social and environmental decision-making, performance monitoring, outcome evaluation and sanction of unacceptable performance are likely to compel firms to engage in CSR programmes that help in improving environmental conditions and mitigating firms' negative social impacts.

3 Applying the Framework to the Context of Nigeria's Oil and Gas Industry

In Nigeria, the impacts of oil and gas activities on the locals can be observed at all levels of operation (i.e., from exploration through production to distribution). For instance, on-the-surface oil pipelines that traverse residential areas and gas flares in Okirika, Rivers State, make the industry environmentally visible and risky. Asides, abandoned corrosion-damaged facility sites (e.g., Bomu Flow Station in Gokana) and mass acres of land damaged by oil spills in Sivibilagbara swamp in Ogoni, Rivers State, are visible negative outcomes of oil production in the Niger Delta.

The impact of oil spills is always tremendous (Eweje, 2006). In 2004, the pipeline of Nigerian Liquefied Natural Gas traversing Kala-Akama, Okirika mangrove forest leaked and got ablaze. The fire burnt ceaselessly for three days (Kadafa, 2012) and there was no timely response to the incident by any organisation. The vegetation and wildlife perished, and air was seriously polluted. On 8 October 1998, the ruptured Jesse pipeline explosion took away over one thousand lives (Aroh et al., 2010). Apart from those that died, soil, water, air, ecosystem and human health were also affected.

The impact on the economic life of poor subsistence farmers is also substantial. Whenever major oil spills occur, oil flows many kilometres through various communities for several days. The harvestable crops will be destroyed. Sometimes it takes several years for oil firms to clean up the oil if they do. For instance, the Bodo oil spills of 2008 and 2009 were not dealt with even up to 2014 when authors were on field work. The

THE ROLE OF ACCOUNTABILITY IN CORPORATE ... 365

result was that subsistence farmers who depend on farm produce for their livelihood are terribly impoverished (Babatunde, 2010; Osaghae, 1995).

The spills on creeks and rivers have similar devastating effects on fishermen and fishing occupation. Majority of those living in the creeks engage in fishing business. When there is oil spill, their fishing occupation is negatively affected. A 78-year-old fisherman, an indigene of Kalaba in Bayelsa state, told BBC reporter that 'whenever their creeks are polluted the result is hunger' (BBC, 2013). This demonstrates that even the uneducated natives are aware of the risk of environmental pollution, at least to a reasonable extent.

Drinkable water in most oil producing communities in Niger Delta is polluted (Fagbohun, 2007). UNEP (2011) states that the presence of mere traces of a highly toxic hydrocarbon, such as *benzene*, in water may render it harmful for human consumption; however some communities still use this contaminated water supply for lack of alternatives (Fagbohun, 2007). WHO (2010) reports that human exposure to *benzene* has been associated with a range of acute and long-term adverse health effects and diseases, including cancer and aplastic anaemia. Apart from oil spills, Nigeria is rated high in gas flare, which has polluted the air (Emoyan et al., 2008). Global warming, destruction of natural species and acid rain and its impact on human health and corrugated roofing sheets are reported as the most common effects of gas flare (Ekpoh & Obia, 2010).

As Bowen (2000) argues, observable social and environmental issues related to industry can trigger actions that could lead to corporate improvement in environmental behaviour. These actions can be taken by any group of environmental stakeholders (government, civil society, or business). For example, from the days of Ken Saro-Wiwa (leader of Movement for the Survival of the Ogoni People (MOSOP) till today certain actions are taken against unacceptable level of oil pollution in Niger Delta communities. Ken was the environmental activist who was hung along with eight others for organising mass protest over Shell's environmental pollution in Ogonland. Apart from MOSOP, several other movements and NGOs have sprung up in the past two decades. The recent one is Niger Delta Avengers (NDA), which came up in 2016, years after President Umaru Yar'Adua granted Niger Delta Militants amnesty in 2009.

The declared common objective of these organisations is to bring a change in oil multinationals' environmental behaviour in Niger Delta (Ikelegbe, 2005; Idemudia, 2012). Over the years, they have raised challenging environmental-related issues. They have demonstrated their grievances through protest, denial of oil company workers access to production facilities and challenging oil companies in the court of law (Babatunde, 2010; Edoho, 2008; Fagbohun, 2007; Ikelegbe, 2005; Obi, 2000).

Previous studies with evidence from Niger Delta region of Nigeria attribute poor physical environment to the activities of oil and gas industry (Eweje, 2006; Frynas, 2001, 2012). It is the poor environmental condition that shows oil companies non-compliance with environmental standards in Nigeria. The *fairness theory* holds that where the unfavourable condition exists (i.e., a negative state of events relative to a given frame of reference), and such negative event is due to someone's volitional or discretionary conducts that violate ethical principle of interpersonal conduct, then the need for accountability arises (Folger & Cropanzano, 2001). In other words, demand for accountability strategy follows closely the existence of an *unfavourable condition* that is *attributable* to person(s') discretionary conducts that *violate* applicable moral principle.

Viewing the deplorable condition of Niger Delta environment in the lens of fairness theory, indicates existence of these three basic prerequisite assumptions that precede the need for a system of environmental accountability. The voice of the people of Niger Delta has echoed the *unfavourable condition* of environment to the international community (Babatunde, 2010; Edoho, 2008; Fagbohun, 2007; Ikelegbe, 2005). Poor pipeline integrity also demonstrates *discretionary conducts* of oil multinationals that *violate* sound environmental moral behaviour of their managers. Therefore, the need for EAS that involves the affected stakeholders emerges. Poor 'pipeline integrity' portrays this lack of accountability. The best practice considers the integrity of pipelines as crucial. Pipeline integrity connotes the concepts of failure prevention, inspection and repair. This study argues that a resilient system of accountability could lead to improvement in environmental performance.

4   Conclusion

The chapter discussed the middle-level role of accountability in enhancing corporate response to social and environmental concern of stakeholders. The chapter offers a new insight into the ongoing debate on the role of accountability in boosting corporate environmental performance. The models indicate what instigates stakeholders' demand for accountability. It further illustrates the possibilities of a careful implementation of a sound system of accountability.

As the knowledge of the impact of climate change and green gas emission deepens, many firms in pollution-intensive industries are facing fierce business resistance from the host communities in many parts of the world. The framework provides means of predicting such resistance. It lays out the more informed steps that organisations follow to reduce such resistance, and thus, achieve their business objectives.

The framework begins with stakeholder engagement in a robust system of accountability. The system captures past performance, and it also lays down the minimum environmental standards organisation should comply with. That is, the framework highlights the possibilities of retrospective and prospective accountability. While retrospective focuses on information about past performance, prospective is concerned with plans about the future physical environment and how the plans will be achieved. The framework portrays crucial role of stakeholders in achieving the desired level of environmental sustainability. The argument is that in a normal environmental accountability system, stakeholders are expected to participate in making decisions on environmental issues that affect them, monitoring compliance with the environmental standards and participating in enforcing compliance with the standards.

Thus, corporate responsiveness to social and environmental issues under accountability procedure will be greater than under traditional voluntarily approach. More importantly, stakeholders' participation in accountability procedures will likely increase the level of their trust in corporation and satisfaction with corporate environmental sustainability policies and practices, even when all the planned objectives are not achieved. The quality of social and environmental impact information disclosure will be better under this kind of accountability procedure. This framework is tested empirically in the next study.

In terms of contribution, the framework provides fresh insight into variety of actors, processes, behaviours and actions that help achieving environmental sustainability. It sets out the mechanism that aids delivery of mutually beneficial social and environmental sustainability outcomes. It lays out a roadmap for researchers who are interested in investigating corporate environmental sustainability practices, particularly in the context of business resistance and weakness in regulatory institutions.

The practical implication revolves around escalating cases of business resistance and the conflicts between host communities and corporations over social and environmental issues. It provides the means to investigate the outcome of such resistance, and the extent to which stakeholder engagement in a robust system of accountability could lead to improved corporate social and environmental responsiveness. It also provides the means of analysing viable outcomes of environmental management system to deal with environmental issues knowing that non-compliance could lead to series of actions from the affected stakeholders. Further studies could be conducted to assess these hypothetical relationships in various contexts.

References

Aaron, K. K., & Patrick, J. M. (2013). Corporate social responsibility patterns and conflicts in Nigeria's oil-rich region. *International Area Studies Review, 16*(4), 341–356.

AccountAbility. (1999). *Accountability 1000: The Foundation Standard—An Overview*. AccountAbility.

AccountAbility. (2008). *Accountability 1000: AccountAbility Principles Standard*. AccountAbility.

Agyenim-Boateng, C., Stafford, A., & Stapleton, P. (2017). The role of structure in manipulating PPP accountability. *Accounting, Auditing & Accountability Journal, 30*(1).

Alrazi, B., de Villiers, C., & van Staden, C. J. (2015). A comprehensive literature review on, and the construction of a framework for, environmental legitimacy, accountability, and proactivity. *Journal of Cleaner Production, 102*, 44–57.

Amoako, G. K., Adam, A. M., Arthur, C. L., & Tackie, G. (2021). Institutional isomorphism, environmental management accounting and environmental accountability: A review. *Environment, Development and Sustainability, 23*(8), 11201–11216.

Anton, W. R. Q., Deltas, G., & Khanna, M. (2004). Incentives for environmental self-regulation and implications for environmental performance. *Journal of Environmental Economics and Management, 48*(1), 632–654.

Babatunde, A. (2010). The Impact of oil exploitation on the socioeconomic life of the Ilaje Ugbo people of Ondo State, Nigeria. *Journal of Sustainable Development in Africa, 2*(5).

BBC (2014). *Shell 'Warned Nigeria pipeline could leak before spills'* https://www.bbc.co.uk/news/business. Accessed on 13th November 2014.

Benner, T., Reinicke, W. H., & Witte, J. M. (2004). Multisectoral networks in global governance: Towards a pluralistic system of accountability 1. *Government Andopposition, 39*(2), 191–210.

Boele, R., Fabig, H., & Wheeler, D. (2001b). Shell, Nigeria and the Ogoni. A study in unsustainable development: II. Corporate social responsibility and 'stakeholder management' versus a rights-based approach to sustainable development. *Sustainable Development, 9*(3), 121–135.

Boele, R., Fabig, H., & Wheeler, D. (2001a). Shell, Nigeria and the Ogoni. A study in unsustainable development I: The story of shell, Nigeria and the Ogoni people environment, economy, relationships: Conflicts and prospect for resolution. *Sustainable Development, 9*, 74–86.

Bowen, F. E. (2000). Environmental visibility: A trigger of green organizational response? *Business Strategy and the Environment, 9*(2), 92.

Bowles, P., & MacPhail, F. (2017). The town that said "No" to the Enbridge Northern Gateway pipeline: The Kitimat plebiscite of 2014. *The Extractive Industries and Society, 4*(1), 15–23.

Burritt, R. L., & Welch, S. (1997). Accountability for environmental performance of the Australian Commonwealth public sector. *Accounting, Auditing & Accountability Journal, 10*(4), 532–561.

Carman, J. G. (2010). The accountability movement: What is wrong with this theory of change? *Nonprofit and Voluntary Sector Quarterly, 39*(2), 256–274.

Christman, P. (2004). Multinational companies and the natural environment: Determinants of global environmental policy. *Academy of Management Journal, 47*(5), 747–760.

Ciupa, K., & Zalik, A. (2020). Enhancing corporate standing, shifting blame: An examination of Canada's Extractive Sector Transparency Measures Act. *The Extractive Industriesand Society, 7*(3), 826–834.

Clarkson, M. E. (1995). A stakeholder framework for analyzing and evaluating corporate social performance. *Academy of Management Review, 20*(1), 92–117.

Conde, M. (2017). Resistance to ming: A review. *Ecological Economics, 132*, 80–90.

Conde, M., & Le Billon, P. (2017). Why do some communities resist mining projects while others do not? *The Extractive Industries and Society, 4*(3), 681–697.

Crane, A., & Matten, D. (2007). *Business Ethics* (2nd ed.). Oxford University Press Inc.

Edino, M. O., Nsofor, G. N., & Bombom, L. S. (2010). Perceptions and attitudes towards gas flaring in the Niger Delta, Nigeria. *The Environmentalist, 30*(1), 67–75.

Edoho, F. M. (2008). Oil transnational corporations: Corporate social responsibility and environmental sustainability. *Corporate Social Responsibility and Environmental Management, 15*(4), 210–222.

Egbon, O., & Mgbame, C. O. (2020). Examining the accounts of oil spills crises in Nigeria through sensegiving and defensive behaviours. *Accounting, Auditing & Accountability Journal, 33*(8), 2053–2076.

Eisenhardt, K. M. (1989). Agency theory: An assessment and review. *Academy of Management Review, 14*(1), 57–74.

Ekpoh, I. J., & Obia, A. E. (2010). The role of gas flaring in the rapid corrosion of zinc roofs in the Niger Delta Region of Nigeria. *The Environmentalist, 30*(4), 347–352.

Emoyan, O. O., Akpoborie, I. A., & Akporhonore, E. E. (2008). The oil and gas industry and the Niger Delta: Implications for the environment. *Journal of Applied Sciences and Environmental Management, 12*(3), 29–37.

Epstein, M. J., & Roy, M. J. (2001). Sustainability in action: Identifying and measuring the key performance drivers. *Long Range Planning, 34*(5), 585–604.

Eweje, G. (2006). Environmental costs and responsibilities resulting from oil exploitation in developing countries: The case of the Niger Delta of Nigeria. *Journal of Business Ethics., 69*, 27–56.

Eweje, G. (2007). Multinational oil companies' CSR initiatives in Nigeria: The scepticism of stakeholders in host communities. *Managerial Law, 49*(5/6), 218–315.

Fagbohun, O. (2007). Imperatives of environmental restoration due to oil pollution in Nigeria. *The. Stellenbosch l. Rev., 18*, 347.

Folger, R., & Cropanzano, R. (2001). Fairness theory: Justice as accountability. *Advances in Organizational Justice, 1*, 1–55.

Franks, D. M., Davis, R., Bebbington, A. J., Ali, S. H., Kemp, D., & Scurrah, M. (2014). Conflict translates environmental and social risk into business costs. *Proceedings of the National Academy of Sciences, 111*(21), 7576–7581.

Freeman, R. E. (1984). *Strategic management: A stakeholder approach.* Pitman.

Frynas, J. G. (2001). Corporate and state responses to anti-oil protests in the Niger Delta. *African Affairs, 100*(398), 27–54.

Frynas, J. G. (2012). Corporate social responsibility or government regulation? Evidence on oil spill prevention. *Ecology and Society, 17*(4), 4.

Giddens, A. (1994). Living in a post-traditional society. In U. Beck, A. Giddens, & S. Lash (Eds.), *Reflexive modernization: Politics, tradition and aesthetics in the modern social order* (pp. 56–109). Polity Press.

Graham, D., & Woods, N. (2006). Making corporate self-regulation effective in developing countries. *World Development, 34*(5), 868–883.

THE ROLE OF ACCOUNTABILITY IN CORPORATE ... 371

Gray, R., Adams, C., & Owen, D. (2014). *Accountability, social responsibility and sustainability: Accounting for society and the environment.* London: Pearson Higher Ed.

Gray, R., Dey, C., Owen, D., Evans, R., & Zadek, S. (1997). Struggling with the praxis ofsocial accounting: Stakeholders, accountability, audits and procedures. *Accounting, Auditing & Accountability Journal, 10*(3), 325–364.

Gray, R., Owen, D., & Adams, C. (1996). *Accounting & Accountability: Changes and Challenges in Corporate Social and Environmental Reporting.* Prentice Hall.

Greenwood, M. (2007). Stakeholder engagement: Beyond the myth of corporate responsibility. *Journal of Business Ethics, 74*(4), 315–327.

Hart, S. L. (1995). A natural-resource-based view of the firm. *Academy of Management Review, 20*(4), 986–1014.

Hettige, H., Huq, M., Pargal, S., & Wheeler, D. (1996). Determinants of pollution abatement in developing countries: Evidence from South and Southeast Asia. *World Development, 24*(12), 1891–1904.

Hooghiemstra, R. (2000). Corporate communication and impression management–new perspectives why companies engage in corporate social reporting. *Journal of Business Ethics, 27*(1), 55–68.

Idemudia, U. (2009a). Assessing corporate–community involvement strategies in the Nigerian oil industry: An empirical analysis. *Resources Policy, 34*(3), 133–141.

Idemudia, U. (2009b). Oil extraction and poverty reduction in the Niger Delta: A critical examination of partnership initiatives. *Journal of Business Ethics, 90*(1), 91–116.

Ikelegbe, A. (2005). The Economy of conflict in oil rich Niger Delta region of Nigeria. *Nordic of African Studies, 14*(2), 208–234.

Jenkins, H. (2004). Corporate social responsibility and the mining industry: Conflicts and constructs. *Corporate Social Responsibility and Environmental Management, 11*(1), 23–34.

Jeremiah, M. S., Woldesenbet Beta, K., & Etim, R. S. (2023). Issue-based environmental sustainability factors in Nigeria's oil and gas industry: The perspectives of academics. *Critical Perspectives on International Business, 19*(1), 113–151.

Johnston, R., & Pongatichat, P. (2008). Managing the tension between performancemeasurement and strategy: Coping strategies. *International Journal of Operations & Production Management, 28*(10), 941–967.

Jos, P. H., & Tompkins, M. E. (2004). The accountability paradox in an age of reinvention the perennial problem of preserving character and judgment. *Administration & Society, 36*(3), 255–281.

Kassinis, G., & Vafeas, N. (2006). Stakeholder pressures and environmental performance. *Academy of Management Journal, 49*(1), 145–159.

Kolk, A., & Mauser, A. (2002). The evolution of environmental management: From stagemodels to performance evaluation. *Business Strategy and the Environment, 11*(1), 1431.

López-Gamero, M. D., Molina-Azorín, J. F., & Claver-Cortés, E. (2010). The potential of environmental regulation to change managerial perception, environmentalmanagement, competitiveness and financial performance. *Journal of CleanerProduction, 18*(10), 963–974.

Melnyk, S. A., Sroufe, R. P., & Calantone, R. (2003). Assessing the impact of environmental management systems on corporate and environmental performance. *Journal of Operations Management, 21*(3), 329–351.

Mitchell, R. K., Agle, B. R., & Wood, D. J. (1997). Toward a theory of stakeholder identification and salience: Defining the principle of who and what really counts. *Academy of Management Review, 22*(4), 853–886.

Mutti, D., Yakovleva, N., Vazquez-Brust, D., & Di Marco, M. H. (2012). Corporate social responsibility in the mining industry: Perspectives from stakeholder groups in Argentina. *Resources Policy, 37*(2), 212–222.

Obi, C. I. (2000). Globalisation and local resistance: The case of Shell versus the Ogoni. In *Globalisation and the politics of resistance* (pp. 280–294). Palgrave Macmillan UK

Öge, K. (2016). Which transparency matters? Compliance with anti-corruption efforts in extractive industries. *Resources Policy, 49*, 41–50.

Ogunmokun, O. C., Mafimisebi, O., & Obembe, D. (2022). Bank lending behaviour and small enterprise debt financing. *Journal of Entrepreneurship in Emerging Economies*. https://doi.org/10.1108/JEEE-02-2022-0043

O'Riordan, T. (1989). Electricity privatization and environmental accountability. *Energy Policy, 17*(2), 141–148.

Osaghae, E. E. (1995). The Ogoni uprising: Oil politics, minority agitation and the future of the Nigerian state. *African Affairs, 94*(376), 325–344.

Özkaynak, B., Rodriguez-Labajos, B., & Erus, B. (2021). Understanding activist perceptions of environmental justice success in mining resistance movements. *The Extractive Industries and Society, 8*(1), 413–422.

Paddock, L. C. (2004). Environmental accountability and public involvement. *Pace Environmental Law Review, 21*(243).

Palma-Oliveira, J. M., Trump, B. D., Wood, M. D., & Linkov, I. (2018). Community-driven hypothesis testing: A solution for the tragedy of the anticommons. *Risk Analysis, 38*(3), 620–634.

Parker, L. D. (2005). Social and environmental accountability research: A view from the commentary box. *Accounting, Auditing & Accountability Journal, 18*(6), 842–860.

THE ROLE OF ACCOUNTABILITY IN CORPORATE ... 373

Phuong, P. T., & Mol, A. P. (2004). Communities as informal regulators: New arrangements in industrial pollution control in Viet Nam. *Journal of Risk Research, 7*(4), 431–444.

Reed, M. S. (2008). Stakeholder participation for environmental management: A literaturereview. *Biological Conservation, 141*(10), 2417–2431.

Sarkis, J., Gonzalez-Torre, P., & Adenso-Diaz, B. (2010). Stakeholder pressure and the adoption of environmental practices: The mediating effect of training. *Journal of Operations Management, 28*(2), 163–176.

Schedler, A. (1999). Conceptualising accountability. In A. Schedler, L. Diamond, & M. F. Platter (Eds.), *The Self-Restraining State: Power and accountability in new democracies* (pp. 13–28). Lynne Reinner Publishers.

Schwartz, M. S., & Carroll, A. B. (2003). Corporate social responsibility: A three-domain approach. *Business Ethics Quarterly, 13*(04), 503–530.

Strange, S. (1996). *The retreat of the state: The diffusion of power in the world economy*. Cambridge University Press.

Stringer, L. C., Reed, M. S., Dougill, A. J., Rokitzki, M., & Seely, M. (2007). Enhancing participation in the implementation of the United Nations Convention to Combat Desertification. In *Natural Resources Forum* (Vol. 31, pp. 198–211).

Swift, T. (2001). Trust, reputation and corporate accountability to stakeholders. *Business Ethics: A European Review, 10*(1), 16–26.

Tsikata, F. S. (1997). The vicissitudes of mineral policy in Ghana. *Resources Policy, 23*(1–2), 9–14.

Uldam, J., & Hansen, H. K. (2017). Corporate responses to stakeholder activism: Partnerships and surveillance. *Critical Perspectives on International Business, 13*(2), 151–165.

Unerman, J., & O'Dwyer,. (2007). The business case for regulation of corporate social responsibility and accountability. *Accounting Forum, 31*, 332–353.

United Nations Environment Programme. (2011). UNEP Annual Report 2011. *UNEP Division of Communications and Public Information*, UNEP.

United Nations Industrial Development Organization. (2006). Available at https://stat.unido.org

Utting, P. (2008). The struggle for corporate accountability. *Development and Change, 39*(6), 959–975.

Vazquez-Brust, D. A., Liston-Heyes, C., Plaza-Ubeda, J. A., & Burgos-Jiménez, J. (2010). Stakeholders' pressures and strategic prioritisation: An empirical analysis of environmental responses in Argentinean firms. *Journal of Business Ethics, 91*, 171192.

Wakefield, S. E., Elliott, S. J., Cole, D. C., & Eyles, J. D. (2001). Environmental risk and (re)action: Air quality, health, and civic involvement in an urban industrial neighbourhood. *Health & Place, 7*(3), 163–177.

WHO. (2010). Preventing disease through healthy environments. http://www.who.int/ipcs/features/benzene.pdf. (Accessed on 15 November 2019).

Wood, D. J., & Jones, R. E. (1995). Stakeholder mismatching: A theoretical problem in empirical research on corporate social performance. *International Journal of Organizational Analysis, 3*(3), 229–267.

World Bank (2018). World Governance Indicators Database, World Bank, Washington: DC.

World Bank (2000). Greening industry, new roles for communities, markets and governments. *World Bank Policy Research Report.* New York: Oxford University Press.

Zeithaml, C. P., & Zeithaml, V. A. (1984). Environmental management: Revising the marketing perspective. *Journal of Marketing, 48*(2), 46–53.

Sustainability: Concept Clarification and Theory

Sara Omair, Hafiz Muhammad Usman Khizar, Omair Majeed, and Muhammad Jawad Iqbal

1 INTRODUCTION

In today's world, sustainability has gained widespread attention and has become one of the most commonly used terms as individuals, organizations, and governments strive to achieve a sustainable future. The need for sustainability arises due to the increasing depletion of natural resources, environmental degradation, and social inequalities. Sustainability is a complex and multifaceted concept that encompasses environmental protection, economic development, social equity, and resource

---

S. Omair (✉)
Department of Management Sciences, National University of Modern Languages Islamabad, Multan campus, Pakistan
e-mail: sara.omair@numl.edu.pk

H. M. U. Khizar
Institute of Business, Management and Administrative Sciences, The Islamia University of Bahawalpur, Bahawalpur, Pakistan
e-mail: usman.khizar@iub.edu.pk

O. Majeed · M. J. Iqbal
Institute of Banking Finance, Bahauddin Zakariya University, Multan, Pakistan
e-mail: jawad.iqbal@iub.edu.pk

© The Author(s), under exclusive license to Springer Nature Switzerland AG 2023
S. Adomako et al. (eds.), *Corporate Sustainability in Africa*, Palgrave Studies in African Leadership,
https://doi.org/10.1007/978-3-031-29273-6_17

conservation. Although the concept of sustainability is not new, and it has been defined and debated over the years, there are many different viewpoints on the conceptualization of sustainability and how this can be achieved. This chapter explores the conceptual domains of environmental sustainability. Specifically, the chapter examines in detail the meaning of corporate sustainability and explores the four (4) distinct areas of sustainability: human, social, economic, and environmental—known as the four pillars of sustainability. Various theories pertaining to sustainability are also explored in this chapter.

2 EVOLUTION OF SUSTAINABILITY—A BRIEF HISTORY

The term "sustain" comes from the Latin word meaning "to hold up" or "to support." This term has been in use for centuries and refers to anything that helps keep something running or extends its duration by providing the necessary support or resources. The closest synonym for "sustain" is the word "maintain." Today, the words "sustain," "sustainability," "sustainable," and "sustaining" are commonly used in literature to describe various aspects of sustainability. However, it was the Germans and Swiss who first developed the concept of sustainable forestry as a way to maintain forests for future generations. This gave rise to the idea of sustainable fisheries, and it brought environmental concerns to the forefront on a larger scale (Sutton, 2004). One of the key aspects proposed by forestry specialists of the seventeenth and eighteenth centuries was the idea of sustainability in terms of diminishing forest resources throughout Europe (Grober & Cunningham, 2012).

The concept of sustainability is not new and has been defined and debated over the years. The roots of sustainability can be traced back to the eighteenth and nineteenth centuries when the Industrial Revolution led to environmental degradation and social inequality. However, the modern concept of sustainability emerged in the twentieth century, when concerns about environmental degradation and resource depletion gained prominence. In 1962, Rachel Carson's book *Silent Spring* raised concerns about the harmful effects of pesticides and initiated the modern environmental movement. Furthermore, early political economists like Smith, Mill, Ricardo, and Malthus emphasized the trade-offs between social justice and wealth creation by advocating for limited demographic and economic expansion in the wake of the industrial revolution (Caradona, 2014). Several ecologists and natural scientists in the late nineteenth and early twentieth centuries also stressed the division among distinct anthropocentric conservationists, emphasizing the importance of protecting natural resources for sustainable consumption and development. These foundational ideas support the contemporary notion of sustainability, which first emerged in the late twentieth century and is now recognized worldwide.

The concept of sustainability shifted from the micro to the macro context, giving rise to the term "sustainable development," which was explained in detail in the book "World Conservation Strategy" jointly produced in 1980 by three organizations: the International Union for the Conservation of Nature and Natural Resources (IUCN), founded in France in 1948; the UN Environmental Program (UNEP), founded in 1972 in Kenya; and the World Wide Fund for Nature (WWF), founded in 1961 in Switzerland (International Union for Conservation of Nature & World Wide Fund for Nature, 1980, p. 6). These organizations work to conserve natural resources and promote their sustainable use, and they defined "sustainable development" as development for sustaining biodiversity and the ecosystem. Notably, the United Nations Conference on the Human Environment in Stockholm, Sweden, in 1972 was a turning point in the evolution of sustainability as it brought global attention to the need for sustainable development. And later, in 1987, the World Commission on Environment and Development published the Brundtland Report, which defined sustainable development as "development that meets the needs of the present without compromising the ability of future generations to meet their own needs."

Another example from the early 1970s might be brought up here when the World Council of Churches' commission on "The Future of Man and Society" talked about the idea of a "sustainable society" (Grober & Cunningham, 2012). The British Green Party, previously known as The Ecology Party, adopted the "Manifesto for a Sustainable Society" in 1975 and published a series of books prominently featuring the language of sustainability (Stivers, 1976). Politicians worldwide began to pay attention to the urgent need for establishing and maintaining sustainability as soon as Prime Minister Gro Harlem Brundtland and the UN panel did. As a result, interest in the idea has greatly increased during the past 20 years and numerous prestigious journals published research pieces on "sustainability," which led to the concept being constructed for analysis. Today, sustainability is a key idea in governance, public administration, and policy development. Despite this, the term "sustainability" is still an open concept with numerous definitions.

3 What Is Sustainability?—Understanding the Concept

Sustainability is a term used to describe a wide range of ideas and concepts related to the protection of the environment, economic development, and social equity (Montiel & Delgado-Ceballos, 2014). A review of the sustainability literature shows that there are many different definitions and conceptualizations of sustainability, which have evolved over time. Some definitions focus on environmental sustainability, while others emphasize social and economic sustainability. However, there is ambiguity and perplexity in the understanding of the terminology of sustainability.

One major source of confusion is the use of the terms "sustainability" and "sustainable development" interchangeably, despite arguments that they have distinct meanings and implications (Koglin, 2009; Mebratu, 1998). Different scholars have presented different viewpoints about sustainability and sustainable development, with some linking the term sustainable development with economic growth, while others warn that economic growth is incompatible with sustainability as an infinite growth process is impossible on a finite planet. However, some argue that economic growth is necessary for obtaining the resources required to attain desired sustainability. Moreover, the need to differentiate between sustainable growth and sustainable development has also been emphasized, considering the differing conceptualization of development (Ruggerio, 2021). In this regard, the lack of precision and clarity in defining sustainability and sustainable development has led to the emergence of various theoretical perspectives and strands of research, including sustainability science and sustainability communication, which emphasize different indicators and domains of sustainability.

One of the earliest and most widely accepted definitions of sustainability is that of sustainable development, as defined in the Brundtland Report by the World Commission on Environment and Development in 1987. This report defined sustainable development as development that meets the needs of the present without compromising the ability of future generations to meet their own needs (WCED, 1987). This definition emphasizes the balance between economic development, social equity, and environmental protection. In June 1992, the UN Conference on Environment and Development (UNCED) in Rio posited that sustainability is the integration or balancing of environmental, social, and economic issues, or simultaneous progress in the environmental, social, and economic domains (Declaration, 1992).

Sustainability demands "firms to encompass a focus on human as well as physical resources" (Pfeffer, 2010, p. 35). Montiel and Delgado-Ceballos (2014) suggest that the concept of sustainability can be defined from two perspectives. They obtained one definition from academic journals and the others from the practitioner's management journals. According to academic management journals, sustainability is defined as "building a society in which a proper balance is created between economic, social, and ecological aims. For businesses, this involves sustaining and expanding economic growth, shareholder value, prestige, corporate reputation, customer relationships, and the quality of products and services. It also means adopting and pursuing ethical business practices, creating sustainable jobs, building value for all of the company's stakeholders, and attending to the needs of the underserved" (Székely & Knirsch, 2005, p. 628). On the other hand, in the practitioner's journals, sustainability is defined as "firms need to integrate six perspectives: (i) regulatory compliance, (ii) incremental mitigation, (iii) value alignment, (iv) whole system design, (v) business model innovation, and (vi) mission transformation" (Markevich, 2009, pp. 13–14). This implies that academics have defined sustainability with diverse meanings.

Some conceptualization of sustainability focuses on environmental sustainability which emphasizes the need to protect natural resources and ecosystems while minimizing the human impact on the planet. Another dominant conceptualization is corporate sustainability, which focuses on the role that businesses and corporations play in creating a sustainable future by balancing the economic, social, and environmental impacts of business operations and creating long-term value for all stakeholders (Montiel & Delgado-Ceballos, 2014). There also exist terminological confusion and overlap between sustainability and sustainable development. It is important to mention that both the terms "sustainable development" and "sustainability" are interchangeable and almost synonymous with each other in theory and practice. However, certain schools of thought point out that sustainable development is contradictory regarding the sustainability of limited economic resources. Hence, scholars claimed that sustainability might be considered a different concept that is more relevant to environmental factors. Therefore, this debate is open even now, and there is a need to explore this difference in the academic discussion to gain an insight into their meanings. However, a predominant consensual argument suggests that "sustainability" is a broader concept that is more relevant to environmental factors, while "sustainable development" emphasizes the importance of social and economic development alongside environmental sustainability.

We can sum up our discussion by concluding that there are various viewpoints on sustainability, which can be broadly categorized into two groups: the anthropocentric and the biocentric perspectives. The anthropocentric perspective is focused on human needs and interests and considers environmental protection and conservation as means to achieve economic and social development. The biocentric perspective, on the other hand, views environmental protection as a fundamental value in its own right and seeks to protect the earth and its ecosystems for their own sake, regardless of their economic or social value (Keitsch, 2018).

4 Domains of Sustainability—Four Pillars

Sustainability is often discussed in terms of three main domains or pillars: (i) the economy, (ii) the society, and (iii) the environment (Gomes Silva et al., 2022; James & Magee, 2016; Ranjbari et al., 2021). These pillars can be represented by three intersecting circles, with sustainability in the center (Purvis et al., 2019). However, it is important to note that each pillar should be strong enough to deliver sustainability, otherwise, the entire structure becomes impervious even if just one pillar is weak (Hansmann et al., 2012). Hence, these pillars are interconnected, and they work in synergy to deliver sustainability (Clune & Zehnder, 2018; Gomes Silva et al., 2022).

The three pillars of sustainability have certain qualities that contribute to the business's strategic decision-making and allow for the effective development and implementation of sustainability policies and processes (Pereira-Moliner et al., 2021; Purvis et al., 2019). Although these pillars overlap, it is impossible to attain sustainability by prioritizing one pillar over another among the three pillars-framework. Therefore, firms must aim to achieve integrated sustainability that integrates the business's environmental, social, and economic responsibilities (Baumgartner, 2014; Dao et al., 2011; Muñoz-Torres et al., 2019). In addition to the three traditional pillars, scholars have also suggested the *"human pillar"* as another engine of growth and sustainable development (Luetz & Walid, 2019; Srivastava et al., 2020). It is important to recognize that the inclusion of the human pillar emphasizes the importance of social and cultural factors in achieving sustainability (Diaconu & Popescu, 2016; Wang et al., 2022).

Economic Pillar of Sustainability

The economic pillar of sustainability focuses on generating economic growth in a way that has no adverse effects on the environment, society, or culture (Grob & Benn, 2014). Businesses form the economy's productive resource and without their support, sustainable development is unachievable (Barkemeyer et al., 2014). This is accomplished by reducing or ceasing the usage of finite resources while keeping public openness. Therefore, the best economic course of action is to boost revenue while cutting back on carbon emissions. However, economic sustainability challenges the capitalist axiom that bigger growth is better and development that threatens to degrade natural and social systems is bad (Elkington, 1997; Grob & Benn, 2014). This demonstrates that when seen in the context of business, economic sustainability refers to the effective use of resources to sustain firm profitability over the long term.

Social Pillar of Sustainability

The social pillar of sustainability concerns how a business affects its direct and indirect stakeholders, such as clients, employees, and neighborhood groups, and is the most conceptually elusive pillar (Murphy, 2012). Hence, social sustainability attempts to protect social capital by investing in and developing the services that make up the framework of our society and considering a broader perspective of the world that considers communities, cultures, and globalization (Boström, 2012). Companies hope to protect future generations through social sustainability and recognize that our actions can affect other people and the entire globe (Sood, 2016). The social pillar has been linked to its environmental implications in terms of four policy sectors, which include equity, awareness for sustainability, participation, and social cohesion. Social sustainability companies uphold and enhance social quality through notions like cohesion, reciprocity, and honesty, as well as the development of relationships between people by promoting and supporting laws, information, and commonly held beliefs about equality and rights (Murphy, 2012).

Environmental Pillar of Sustainability

The environmental pillar of sustainability covers the tactics for decreasing greenhouse gas emissions and offsetting them, using renewable energy, removing hazardous dangers, reusing or recycling materials, and managing packaging waste to minimize the carbon footprint across the entire value chain (Kuhlman & Farrington, 2010). Environmental sustainability focuses on how companies can obtain favorable economic results without causing short- or long-term environmental damage (Mikulčić et al., 2017). Understanding what is meant by the environment in this context is crucial to understanding the idea of environmental sustainability (Linnenluecke & Griffiths, 2013). When we talk about the environment, we don't only mean the external ecosystem, but also the experienced ecosystem that people are knowingly and purposefully connected to. As a result, the experienced environment is made up of a complex ecosystem that is characterized by conscious life centered on humans. It aims to improve human welfare by protecting natural capital (such as land, air, water, minerals, etc.) and ensuring that the needs of the present generation are met without endangering those of future generations (Kuhlman & Farrington, 2010; Purvis et al., 2019).

Human Pillar of Sustainability

The human pillar of sustainability is the upkeep of human capital by providing services like health, education, skill development, leadership, and knowledge, which make up the human capital (Benn et al., 2014). Human sustainability attempts to preserve and enhance the human capital in society by investing in these systems (Diaconu & Popescu, 2016). Anyone directly or indirectly involved in the creation of goods, the delivery of services, or larger stakeholders is important to consider under the general heading of human sustainability (Grob & Benn, 2014). To promote business ideals that respect human capital, a business organization must see itself as a member of society (Wang et al., 2022). As a result, human sustainability groups ensure that corporate operations do not harm the planet. Therefore, human sustainability includes the growth of capacities and skills necessary to support an organization's operations and sustainability and advance the community's social and economic well-being.

Comparison of the Four Pillars of Sustainability

A critical review of these four pillars of sustainability allows us to compare and contrast these domains. First, economic sustainability is concerned with maintaining economic capital in the form of income and profit. It emphasizes the efficient allocation of resources and economic growth without compromising the future. Economic sustainability is closely linked to the concept of throughput growth, which is the flow of material and energy from environmental sources. However, economic sustainability must not be restricted by throughput growth. It should focus on maintaining a stable economy while also protecting natural resources. Second, social sustainability is centered on maintaining and enhancing social capital, which includes shared values, beliefs, norms, and institutions that facilitate cooperation and foster trust within a society. Social sustainability requires that people have access to basic needs such as education, healthcare, and housing. It also emphasizes equality, diversity, and human rights. Social sustainability recognizes that social capital is essential for a society to function properly. Third, environmental sustainability aims to protect the natural environment by reducing human impact on it. It recognizes that the planet's natural resources are finite and need to be conserved for future generations. It involves maintaining a balance between the use and preservation of natural resources. Environmental sustainability focuses on the efficient use of resources and waste reduction. It also recognizes the importance of biodiversity and ecosystems in maintaining a healthy planet. Fourth, human sustainability focuses on improving the quality of human life by enhancing access to education, healthcare, and basic needs such as food and water. It recognizes that human capital is an important resource that needs to be developed and maintained. Human sustainability aims to create a society that is healthy, educated, and productive. It emphasizes the importance of individual well-being and the development of skills necessary to support an organization's operations and sustainability.

On the whole, we can conclude our discussion on the comparisons among the four pillars of sustainability as follows: economic sustainability focuses on maintaining a stable economy while also protecting natural resources, social sustainability emphasizes the importance of social capital and equality, environmental sustainability aims to protect the natural environment and reduce human impact on it, and human sustainability focuses on improving the quality of human life and developing human capital. However, all four pillars of sustainability are interconnected and must be balanced to achieve a sustainable future.

5   Sustainability-Related Theoretical Frameworks and Approaches

The concept of sustainability has become increasingly relevant in recent times due to the challenges posed by climate change, biodiversity loss, and resource depletion. Sustainability theories provide a framework for understanding and addressing these challenges by guiding the development of sustainable practices and policies. There are numerous sustainability theories, each with its unique focus and approach. This chapter explores some of the most prominent theories of sustainability. These theories range from traditional ones, such as stakeholder theory, institutional theories, and resource-based views, to contemporary ones, including sustain-centrism, green economics, ecological theory, cybernetics, systems theory, and positive, weak, and strong sustainability. The literature on sustainability reveals that the concept of sustainability has shifted from a focus on defining sustainability to a more practical approach to how organizations can promote sustainability. Theories on sustainability can provide valuable insights into the most effective ways to promote sustainable development and create a more sustainable future for all.

Stakeholder Theory

Stakeholder theory is a theoretical framework that underscores the importance of considering the perspectives and interests of all stakeholders in decision-making processes. According to this theory, organizations that can balance the interests of all stakeholders—including employees, customers, suppliers, shareholders, and the broader community—are more likely to achieve long-term success and sustainability (Parmar et al., 2010). In his seminal work, "Strategic Management-A Stakeholder Approach," Freeman defined a stakeholder as "any group or individual who can affect or is affected by the attainment of the organization's objectives." He identified two categories of stakeholders: primary and secondary. Primary stakeholders directly affect the business, such as suppliers, customers, and employees, while secondary stakeholders indirectly affect the business, such as the government, environmentalists, and special interest organizations (Freeman, 2010). Freeman argued that businesses must comprehend their interactions with these stakeholders to theorize a new role for corporations. The stakeholder theory, introduced by Freeman during the late 1970s, posits that environmental challenges are addressed by both social and non-social stakeholders. To accomplish their strategic goals, corporations must respond to pressure and requests from their stakeholders (Chang et al., 2017).

The stakeholder theory, which is one of the contemporary theories of sustainability demonstrates that CSR has significantly impacted the firm's performance because of its unique approach to striving for sustainability (Laine, 2014). Previous studies have contributed to the stakeholder theory and environmental sustainability literature by ascertaining that stakeholder integration may help build the structural support required to mitigate weak institutions and enhance the firm's financial performance (Danso et al., 2020). Moreover, another recent study confirmed the role of stakeholder integration in strengthening the relationship between entrepreneurial orientation and the performance of these new ventures through environmental sustainability orientation (Amankwah-Amoah et al., 2019). In general, stakeholder theory emphasizes the importance of taking a broad perspective on sustainability and considering the interests of all stakeholders in decision-making processes. By doing so, organizations can create more sustainable practices that lead to long-term success and benefits for all stakeholders involved.

Corporate Sustainability

Corporate sustainability is an approach to business that seeks to balance economic, environmental, and social concerns while meeting the needs of stakeholders. Although there is no single definition of corporate sustainability, it is widely recognized that businesses must address these three factors to achieve sustainable development. This approach is often operationalized through the "Triple Bottom Line (TBL)" framework (Elkington, 1997), which recognizes the importance of social, environmental, and financial factors in business performance. One key benefit of incorporating TBL into management strategies is the potential for sustained growth and competitive advantage, both in established and emerging markets. Sustainable business models (SBMs) that consider the interests of multiple stakeholders can help organizations integrate sustainability into their operational procedures, leading to long-term success.

Studies have shown that adopting SBMs can help companies maintain a competitive edge (Chang et al., 2017). In particular, corporate sustainability and the TBL framework are important approaches to promoting sustainable development in the business world. By balancing economic, environmental, and social concerns, businesses can meet the needs of stakeholders, achieve long-term growth, and contribute to a more sustainable future (Khizar et al., 2021). Managers have started to recognize the significance of developing a corporate sustainability strategy since they present the business' strategic position (Kitsios et al., 2020). Corporate sustainability enables sustainability-oriented firms to multiply their capacity to generate more investment, invest in human capital, create jobs, and build international business standards through the use of eco-friendly and resource-efficient technologies (Murthy, 2012). However, developing and implementing corporate sustainability strategies enables firms to tackle social and environmental challenges (Engert et al., 2016). Therefore, a business needs to select the appropriate sustainability strategy and its alignment with the business strategy.

Institutional Theory

Institutional theory is a theoretical framework that highlights the role of institutions, norms, and values in shaping human behavior and decision-making. It suggests that sustainable development requires the creation of effective institutions that can regulate human behavior and promote sustainable practices (Scott, 2008). The institutional theory also underscores the significance of institutional change and evolution in response to changing environmental and social conditions. According to the theory, institutional forces have more impact than strategic analysis of stakeholders. Scholars have used this theory to understand how socially responsible actions differ between nations (Brammer et al., 2012). In addition, institutional theory has been applied to describe the dynamics of the environmental component of sustainability, such as by analyzing the evolution of corporate environmentalism (Hoffman & Jennings, 2015). Researchers have also found that ecologically responsible companies face less stock market risk compared to environmentally irresponsible ones, based on an extensive analysis of 100 companies over 5 years (Bansal & Clelland, 2004). Furthermore, institutional conditions that influence the likelihood of businesses in various industry sectors implementing ecologically sustainable practices, either symbolically or significantly, have been predicted (Montiel & Delgado-Ceballos, 2014). Hence, this theory is useful in explaining the institutionalization processes that lead to sustainable companies, the adoption of sustainability-related practices, and the analysis of sustainability reporting.

RBV and NRBV

The Resource-Based View (RBV) is a theoretical framework that suggests that an organization's resources and capabilities are the primary sources of its competitive advantage (Barney, 1991). These resources can include static, dynamic, tangible, financial, human, and intellectual capital. RBV emphasizes the importance of developing and leveraging unique resources and capabilities that cannot be easily replicated by competitors (Armstrong & Shimizu, 2007). In 1995, Hart expanded RBV to include the external environment, creating the Natural Resource-Based View (NRBV).

The NRBV framework emphasizes the importance of natural resources in creating and sustaining competitive advantage (Hart, 1995). According to NRBV, organizations that can efficiently and sustainably manage their natural resources are more likely to achieve long-term success. NRBV focuses on strategic competencies such as pollution prevention, product stewardship, and clean technology, which are developed through the company's interaction with the natural environment (de Almeida et al., 2021). Previous studies have utilized the RBV and NRBV to explain the firm's environmental sustainability orientation stance (Adomako et al., 2019). For instance, NRBV has been used to assess the role of competitive strategies, such as low cost, differentiation, and integration in the association of environmental sustainability orientation and performance of the firm (Danso et al., 2019). Hence, both RBV and NRBV consider sustainability orientation as an organizational resource and a dynamic capability that can be used to achieve competitive advantage and lead to higher firm performance (Jusoh et al., 2021; Khizar et al., 2022).

Systems Theory

Systems theory is a theoretical framework that can be applied to the concept of sustainability, as suggested in a study by Gallopín (2003). In this theory, sustainability is viewed as an open system that exchanges information, matter, and energy with its environment through input and output variables. These variables can predict the system's current state, which is influenced by its past state. To evaluate system performance, output variables are used to develop a general equation for sustainability (Ruggerio, 2021). This equation suggests that a system is sustainable if its' overall output value remains constant over time. However, there may be subjectivity around the definition of sustainability, which can affect the interpretation of the equation.

Other scholars have built on this idea by focusing on three fundamental assumptions about sustainability, which include the emergent nature of complex systems, the accumulation and shifting of the entire network, and the hierarchical structure of organizations (Crojethovich Martín & Rescia Perazzo, 2007). Additionally, Ben-Eli (2018) used systems theory to explain sustainability by emphasizing the understanding of a system's carrying capacity and its relationship to its internal demographic dynamics. Overall, systems theory provides a useful framework for understanding the interconnectedness of sustainability and how it is affected by various factors within a system.

Sustaincentrism

Sustaincentrism is a theoretical framework that places sustainability at the forefront of decision-making processes. It emphasizes the need for a fundamental shift in the way individuals, organizations, and societies prioritize their goals and objectives to achieve sustainable development. According to this theory, sustainability must be given priority over economic, social, or political interests. Gladwin first used the term "sustaincentrism" to describe the process of achieving human development in a way that is inclusive, connected, equitable, cautious, and secure. The essential elements of sustainable development, as outlined by Gladwin et al. (1995), include inclusivity (considering environmental and human systems, present and future), connectivity (acknowledging the interconnection and interdependence of global issues), equity (promoting equitable distribution of resources and property rights), prudence (fulfilling duties of care and prevention), and security (ensuring safety from chronic threats).

To investigate the factors that have contributed to the popularity of this framework, researchers have conducted experimental studies. For instance, Laine (2014) analyzed the elements of sustaincentrism and explored their impact on sustainability. These studies enhance our understanding of how this theory can be implemented in practice to promote sustainable development. However, sustaincentrism provides a valuable framework for prioritizing sustainability and ensuring that the long-term needs of the planet and its inhabitants are met.

Green Economics

Green economics is an approach to economic development that emphasizes the importance of environmental sustainability, social fairness, and human well-being (Ruggerio, 2021). The concept of a green economy has gained significant importance and recognition in both domestic and global policymaking since the Fifth Ministerial Conference on Environment and Development (MCED) in 2005. According to the United Nations Environment Programme (UNEP), a green economy is an economy that focuses on enhancing human well-being and social fairness while simultaneously reducing environmental risks and ecological scarcities (Green Economy, 2010). Green growth and a green economy are prerequisites for poverty reduction and sustainable development, as recognized by the United Nations Economic and Social Commission for Asia and the Pacific (ESCAP) (Chang et al., 2017).

Green growth emphasizes the interconnection between environmental concerns and economic growth and development. However, green growth does not come at the cost of sustainability (Chang et al., 2017). It requires wise investment in modernizing and improving every aspect of the production process to conserve resources for the environment (Jacobs, 2013). A green economy acts as a means of achieving sustainability, rather than substituting it. To transition from environmentally destructive practices to more environmentally friendly ones, active policies and proper rules for technology and other voluntary initiatives are necessary (Loiseau et al., 2016). For instance, firms require supportive policies to modify their business environment to engage in activities that promote environmental sustainability (Ruggerio, 2021). In summary, green economics promotes the integration of environmental, social,

390 S. OMAIR ET AL.

and economic considerations in decision-making to achieve sustainable development. The concept of a green economy is essential for poverty reduction and social justice while preserving the environment for future generations.

Cybernetics

The Cybernetics theory offers valuable insights into understanding the interrelationship between a system's structure and its behavior in the context of sustainability. By emphasizing the importance of changing underlying structures to achieve sustainable outcomes, it provides a useful framework for developing more effective sustainability strategies. The Cybernetics theory explores how systems control, adapt, change, and self-organize, the structures and mechanisms that mediate their performance and conduct (Ben-Eli, 2012). This concept can be traced back to Norbert Wiener and his associates, who demonstrated the crucial link between a system's output, the observed behavior, and its underlying structure, and applied it to operationalize the concept of sustainability (Ben-Eli, 2012). Although the concept may seem straightforward, many reform or improvement initiatives focus on controlling results rather than changing the structures that give rise to those outcomes, making it complex (Schwaninger, 2015).

According to the Cybernetics theory, two aspects are crucial to this viewpoint: firstly, sustainability is viewed as a specific system state arising from a specific underlying structure, and secondly, sustainability can be seen as a type of stability characterized by some quantity that remains invariant (Ben-Eli, 2012). The theory postulates that sustainability is a specific type of equilibrium that arises between the population and its surroundings. This equilibrium is a critical characteristic of the state of sustainability that is consistent with Cybernetics theory. It forms a two-way circular structure, or loop, in which the main variables, population and carrying capacity, continuously influence each other. Therefore, Ben-Eli (2012) theorized sustainability as "A dynamic equilibrium in the processes of interaction between a population and the carrying capacity of its environment, such that the population develops to express its full potential without producing irreversible adverse effects on the carrying capacity of the environment upon which it depends" (p. 6).

Corporate Sustainable Development

Bansal introduced "corporate sustainable development" as a tridimensional construct made up of (a) economic prosperity attained through value creation, (b) social equity through corporate social responsibility, and (c) environmental integrity through corporate environmental management in an additional effort to incorporate sustainable development into the business world. The three separate management domains of value creation, CSR, and environmental management may be combined to yield multiple financial and non-financial benefits for the firms (Bansal, 2005). CSD is viewed as a business strategy that can help meet the needs of the stakeholders of an organization in a way that the interests of local communities are not compromised (Chow & Chen, 2012).

Contemporary Ecological Theory

The contemporary ecological theory recognizes the importance of sustainability, which is often used interchangeably with other terms such as ecological sustainability, social sustainability, economic sustainability, and project sustainability. Unlike the neoclassical theory, ecology cannot predict the human economy, but it is viewed as a component of an open system that encourages strong sustainability stances through information and element exchange. Academics agree that ecological systems can be used to understand socio-ecological systems better, including society, which is considered a key factor in shifts in the health of ecosystems (Ruggerio, 2021). According to contemporary ecological theory, ecosystems are self-organized dynamic systems that can experience rapid transitions between states with varying degrees of stability and equilibrium (Haberl et al., 2004). Achieving ecological sustainability requires combining four methods, including (i) comprehensive quality environmental management, (ii) ecological sustainable competitive strategies, (iii) technology-for-nature swaps, and (iv) corporate population impact control (Shrivastava, 1995). It is essential to note that environmental sustainability and ecological sustainability are not interchangeable. While environmental sustainability refers to preserving natural resources, ecological sustainability refers to everything connected with the Earth's ecosystem and the functioning of its biogeochemical systems (Ruggerio, 2021).

Ecological Footprint Framework and Ecological Modernization Theory

The ecological footprint model suggests that the impact of human activity on the environment can be measured by the number of natural resources required to sustain human activities (Işık et al., 2021). Therefore, it is essential to reduce resource consumption and minimize waste in order to achieve sustainable development. Moreover, the ecological modernization theory emphasizes the role of technological innovation and economic growth in solving environmental problems, promoting cleaner technologies, and sustainable production and consumption patterns. It recognizes the importance of state policies and regulations, as well as the role of businesses in developing and implementing sustainable practices (York et al., 2010).

Positive Sustainability (and Negative Sustainability)

Scholars have provided a nuanced explanation of sustainability, which is defined as the capacity to endure, persist, or have a future (James & Magee, 2016). Negative sustainability is not meant to be interpreted as evil, but rather refers to the process of minimizing the negative consequences of past development or human behavior that can jeopardize our future. In contrast, positive sustainability entails promoting human involvement practices and meanings that support ongoing ecological and social processes. This requires developing strategies that ensure a stable future and re-evaluating our relationship with the material and social surroundings, refraining from viewing them merely as resources for investment and exploitation. The authors emphasize the global community's responsibility toward future generations (Ruggerio, 2021).

Weak Sustainability (and Strong Sustainability)

Sustainability has been conceptualized by several schools of thought in various ways, including very weak, weak, strong, and very strong sustainability. However, although they are measured in the same breadth, their formalization differs (Ayres et al., 1998). They form two opposing extremes of economic sustainability, but both are adopted to address the idea of sustainability (Neumayer, 2003). While sustainable development is defined by a circular and green economy, innovations in environmental methods, although having more distinct inventions, are based on a poor basis (Ruggerio, 2021). This is due to several unknown exogenous and endogenous processes and the high level of uncertainty associated with ecosystem changes, resulting in a seeming equilibrium state.

The concept of weak sustainability versus strong sustainability is one of the earliest theoretical frameworks for sustainability. Weak sustainability suggests that environmental resources are interchangeable and that economic growth can be sustained as long as total wealth is maintained. On the other hand, strong sustainability suggests that natural capital is non-substitutable and that economic growth cannot be sustained if environmental resources are depleted (Ruggerio, 2021). Hence, this theory highlights the need for conservation and the protection of natural capital.

Moreover, neoclassical economics presupposes that energy and matter (commodities) circulate in a nearly closed system with limitless resources (inputs) and an infinite ability to handle wastes (outputs), which economists refer to as negative externalities. The circular economy (Wanner, 2015) and green economy (Schroeder et al., 2019) are two of the most recent conceptual proposals emerging from the weak sustainability approach. They both adhere to the premises of sustainable development and posit that environmental issues can be resolved by technological and scientific means. However, some characteristics of nature cannot be replaced by artificial capital, which is why the "precautionary principle" must take precedence over the neoclassical theory's economic logic. This does not imply taking a conservationist stance toward nature supervising human societies (referred to as extremely strong sustainability), but rather recognizing that the survival of a business depends on reversing the trend toward the degradation of Earth's surroundings (Ruggerio, 2021).

6 Corporate Sustainability—What It Is and Why It Is Important?

In today's rapidly changing and challenging environment, sustainability issues have become the center of interest in business theory and practices around the world. Previously, the concepts such as *sustainability, responsibility, ethics, and accountability* were not being prioritized in businesses; however, corporate sustainability issues are becoming crucial in response to the calls for sustainable development as well as due to the constant pressure from the multiple stakeholders to behave in a socially and environmentally responsible way (Schmitz et al., 2019).

Corporate sustainability is an essential aspect of sustainability that is gaining significant attention. Business organizations are major contributors to environmental and social issues and have a significant impact on the natural environment and communities in which they operate. Corporate sustainability involves integrating sustainability principles into a company's operations, products, and services to achieve long-term economic success while also contributing to sustainable development. It is about creating shared value for all stakeholders, including shareholders, employees, customers, and the wider community. Moreover, sustainability is often defined in the triple bottom line (TBL) model in the business context (Elkington, 2013). TBL framework considers sustainability in three dimensions: (i) economic, (ii) social, and (iii) environmental (Elkington, 1997). The TBL framework suggests that business goals are inseparable from the societies and environments in which they operate. Therefore, business sustainability should not only be measured in financial terms but also social and environmental aspects should also be considered. To this end, integration of the triple bottom line (i.e., profit, people, and the planet) considerations in businesses has increasingly been recognized as an important field of research and practice (Tate & Bals, 2018).

Corporate sustainability has gained significant consideration around the world due to the positive results of incorporating sustainable practices in organizations (e.g., Calabrese et al., 2019). In this regard, the private sector is increasingly being inspired by the long-term benefits of integrating sustainability elements in their business models (Calabrese et al., 2019; Schaltegger et al., 2019). However, there are many reasons why corporate sustainability is significant. First, it enables companies to meet the changing expectations of various stakeholders such as customers and investors who are increasingly demanding sustainable practices. Second, it helps companies to reduce risks and increase resilience by addressing environmental and social issues that could impact their operations. Third, it provides companies with a competitive advantage by enhancing their reputation and brand value. Finally, corporate sustainability is essential for achieving the United Nations Sustainable Development Goals (SDGs), which are aimed at eradicating poverty, protecting the planet, and promoting sustainable development. The United Nations SDGs provide a framework for achieving sustainable development and highlight the importance of sustainability in every sphere of life. The SDGs call for an urgent response from countries to ensure access to clean water and clean energy use, reduce inequalities, promote peace and justice, and protect the climate, and life underwater and on land, among other goals. Corporate sustainability plays a critical role in achieving these goals by aligning business strategies with sustainable development objectives. In this regard, it is generally assumed that—without sustainable organizations, there is no sustainable development, and thus, no future (Weidinger et al., 2014).

7 CONCLUSION AND FUTURE RESEARCH TRAJECTORIES

This chapter provides a comprehensive overview of historical developments, various definitions, theories, and dimensions of sustainability, as well as the importance of corporate sustainability in light of UN Agenda 2030. We discovered how the concept of sustainability emerged from the late 1940s to the 1980s when the UN Brundtland Commission used the concept of sustainable development to comprehensively define sustainability. This prompted other scholars to put forward their proposed definitions of sustainability; however, sustainability established itself as a complex construct, as evident from the academic and practitioner journals. An ambiguity seems to exist regarding whether sustainability is synonymous only with environmental management or whether it must be tri-dimensional. It is important to mention here that the majority of scholars agree to include social and economic aspects along with the environmental factor in sustainability (Abbas et al., 2019; Hysa et al., 2020). The comparison of definitions indicates very less differences; however, some definitions provide guidelines to managers on pursuing sustainability at the corporate level, while others are more holistic and philosophical. The major consensus of the scholars for the general definition of sustainability remains with meeting the needs of the present generation in a way that does not compromise on the resources for the provision of needs for future generations.

In addition, this chapter delves into sustainability in-depth, drawing on various organizational theories to shed light on the topic. Traditional theories such as stakeholder theory, institutional theory, and RBV offer valuable insights into sustainable practices. In addition, contemporary theories like sustaincentrism and green economics challenge the prevailing human-centric business paradigm and advocate for nature-focused practices. Scholars have also emphasized the importance of both positive and negative sustainability, which can eradicate negative consequences of previous human behavior and support practices that benefit society and ecology. Systems theory and cybernetics theory provide a framework for controlling and organizing sustainable practices, while contemporary ecological theory highlights the dynamic nature of sustainability. Finally, sustainability can range from very weak to very strong and requires a balance between economic, environmental, and social performance through the Triple Bottom Line approach.

The importance of sustainability can also be attributed due to its applicability in achieving the UN Global Agenda 2030 for the nations to put the sustainability essence into practice. As discussed in this chapter, sustainability stands strongly on four pillars (i.e., economic, social, environmental, and human) that work synergistically to create a balance and deliver the desired objectives, leading to integrated sustainability. The economic dimension links individuals and institutions with economic growth, while the pillar of society dictates the association with the primary and secondary stakeholders. The most important pillar of the environment highlights how the actions of institutions affect natural resources and ecosystems. Lastly, the human sustainability pillar targets to improve and maintain the human capital in society by investing in welfare sectors.

Future Research Directions

Although this chapter provides a valuable overview of sustainability definitions, theories, and dimensions, there is a need for more critical evaluation for further knowledge development. Future research should focus on the trade-offs and synergies between economic, social, and environmental sustainability, the role of technology and innovation, and the role of individuals and communities in promoting sustainability.

One aspect that deserves further examination is the potential tension between economic growth and sustainability, which is a common theme in the literature. While many scholars agree that economic growth is necessary for sustainable development (Eisenmenger et al., 2020; Kurniawan & Managi, 2018), others argue that a paradigm shift is required toward a more sustainable and equitable economic system (Chasi & Heleta, 2022; Shah, 2013). This debate highlights the need for further research on the trade-offs and synergies between economic, social, and environmental sustainability. Moreover, integrated sustainability is a relatively under-researched area, especially the eco-economic sustainability dimension. Therefore, scholars can conduct studies investigating this field. Another area for future research is the cross-cultural and sectoral investigations of four pillars of sustainability, such as textile, healthcare, education, and tourism. Sector-specific sustainability goals can be redesigned, and sustainability action plans, if required, may be suggested for better resilience.

Despite advances in sustainability research and practice, our understanding of the role of technology and innovation in promoting sustainability is limited (Godil et al., 2021; Zhang et al., 2019). Advances in technology have the potential to reduce environmental impact, enhance social equity, and stimulate economic growth (Cisneros-Montemayor et al., 2019; Mastini et al., 2021). However, technological innovation can also have unintended consequences (Ahmed et al., 2021; Lichtenthaler, 2021), and there is a need to evaluate the sustainability implications of emerging technologies. Finally, there is a need for more research on the role of individuals and communities in promoting sustainability. While much of the literature focuses on the role of institutions and corporations (Bag et al., 2021; Polasky et al., 2019), individuals and communities also have an important role to play in promoting sustainability. Future research could explore the factors that influence individual and community engagement in sustainability, and identify strategies to promote more sustainable behaviors and lifestyles.

References

Abbas, J., Mahmood, S., Ali, H., Ali Raza, M., Ali, G., Aman, J., Bano, S., & Nurunnabi, M. (2019). The effects of corporate social responsibility practices and environmental factors through a moderating role of social media marketing on sustainable performance of business firms. *Sustainability, 11*(12), 3434.

Adomako, S., Amankwah-Amoah, J., Danso, A., Konadu, R., & Owusu-Agyei, S. (2019). Environmental sustainability orientation and performance of family and nonfamily firms. *Business Strategy and the Environment, 28*(6), 1250–1259.

Ahmed, Z., Nathaniel, S. P., & Shahbaz, M. (2021). The criticality of information and communication technology and human capital in environmental sustainability: Evidence from Latin American and Caribbean countries. *Journal of Cleaner Production, 286*, 125529.

Amankwah-Amoah, J., Danso, A., & Adomako, S. (2019). Entrepreneurial orientation, environmental sustainability and new venture performance: Does stakeholder integration matter? *Business Strategy and the Environment, 28*(1), 79–87.

398 S. OMAIR ET AL.

Armstrong, C. E., & Shimizu, K. (2007). A review of approaches to empirical research on the resource-based view of the firm. *Journal of Management, 33*(6), 959–986.

Ayres, R. U., Van Den Bergh, J. C., & Gowdy, J. M. (1998). *Weak versus strong sustainability* (Tinbergen Institute Discussion Papers 98-103/3). Tinbergen Institute.

Bag, S., Pretorius, J. H. C., Gupta, S., & Dwivedi, Y. K. (2021). Role of institutional pressures and resources in the adoption of big data analytics powered artificial intelligence, sustainable manufacturing practices and circular economy capabilities. *Technological Forecasting and Social Change, 163*, 120420.

Bansal, P. (2005). Evolving sustainably: A longitudinal study of corporate sustainable development. *Strategic Management Journal, 26*, 197–218.

Bansal, P., & Clelland, I. (2004). Talking trash: Legitimacy, impression management, and unsystematic risk in the context of the natural environment. *Academy of Management Journal, 47*(1), 93–103.

Barkemeyer, R., Holt, D., Preuss, L., & Tsang, S. (2014). What happened to the 'development' in sustainable development? Business guidelines two decades after Brundtland. *Sustainable Development, 22*(1), 15–32.

Barney, J. (1991). Firm resources and sustained competitive advantage. *Journal of Management, 17*(1), 99–120.

Baumgartner, R. J. (2014). Managing corporate sustainability and CSR: A conceptual framework combining values, strategies and instruments contributing to sustainable development. *Corporate Social Responsibility and Environmental Management, 21*(5), 258–271.

Ben-Eli, M. (2012). The cybernetics of sustainability: Definition and underlying principles. In *Enough for all forever: A handbook for learning about sustainability* (pp. 255–268). Common Ground.

Ben-Eli, M. U. (2018). Sustainability: Definition and five core principles, a systems perspective. *Sustainability Science, 13*(5), 1337–1343.

Benn, S., Edwards, M., & Williams, T. (2014). *Organizational change for corporate sustainability*. Routledge

Boström, M. (2012). A missing pillar? Challenges in theorizing and practicing social sustainability: Introduction to the special issue. *Sustainability: Science, Practice and Policy, 8*(1), 3–14.

Brammer, S., Jackson, G., & Matten, D. (2012). Corporate social responsibility and institutional theory: New perspectives on private governance. *Socio-Economic Review, 10*(1), 3–28.

Calabrese, A., Costa, R., Levialdi, N., & Menichini, T. (2019). Integrating sustainability into strategic decision-making: A fuzzy AHP method for the selection of relevant sustainability issues. *Technological Forecasting and Social Change, 139*, 155–168.

Caradona, J. (2014). *Is 'progress' good for humanity?* The Atlantic. In.

Chang, R.-D., Zuo, J., Zhao, Z.-Y., Zillante, G., Gan, X.-L., & Soebarto, V. (2017). Evolving theories of sustainability and firms: History, future directions and implications for renewable energy research. *Renewable and Sustainable Energy Reviews, 72,* 48–56.

Chasi, S., & Heleta, S. (2022). Towards more sustainable, equitable and just internationalisation practices: The case of internationalisation conferences. *Journal of Studies in International Education.* https://doi.org/10.1177/102 83153221139924

Chow, W. S., & Chen, Y. (2012). Corporate sustainable development: Testing a new scale based on the mainland Chinese context. *Journal of Business Ethics, 105,* 519–533.

Cisneros-Montemayor, A. M., Moreno-Báez, M., Voyer, M., Allison, E. H., Cheung, W. W., Hessing-Lewis, M., Oyinlola, M. A., Singh, G. G., Swartz, W., & Ota, Y. (2019). Social equity and benefits as the nexus of a transformative Blue Economy: A sectoral review of implications. *Marine Policy, 109,* 103702.

Clune, W. H., & Zehnder, A. J. (2018). The three pillars of sustainability framework: Approaches for laws and governance. *Journal of Environmental Protection, 9*(3), 211–240.

Crojethovich Martín, A. D., & Rescia Perazzo, A. J. (2007). Organización y sostenibilidad en un sistema urbano socio-ecológico y complejo. *Revista Internacional de Tecnología, Sostenibilidad y Humanismo* (1) (diciembre 2006), 103–121.

Danso, A., Adomako, S., Amankwah-Amoah, J., Owusu-Agyei, S., & Konadu, R. (2019). Environmental sustainability orientation, competitive strategy and financial performance. *Business Strategy and the Environment, 28*(5), 885–895.

Danso, A., Adomako, S., Lartey, T., Amankwah-Amoah, J., & Owusu-Yirenkyi, D. (2020). Stakeholder integration, environmental sustainability orientation and financial performance. *Journal of Business Research, 119,* 652–662.

Dao, V., Langella, I., & Carbo, J. (2011). From green to sustainability: Information Technology and an integrated sustainability framework. *The Journal of Strategic Information Systems, 20*(1), 63–79.

de Almeida, J. M. G., Gohr, C. F., Morioka, S. N., & da Nobrega, B. M. (2021). Towards an integrative framework of collaborative capabilities for sustainability: A systematic review and research agenda. *Journal of Cleaner Production, 279,* 123789.

Diaconu, L., & Popescu, C. C. (2016). Human capital—A pillar of sustainable development. Empirical evidences from the EU states. *European Journal of Sustainable Development, 5*(3), 103–103.

Eisenmenger, N., Pichler, M., Krenmayr, N., Noll, D., Plank, B., Schalmann, E., Wandl, M. T., & Gingrich, S. (2020). The Sustainable Development Goals prioritize economic growth over sustainable resource use: A critical reflection on the SDGs from a socio-ecological perspective. *Sustainability Science, 15*, 1101–1110.

Elkington, J. (1997). The triple bottom line. *Environmental Management: Readings and Cases, 2*, 49–66.

Elkington, J. (2013). Enter the triple bottom line. In *The triple bottom line: Does it all add up?* (pp. 1–16). Routledge.

Engert, S., Rauter, R., & Baumgartner, R. J. (2016). Exploring the integration of corporate sustainability into strategic management: A literature review. *Journal of Cleaner Production, 112*, 2833–2850.

Freeman, R. E. (2010). *Strategic management: A stakeholder approach.* Cambridge University Press.

Gallopín, G. C. (2003). *A systems approach to sustainability and sustainable development.* ECLAC.

Gladwin, T. N., Kennelly, J. J., & Krause, T. S. (1995). Shifting paradigms for sustainable development: Implications for management theory and research. *Academy of management Review, 20*(4), 874–907.

Godil, D. I., Yu, Z., Sharif, A., Usman, R., & Khan, S. A. R. (2021). Investigate the role of technology innovation and renewable energy in reducing transport sector CO_2 emission in China: A path toward sustainable development. *Sustainable Development, 29*(4), 694–707.

Gomes Silva, F. J., Kirytopoulos, K., Pinto Ferreira, L., Sá, J. C., Santos, G., & Cancela Nogueira, M. C. (2022). The three pillars of sustainability and agile project management: How do they influence each other. *Corporate Social Responsibility and Environmental Management, 29*(5), 1495–1512.

Green Economy. (2010). *Developing countries success stories.* UNEP. https://www.greengrowthknowledge.org/sites/default/files/downloads/resource/GE_developing_countries_success_stories_UNEP.pdf (дата обращения 14.12.2020).

Grober, U., & Cunningham, R. (2012). *Sustainability: A cultural history.* Green Books.

Grob, S., & Benn, S. (2014). Conceptualising the adoption of sustainable procurement: An institutional theory perspective. *Australasian Journal of Environmental Management, 21*(1), 11–21.

Haberl, H., Fischer-Kowalski, M., Krausmann, F., Weisz, H., & Winiwarter, V. (2004). Progress towards sustainability? What the conceptual framework of material and energy flow accounting (MEFA) can offer. *Land Use Policy, 21*(3), 199–213.

Hansmann, R., Mieg, H. A., & Frischknecht, P. (2012). Principal sustainability components: Empirical analysis of synergies between the three pillars of sustainability. *International Journal of Sustainable Development & World Ecology, 19*(5), 451–459.

SUSTAINABILITY: CONCEPT CLARIFICATION AND THEORY 401

Hart, S. L. (1995). A natural-resource-based view of the firm. *Academy of Management Review, 20*(4), 986–1014.

Hoffman, A. J., & Jennings, P. D. (2015). Institutional theory and the natural environment: Research in (and on) the Anthropocene. *Organization & Environment, 28*(1), 8–31.

Hysa, E., Kruja, A., Rehman, N. U., & Laurenti, R. (2020). Circular economy innovation and environmental sustainability impact on economic growth: An integrated model for sustainable development. *Sustainability, 12*(12), 4831.

International Union for Conservation of Nature, & World Wide Fund for Nature. (1980). *World conservation strategy: Living resource conservation for sustainable development* (Vol. 1). IUCN.

Işık, C., Ahmad, M., Ongan, S., Ozdemir, D., Irfan, M., & Alvarado, R. (2021). Convergence analysis of the ecological footprint: Theory and empirical evidence from the USMCA countries. *Environmental Science and Pollution Research, 28*, 32648–32659.

Jacobs, M. (2013). Green growth. In *The handbook of global climate and environment policy* (pp. 197–214). Wiley.

James, P., & Magee, L. (2016). Domains of sustainability. In *Global encyclopedia of public administration, public policy, and governance* (pp. 1–17). Springer.

Jusoh, R., Yahya, Y., Zainuddin, S., & Asiaei, K. (2021). Translating sustainability strategies into performance: Does sustainability performance management matter? *Meditari Accountancy Research, 31*, 258–293 (ahead-of-print).

Keitsch, M. (2018). Structuring ethical interpretations of the sustainable development goals—Concepts, implications and progress. *Sustainability, 10*(3), 829.

Khizar, H. M. U., Iqbal, M. J., Khalid, J., & Adomako, S. (2022). Addressing the conceptualization and measurement challenges of sustainability orientation: A systematic review and research agenda. *Journal of Business Research, 142*, 718–743.

Khizar, H. M. U., Iqbal, M. J., & Rasheed, M. I. (2021). Business orientation and sustainable development: A systematic review of sustainability orientation literature and future research avenues. *Sustainable Development, 29*(5), 1001–1017.

Kitsios, F., Kamariotou, M., & Talias, M. A. (2020). Corporate sustainability strategies and decision support methods: A bibliometric analysis. *Sustainability, 12*(2), 521.

Koglin, T. (2009). *Sustainable development in general and urban context: A literature review* (pp. 8–12). Department of Technology and Society, Lund University.

Kuhlman, T., & Farrington, J. (2010). What is sustainability? *Sustainability, 2*(11), 3436–3448.

Kurniawan, R., & Managi, S. (2018). Economic growth and sustainable development in Indonesia: An assessment. *Bulletin of Indonesian Economic Studies, 54*(3), 339–361.

Laine, M. (2014). Defining and measuring corporate sustainability: Are we there yet? *Social and Environmental Accountability Journal, 34*(3), 187–188.

Lichtenthaler, U. (2021). Digitainability: The combined effects of the megatrends digitalization and sustainability. *Journal of Innovation Management, 9*(2), 64–80.

Linnenluecke, M. K., & Griffiths, A. (2013). Firms and sustainability: Mapping the intellectual origins and structure of the corporate sustainability field. *Global Environmental Change, 23*(1), 382–391.

Loiseau, E., Saikku, L., Antikainen, R., Droste, N., Hansjürgens, B., Pitkänen, K., Leskinen, P., Kuikman, P., & Thomsen, M. (2016). Green economy and related concepts: An overview. *Journal of Cleaner Production, 139*, 361–371.

Luetz, J. M., & Walid, M. (2019). Social responsibility versus sustainable development in United Nations policy documents: A meta-analytical review of key terms in human development reports. In *Social responsibility and sustainability: How businesses and organizations can operate in a sustainable and socially responsible way* (pp. 301–334). Springer.

Markevich, A. (2009). The evolution of sustainability. *MIT Sloan Management Review, 51*(1), 13.

Mastini, R., Kallis, G., & Hickel, J. (2021). A green new deal without growth? *Ecological Economics, 179*, 106832.

Mebratu, D. (1998). Sustainability and sustainable development: Historical and conceptual review. *Environmental Impact Assessment Review, 18*(6), 493–520.

Mikulčić, H., Duić, N., & Dewil, R. (2017). Environmental management as a pillar for sustainable development. *Journal of Environmental Management, 203*, 867–871.

Montiel, I., & Delgado-Ceballos, J. (2014). Defining and measuring corporate sustainability: Are we there yet? *Organization & Environment, 27*(2), 113–139.

Muñoz-Torres, M. J., Fernández-Izquierdo, M. Á., Rivera-Lirio, J. M., & Escrig-Olmedo, E. (2019). Can environmental, social, and governance rating agencies favor business models that promote a more sustainable development? *Corporate Social Responsibility and Environmental Management, 26*(2), 439–452.

Murphy, K. (2012). The social pillar of sustainable development: A literature review and framework for policy analysis. *Sustainability: Science, Practice and Policy, 8*(1), 15–29.

Murthy, V. P. (2012). Integrating corporate sustainability and strategy for business performance. *World Journal of Entrepreneurship, Management and Sustainable Development, 8*, 5–17.

Neumayer, E. (2003). *Weak versus strong sustainability: Exploring the limits of two opposing paradigms.* Edward Elgar.

Parmar, B. L., Freeman, R. E., Harrison, J. S., Wicks, A. C., Purnell, L., & De Colle, S. (2010). Stakeholder theory: The state of the art. *Academy of Management Annals, 4*(1), 403–445.

Pereira-Moliner, J., López-Gamero, M. D., Font, X., Molina-Azorín, J. F., Tarí, J. J., & Pertusa-Ortega, E. M. (2021). Sustainability, competitive advantages and performance in the hotel industry: A synergistic relationship. *Journal of Tourism and Services, 12*(23), 132–149.

Pfeffer, J. (2010). Building sustainable organizations: The human factor. *Academy of Management Perspectives, 24*(1), 34–45.

Polasky, S., Kling, C. L., Levin, S. A., Carpenter, S. R., Daily, G. C., Ehrlich, P. R., Heal, G. M., & Lubchenco, J. (2019). Role of economics in analyzing the environment and sustainable development. *Proceedings of the National Academy of Sciences, 116*(12), 5233–5238.

Purvis, B., Mao, Y., & Robinson, D. (2019). Three pillars of sustainability: In search of conceptual origins. *Sustainability Science, 14*(3), 681–695.

Ranjbari, M., Esfandabadi, Z. S., Zanetti, M. C., Scagnelli, S. D., Siebers, P.-O., Aghbashlo, M., Peng, W., Quatraro, F., & Tabatabaei, M. (2021). Three pillars of sustainability in the wake of COVID-19: A systematic review and future research agenda for sustainable development. *Journal of Cleaner Production, 297*, 126660.

Ruggerio, C. A. (2021). Sustainability and sustainable development: A review of principles and definitions. *Science of the Total Environment, 786*, 147481.

Schaltegger, S., Hörisch, J., & Freeman, R. E. (2019). Business cases for sustainability: A stakeholder theory perspective. *Organization & Environment, 32*(3), 191–212.

Schmitz, E. A., Baum, M., Huett, P., & Kabst, R. (2019). The contextual role of regulatory stakeholder pressure in proactive environmental strategies: An empirical test of competing theoretical perspectives. *Organization & Environment, 32*(3), 281–308.

Schroeder, P., Anggraeni, K., & Weber, U. (2019). The relevance of circular economy practices to the sustainable development goals. *Journal of Industrial Ecology, 23*(1), 77–95.

Schwaninger, M. (2015). Organizing for sustainability: A cybernetic concept for sustainable renewal. *Kybernetes, 44*(6/7), 935–954.

Scott, W. R. (2008). Approaching adulthood: The maturing of institutional theory. *Theory and Society, 37*, 427–442.

Shah, M. (2013). Water: Towards a paradigm shift in the twelfth plan. *Economic and Political Weekly, 48*, 40–52.

Shrivastava, P. (1995). The role of corporations in achieving ecological sustainability. *Academy of Management Review, 20*(4), 936–960.

Sood, N. (2016). Social sustainability: A global perspective. *ACADEMICIA: An International Multidisciplinary Research Journal, 6*(3), 322–326.

Srivastava, A., Sharma, R. K., & Suresh, A. (2020). Impact of Covid-19 on sustainable development goals. *International Journal of Advanced Science and Technology, 29*(9), 4968–4972.

Stivers, R. L. (1976). *The sustainable society: Ethics and economic growth.* Westminster Press.

Sutton, P. (2004). A perspective on environmental sustainability. *Paper on the Victorian Commissioner for Environmental Sustainability, 1*, 32.

Székely, F., & Knirsch, M. (2005). Responsible leadership and corporate social responsibility: Metrics for sustainable performance. *European Management Journal, 23*(6), 628–647.

Tate, W. L., & Bals, L. (2018). Achieving shared triple bottom line (TBL) value creation: Toward a social resource-based view (SRBV) of the firm. *Journal of Business Ethics, 152*, 803–826.

Wang, S., Lin, X., Xiao, H., Bu, N., & Li, Y. (2022). Empirical study on human capital, economic growth and sustainable development: Taking Shandong province as an example. *Sustainability, 14*(12), 7221.

Wanner, T. (2015). The new 'passive revolution' of the green economy and growth discourse: Maintaining the 'sustainable development' of neoliberal capitalism. *New Political Economy, 20*(1), 21–41.

WCED, S. W. S. (1987). World commission on environment and development. Our common future, 17(1), 1-91.

Weidinger, C., Fischler, F., & Schmidpeter, R. (2014). *Sustainable entrepreneurship: Business success through sustainability.* Springer. https://doi.org/10.1007/978-3-642-38753-1

York, R., Rosa, E. A., & Dietz, T. (2010). Ecological modernization theory: Theoretical and empirical challenges. In *The international handbook of environmental sociology* (2nd ed.). Edward Elgar.

Zhang, Y., Khan, U., Lee, S., & Salik, M. (2019). The influence of management innovation and technological innovation on organization performance. A mediating role of sustainability. *Sustainability, 11*(2), 495.

Corporate Governance and Sustainability Reporting in Africa

Waseem Ahmad Khan, Muhammad Farooq Shabbir, Hafiz Muhammad Usman Khizar, and Dacosta Omari

1 Introduction

Since the UN introduced its sustainable development goals (SDGs), the countries have been pushing to achieve these goals through multiple regulatory measures. These goals include improving poverty, education, climate, and green energy (United Nations, 2016). The SDGs compliance requires corporates to report their progress on the environmental, social, and governance (ESG) objectives. While sustainability reporting

---

W. A. Khan (✉) · M. F. Shabbir · H. M. U. Khizar
Institute of Business, Management & Administrative Sciences, The Islamia University of Bahawalpur, Bahawalpur, Pakistan
e-mail: waseem.khan@iub.edu.pk

M. F. Shabbir
e-mail: farooq.shabbir@iub.edu.pk

H. M. U. Khizar
e-mail: usman.khizar@iub.edu.pk

D. Omari
Durham University Business School, Durham, UK
e-mail: dacosta.omari@durham.ac.uk

© The Author(s), under exclusive license to Springer Nature Switzerland AG 2023
S. Adomako et al. (eds.), *Corporate Sustainability in Africa*,
Palgrave Studies in African Leadership,
https://doi.org/10.1007/978-3-031-29273-6_18

405

could benefit corporate reputation and build consumer confidence in them, it can also help governments and regulatory authorities to achieve SDGs. Hence, transparent sustainability reporting is crucial to achieving sustainable development goals.

There has been a paradigm shift due to which sustainability reporting is now emphasized more than in the past. Corporations, these days, are increasingly under pressure for good governance and sustainability due to increasing competition. The increasing competition has provoked businesses to develop a sustainable business model, stimulating sustainability reporting. Much research was conducted to link the governance variables and sustainability reporting to fill the gap in the potential linkage between corporate governance and sustainability reporting (Aguilar-Fernández & Otegi-Olaso, 2018; Hamad et al., 2020; Husnaint & Basuki, 2020). Due to its growing importance, many organizations have been involved in sustainability reporting, such as the Global Reporting Initiative (GRI) and the International Federation of Accountants (IFAS). The significance of sustainability reporting for businesses has emerged for many reasons. Firstly, firms with sustainable reporting practices tend to have a competitive edge over those with little or no reporting. Secondly, it is perceived to strengthen the link between an organization and its stakeholders.

While many developed continents like America and Europe have progressed a lot in their sustainability reporting, Africa, on the other hand, has been a little slow toward reporting on ESGs. Many studies cover the numerous aspects of sustainability reporting in America, Europe, and Asia. However, very few authors have analyzed about the sustainability reporting regimes in sub-Saharan Africa. The lack of research on Africa may be caused by the fact that African countries have unique social and environmental contexts (Tilt et al., 2021). Additionally, since African countries have been more exposed to the global climate issue (Adelle, 2016), the escalating need for African countries to do sustainability reporting has also grown with time. Like Asia, the continent faces limited access to clean water, deforestation, poverty, and pollution. Despite these concerning issues, Africa still lacks effective policies and regulations to deal with these problems. Moreover, the conflicting nature of sustainability reporting standards calls for a broader reform strategy or policy harmonization.

The rest of the chapter is organized into the following sections. Section 2 provides a brief overview of the contextual background of sustainability reporting. The Section 3 gives a detailed description of different sustainability reporting regimes in Africa. Section 4 elaborates on the role of corporate governance in streamlining sustainability reporting. Section 5 reports the conflicts in sustainability reporting and how to resolve them through standardization. Finally, Section 6 concludes the chapter by outlining the current trends in sustainability reporting and future directives for African countries to achieve SDGs.

2 Contextual Background

The United Nations 2030 agenda on sustainable development and reporting provides a framework for companies to use their financial and technological resources to achieve sustainability. The 2030 Agenda puts the responsibility on corporations and governments to formulate necessary regulatory models and reporting standards on sustainability (United Nations, 2015). This agenda emphasizes the need to consider the people, planet, peace, and prosperity to achieve sustainable development. Sustainable Development Goals (SDGs) facilitate firms to identify and prioritize their sustainability issues and then mold their strategies to achieve those objectives (Adams, 2017).

The African continent is one of the most populous regions, with over one billion in the population (Amaeshi et al., 2016). Most of these countries gained independence in the 1950s, and a significant chunk of their population is rural, with only 37% living in big cities. These countries have primarily faced governance problems, civil riots, unstable economic performance, policy credibility problems, and improper foreign aid utilization. Governments and corporations must formulate strategies to address the growing concerns regarding the environmental and social impact of the firms' actions. Hence Africa's Development Agenda (Agenda 2063) regarding the UN's SDGs lays out guidelines for corporate efforts to achieve social and environmental objectives (United Nations, 2016), also known as sustainable development.

Sustainability reporting is defined as firms' ESG disclosures and their effects on their ability to achieve sustainability reporting. Historically, firms were mainly required to do financial reporting only (Gouws & Cronje, 2008). However, enhancing transparency regarding firms' ESG goals has made sustainability reporting critical because many potential investors look for ethical and less risky investments. However, there has been an increasing consensus that the quality of sustainability reporting is usually low for corporations operating in developing countries. Winkler

(2017) has argued that more prominent companies tend to report more, while Dissanayake et al. (2016) have reported that corporates in sensitive industries do the same.

An integrated framework is provided by Global Reporting Initiative (GRI), registering sustainability objectives, which involve social, environmental, and economic standards. The GRI standards can help corporates to report their progress on SDGs. The importance of sustainability reporting can be seen in the fact that 80% of the companies in the World now maintain sustainability reporting practices, with North America having the highest reporting rate on sustainability (KPMG, 2020). The KPMG (2020) report argues that SDGs reporting is primarily unbalanced and is not aligned with the corporates' business goals. This could be caused by inflexibility, ineffectiveness, and a single non-custom approach to compulsory sustainability reporting standards (Musaali & Wilcox, 2007). Hence, sustainability reporting seems inefficient, practiced only to please the regulators and investors for business growth.

Meanwhile, the regulators may not be well-equipped to articulate relevant regulations for sustainability reporting. Despite these potential weaknesses, the authors still advocate the idea of developing a set of rules and regulations that could help achieve the potential SDGs via sustainability reporting. One major challenge to developing regulations on sustainability reporting is the standardization of these frameworks, as there are 100 reporting frameworks on 1500 indicators for almost 600 potential problems (Guthrie, 2012). Such complicated frameworks could undermine the reliability and effectiveness of sustainability reporting.

To counter the above-described problems, Integrated reporting was introduced in Africa in 2009, covering organizations' financial and non-financial progress (IoDA, 2009). This integrated reporting framework covers a company's governance mechanism, leading progress indicators, business plan, opportunities and risks, policy approach, and overall prospects.

CORPORATE GOVERNANCE AND SUSTAINABILITY ... 409

3 Sustainability Reporting Regimes in Selected African Countries

Zambia

Being an East African country, Zambia was the fastest-growing African economy during the first decade of the twenty-first century. However, the economic growth of Zambia halted recently, mainly caused by falling copper prices, energy shortfalls, and large fiscal deficits (African Development Bank, 2021). Despite these troubling indicators, Zambia still ranks 8th most competitive state in Africa (Lusaka Times, 2018). COVID-19 has further pushed back the economy of Zambia, which is already in crisis due to constant droughts (World Bank, 2021a). Zambia's leading stock exchange is the Lusaka Stock Exchange (LuSE), founded in 1993 and is a member of the African Stock Exchanges Association. LuSE has issued Corporate Governance Guidelines 2005 for the listed firms. These guidelines require listed public firms to report compliance with these rules in their annual reports.

Regarding sustainability reporting in Zambia, there are no legal requirements that require investors and companies to follow ESG protocols while investing (Sakuwaha, 2022). The only ESG-related reporting framework is LuSE's 2005 Corporate Governance Guidelines. The framework has an integrated sustainability reporting mechanism that mandates companies to adopt specific sustainability measures and report their progress periodically (Moira Mukuka Legal Practitioners, 2020). However, these only apply to the companies listed on the stock exchange. Since these are just guidelines and are not compulsory to be followed, most of the reporting on sustainability in Zambia is done voluntarily. For example, Institute for Sustainability Africa (INSAF) and BDO Zambia launched a sustainability reporting initiative to enhance this voluntary reporting. Also, the Zambia Institute of Chartered Accountants (ZICA) has emphasized that a firm's sustainability report can be a critical document for communicating the sustainability performance and its effect (Mbale, 2015).

Mizuno (2021) has argued that despite the global agreement to adopt and report on SDGs, the corporates' reporting on sustainability is insufficient. While the sustainability commitments by companies and investors have increased, the author said that carbon emissions from companies increased by 10% from 2015 to 2019. The phenomena have been endorsed by Mutale et al. (2019), who attributed that corporate sustainability performances slightly or insignificantly affect most SDGs. The authors have suggested adopting sustainability frameworks customized to the Zambian context, which should be formed with the consent of all stakeholders. Zambia's first Voluntary National Review has shown that the country has underscored its SDG commitment (UNDP, 2020). So, the country's current national plan has domesticated the SDGs.

Algeria

Algeria is selected as a case study for North Africa. The state mostly dominates the country's economic policies. Though the country implemented nationalization in the first two decades after it gained independence, it shifted its focus to privatization in the early 80s. However, Algeria has suspended the privatization process in recent years and put restraints on foreign investments. These restrictions are now being reduced gradually. Although the Algerian economy was depressed by the COVID-19 pandemic, World Bank (2021b) argued that it is expected to recover in 2021 partially. The only stock exchange in Algeria, "Bourse d'Algérie" (SGBV), started its operations in 1997. While the SGBV grew significantly (62% in just one year), it remains one of the World's smallest exchanges.

North Africa, particularly Algeria, is primarily affected by climate change. The country suffers from droughts and limited water resources. These issues have a substantial impact on the agriculture sector of Algeria. Consequently, the country had to make policies for climate change adjustment and extenuation methods (Nachmany et al., 2015). These include (i) implementing sustainable socio-economic growth, (ii) reducing Carbon emissions through renewable energy resources and plantation attempts, and (iii) making new and empowering current institutes and workforce. In 2002, European Union and the Swiss Agency for Development and Cooperation (SDC), along with World Bank, the German Technical Cooperation Agency (GTZ), and Mediterranean Environment Technical Assistance Program (METAP), funded Algeria's first National Plan for Environment and Sustainable Development. Despite these attempts, Algeria still ranks low on the global Environmental Sustainability Index due to its weak performance in securing biodiversity, pollution, and water shortage (Euromonitor, 2021).

Algeria has developed the Sustainable Consumption and Production National Action Plan (SCP-NAP), which is part of its attempt to accomplish Agenda 2030 and SDGs (Euromonitor, 2021). The plan is comprised of 42 actions in three main aspects; (i) integrate sustainable production and consumption forms into state procedures and strategies, (ii) promote energy efficiency and produce renewable energy, and (iii) become a zero-waste country by 2030. The effectiveness of this plan can be seen in the years to come. Despite these policies and programs, most corporate reporting on sustainability in Algeria is voluntary, like in many African countries. Academics have recommended that Algeria develop a sustainable reporting framework for the firms. However, there is an evident lack of communication and coordination between concerned stakeholders and the Algerian Government (Gherbi, 2012). These issues could create complications for the accomplishment of Agenda 2030 and SDGs.

Equatorial Guinea

Central African country Equatorial Guinea has seen accelerated economic growth due to substantial oil resources. The country's corporate governance structure is primarily influenced by the Organization of Business Law in Africa (OHADA), which was formed to standardize investment regulations in Africa (Krotoff, 2014). However, OHADA is mainly concentrated on financial reporting, such as profits/losses, assets, and liabilities of a corporation, and it does not cover the ESG reporting aspect of the organization. Therefore, ESG reporting is the sole discretion of the firms.

Equatorial Guinea is now gearing up to formulate regulations on sustainability reporting. However, the regime is still in the evolution phase. Meanwhile, corporations follow international reporting frameworks such as GRI while reporting their progress on ESG goals. At present, sustainability reporting in the country is mostly done voluntarily. While work on corporate regulations for sustainability reporting is still in progress, Equatorial Guinea has taken the initiative with the help of the UN Food and Agriculture Organization (UNFAO). It has launched RDD (Reducing Emissions from Deforestation and Forest Degradation) and National Investment Plan for Sustainable Development 2035 (UNFAO, 2020). The initiative aims to preserve the country's forests and fight climate change and sustainable development. While multinationals like

Equatorial Coca-Cola Company do some voluntary reporting on ESG progress, this move isn't enough to support sustainability reporting.

According to a report by US State Department (n.d.) Equatorial Guinea's accounting, legal, and regulatory standards aren't transparent and do not meet international standards. The 2018 Fiscal Transparency report validates this by stating that the country failed to meet the minimum fiscal transparency standards. The good news is that the country's Ministry of Mines and Hydrocarbons has set up regulations that require specific industries to have at least minimum CSR contributions. Therefore, the county is considering increasing these rates. Equatorial Guinea also applied to join the Extractive Industries Transparency Initiative (EITI) in 2019. However, the country withdrew its application in 2020 due to incomplete documentation (US State Department, 2021). The country must do more if it wishes to be recognized for its ESG efforts and sustainability reporting.

Namibia

The authors selected Namibia as a case study for Southern Africa. Namibia is considered an emerging African economy, classified as an upper-middle-income country by the World Bank. The Namibian Government has a free-market principle which has helped create many jobs. The Foreign Investment Act 1990 protects multinationals against nationalization, allows them to remit profits, and facilitates equitable dispute resolutions. The Namibian economy mainly depends on the proceeds generated from the export of minerals, livestock, and fish (CIA, 2022). In 2021, the Namibian President established the Namibia Investment Promotion and Development Board (NIPDB) to bring economic reforms.

Namibia's Corporate Governance Code (NamCode), introduced in 1994 and improved & implemented in 2014, gives a list of the best rules to help directors make the right decisions for corporates. The NamCode is based on King III and provides corporate guidance for all Namibian companies. The good thing about NamCode is that it's based upon the rules of the triple bottom line by focusing on sustainability. Introducing the triple bottom line into the NamCode makes companies focus on social, environmental, economic, and financial problems. NamCode has concentrated on changing the direction of corporates from a balance sheet-based economic value to an ESG-based future-oriented strategy (Deloitte, n.d.). In addition, NamCode has specific guidelines for the directors and has placed responsibility on the board of Directors to be collectively liable for the Corporate to operate ethically and with integrity.

The Namibian Government is steadily progressing toward achieving the UN's SDGs and playing its role in sustainable development through various measures. For example, it has recently secured financing from African Development Bank for ESTA (Environmental, Social and Cross-Cutting Issues Technical Assistant) project. The project mainly focuses on evaluating the risks posed to human lives and the environment caused by different projects and corporations. The program will also ensure that the implementation of various projects conforms with Namibia's commitment to SDGs (African Development Bank, 2020). Namibia's mining sector has CSR programs concentrating on well-being, environmental stability, education, and community resources administration (US State Department, 2021). Despite Namibia's accelerated growth in ESG and sustainability reporting, the country still lacks an effective reporting framework. Marenga and Kakujaha-Matundu (2019) have reported that Namibia's legal and policy framework on CSR is still vague, particularly concerning foreign investors.

Ghana

Ghana has been selected as a case study for West Africa. Ghana is regarded as one of the leading African countries because it has sizeable natural wealth and was the first country in South Sahara to gain independence. The Ghana Stock Exchange was incorporated in 1989 and commenced trading in 1990. The Ghanaian economy is comprised of both private and public firms. Almost half of the country's GDP is derived from the services sector, with a 20% contribution from the industry. Agriculture constitutes a large part of Ghana's economy. In addition to the services and agriculture sectors, mining is another major contributor to the country's economy. According to the data, mining accounts for 5% of Ghana's GDP and makes up 37% of the country's exports.

Governance of listed companies in Ghana was previously regulated under the Companies Act 1963. The Act included general and special provisions for financial reporting and appointment of the directors. In addition to this Act, other laws that impact the governance of listed firms include the Securities and Exchange Commission Regulations, 2003, and the Securities Industry Act 2016. These frameworks cover listed firms' disclosure requirements and financial reporting (ECGI, n.d.). However, to modernize the management of companies in Ghana, the country passed a new Companies Act 2019 along with directives issued by the Bank of Ghana, the Registrar of Companies, and the Securities and Exchange Commission. In addition, the new regulations have rules for the use of modern technology in the regulatory affairs of the firm, increased responsibilities of the directors, and recognition of minority rights of stockholders (Bright & Amihere, 2021).

Despite the country's attempt to encourage corporates to do sustainability reporting, the progress on the agenda is still in progress. A recent study on the assessment of sustainability reporting in Ghana has reported that the sustainability reporting quality of the firms is poor (Ahenkan et al., 2018). The authors have blamed it on the fact that sustainability reporting in Ghana is still voluntary and have recommended that reporting should be mandatory. In their research, the argument is also supported by Pobbi et al. (2020), who narrated that the overall performance scores do not meet international standards despite an increasing trend in voluntary environmental disclosures.

On the other hand, Arthur et al. (2017) have reported that there has been an increasing tendency of sustainability reporting by mining companies according to the GRI directives. The Director-General of the Ghanaian Security and Exchange Commission has also urged listed firms to place sustainability reporting above their profit-seeking objectives for a better environment (Adadevoh, 2020). The Director-General has also pleaded with the firms to accelerate their sustainability reporting by following global standards. The popularity of sustainability reporting has also encouraged Ghanaian Universities to voluntarily report on their sustainability performance. A study conducted by (Hinson et al., 2015) has given some interesting facts about the phenomenon. They discovered that despite none of the Universities claiming to address the sustainability issue, almost all of them have reported about their sustainability performance on their websites and reports.

Looking at the current trends in sustainability reporting in Ghana, it seems that voluntary reporting isn't enough to make an impact. Instead, the Ghanaian Government has to devise specific reporting standards to improve the pace of sustainability reporting in Ghana.

4 Corporate Governance and Sustainability Reporting

With the increased focus on sustainability, firms must formulate management strategies for creating social, economic, and environmental values. These objectives can be achieved by incorporating sustainability into business planning (Accenture, 2011). Once sustainability becomes part of the business process, the next step would be to measure the effect of these actions on the financial performance of the firms (Dyllick & Hockerts, 2002). Finally, firms must identify social, environmental, and economic indicators that can affect a firm's success (Epstein & Roy, 2001).

Bandyopadhyay (n.d.) believes that laws can only outline the basic framework. However, best corporate governance practices are voluntary. Hence, implementing these laws would mainly depend on the corporates' will to adopt good practices. A similar argument was made by So et al. (2021), who concluded that human governance is the key element of sustainability reporting. Therefore, it can be safely assumed that an effective corporate governance structure encourages sustainability reporting (Janggu et al., 2014).

The increased emphasis on sustainability agenda has redefined the relationship between companies and their concerned stakeholders. Hence, corporates are expected to embrace this change and act proactively. Farnham (2020) has argued that legislative frameworks are articulated to safeguard societies from threats and prevent problems. The effective implementation of these legislative frameworks primarily lies on the shoulder of corporate governance. Therefore, there has been an increasing consensus that corporates must improve their corporate governance practices to improve their relationship with their stakeholders. The fact that focusing on sustainability can enhance their ability to grow can be the biggest motivation for corporates. This has been endorsed by Teigland and Hobbs (2022), who narrated that robust corporate governance can be crucial for grasping the growth prospects of the ESG agenda.

No matter how strong regulations a country introduces for sustainability, their outcome can never be productive unless organizations have a solid corporate governance structure to implement these regulations. There has been an increasing consensus regarding strong corporate governance mechanisms for managing corporates to help achieve corporate profits with proper social accountability and responsibility. Good governance practices help monitor, control, and promote sustainability reporting (Mahmood et al., 2018). Onga and Djajadikertaa (2017) found a positive relationship between strong governance mechanisms and sustainability reporting practices. Since corporate governance's underlying objective is to protect shareholders' interests, push the management to disclose information on every aspect of business (Abdelfattah & Aboud, 2020). Fama and Jensen (1983) posits attention toward the critical dimension of corporate governance, i.e., board composition, which plays a vital role in monitoring a firm's management. The board composition has been studied with board independence, gender diversity, and CEO Duality.

The diversity in board composition protects stakeholders' concerns that satisfy stakeholders' requirements for relevant information (García-Izquierdo et al., 2018; Rupley et al., 2012). Therefore, companies become more responsible and adopt the voluntary discourse of information, including sustainability reporting (Haniffa & Cooke, 2005). Gender diversity on the board of directors provokes the strong monitoring role of the board. Perceptual differences between men and women allow the female board members to present contradictory arguments and urge social responsibility (Kang & Gray, 2011; Nguyen et al., 2015; Saeed et al., 2018; Shabbir et al., 2020). It is also noted that female directors are more concerned about companies' environmental performance than financial performance (Adams & Ferreira, 2009). Similarly, Fernandez-Feijoo et al. (2014) reported a positive link between sustainability reporting and female participation in the boardroom of global fortune 250 companies.

Another dimension of board composition is the independent director. Many outsider directors can resolve managers'and stakeholders' conflicts (Andreou et al., 2014; Coles et al., 2008; Michelon & Parbonetti, 2012). Wang and Dewhirst (1992) mentioned that the presence of independent directors tends to have diverse knowledge and perspective that extends the engagement of stakeholders. Independent directors are more inclined to disclose information to a broader group of stakeholders since they are more concerned about their reputations. Independent directors are more open to sustainability reporting to offset the opportunistic trend of insider directors (Haniffa & Cook, 2005). Independent directors stress the company's reputation and environmental performance to enhance their reputation and societal prestige.

5 SUSTAINABILITY REPORTING CONFLICTS AND POLICY HARMONIZATION IN AFRICA

After reviewing the reporting regimes in different African countries, it can be concluded that every country has its strategy for sustainability reporting. While most countries follow the international ESG frameworks, almost all do it voluntarily, in their comfort. The African region is far behind many countries on sustainability reporting. These conflicts in sustainability reporting among African regimes call for policy harmonization. In this regard, the following initiatives have been started.

African Peer Review Mechanism

Established in 2003, the APRM encourages member states to self-assess their governance progress. The move aims to promote the self-review mechanism in member states to check their progress on African and international governance obligations. The areas in which reporting is required are; political governance, economic governance, corporate governance, and socio-economic development. The APRM has support from many African and International forums like African Development Bank, UNDP Bureau for Africa, and African Capacity Building Foundation (African Union, n.d.). Gruzd (2014) advocated that APRM has successfully created a common governance vocabulary in Africa and has assisted governance activists in upholding their government promises.

Regional Economic Communities

These are the regional groups of different African States. Their purpose is to facilitate economic integration between member states. RECs coordinate common interests in areas like security, growth, and governance. The African region currently has more than ten RECs that help coordinate efforts on the common interests of African countries. One of the major efforts is the African Economic Community (AEC), established in 1991. The purpose was to enhance intra-African trade, lesser imports, and lower poverty. However, the AEC and different RECs are wrestling with multiple challenges. The integration process has been slow, and many RECs haven't achieved their targets (Rettig et al., 2013). The authors have suggested the African Union hold more joint meetings than the biannual ones for coordinated efforts to boost regional trade. Moreover, the AU can consider using scorecards to measure the member states' performance and penal actions for underperformers to motivate them to achieve their goals.

African Continental Free Trade Area

The African Continental Free Trade Area (AfCFTA) is a trade agreement to create the World's biggest free trade area in 54 African Countries. The purpose is to create a common market and enhance Africa's economic integration. The combined GDP of these countries is almost $3.4 trillion. To reap its full potential, major policy changes and trade facilitation steps are needed among the member countries (Thomas, 2022). The agreement has enormous scope and aims to reduce tariffs among member states. The agreement focuses on reducing technical trade barriers and boosting sanitary standards and ESG progress. In addition, the contract can speed up growth, diversification of exports, and attraction of foreign direct investment to Africa (World Bank, 2020).

6 Conclusion

This chapter reviews sustainability reporting practices in Africa and the importance of adopting ESG goals for sustainable development. The chapter broadly covers different sustainability reporting regimes in Africa and sheds light on the evolution of sustainability reporting and its relevance in the African context. Though most African firms report their performance on ESG goals voluntarily, there has been an increasing trend toward mandatory reporting. The move comes after the slow progress of African states on sustainable development. Most African countries use a voluntary reporting framework or a hybrid framework involving voluntary and mandatory reporting.

Due to these conflicts in sustainability reporting, the need for a harmonized reporting framework has emerged over time. A harmonized sustainability reporting framework is crucial for sustained socio-economic development. It can also facilitate comparability and accurately measure the progress being made by African countries. Despite a global initiative such as GRI for reporting on social, environmental, and economic objectives, there has been an increasing consensus that the quality of sustainability reporting is low in developing countries, particularly in the African region. A recent report by KPMG has shared insights by narrating that most corporates' sustainability reporting is not associated with their business objectives. The report argued that most sustainability reporting is only to please the regulators and investors and lacks a social perspective. To counter such problems, integrated reporting was introduced in Africa. However, the project wasn't much successful in terms of sustainability prospects.

The first attempt to harmonize sustainability reporting in Africa was made in 2003 by introducing African Peer Review Mechanism (APRM). APRM aims to improve the African countries' corporate governance standards on sustainability. This mechanism tracks compliance on sustainability reporting, checks for potential policy conflicts, and ultimately provides proper resolution for harmonized reporting. Another possible solution could be the Regional Economic Communities for harmonizing sustainability reporting in Africa. The African region currently has more than ten RECs that help coordinate efforts on African countries' common interests. Among these RECs, the East African Community has issued a directive on the corporate governance of listed firms. This directive requires the firms to know their ESG policies and report progress on these ESG objectives. The most recent initiative toward formulating a harmonized policy framework is the African Continental Free Trade Agreement (AfCFTA). The agreement mainly focuses on reducing tariffs among member states and trade barriers. For example, the AfCFTA could use the work of the Integrated Reporting Committee of Africa to promote harmonized sustainable reporting.

Since non-integrated sustainability reporting can pose many threats to the African region, it can significantly reduce comparability and accountability. Therefore, it is argued that integrated reporting can improve corporate performance and help achieve better sustainability. Integrated reporting combines financial and ESG reporting and includes integrated thinking and value creation (IIRC, 2011). Based on the reviewed reporting regimes in Africa, it can be assessed that none of these reporting frameworks would work unless there is some punishment for non-compliance. Furthermore, the self-regulatory models cannot work as corporates would opt for selective compliance. Songi and Dias (2019) recommended that Africa adopt a reporting framework based on compliance. This hybrid framework may comprise mandatory and voluntary methods that impose sanctions on non-compliance.

REFERENCES

Abdelfattah, T., & Aboud, A. (2020). Tax avoidance, corporate governance, and corporate social responsibility: The case of the Egyptian capital market. *Journal of International Accounting, Auditing and Taxation, 38*, 100304. https://doi.org/10.1016/j.intaccaudtax.2020.100304

Accenture. (2011). *Sustainability performance management: How CFOs can unlock value*. London.

Adadevoh, D. (2020, March 9). *Ghana: Put sustainability reporting above profit motives—Listed companies urged*. Retrieved from https://allafrica.com/sto ries/202003090706.html

Adams, C. A. (2017). Conceptualising the contemporary corporate value creation process. *Accounting, Auditing & Accountability Journal, 30*(4), 906–931. https://doi.org/10.1108/AAAJ-04-2016-2529

Adams, R. B., & Ferreira, D. (2009). Women in the boardroom and their impact on governance and performance. *Journal of Financial Economics, 94*(2), 291–309. https://doi.org/10.1016/j.jfineco.2008.10.007

Adelle, C. (2016, February 11). *How Africa can up its game to meet environmental challenges*. Retrieved from https://theconversation.com/how-africa-can-up-its-game-to-meet-environmental-challenges-54204

African Development Bank. (2020). *EOI—Namibia—Environmental, social and cross cutting issues technical assistant for the Namibia water sector support program | African Development Bank—Building today, a better Africa tomorrow*. Retrieved April 7, 2022, from https://www.afdb.org/en/docume nts/eoi-namibia-environmental-social-and-cross-cutting-issues-technical-assist ant-namibia-water-sector-support-program

African Development Bank. (2021). *Zambia Economic Outlook | Building today, a better Africa tomorrow*. Retrieved March 9, 2023, from https://www.afdb. org/en/countries-southern-africa-zambia/zambia-economic-outlook

African Union. (n.d.). *The African Peer Review Mechanism | African Union*. Retrieved April 15, 2022, from https://au.int/en/aprm

Aguilar-Fernández, M. E., & Otegi-Olaso, J. R. (2018). Firm size and the business model for sustainable innovation. *Sustainability (Switzerland), 10*(12). https://doi.org/10.3390/su10124785

Ahenkan, A., Aboagye, A. A., & Boon, E. K. (2018). Corporate environmentalism: An assessment of sustainability reporting among firms in Ghana. *International Journal of Environmental Technology and Management, 21*(5–6), 319–339. https://doi.org/10.1504/IJETM.2018.100591

Amaeshi, K., Okupe, A., & Ismail, T. (2016). Sub-Saharan Africa. In W. Visser (Ed.), *The world guide to sustainable enterprise* (1st ed., p. 246). Routledge. https://doi.org/10.4324/9781351284448

Andreou, P. C., Louca, C., & Panayides, P. M. (2014). Corporate governance, financial management decisions and firm performance: Evidence from the maritime industry. *Transportation Research Part e: Logistics and Transportation Review, 63*, 59–78. https://doi.org/10.1016/j.tre.2014.01.005

Arthur, C. L., Wu, J., Yago, M., & Zhang, J. (2017). Investigating performance indicators disclosure in sustainability reports of large mining companies in Ghana. *Corporate Governance (Bingley), 17*(4), 643–660. https://doi.org/10.1108/CG-05-2016-0124

Bandyopadhyay, R. (n.d.). *Going beyond corporate governance: Sustainability reporting*. IOD Global.

Bright, V., & Amihere, M. (2021, June 22). *Corporate governance 2021—Ghana*. Retrieved April 8, 2022, from https://practiceguides.chambers.com/practice-guides/corporate-governance-2021/ghana/trends-and-developments

CIA. (2022, March 22). *Namibia—The World Factbook*. Retrieved April 6, 2022, from https://www.cia.gov/the-world-factbook/countries/namibia/#economy

Coles, J. L., Daniel, N. D., & Naveen, L. (2008). Boards: Does one size fit all? *Journal of Financial Economics, 87*(2), 329–356. https://doi.org/10.1016/j.jfineco.2006.08.008

Deloitte. (n.d.). *NamCode: The corporate governance code for Namibia*. Retrieved from https://www2.deloitte.com/za/en/namibia/pages/risk/articles/namcode-overview.html

Dissanayake, D., Tilt, C., & Xydias-Lobo, M. (2016). Sustainability reporting by publicly listed companies in Sri Lanka. *Journal of Cleaner Production, 129*, 169–182. https://doi.org/10.1016/j.jclepro.2016.04.086

Dyllick, T., & Hockerts, K. (2002). Beyond the business case for corporate sustainability. *Business Strategy and the Environment, 11*, 130–141. https://doi.org/10.1002/bse.323

ECGI. (n.d.). *Corporate governance in Ghana*. Retrieved April 8, 2022, from https://ecgi.global/content/corporate-governance-ghana

Epstein, M. J., & Roy, M.-J. (2001). Sustainability in action: Identifying and measuring the key performance drivers. *Long Range Planning, 34*, 585–604.

Euromonitor. (2021, September). *Sustainability: Algeria*. Retrieved April 9, 2022, from https://www.euromonitor.com/sustainability-algeria/report

Fama, E. F., & Jensen, M. C. (1983). Separation of ownership and control separation of ownership and control. *Journal of Law and Economics, 26*(2), 301–325. https://doi.org/10.1086/467037

Farnham, K. (2020). *What is the relationship between corporate governance and sustainability?* Retrieved April 15, 2022, from https://www.diligent.com/insights/esg/what-is-the-relationship-between-corporate-governance-sustainability/

Fernandez-Feijoo, B., Romero, S., & Ruiz-Blanco, S. (2014). Women on boards: Do they affect sustainability reporting? *Corporate Social Responsibility and*

422   W. A. KHAN ET AL.

Environmental Management, 21(6), 351–364. https://doi.org/10.1002/csr.
1329

García-Izquierdo, A. L., Fernández-Méndez, C., & Arrondo-García, R. (2018,
August). Gender diversity on boards of directors and remuneration committees: The influence on listed companies in Spain. *Frontiers in Psychology, 9,*
1–14. https://doi.org/10.3389/fpsyg.2018.01351

Gherbi, M. (2012). Problematic of environment protection in Algerian cities.
Energy Procedia, 18, 265–275. https://doi.org/10.1016/j.egypro.2012.
05.038

Gouws, D. G., & Cronje, C. J. (2008). Corporate annual reports: Accounting
practices in transition. *Southern African Business Review, 12*(2), 108–133.

Gruzd, S. (2014). *The African Peer Review Mechanism: Development lessons
from Africa's remarkable governance assessment system.* Retrieved from https:/
/gsdrc.org/document-library/the-african-peer-review-mechanism-develo
pment-lessons-from-africas-remarkable-governance-assessment-system/

Guthrie, L. (2012). *The case for consistency in corporate climate change-related
reporting.* Retrieved from http://www.cdsb.net/sites/cdsbnet/files/the-case-
for-consistency-in-climate-change-related-reporting.pdf

Hamad, S., Draz, M. U., & Lai, F. W. (2020). The impact of corporate
governance and sustainability reporting on integrated reporting: A conceptual framework. *SAGE Open, 10*(2). https://doi.org/10.1177/215824402
0927431

Haniffa, R. M., & Cooke, T. E. (2005). The impact of culture and governance
on corporate social reporting. *Journal of Accounting and Public Policy, 24*(5),
391–430. https://doi.org/10.1016/j.jaccpubpol.2005.06.001

Hinson, R., Gyabea, A., & Ibrahim, M. (2015). Sustainability reporting among
Ghanaian universities. *Communicatio, 41*(1), 22–42. https://doi.org/10.
1080/02500167.2015.1024391

Husnaint, W., & Basuki, B. (2020). ASEAN corporate governance scorecard:
Sustainability reporting and firm value. *Journal of Asian Finance, Economics
and Business, 7*(11), 315–326. https://doi.org/10.13106/jafeb.2020.vol7.
no11.315

IIRC. (2011). *Towards integrated reporting: Communicating value in the 21st
century. Integrated reporting.* Retrieved from www.theiirc.org

IoDA. (2009). *The King Report on Governance for South Africa. Code of
Governance for South Africa.* Johannesburg. Retrieved from https://cdn.
ymaws.com/www.iodsa.co.za/resource/resmgr/king_iii/King_Report_on_
Governance_fo.pdf

Janggu, T., Darus, F., Mohamed, M., & Sawani, Y. (2014). Does good corporate
governance lead to better sustainability reporting? An analysis using structural
equation modeling. In *Procedia - Social and Behavioral Sciences* (Vol. 145,
pp. 138–145). Elsevier B.V. https://doi.org/10.1016/j.sbspro.2014.06.020

Kang, H. H., & Gray, S. J. (2011). Reporting intangible assets: Voluntary disclosure practices of top emerging market companies. *International Journal of Accounting, 46*(4), 402–423. https://doi.org/10.1016/j.intacc.2011.09.007

KPMG. (2020). *The time has come: The KPMG survey of sustainability reporting 2020* (Vol. 17). Retrieved from https://home.kpmg/xx/en/home/insights/2020/11/the-time-has-come-survey-of-sustainability-reporting.html

Krotoff, F. (2014, May 14). *OHADA: Revised uniform act on commercial companies and economic interest groups | Gide Loyrette Nouel.* Retrieved April 4, 2022, from https://www.gide.com/en/news/ohada-revised-uniform-act-on-commercial-companies-and-economic-interest-groups

Mahmood, Z., Kouser, R., Ali, W., Ahmad, Z., & Salman, T. (2018). Does corporate governance affect sustainability disclosure? A Mixed Methods Study. *Sustainability (switzerland), 10*(1), 1–20. https://doi.org/10.3390/su10010207

Marenga, R., & Kakujaha-Matundu, O. (2019). Sustainable development and corporate social responsibilities of foreign investors in namibia: Is there a need for a mercantile refocus? *Journal of International Business and Economics, 7*(2). https://doi.org/10.15640/jibe.v7n2a8

Mbale, T. (2015, April 9). *BDO Zambia launches reporting initiative—Zambia Daily Mail.* Retrieved April 9, 2022, from http://www.daily-mail.co.zm/bdo-zambia-launches-reporting-initiative/

Michelon, G., & Parbonetti, A. (2012). The effect of corporate governance on sustainability disclosure. *Journal of Management and Governance, 16*(3), 477–509. https://doi.org/10.1007/s10997-010-9160-3

Mizuno, H. (2021, July 15). Can business work for both people and planet? *Zambia Daily Mail.* Retrieved from http://www.daily-mail.co.zm/can-business-work-for-both-people-and-planet/

Moira Mukuka Legal Practitioners. (2020, September 26). *At a glance: ESG and investing in Zambia—Lexology.* Retrieved April 9, 2022, from https://www.lexology.com/library/detail.aspx?g=6ffc619f-42d4-4317-a540-5039b7ddad9e

Mutale, I., Franco, I. B., & Jewette, M. (2019). Corporate sustainability performance: An approach to effective sustainable community development or not? A case study of the luanshya copper mine in zambia. *Sustainability, 11*(20), 5775. https://doi.org/10.3390/su11205775

Musaali, M. E., & Wilcox, V. (2007). From "comply or explain" to "comply or else." *SSRN Electronic Journal,* 1–11. https://doi.org/10.2139/ssrn.1407444

Nachmany, M., Fankhauser, S., Davidová, J., Kingsmill, N., Landesman, T., Roppongi, H., Schleifer, P., Setzer, J., Sharman, A., Singleton, C. S., Sundaresan, J., & Townshend, T. (2015). *The 2015 global climate legislation study: A review of climate change legislation in 99 countries: Summary for policy-makers.* Grantham Research Institute on Climate Change and the Environment, GLOBE International.

Nguyen, T., Locke, S., & Reddy, K. (2015). Does boardroom gender diversity matter? Evidence from a transitional economy. *International Review of Economics and Finance, 37*, 184–202. https://doi.org/10.1016/j.iref.2014.11.022

Onga, T., & Djajadikertaa, H. G. (2017). Impact of corporate governance on sustainability reporting: Empirical study in the Australian resources industry. *School of Business and Law, Edith Cowan University, Australia,* 1–20.

Pobbi, M., Anaman, E. A., & Quarm, R. S. (2020). Corporate sustainability reporting: Empirical evidence from Ghana. *Journal of Economics and Business, 3*(3), 1005–1013. https://doi.org/10.31014/aior.1992.03.03.256

Rettig, M., Kamau, A. W., & Muluvi, A. S. (2013, May 17). The African union can do more to support regional integration. *Brookings.* Retrieved from https://www.brookings.edu/blog/up-front/2013/05/17/the-african-union-can-do-more-to-support-regional-integration/

Rupley, K. H., Brown, D., & Marshall, R. S. (2012). Governance, media and the quality of environmental disclosure. *Journal of Accounting and Public Policy, 31*(6), 610–640. https://doi.org/10.1016/j.jaccpubpol.2012.09.002

Saeed, A., Sameer, M., Raziq, M. M., Salman, A., & Hammoudeh, S. (2018). Board gender diversity and organizational determinants: Empirical evidence from a major developing country. *Emerging Markets Finance and Trade, 54,* 1–18. https://doi.org/10.1080/1540496X.2018.1496421

Sakuwaha, S. (2022, August 22). *At a glance: ESG and investing in Zambia—Lexology.* Retrieved March 9, 2023, from https://www.lexology.com/library/detail.aspx?g=05cff30d-0c1f-429b-9906-1852e0880fab

Shabbir, M. F., Xin, Y., & Hafeez, S. (2020). Corporate governance and firm efficiency: An application of internet companies of China. *Emerging Markets Finance and Trade, 56*(12), 2874–2890. https://doi.org/10.1080/1540496X.2019.1667768

So, I. G., Haron, H., Gui, A., Princes, E., & Sari, S. A. (2021). Sustainability reporting disclosure in islamic corporates: Do human governance, corporate governance, and IT usage matter? *Sustainability, 13*(23). https://doi.org/10.3390/su132313023

Songi, O., & Dias, A. K. (2019). Sustainability reporting in Africa: A comparative study of Egypt, equatorial Guinea, Kenya, Nigeria, Botswana and South Africa. In *The Cambridge handbook of corporate law, corporate governance and sustainability* (pp. 536–550). https://doi.org/10.1017/9781108658386

Teigland, J. L., & Hobbs, A. (2022, February 17). *How can boards strengthen governance to accelerate their ESG journeys? | EY—Global.* Retrieved April 15, 2022, from https://www.ey.com/en_gl/attractiveness/22/how-can-boards-strengthen-governance-to-accelerate-their-esg-journeys

Thomas, D. (2022, February 10). *What you need to know about the African continental free trade area—African business*. Retrieved April 15, 2022, from https://african.business/2022/02/trade-investment/what-you-need-to-know-about-the-african-continental-free-trade-area/

Tilt, C. A., Qian, W., Kuruppu, S., & Dissanayake, D. (2021). The state of business sustainability reporting in sub-Saharan Africa: An agenda for policy and practice. *Sustainability Accounting, Management and Policy Journal, 12*(2), 267–296. https://doi.org/10.1108/SAMPJ-06-2019-0248

Times, L. (2018, April 5). *Zambia: Quantum Global Group says that Zambia Economy is Africa's 8th best*. Retrieved from https://www.lusakatimes.com/2018/04/05/quantum-global-group-says-that-zambia-economy-is-africas-8th-best/

UNDP. (2020). *Zambia: Sustainable development knowledge platform*. Retrieved April 9, 2022, from https://sustainabledevelopment.un.org/memberstates/zambia

UNFAO. (2020, July 21). *Equatorial Guinea launches its REDD+ National investment plan | REDD+ Reducing emissions from deforestation and forest degradation | Food and Agriculture Organization of the United Nations*. Retrieved April 4, 2022, from https://www.fao.org/redd/news/detail/en/c/1300064/

United Nations. (2015). *Transforming our world: the 2030 agenda for sustainable development A/RES/70/1. UN General Assembly*. Retrieved from https://www.un.org/ga/search/view_doc.asp?symbol=A/RES/70/1&Lang=E

United Nations. (2016). *United Nations sustainable development agenda*. Retrieved from http://www.un.org/sustainabledevelopment/development-agenda/

US State Department. (n.d.). *2019 Investment climate statements: Equatorial Guinea*. Retrieved April 5, 2022, from https://www.state.gov/reports/2019-investment-climate-statements/equatorial-guinea/

US State Department. (2021). *2021 Investment climate statements: Equatorial Guinea*. Retrieved April 5, 2022, from https://www.state.gov/reports/2021-investment-climate-statements/equatorial-guinea/

Wang, J., & Dewhirst, H. D. (1992). Boards of directors and stakeholder orientation. *Journal of Business Ethics, 11*(2), 115–123. https://doi.org/10.1007/BF00872318

Winkler, D. (2017). *How do multinationals report their economic, social, and environmental impacts? Evidence from global reporting initiative data* (No. 827). Policy Research Working Paper. Retrieved from http://hdl.handle.net/10986/29010

World Bank. (2020). *The African continental free trade area*. Retrieved from https://www.worldbank.org/en/topic/trade/publication/the-african-continental-free-trade-area

World Bank. (2021a, September 23). *Zambia overview: Development news, research, data.* Retrieved April 9, 2022, from https://www.worldbank.org/en/country/zambia/overview#1

World Bank. (2021b). *Algeria Overview: Development news, research, data.* Retrieved April 9, 2022, from https://www.worldbank.org/en/country/algeria/overview#1

Green Human Resource Practices and Sustainability Performance: Evidence from Ghana

Gladys Esinu Abiew, George Kofi Amoako, and Emem Anwana

1 Introduction

Globally, the acknowledgment of the fact that the natural environment is greatly being affected by pollution has stimulated the interest of scholars to conduct investigations in relation to the issues of environmental sustainability also known as "green" (Yusoff et al., 2015). Consequently,

---

G. E. Abiew (✉)
Koforidua Technical University, Koforidua, Ghana
e-mail: esinu.abiew@ktu.edu.gh

Kwame Nkrumah University of Science and Technology, Kumasi, Ghana

G. K. Amoako
Ghana Communication Technology University, Accra, Ghana

Durban University of Technology, Durban, South Africa

E. Anwana
Faculty of Management Sciences, Durban University of Technology, Durban, South Africa
e-mail: emema@dut.ac.za

© The Author(s), under exclusive license to Springer Nature Switzerland AG 2023
S. Adomako et al. (eds.), *Corporate Sustainability in Africa*,
Palgrave Studies in African Leadership,
https://doi.org/10.1007/978-3-031-29273-6_19

427

there is a quest for sustainable policies and actions, which is greatly demanded all over the world (Zubair & Khan, 2019), and an increasing demand by stakeholders for firms to reduce carbon footprints and greenhouse gas emissions caused by them (Bhardwaj, 2016). This affects all departments of firms including human resource department.

The concept of green HRM has been defined as a process that involves reducing environmentally unfriendly practices through less printing while communicating through video conferencing, among others (Margaretha & Saragih, 2013).

Ironically, literature repeatedly emphasized that since the cause of environmental challenges is the doings of organizations, they thus need to take greater responsibility in addressing environmental management issues (Yusoff et al., 2015). Zubair and Khan (2019) assert that diverse parts of organizations can contribute to greater green goals through the reorganization of their routine practices. Subsequently, the human resource department is noted as one such department that can contribute to these green goals within an organization because green HRM is currently a critical corporate strategy for organizations; moreover, the department plays a relevant role in going "green."

However, despite HRM gaining an essence in the last couple of decades (Jabbour & de Sousa Jabbour, 2016), there is a relatively scarce study on green HRM practices, a facet of ecological sustainability (Yusoff et al., 2015). This observation was further supported by Paillé et al. (2020) who indicated that although the topic of HRM has been researched on in the last decades, only a few studies have been conducted to test how green HRM practices will lead to the realization of workplace goals to achieve environmental stability even though HRM has been identified as the most significant element of sustainability because it pertains to the most valued asset of firms, which is the labor force (Ahmad, 2015).

Conversely, it has been realized that without the incorporation of green HRM practices the implementation of green processes cannot excel (Jabbour & de Souza Jabbour, 2016) because green HRM influences sustainable performance (Siyambalapitiya et al., 2018).

This gap has led to few studies investigating how unidimensional green HRM practices, including training and development, reward and compensation, and performance management (Amjad et al., 2021), can affect environmental stability.

It must further be noted that although several researchers conceptualized and reviewed the concept in diverse contexts, most studies have treated green HRM practices as a unidimensional concept (e.g., Mukherjee & Chandra, 2018; Siyambalapitiya et al., 2018) even though each of the practices may have a different effect on a specific outcome.

Again, extant literature revealed that even those studies that tried to investigate the effect of some of the multi-dimensions of green HRM practices on eco-friendly performance had mixed findings. For instance, Yong et al. (2020) found that environmentally friendly recruitment and training have a positive relationship with eco-friendly practices. However, green selection and green reward had no significant influence on sustainability. Other studies likewise found green training as one identified dimension of green HRM practices to be crucial in the conduct of ecological management in organizations (Gupta, 2018). Jackson and Seo (2010) further emphasized that it is essential to treat green HRM practices as multi-dimensional concepts because HRM is made up of a set of practices that organizations adopt to implement policies that will lead to environmental sustainability.

Nevertheless, evidence of how each green HRM practice, such as recruitment, recruitment processes, and sustainable policy designs, relates to sustainable organizational performance in solo research is absent in the literature. A further comparison of other green HRM practices with job descriptions and recruitment will again bring one to the realization that knowledge of green recruitment and selection, for instance, is still scanty (Amjad et al., 2021).

Again, even though sustainable HRM activities can influence organizational performance (Siyam Siyambalapitiya et al., 2018), it has been emphasized that such relationships could be shaped by contextual situations (Leidner et al., 2019).

Nevertheless, very little knowledge exists on the moderating influence of variables such as green leadership in relation to green HRM practices and sustainability accomplishment. This green leadership is defined as a leadership style that is eco-friendly, which encourages and practices climate change mitigation and a style which takes resilience actions Gole (2012). In other words, it is a kind of leadership style that champions global environmental protection and reflects climate change mitigation and resilience as a means of eco-friendly development. Nevertheless research suggests that leaders play a pivotal role in climate change education and initiatives (Ali, 2019).

It is based on the identified gaps that this study is making a proposition for the link between sustainable recruitment, sustainable recruitment processes, green policy, and sustainable performance to be investigated and to further find out how green leadership could help strengthen this relationship. Concisely, the paper expands on the green HRM practices literature by proposing its multi-dimension association with sustainable firm performance while proposing that green leadership serves as a boundary condition to link these practices to sustainable organizational performance. The embracing and incorporation of green practices in HRM to achieve sustainability performance is critical for managers.

2 DEVELOPMENT OF PROPOSITION AND CONCEPTUAL FRAMEWORK

Green Recruitment and Organizational Sustainability Performance

Currently, several job seekers, as well as employees, are sensitive to environmental issues such that they apply for and accept job offers based on how companies value the environment (Paillé, 2022). Prospective job applicants perceive that actions taken by their proposed firms project their images. Therefore, it is expected of recruiters to ensure they make their environmentally sustainable initiatives a vital element to entice job applicants who love sustainability (Aranganathan, 2018). Nevertheless, human resource teams are currently designing recruitment in such a way that the cost, time, and energy required in hiring a prospective applicant will be reduced (Aranganathan, 2018) because new data has revealed an intense interest for sustainable package by consumers (Global Buying Green Report, 2022). The implication is that recruiting teams who believe in sustainability now do not print and advertise their needs in newsletters and print rather they resort to the use of online platforms and media which is a reflection of sustainability.

Recruiting teams not printing out documents means not using paper and hence less or no cutting down of trees thereby helping in sustainability. This also leads to less cost, no energy in printing, and less time is used in making product leading to cheaper goods and consumers. Moreover consumers will perceive such companies as doing better to protect the environment which will increase their sustainability credentials and enhance their reputation. This assertion is supported by the 2022 Global Buying Green Report released by Trivium Packaging which was revealed through a survey of 15,000 consumers across North and South Americas and Europe. The study pointed out that 85% of people below the age of

45 years are willing to pay more for eco-friendly packaged goods, interestingly the study showed that 57% of consumers do not want to engage with businesses whose activities are not eco-friendly. Finally the study revealed that 68% of respondents engaged with businesses based on their sustainability credentials in the last six months. This goes to support the idea that firms who practice green recruitment are likely to be perceived as eco-friendly.

Accordingly, the concept of green recruiting has become a notable dimension of green HRM practices where Zaid et al. (2018), for instance, reported that green HRM practices, which included recruitment, provide a competitive advantage in the accomplishment of sustainable performance. The concept of green recruitment has therefore become an evolving green human resource activity that is drawing considerable attention from researchers in the sector of HRM (Jepsen & Grob, 2015). However, diverse definitions of recruitment exist in literature (Aranganathan, 2018). Aranganathan (2018), for instance, defined it as the process of enticing a prospective job applicant who possesses the understanding, competencies, approaches, and attitude that are in line with ecological management systems within firms.

Others describe it as the process of posting jobs on the internet as well as submitting job applications through the use of the internet, job vacancy announcement that shows ecologically sustainable values and standards, and interviews through the use of telephones and video conferencing (Mukherjee et al., 2020), and job description that depicts the sustainability agenda (Opatha, 2013), among others. The HR division, therefore, has a vital duty in changing firms into green because they have the responsibility of enticing, hiring, and managing turnover while being cognisant of environmental sustainability (Aranganathan, 2018). The recruiting process concisely emphasizes less reliance on the use of paper to attract job applicants to guarantee less impact on the environment where environmental protection is given more attention within firms. Nevertheless, a study by Martins et al. (2021) put forward that sustainable recruitment or hiring has a positive and noteworthy effect on sustainable ecological accomplishment.

This finding corroborates the findings of previous studies in the area of sustainable HRM where it was evident that recruitment, training, and development, for instance, positively affect an organization's accomplishment (Obaid, 2015). Yong et al. (2019) provided further support

432   G. E. ABIEW ET AL.

that sustainable recruitment has a positive effect on a firm's green achievement. Thus, we proposed that;

Proposition 1: *Green recruiting has a direct and positive influence on sustainability performance.*

Green Recruitment Processes and Organizational Sustainability Performance

The green recruitment process goes beyond the process of attracting job applicants who value sustainable environmental practices. The process, conceptualized as environmentally sustainable recruitment and selection involves the practice of recruiting and choosing prospective job applicants who are abreast with issues pertaining to environmental sustainability and are enthusiastic to realize environmental sustainability performance (Tang et al., 2018). The process of green recruitment and selection is said to enhance the advanced stages of organizational entry (Pham et al., 2019). Notwithstanding, while some organizations decide to apply green standards when choosing prospective employees, others do not; however, it is important to note that communicating an organization's environmental beliefs and refresher training is very vital during the stage of attraction and selecting of job applicants (Pham et al., 2019). It is therefore expected of firms and persons to exhibit their roles toward sustaining the environment by putting up behaviors that depict environmentally welcoming citizens while partaking in environmentally sustainable accomplishments (Pham et al., 2019).

This is because Pham et al. (2019) found that the possession of a pro-ecological workforce is essential for the realization of ecological achievement because workers' sustainable behaviors determine sustainability performance.

They further asserted that green recruitment and selection contribute to the attainment of eco-friendly sustainability performance by assisting to locate and recruit the right candidates with a pro-environmental mentality. This study thus proposed that;

Proposition 2: *Green recruiting processes have a direct and positive influence on ssustainability performance.*

Green HRM Policy Designs and Sustainability Performance

HR policies entail the guidelines by which candidates are hired, work procedures, reward, leave, training, promotion, work environments, termination, and other important functions. Incorporating green thinking into these guidelines is referred to as green HRM policies (Mukherjee et al., 2020). Consequently, it is expected of employees to show appreciation for the sustainability policies and practices of their respective organizations after joining (Mehta & Chugan, 2015). These green policies are related to human resource practices such as green training and development, green employee relations, sustainability performance management, and green exit (Mukherjee et al., 2020).

Under environmentally sustainable training and development, the green policies entail the deliberation on eco-friendly issues in an orientation program where fresh employees are alerted of their firm's ecological objectives, the need to conduct green training needs analysis, the need for employees to be given training on sustainable practices like recycling, and making training material available online (Mukherjee et al., 2020). In terms of green performance management, the green policy concerns putting up sustainable objectives and aims for the workers and measuring their accomplishment in relation to these set standards. Over here, the policy is to ensure that environmentally sustainable goals indicated in the job description are related to performance appraisal systems (Mehta & Chugan, 2015).

The implication is that linking green policies, which relate to performance management systems, to the performance appraisal of employees will enhance their zeal to take issues of green seriously since their green attitude will be judged through performance appraisal.

Green policies relating to compensation and benefits entail designing compensation and reward systems to stimulate personnel who attain ecologically sustainable goals and who have adopted innovative ideas to defend the environment with the least use of resources.

Awarding candidates who have achieved these green goals would therefore increase their loyalty, motivate them, improve their satisfaction, and accelerate their sustainability performance (Berber & Aleksić, 2016). For better employee productivity and performance, the employee–employer relationship has been recognized as one of the most essential things to be maintained. This is because it is the duty of human resource managers to maintain a job atmosphere where workers are not intimidated to bring forth their ideas. The enabling environment, which will enhance employee participation, will thus promote their productivity and performance (Mukherjee et al., 2020).

Green exit, another green HRM policy, refers to how employees leave an organization; however, most organizations are making an effort to amend their exit policies in terms of sustainability. To gain positively through employee existence, these green policies have been projected in HRM to include the resignation of employees through online portals and mail and conducting exit interviews, which include discussions on employees' achievement of their aims (Nijhawan, 2014). Others include criticizing personnel who are unable to realize their sustainability aims and giving out certificates to people who were active in undertaking sustainability activities during their stay within their firms. Carrying out these green policies revitalizes the culture and interest of organizations as well as their efficiency leading to better sustainability performance (Mukherjee et al., 2020). Thus, we propose that:

Proposition 3: *Green HRM policies have a direct and positive influence on sustainability performance.*

The Moderating Role of Green Leadership

The leadership style in an organization has been identified as a substantial factor that impacts the achievement of organizational goals and objectives as well as the daily operations of a company (Ayandibu, 2019). It has also been proposed that green HRM will lead to higher levels of green competitive advantage under varying organizational context conditions (Zhou & Shalley, 2011).

Since green leadership is a notable organizational context condition, the implication is that when top management exhibits high green leadership standards, it may accelerate green HRM practices such as green recruitment, green recruitment processes, and green policy designs to achieve sustainable performance.

Talking of how green leadership could essentially strengthen the link between sustainability practices and sustainable organizational performance, Awan et al. (2022) found that green transformational leadership, for instance, reinforces the link between sustainability ability and green innovation. However, making leadership a potential moderator of the proposed linkage between green practices and green organizational performance though this effect is yet to be empirically tested.

Other studies revealed that green transformational leadership, as one type of green leadership, is significant in predicting green human resource activities such as sustainability behaviors through green HRM practices to achieve organizational aims (Farrukh et al., 2022).

The implication is that green leadership has a potential moderating effect on green HRM practices and sustainability performance. From the discussion, the following proposition is suggested:

Proposition 4a: Green leadership moderates the link between green recruitment and sustainability performance.

Proposition 4b: Green leadership moderates the relationship between green recruitment processes and sustainability performance.

Proposition 4c: Green leadership moderates the relationship between green HRM policy designs and sustainability performance.

3 RESEARCH DESIGN AND METHODOLOGY

Established knowledge proposes that HRM practices augment sustainability performance. Moreover, there is an agreement among researchers on the effect of green HRM practices on performance. However, we suggest that the effect of green HRM practices on firms' performance will be moderated by different factors such as green leadership. In the earlier discussions, this research adopted the research approach known as the desk approach. This approach entails the summary, collection, and amalgamation of previous studies. This is a very popular and accepted investigative research tool that collates a number of vital studies under one conceptual framework.

In order to enhance our comprehension of sustainability performance, we dwelt on several databases. In addition, this study depended on the use of secondary research including books, journals, and other electronic sources. Studies that do not relate to our framework were excluded. The following procedure was followed to collect data.

1. We undertook an electronic search with the keywords (green HRM practices, green recruitment, green recruitment processes,

green HRM policy designs, sustainability performance) in renowned database such as Springer Online Journals; Elsevier Online Journals, Wiley Online Library, Emerald Online Journals; Mdpi, etc., across disciplines, such as HRM and sustainability.

2. Additional search was done in notable journals such as International Journal of Business Management & Economic Research; Journal of Environmental Management, International Journal of Environmental Research and Public Health, and Journal of Cleaner Production.

The search of the above-mentioned journals was accompanied by the use of a manual search to guarantee the non-exclusion of important studies. In all this, we are confident that we conducted a thorough exploration of the literature to undertake this study.

4 Discussion of Proposed Conceptual Framework

Figure 1 depicts the proposed model of the study, demonstrating the reviewed literature. The dependent variable is sustainable organizational performance, which represents the outcome variable of the model. Green HRM practices are the independent variables and are presented as a multidimensional concept that includes green recruitment, green recruitment processes, and green HRM policies. The moderating variable in the model is green leadership. The conceptual model explains how organizations can gain sustainable performance through green recruitment, green recruitment processes, and green HRM policy designs.

The model also proposes that green leadership moderated the association between green HRM practices (green recruitment, green recruitment processes, green HRM policy designs) and sustainable organizational performance.

The proposed conceptual framework suggests that sustainability practices in organizations can be improved through green HRM policy designs, green recruitment processes, and green recruitment efforts. The proposed model also suggests that achieving sustainability performance can be improved through green leadership. This implies that the model underscores the importance of green leadership in sustainability achievement in all three green activities namely green HRM policy designs, green recruitment processes, and green recruitment.

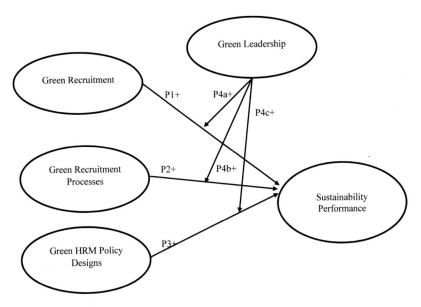

Fig. 1 Conceptual model

5 Theoretical and Managerial Implications

From a theoretical and managerial point of view, a number of implications could be garnered from this paper. Firms in Africa especially need to be abreast with issues of sustainability and how it could affect their sustainability performance. This model explores how the ability of organizations to engage in green HRM practices affects their sustainability performance. Theoretically, this study will enlighten researchers on how green recruitment could influence sustainable organizational performance.

Our conceptual model, when empirically tested, could yield empirical evidence to improve our understanding of the role green HRM practices place in achieving sustainable performance. This is consistent with the proposal of the resource-based view theory, which suggests that a firm can obtain sustained competitive advantage through its resources and capability (Barney, 1991).

This study has shown that green recruitment can potentially influence sustainable performance; and reveals how the implication of green HRM policies could influence sustainability performance. Furthermore, the study highlights that green recruitment processes could influence sustainability performance.

In addition, this study broadens the literature by scrutinizing how green leadership moderates the relationship between green recruitment and sustainable performance, green recruitment processes and sustainable performance, and green HRM policy designs and sustainable performance.

The knowledge gap is filled by extending literature to a developing market perspective and making a contribution to theory. We have also contributed to the knowledge gap by demonstrating when green HRM practices-sustainable performance relationships will work in the Sub-Saharan Africa context. What was known about this relationship was largely limited to the developed economies' environment. This model explores how the engagement of organizations in green HRM practices affects their sustainability performance.

The conceptual framework clearly shows the need for organizations to adopt eco-friendly HRM practices; and that there is a need for government and institutional policies to overcome the hindrances to eco-friendly HRM practices. This study has a noteworthy repercussion for firms in Ghana and other emerging economies with similar eco-friendly issues. The result that would be derived from the empirical testing of this paper will therefore enable firms to comprehend the fluctuating trends in eco-friendly practices and offer useful reference points for future studies in the emerging economies context.

The study offers several useful managerial and practical implications for managers at least within the study context. Discoveries from this study, therefore, will bring to light several essential implications for managers who are in charge of managing green recruitment practices to impact sustainable organizational performance. It is proposed that the finding from the study will establish that green HRM practices (green recruitment, green recruitment processes, green HRM policy designs) will lead to firms' sustainable performance. This suggests that managers must invest in green HRM practices. Moreover, managers are encouraged to be aware of the environment within which they operate since the environment has a significant impact on the success of their green HRM practices. Even though this study has established that green HRM positively and directly relates to sustainable organizational performance, this relation is affected by certain internal environmental factors such as green leadership.

Therefore, managers must pay serious attention to how their belief and acceptance of issues of green affect their green HRM practices; bearing in mind that higher levels of green leadership would help them to effectively implement green HRM practices such as green recruitment, green recruitment processes, and green HRM policy designs.

From a further applied point of view, there is a need for supportive leadership who believes in "green" so as to inspire human resource managers and employees to engage in sustainable green HRM practices. The conceptual framework indicates a need for green leadership toward accelerating green HRM practices.

The study concisely has a substantial inference for the corporate practice among firms in Ghana and other developing economies with similar sustainability issues. Its empirical findings will therefore enable firms to better understand the changing trends in sustainability issues and offer a useful reference point for further studies in an emerging country context.

6   Conclusions, Limitations, and Directions for Future Research

Comprehending how organizations can achieve sustainable organizational performance is very important because it is established knowledge in the literature that sustainable organizational performance improves the competitive advantage of businesses. This paper deduced the fact that several businesses are faced with sustainability issues. This requires the adoption of appropriate environmental practices to adequately implement these green human resource practices to achieve a competitive advantage for businesses. Again, this paper discovered that the workforce of organizations is a vital element in gaining environmental sustainability. Therefore adopting the right processes and practices such as green recruitment, green recruitment processes, and green HRM policy designs will enable organizations to reap sustainability advantages since people with a green mindset will be recruited, passed through the green recruitment processes, and would be made to follow the green policies.

Therefore, organizations need to focus on the RBV theory since the imitable resources, which are immovable across firms like their green abilities to recruit, engage in green recruitment processes, and implement green policy designs, can enable them to gain a sustainable organization. The rapidly growing demand for organizational sustainability can thus be realized when organizations engage in green recruitment, green recruitment processes, and green HRM policy designs. Notwithstanding the valuable contributions of this study, the study faced several limitations.

First, the study solely focused on Ghana and, moreover, it is purely a conceptual paper. It would thus be thought-provoking to empirically examine the framework in Ghana as well as other jurisdictions in Sub-Saharan Africa so as to get more insight into the relationships between the variables within the framework. This is because the diversity within the region could influence these results in different ways.

Second, the study focused on green leadership as a contingency factor influencing the green HRM practices-sustainable organizational performance relationship. It would therefore be necessary for future research to ascertain and discover other possible contingency factors that could influence the HRM practices-sustainable organizational performance relationship.

For example, organizational culture and supportive leadership could be explored as the contingency factors that could influence this relationship. This would offer a more solid and broader clarification of the HRM practices-sustainable organizational performance relationship.

References

Ahmad, S. (2015). Green human resource management: Policies and practices. *Cogent Business & Management, 2*(1), 1030817.

Ali, W. (2019). Green leadership as an emerging style for addressing climate change issues in schools. *Journal of Social Sciences, 15*, 58–68.

Amjad, F., Abbas, W., Zia-UR-Rehman, M., Baig, S. A., Hashim, M., Khan, A., & Rehman, H. U. (2021). Effect of green HRM practices on organizational sustainability: The mediating role of environmental and employee performance. *Environmental Science and Pollution Research, 28*(22), 28191–28206.

Aranganathan, P. (2018). Green recruitment: A new-fangled approach to attract and retain talent. *International Journal of Business Management & Research, 8*(2), 69–76.

Awan, F. H., Dunnan, L., Jamil, K., & Gul, R. F. (2022). Stimulating environmental performance via green human resource management, green transformational leadership, and green innovation: A mediation-moderation model. *Environmental Science and Pollution Research*, 1–19.

Ayandibu, A. O. (2019). Green transformational leadership and organizational behavior effectiveness. In *Contemporary multicultural orientations and practices for global leadership* (pp. 225–244). IGI Global.

Barney, J. (1991). Firm resources and sustained competitive advantage. *Journal of Management, 77*(1), 99–120.

Berber, N., & Aleksic, M. (2016). Green human resource management: Organizational readiness for sustainability. In *International scientific conference the priority directions of national economy development* (pp. 271–282). Faculty of Economics, University of Niš.

Bhardwaj, B. R. (2016). Role of green policy on sustainable supply chain management: A model for implementing corporate social responsibility (CSR). *Benchmarking: An International Journal.*

Buying Green Report 2022. (2022). *Trivium packaging buying green report 2022.* https://www.triviumpackaging.com/news-media/reports/buying-green-report-2022/. Accessed on March 16, 2023.

Farrukh, M., Ansari, N., Raza, A., Wu, Y., & Wang, H. (2022). Fostering employee's pro-environmental behavior through green transformational leadership, green HRM and environmental knowledge. *Technological Forecasting and Social Change, 179*, 121643.

Gole, P. (2012). Green leadership: Ways of practicing it. In *2nd International conference on computer and software modeling.* IACSIT Press. http://www.ipcsit.com/vol54/018-ICCSM2012-S2008.pdf.

Gupta, H. (2018). Assessing organizations performance on the basis of GHRM practices using BWM and Fuzzy TOPSIS. *Journal of Environmental Management, 226*, 201–216.

Jabbour, C. J. C., & de Sousa Jabbour, A. B. L. (2016). Green HRM and green supply chain management: Linking two emerging agendas. *Journal of Cleaner Production, 112*, 1824–1833.

Jackson, S. E., & Seo, J. (2010). The greening of strategic HRM scholarship. *Organization Management Journal, 7*, 278–290.

Jepsen, D. M., & Grob, S. (2015). Sustainability in recruitment and selection: building a framework of practices. *Journal of Education for Sustainable Development, 9*(2), 160–178.

Leidner, S., Baden, D., & Ashleigh, M. J. (2019). Green (environmental) HRM: Aligning ideals with appropriate practices. *Personnel Review, 48*(5), 1169–1185.

Margaretha, M., & Saragih, S. (2013). Developing new corporate culture through green human resource practice. In *International Conference on Business, Economics, and Accounting* (Vol. 1, No. 10).

Martins, J. M., Aftab, H., Mata, M. N., Majeed, M. U., Aslam, S., Correia, A. B., & Mata, P. N. (2021). Assessing the impact of green hiring on sustainable performance: Mediating role of green performance management and compensation. *International Journal of Environmental Research and Public Health, 18*(11), 5654.

Mehta, K., & Chugan, P. K. (2015). Green HRM in pursuit of environmentally sustainable business. *Pursuit of Environmentally Sustainable Business (June 1, 2015). Universal Journal of Industrial and Business Management, 3*(3), 74–81.

Mukherjee, B., & Chandra, B. (2018). Conceptualizing green human resource management in predicting employees' green intention and behaviour: A conceptual framework. *Prabandhan: Indian Journal of Management, 11*(7), 36–48.

Mukherjee, S., Bhattacharjee, S., Paul, N., & Banerjee, U. (2020). Assessing green HRMpractices in higher educational institute. *TEST Engineering & Management, 82.*

Nijhawan, G. (2014). Green HRM—A requirement for sustainable organization. *Indian Journal of Research, 3*, 69–70.

Obaid, T. (2015). The impact of green recruitment, green training and green learning on the firm performance: Conceptual paper. *International Journal of Applied Research, 1*(12), 951–953.

Opatha, H. H. P. (2013). Green human resource management: A simplified introduction. *Proceedings of the HR Dialogue*, 12–20.

Paillé, P. (2022). Managing green recruitment for attracting pro-environmental job seekers: Toward a conceptual model of "Handicap" principle. In *Sustainable human resource management* (pp. 57–89). River Publishers.

Paillé, P., Valéau, P., & Renwick, D. W. (2020). Leveraging green human resource practices to achieve environmental sustainability. *Journal of Cleaner Production, 260*, 121137.

Pham, D. D. T., Paillé, P., & Halilem, N. (2019). Systematic review on environmental innovativeness: A knowledge-based resource view. *Journal of Cleaner Production, 211*, 1088–1099.

Siyambalapitiya, J., Zhang, X., & Liu, X. (2018). Green human resource management: A proposed model in the context of Sri Lanka's tourism industry. *Journal of Cleaner Production, 201*, 542–555.

Tang, G., Chen, Y., Jiang, Y., Paillé, P., & Jia, J. (2018). Green HRM practices: Scale development and validity. *Asia Pacific Journal of Human Resources, 56*(1), 31–55.

Yong, J. Y., Yusliza, M. Y., Ramayah, T., & Fawehinmi, O. (2019). Nexus between green intellectual capital and green human resource management. *Journal of Cleaner Production, 215*, 364–374.

Yong, J. Y., Yusliza, M. Y., Ramayah, T., Chiappetta Jabbour, C. J., Sehnem, S., & Mani, V. (2020). Pathways towards sustainability in manufacturing organizations: Empirical evidence on the role of green human resource management. *Business Strategy and the Environment, 29*(1), 212–228.

Yusoff, Y. M., Othman, N. Z., Fernando, Y., Amran, A., Surienty, L., & Ramayah, T. (2015). Conceptualization of green human resource management: An exploratory study from Malaysian-based multinational companies. *International Journal of Business Management & Economic Research, 6*(3), 158–166.

Zaid, A. A., Jaaron, A. A., & Bon, A. T. (2018). The impact of green HRM and green supply chain management practices on sustainable performance: An empirical study. *Journal of Cleaner Production, 204*, 965–979.

Zhou, J., & Shalley, C. E. (2011). Deepening our understanding of creativity in the workplace: A review of different approaches to creativity research. In *Zedeck Sheldon APA handbook of industrial & organizational psychology* (pp. 275–302). American Psychological Association.

Zubair, D. S. S., & Khan, M. (2019). Sustainable development: The role of green HRM. *International Journal of Research in Human Resource Management, 1*(2), 1–6.

INDEX

A
Access to financial resources, 258, 265
African Continental Free Trade Area (AfCFTA), 418
African Peer Review Mechanism (APRM), 417, 419
Agency theory, 153, 154, 158, 354
Algeria, 22, 30, 86, 88, 410, 411

B
Basis for environmental accountability system, 359
Bribery and corruption theories, 153
Business-and-society relationship, 70

C
Circular economy, 11, 12, 15, 16, 23, 25, 26, 31, 38, 39, 134, 216, 393
Climate change realities, 215
Comparison of the four pillars of sustainability, 383

Contemporary Ecological Theory, 391, 396

Corporate governance and sustainability reporting, 406, 415

Corporate sustainability (CS), 3, 4, 39, 66, 153, 188, 189, 191, 192, 196, 197, 200–202, 298, 299, 304, 305, 309, 312, 322, 339, 376, 379, 385, 386, 393–395, 410

Corporate Sustainable Development, 391

Crowdfunding, 246, 272, 288

Cultural theory, 155, 158

Culture, 4, 155, 156, 188–190, 192–197, 202, 239, 241–243, 245, 247, 248, 277, 283, 287, 303, 306, 325, 332, 339, 381, 440

Cybernetics, 384, 390, 396

© The Editor(s) (if applicable) and The Author(s), under exclusive license to Springer Nature Switzerland AG 2023
S. Adomako et al. (eds.), *Corporate Sustainability in Africa*, Palgrave Studies in African Leadership, https://doi.org/10.1007/978-3-031-29273-6

445

446 INDEX

D

Degrowth and the Global South, 162, 167

Demographic pressures, 48, 51, 54

Dependency theory, 48–50, 53, 55, 56, 59

Domains of Sustainability, 378, 380

Drivers of gender inequality, 321, 330

E

Ease of doing business index (EDBI), 106–110, 116, 117

Economic growth and poverty reduction, 109

Economic pillar of sustainability, 381

Education and poverty reduction, 111

Entrepreneurial branding, 283, 284, 286, 291

Entrepreneurial Ecosystem in Africa, 240

Entrepreneurship and sustainability, xx, 4, 238, 248

Environmental degradation, 2, 10, 11, 48, 50, 53, 69, 102, 104, 154, 155, 157–159, 323, 326, 327, 330, 356, 375, 376

Environmental pillar of sustainability, 382

Equatorial Guinea, 105, 107, 109, 411, 412

Evolution of corporate sustainability, 191

Evolution of Organizational Culture, 193

Expected SDG gaps, 90

F

Financing SDGs, 48, 94

Forest preservation, 215

G

Gender and sustainability, 322–325, 330, 338, 339

Gender inequality in Africa, 321, 328

Ghana, xi, xii, 2, 18, 21, 23, 28, 30, 89, 231, 241, 258–261, 269, 285, 286, 289, 298, 299, 305–311, 333, 334, 413, 414, 438–440

Governance and corruption, 52, 116

Governments and MNEs, 72

Green economics, 384, 389, 395

H

Healthcare and poverty reduction, 112

Human capital, 93, 94, 111–114, 160, 161, 235, 239, 244, 248, 277, 382–384, 386, 396

Human Pillar of Sustainability, 382

I

Inadequate female Empowerment, 321, 330, 331

Income inequality, 53, 67, 165, 328

Industrial dynamic, 239, 247

Innovation and regulatory framework in Africa, 222

Innovation and Sharing Economy in Africa, 220

Innovation taxonomy and technology paradigms, 209

Institutional pressures and SMEs' Sustainability, 136

Institutional theory, 128, 129, 136, 140, 156, 159, 236, 283, 386, 395

Institutions and sustainable actions, 283

INDEX   447

L

Leapfrogging technology shifts, 219

M

Market, 33, 34, 56, 59, 67, 71, 74, 75, 103, 104, 113, 116, 117, 128, 130–134, 173, 210, 211, 213, 215, 216, 218, 220, 221, 223, 224, 232, 237–239, 241, 243–248, 256, 257, 261, 263, 266, 269–272, 274, 275, 277, 281, 284, 288, 289, 291, 302–305, 307, 312, 321, 328, 386, 412, 418, 438

Multinational enterprises (MNEs), 65–75, 282

N

Namibia, 89, 410, 412, 413

Nigeria, xvii, 2, 17, 18, 21, 23, 24, 28–30, 82, 83, 90–96, 98, 105, 108, 129, 130, 134, 135, 138, 220, 224, 257, 259–261, 267, 269, 271, 276, 287, 302, 335, 336, 364–366

O

Open Innovation in Africa, 211

P

Political economy theory, 157, 159

Poverty, 48, 49, 51–53, 55, 58, 67, 73, 74, 81–88, 90–93, 95, 101–118, 129, 151–153, 162, 166, 167, 169, 176, 190, 212, 214, 235, 256, 257, 261, 277, 278, 327, 331–333, 389, 390, 394, 405, 406, 417

Private Corporations and gender diversity, 309

R

Rational choice theory, 154, 155, 158

RBV and NRBV, 387

Resource-based view (RBV), 128, 129, 131, 140, 384, 387, 395, 437, 439

Resource curse and poverty, 103, 104

Restructuring the Informal Business Sector in Africa, 266

S

Saving the mangroves, 217

SDGs AND AFRICA, 82

SDGs progress and challenges African perspective, 82

Small and Medium Enterprises in Africa, 129

Social pillar of sustainability, 381

Stakeholder's role in a resilient EAS, 360

Stakeholder theory, 128, 192, 352–354, 363, 384, 385, 395

Strategy formulation, 272

Sustainability and Africa, 2

Sustainability and innovation in Africa, 217

Sustainability issues in Africa, 196, 214, 326

Sustainability-oriented innovation, 132, 140

Sustainability reporting, 4, 69, 387, 405–409, 411–419

Sustainable development goals (SDGs), 1, 3, 4, 47–59, 66–69, 73, 74, 81–86, 88–90, 92, 93, 95, 112, 169, 170, 174, 177, 187, 235, 278, 289, 298, 320, 322, 328–331, 394, 405–411, 413

Sustainable entrepreneurship (SE), xvi, xvii, 103, 104, 106, 110, 113,

116–118, 188, 238, 270, 271, 278

Sustaincentrism, 388, 389, 395

Systems theory, 384, 388, 396

T

The concept of sustainability, 1, 233, 321, 376, 377, 379, 384, 388, 390, 395

The opportunities of the digital era, 269, 275

The SWOT analysis, 256, 261

Tyre Pyrolysis and Sustainable Practices in Africa, 15

W

Waste tyre pyrolysis, 12, 26, 27, 31, 38

Women and corporate sustainability, 300

Z

Zambia, 22, 30, 105, 108, 129, 257, 409, 410

Printed in the United States
by Baker & Taylor Publisher Services